Horizon Owners Workshop Manual

John S Mead

Models covered

All Talbot/Chrysler Horizon models, Series I and II, including special and limited edition models; 1118 cc, 1294 cc and 1442 cc

Covers 4- & 5-speed manual gearbox and automatic transmission
Does not cover Diesel engine models

ISBN 1 85010 197 3

© Haynes Publishing Group 1981, 1983, 1985

Printed in England *(473–6L2)*

ABCDE
FGHIJ
KL

Haynes
THE BOOK

Haynes Publishing Group
Sparkford Nr Yeovil
Somerset BA22 7JJ England

Haynes Publications, Inc
861 Lawrence Drive
Newbury Park
California 91320 USA

British Library Cataloguing in Publication Data
Mead, John S.
Talbot/Chrysler Horizon owners workshop manual.
–3rd ed.– (Owners Workshop Manuals)
1. Talbot Horizon automobile
I. Title   II. Series
629.28'722   TL215.T24
ISBN 1-85010-197-3

Acknowledgements

Thanks are due to the Talbot Motor Company for the provision of technical information and certain illustrations. The Champion Sparking Plug· Company supplied the illustrations showing the various spark plug conditions. Sykes-Pickavant provided some of the workshop tools. Thanks are also due to all those people at Sparkford who helped in the production of this manual.

About this manual

Its aim

The aim of this manual is to help you get the best from your car. It can do so in several ways. It can help you decide what work must be done (even should you choose to get it done by a garage), provide information on routine maintenance and servicing, and give a logical course of action and diagnosis when random faults occur. However, it is hoped that you will use the manual by tackling the work yourself. On simpler jobs it may even be quicker than booking the car into a garage and going there twice to leave and collect it. Perhaps most important, a lot of money can be saved by avoiding the costs the garage must charge to cover its labour and overheads.

The manual has drawings and descriptions to show the function of the various components so that their layout can be understood. Then the tasks are described and photographed in a step-by-step sequence so that even a novice can do the work.

Its arrangement

The manual is divided into thirteen Chapters, each covering a logical sub-division of the vehicle. The Chapters are each divided into Sections, numbered with single figures, eg 5; and the Sections into paragraphs (or sub-sections), with decimal numbers following on from the Section they are in, eg 5.1. 5.2 etc.

It is freely illustrated, especially in those parts where there is a detailed sequence of operations to be carried out. There are two forms of illustration: figures and photographs. The figures are numbered in sequence with decimal numbers, according to their position in the Chapter – Fig. 6.4 is the fourth drawing/illustration in Chapter 6. Photographs carry the same number (either individually or in related groups) as the Section or sub-section to which they relate.

There is an alphabetical index at the back of the manual as well as a contents list at the front. Each Chapter is also preceded by its own individual contents list.

References to the 'left' or 'right' of the vehicle are in the sense of a person in the driver's seat facing forwards.

Unless otherwise stated, nuts and bolts are removed by turning anti-clockwise, and tightened by turning clockwise.

Vehicle manufacturers continually make changes to specifications and recommendations, and these, when notified, are incorporated into our manuals at the earliest opportunity.

Whilst every care is taken to ensure that the information in this manual is correct, no liability can be accepted by the authors or publishers for loss, damage or injury caused by any errors in, or omissions from, the information given.

Introduction to the Talbot Horizon

Introduced in 1978, the Horizon received great acclaim from both the motoring press and the public alike and that same year won the Car of the Year Award.

The reason for the Horizon's success is fairly straightforward as the car incorporates all the best features of the well proven Simca 1100 and Chrysler Alpine range, plus many new improvements of its own.

The four-cylinder overhead valve engine is mounted transversely in the engine compartment and inclined rearwards to provide a low bonnet profile. This gives a smooth, low drag airflow over the body and reduces wind noise.

Power from the engine is transmitted through an all-synchromesh gearbox and differential unit attached to the left-hand side of the engine, and then via short driveshafts to the front wheels.

Certain models, fitted with the larger 1442 cc engine, are equipped with automatic transmission as standard equipment.

Torsion bars and wishbone radius arms are used for the front suspension, while the independent rear suspension has trailing arms supported on coil springs. Telescopic dampers are fitted to both front and rear suspension systems.

The front wheel drive layout dispenses with the conventional propeller shaft, rear axle and associated floor bulges. This provides additional foot room in the passenger compartment and considerably increases the luggage area.

Although the Horizon is a fairly large car in terms of roominess, the performance, even with the smaller 1118 cc engine, is very lively. For the customer who requires increased performance the larger 1294 cc and 1442 cc engines are available.

Contents

Horizon GLS

Horizon GL. This is the project car used for this manual

General dimensions, weights and capacities

Dimensions

Overall length:
SX models .... 156.75 in (3980 mm)
All other models .... 156.0 in (3960 mm)
Overall width .... 66 in (1680 mm)
Overall height (at kerb weight) .... 55.5 in (1410 mm)
Wheelbase .... 99.25 in (2520 mm)
Front track:
SX models .... 56.5 in (1434 mm)
All other models .... 55.75 in (1416 mm)
Rear track:
SX models .... 54.75 in (1387 mm)
All other models .... 54.0 in (1369 mm)
Ground clearance (at kerb weight) .... 7 in (180 mm)

Kerb weights

1442 cc engine with automatic transmission .... 2194 to 2260 lb (995 to 1025 kg)
All other models .... 2084 to 2183 lb (945 to 990 kg)
Permissible roof rack load .... 110 lb (50 kg)

Trailer weights

The weights below are the manufacturer's recommended maxima for a laden trailer or caravan; they may be subject to modification according to local regulations

Unbraked trailer:
Manual transmission models .... 1036 lb (470 kg)
Automatic transmission models .... 1091 lb (494 kg)
Braked trailer:
1118 cc models .... 1650 lb (750 kg)
1294 cc models .... 1764 lb (800 kg)
1442 cc models (manual) .... 1874 lb (850 kg)
1442 cc models (automatic) .... 1984 lb (900 kg)

Capacities

Engine oil:
With filter change .... 5.75 pints (3.3 litres)
Without filter change .... 5.25 pints (3.0 litres)

Manual transmission:
Gearbox .... 1.0 pint (0.6 litres)
Final drive .... 0.9 pint (0.5 litres)

Automatic transmission: **Drain and refill**   **From dry**
Gearbox and torque converter .... 5.6 pints (3.2 litres)   11.25 pints (6.4 litres)
Final drive .... 1.85 pints (1.05 litres)   2.0 pints (1.15 litres)

Cooling system (with heater):
All except SX .... 10.6 pints (6.0 litres)
SX .... 10.9 pints (6.2 litres)
Fuel tank .... 9.9 gallons (45 litres)
Washer reservoirs:
Windscreen .... 3.2 pints (1.8 litres)
Windscreen/headlamp .... 8.5 pints (4.8 litres)
Tailgate .... 2.5 pints (1.4 litres)

Buying spare parts and vehicle identification numbers

Buying spare parts

Spare parts are available from many sources, for example: Talbot garages, other garages and accessory shops, and motor factors. Our advice regarding spare part sources is as follows.

Officially appointed Talbot garages – This is the best source of parts which are peculiar to your car and are otherwise not generally available (eg complete cylinder heads, internal gearbox components, badges, interior trim, etc). It is also the only place at which you should buy parts if your car is still under warranty – non-Talbot components may invalidate the warranty. To be sure of obtaining the correct parts it will always be necessary to give the storeman your car's engine and chassis number, and if possible, to take the 'old' part along for positive identification. Remember that many parts are available on a factory exchange scheme – any parts returned should always be clean! It obviously makes good sense to go straight to the specialist on your car for this type of part for they are best equipped to supply you.

Other garages and accessory shops – These are often very good places to buy materials and components needed for the maintenance of your car (eg oil filters, spark plugs, bulbs, drivebelts, oil and greases, touch-up paint, filler paste etc). They also sell general accessories, usually have convenient opening hours, charge lower prices and can often be found not far from home.

Motor factors – Good factors will stock all of the more important components which wear out relatively quickly (eg clutch components, pistons, valves, exhaust systems, brake cylinders/pipes/hoses/seals/shoes and pads etc). Motor factors will often provide new or reconditioned components on a part exchange basis – this can save a considerable amount of money.

Vehicle identification numbers

Always have details of the car, its serial and engine numbers available when ordering parts. If you can take along the part to be renewed, it is helpful. Modifications were and are being continually made and often are not generally publicised. A storeman in a parts department is quite justified in saying that he cannot guarantee the correctness of a part unless these relevant numbers are available.

The vehicle identification plate is located centrally between the bulkhead ribs (photo).

The body serial number is located on the right-hand wing valance.

The engine number is stamped on a plate secured to the cylinder block adjacent to the distributor (photo). For identification purposes, this number should also be quoted when ordering parts for the final drive assembly.

The gearbox number is located on the end of the casing as illustrated.

The paint colour code will be found on the left-hand wing valance.

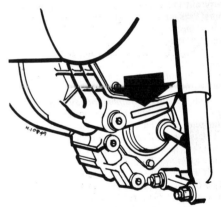

Gearbox serial number (arrowed)

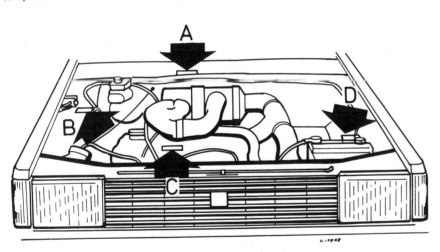

Vehicle identification plates

A *Identification plate*
B *Serial number*
C *Engine number*
D *Paint colour*

Vehicle identification plate

Location of engine number

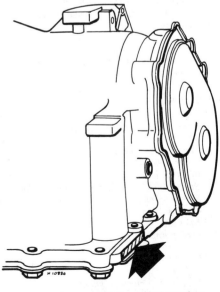

Automatic transmission serial number (arrowed)

Tools and working facilities

Introduction

A selection of good tools is a fundamental requirement for anyone contemplating the maintenance and repair of a motor vehicle. For the owner who does not possess any, their purchase will prove a considerable expense, offsetting some of the savings made by doing-it-yourself. However, provided that the tools purchased are of good quality, they will last for many years and prove an extremely worthwhile investment.

To help the average owner to decide which tools are needed to carry out the various tasks detailed in this manual, we have compiled three lists of tools under the following headings: *Maintenance and minor repair*, *Repair and overhaul*, and *Special*. The newcomer to practical mechanics should start off with the *Maintenance and minor repair* tool kit and confine himself to the simpler jobs around the vehicle. Then, as his confidence and experience grow, he can undertake more difficult tasks, buying extra tools as, and when, they are needed. In this way, a *Maintenance and minor repair* tool kit can be built-up into a *Repair and overhaul* tool kit over a considerable period of time without any major cash outlays. The experienced do-it-yourselfer will have a tool kit good enough for most repair and overhaul procedures and will add tools from the *Special* category when he feels the expense is justified by the amount of use to which these tools will be put.

It is obviously not possible to cover the subject of tools fully here. For those who wish to learn more about tools and their use there is a book entitled *How to Choose and Use Car Tools* available from the publishers of this manual.

Maintenance and minor repair tool kit

The tools given in this list should be considered as a minimum requirement if routine maintenance, servicing and minor repair operations are to be undertaken. We recommend the purchase of combination spanners (ring one end, open-ended the other); although more expensive than open-ended ones, they do give the advantages of both types of spanner.

Combination spanners - 10, 11, 12, 13, 14 & 17 mm
Adjustable spanner - 9 inch
Engine sump/gearbox/rear axle drain plug key
Spark plug spanner (with rubber insert)
Spark plug gap adjustment tool
Set of feeler gauges
Brake adjuster spanner
Brake bleed nipple spanner
Screwdriver - 4 in long x $\frac{1}{4}$ in dia (flat blade)
Screwdriver - 4 in long x $\frac{1}{4}$ in dia (cross blade)
Combination pliers - 6 inch
Hacksaw (junior)
Tyre pump
Tyre pressure gauge
Grease gun
Oil can
Fine emery cloth (1 sheet)
Wire brush (small)
Funnel (medium size)

Repair and overhaul tool kit

These tools are virtually essential for anyone undertaking any major repairs to a motor vehicle, and are additional to those given in the *Maintenance and minor repair* list. Included in this list is a comprehensive set of sockets. Although these are expensive they will be found invaluable as they are so versatile - particularly if various drives are included in the set. We recommend the $\frac{1}{2}$ in square-drive type, as this can be used with most proprietary torque wrenches. If you cannot afford a socket set, even bought piecemeal, then inexpensive tubular box spanners are a useful alternative.

The tools in this list will occasionally need to be supplemented by tools from the *Special* list.

Sockets (or box spanners) to cover range in previous list
Reversible ratchet drive (for use with sockets)
Extension piece, 10 inch (for use with sockets)
Universal joint (for use with sockets)
Torque wrench (for use with sockets)
'Mole' wrench - 8 inch
Ball pein hammer
Soft-faced hammer, plastic or rubber
Screwdriver - 6 in long x $\frac{5}{16}$ in dia (flat blade)
Screwdriver - 2 in long x $\frac{5}{16}$ in square (flat blade)
Screwdriver - 1$\frac{1}{2}$ in long x $\frac{1}{4}$ in dia (cross blade)
Screwdriver - 3 in long x $\frac{1}{8}$ in dia (electricians)
Pliers - electricians side cutters
Pliers - needle nosed
Pliers - circlip (internal and external)
Cold chisel - $\frac{1}{2}$ inch
Scriber
Scraper
Centre punch
Pin punch
Hacksaw
Valve grinding tool
Steel rule/straight-edge
Allen keys
Selection of files
Wire brush (large)
Axle-stands
Jack (strong scissor or hydraulic type)

Special tools

The tools in this list are those which are not used regularly, are expensive to buy, or which need to be used in accordance with their manufacturers' instructions. Unless relatively difficult mechanical jobs are undertaken frequently, it will not be economic to buy many of these tools. Where this is the case, you could consider clubbing together with friends (or joining a motorists' club) to make a joint purchase, or borrowing the tools against a deposit from a local garage or tool hire specialist.

The following list contains only those tools and instruments freely available to the public, and not those special tools produced by the vehicle manufacturer specifically for its dealer network. You will find occasional references to these manufacturers' special tools in the text of this manual. Generally, an alternative method of doing the job without the vehicle manufacturers' special tool is given. However, sometimes, there is no alternative to using them. Where this is the case and the relevant tool cannot be bought or borrowed, you will have to entrust the work to a franchised garage.

> *Valve spring compressor*
> *Piston ring compressor*
> *Balljoint separator*
> *Universal hub/bearing puller*
> *Impact screwdriver*
> *Micrometer and/or vernier gauge*
> *Dial gauge*
> *Stroboscopic timing light*
> *Dwell angle meter/tachometer*
> *Universal electrical multi-meter*
> *Cylinder compression gauge*
> *Lifting tackle*
> *Trolley jack*
> *Light with extension lead*

Buying tools

For practically all tools, a tool dealer is the best source since he will have a very comprehensive range compared with the average garage or accessory shop. Having said that, accessory shops often offer excellent quality tools at discount prices, so it pays to shop around.

Remember, you don't have to buy the most expensive items on the shelf, but it is always advisable to steer clear of the very cheap tools. There are plenty of good tools around at reasonable prices, so ask the proprietor or manager of the shop for advice before making a purchase.

Care and maintenance of tools

Having purchased a reasonable tool kit, it is necessary to keep the tools in a clean serviceable condition. After use, always wipe off any dirt, grease and metal particles using a clean, dry cloth, before putting the tools away. Never leave them lying around after they have been used. A simple tool rack on the garage or workshop wall, for items such as screwdrivers and pliers is a good idea. Store all normal spanners and sockets in a metal box. Any measuring instruments, gauges, meters, etc, must be carefully stored where they cannot be damaged or become rusty.

Take a little care when tools are used. Hammer heads inevitably become marked and screwdrivers lose the keen edge on their blades from time to time. A little timely attention with emery cloth or a file will soon restore items like this to a good serviceable finish.

Working facilities

Not to be forgotten when discussing tools, is the workshop itself. If anything more than routine maintenance is to be carried out, some form of suitable working area becomes essential.

It is appreciated that many an owner mechanic is forced by circumstances to remove an engine or similar item, without the benefit of a garage or workshop. Having done this, any repairs should always be done under the cover of a roof.

Wherever possible, any dismantling should be done on a clean flat workbench or table at a suitable working height.

Any workbench needs a vice: one with a jaw opening of 4 in (100 mm) is suitable for most jobs. As mentioned previously, some clean dry storage space is also required for tools, as well as the lubricants, cleaning fluids, touch-up paints and so on which become necessary.

Another item which may be required, and which has a much more general usage, is an electric drill with a chuck capacity of at least $\frac{5}{16}$ in (8 mm). This, together with a good range of twist drills, is virtually essential for fitting accessories such as wing mirrors and reversing lights.

Last, but not least, always keep a supply of old newspapers and clean, lint-free rags available, and try to keep any working area as clean as possible.

Spanner jaw gap comparison table

Jaw gap (in)	Spanner size
0.250	$\frac{1}{4}$ in AF
0.276	7 mm
0.313	$\frac{5}{16}$ in AF
0.315	8 mm
0.344	$\frac{11}{32}$ in AF; $\frac{1}{8}$ in Whitworth
0.354	9 mm
0.375	$\frac{3}{8}$ in AF
0.394	10 mm
0.433	11 mm
0.438	$\frac{7}{16}$ in AF
0.445	$\frac{3}{16}$ in Whitworth; $\frac{1}{4}$ in BSF
0.472	12 mm
0.500	$\frac{1}{2}$ in AF
0.512	13 mm
0.525	$\frac{1}{4}$ in Whitworth; $\frac{5}{16}$ in BSF
0.551	14 mm
0.563	$\frac{9}{16}$ in AF
0.591	15 mm
0.600	$\frac{5}{16}$ in Whitworth; $\frac{3}{8}$ in BSF
0.625	$\frac{5}{8}$ in AF
0.630	16 mm
0.669	17 mm
0.686	$\frac{11}{16}$ in AF
0.709	18 mm
0.710	$\frac{3}{8}$ in Whitworth, $\frac{7}{16}$ in BSF
0.748	19 mm
0.750	$\frac{3}{4}$ in AF
0.813	$\frac{13}{16}$ in AF
0.820	$\frac{7}{16}$ in Whitworth; $\frac{1}{2}$ in BSF
0.866	22 mm
0.875	$\frac{7}{8}$ in AF
0.920	$\frac{1}{2}$ in Whitworth; $\frac{9}{16}$ in BSF
0.938	$\frac{15}{16}$ in AF
0.945	24 mm
1.000	1 in AF
1.010	$\frac{9}{16}$ in Whitworth; $\frac{5}{8}$ in BSF
1.024	26 mm
1.063	$1\frac{1}{16}$ in AF; 27 mm
1.100	$\frac{5}{8}$ in Whitworth; $\frac{11}{16}$ in BSF
1.125	$1\frac{1}{8}$ in AF
1.181	30 mm
1.200	$\frac{11}{16}$ in Whitworth; $\frac{3}{4}$ in BSF
1.250	$1\frac{1}{4}$ in AF
1.260	32 mm
1.300	$\frac{3}{4}$ in Whitworth; $\frac{7}{8}$ in BSF
1.313	$1\frac{5}{16}$ in AF
1.390	$\frac{13}{16}$ in Whitworth; $\frac{15}{16}$ in BSF
1.417	36 mm
1.438	$1\frac{7}{16}$ in AF
1.480	$\frac{7}{8}$ in Whitworth; 1 in BSF
1.500	$1\frac{1}{2}$ in AF
1.575	40 mm; $\frac{15}{16}$ in Whitworth
1.614	41 mm
1.625	$1\frac{5}{8}$ in AF
1.670	1 in Whitworth; $1\frac{1}{8}$ in BSF
1.688	$1\frac{11}{16}$ in AF
1.811	46 mm
1.813	$1\frac{13}{16}$ in AF
1.860	$1\frac{1}{8}$ in Whitworth; $1\frac{1}{4}$ in BSF
1.875	$1\frac{7}{8}$ in AF
1.969	50 mm
2.000	2 in AF
2.050	$1\frac{1}{4}$ in Whitworth; $1\frac{3}{8}$ in BSF
2.165	55 mm
2.362	60 mm

Jacking and towing

The jack is stowed in the luggage compartment against the rear panel (photo). The wheelbrace is located in the rear of the engine compartment.

The spare wheel is secured beneath the rear end of the car (photo). To remove it, lift up the luggage compartment carpet and slacken the carrier bolt using the wheelbrace until the wheel can be withdrawn from beneath the vehicle.

Before jacking up the car, ensure it is standing on level ground and set the handbrake on firmly. Chock the wheel diagonally opposite the one being raised.

Insert the jack arm into the square socket nearest to the wheel being removed. Ensure the jack is upright and standing on firm ground before raising the car.

If work is to be carried out beneath the vehicle while it is jacked up, axle stands or suitable wooden blocks **must** be placed beneath the car to take its weight in the eventuality of jack failure.

When towing another vehicle or being towed, attach the tow-rope to a sturdy part of the underbody such as the suspension crossmember, never to any part of the steering linkage. Note that the eyes in the front and rear bumper brackets are for lashing the vehicle during transporation only and **must not** be used for towing.

If a vehicle with automatic transmission is to be towed, the towing speed must not exceed 25 mph (40 kph) and the distance towed must not exceed 15 miles (24 km). If these conditions cannot be met, the vehicle must be towed with the front wheels off the ground; this should be done in any case if transmission damage is already suspected. On no account must the vehicle be towed with the rear wheels suspended and the front wheels on the ground.

Location of spare wheel

Location of jack in luggage compartment

Jacking up the car

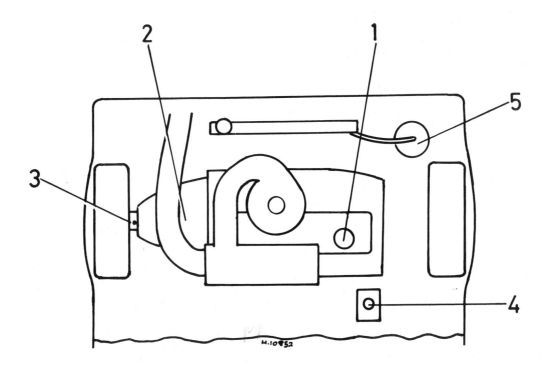

Recommended lubricants and fluids

Component or system	Lubricant type or specification
1 Engine	Multigrade engine oil SAE 20W/50
2 Manual gearbox	SAE 90EP gear oil
3 Final drive (with manual gearbox)	SAE 90EP gear oil
Automatic transmission and final drive	Dexron® automatic transmission fluid
Driveshaft	Multi-purpose lithium-based grease
Hub bearings	Multi-purpose lithium-based grease
Steering unit:	
Early models	Molybdenum grease
Later models	Semi-fluid EP grease
4 Brake and clutch hydraulic systems	Hydraulic fluid to SAE J1703/DOT3
5 Cooling system	Antifreeze to BS 3152

Note: *The above are general recommendations only. Lubrication requirements vary from territory to territory and depend on vehicle usage. Consult the operator's handbook supplied with your vehicle.*

Safety first!

Professional motor mechanics are trained in safe working procedures. However enthusiastic you may be about getting on with the job in hand, do take the time to ensure that your safety is not put at risk. A moment's lack of attention can result in an accident, as can failure to observe certain elementary precautions.

There will always be new ways of having accidents, and the following points do not pretend to be a comprehensive list of all dangers; they are intended rather to make you aware of the risks and to encourage a safety-conscious approach to all work you carry out on your vehicle.

Essential DOs and DON'Ts

DON'T rely on a single jack when working underneath the vehicle. Always use reliable additional means of support, such as axle stands, securely placed under a part of the vehicle that you know will not give way.

DON'T attempt to loosen or tighten high-torque nuts (e.g. wheel hub nuts) while the vehicle is on a jack; it may be pulled off.

DON'T start the engine without first ascertaining that the transmission is in neutral (or 'Park' where applicable) and the parking brake applied.

DON'T suddenly remove the filler cap from a hot cooling system – cover it with a cloth and release the pressure gradually first, or you may get scalded by escaping coolant.

DON'T attempt to drain oil until you are sure it has cooled sufficiently to avoid scalding you.

DON'T grasp any part of the engine, exhaust or catalytic converter without first ascertaining that it is sufficiently cool to avoid burning you.

DON'T syphon toxic liquids such as fuel, brake fluid or antifreeze by mouth, or allow them to remain on your skin.

DON'T inhale brake lining dust – it is injurious to health.

DON'T allow any spilt oil or grease to remain on the floor – wipe it up straight away, before someone slips on it.

DON'T use ill-fitting spanners or other tools which may slip and cause injury.

DON'T attempt to lift a heavy component which may be beyond your capability – get assistance.

DON'T rush to finish a job, or take unverified short cuts.

DON'T allow children or animals in or around an unattended vehicle.

DO wear eye protection when using power tools such as drill, sander, bench grinder etc, and when working under the vehicle.

DO use a barrier cream on your hands prior to undertaking dirty jobs – it will protect your skin from infection as well as making the dirt easier to remove afterwards; but make sure your hands aren't left slippery.

DO keep loose clothing (cuffs, tie etc) and long hair well out of the way of moving mechanical parts.

DO remove rings, wristwatch etc, before working on the vehicle – especially the electrical system.

DO ensure that any lifting tackle used has a safe working load rating adequate for the job.

DO keep your work area tidy – it is only too easy to fall over articles left lying around.

DO get someone to check periodically that all is well, when working alone on the vehicle.

DO carry out work in a logical sequence and check that everything is correctly assembled and tightened afterwards.

DO remember that your vehicle's safety affects that of yourself and others. If in doubt on any point, get specialist advice.

IF, in spite of following these precautions, you are unfortunate enough to injure yourself, seek medical attention as soon as possible.

Fire

Remember at all times that petrol (gasoline) is highly flammable. Never smoke, or have any kind of naked flame around, when working on the vehicle. But the risk does not end there – a spark caused by an electrical short-circuit, by two metal surfaces contacting each other, or even by static electricity built up in your body under certain conditions, can ignite petrol vapour, which in a confined space is highly explosive.

Always disconnect the battery earth (ground) terminal before working on any part of the fuel system, and never risk spilling fuel on to a hot engine or exhaust.

It is recommended that a fire extinguisher of a type suitable for fuel and electrical fires is kept handy in the garage or workplace at all times. Never try to extinguish a fuel or electrical fire with water.

Fumes

Certain fumes are highly toxic and can quickly cause unconsciousness and even death if inhaled to any extent. Petrol (gasoline) vapour comes into this category, as do the vapours from certain solvents such as trichloroethylene. Any draining or pouring of such volatile fluids should be done in a well ventilated area.

When using cleaning fluids and solvents, read the instructions carefully. Never use materials from unmarked containers – they may give off poisonous vapours.

Never run the engine of a motor vehicle in an enclosed space such as a garage. Exhaust fumes contain carbon monoxide which is extremely poisonous; if you need to run the engine, always do so in the open air or at least have the rear of the vehicle outside the workplace.

If you are fortunate enough to have the use of an inspection pit, never drain or pour petrol, and never run the engine, while the vehicle is standing over it; the fumes, being heavier than air, will concentrate in the pit with possibly lethal results.

The battery

Never cause a spark, or allow a naked light, near the vehicle's battery. It will normally be giving off a certain amount of hydrogen gas, which is highly explosive.

Always disconnect the battery earth (ground) terminal before working on the fuel or electrical systems.

If possible, loosen the filler plugs or cover when charging the battery from an external source. Do not charge at an excessive rate or the battery may burst.

Take care when topping up and when carrying the battery. The acid electrolyte, even when diluted, is very corrosive and should not be allowed to contact the eyes or skin.

If you ever need to prepare electrolyte yourself, always add the acid slowly to the water, and never the other way round. Protect against splashes by wearing rubber gloves and goggles.

When jump starting a car using a booster battery, for negative earth (ground) vehicles, connect the jump leads in the following sequence: First connect one jump lead between the positive (+) terminals of the two batteries. Then connect the other jump lead first to the negative (−) terminal of the booster battery, and then to a good earthing (ground) point on the vehicle to be started, at least 18 in (45 cm) from the battery if possible. Ensure that hands and jump leads are clear of any moving parts, and that the two vehicles do not touch. Disconnect the leads in the reverse order.

Mains electricity

When using an electric power tool, inspection light etc, which works from the mains, always ensure that the appliance is correctly connected to its plug and that, where necessary, it is properly earthed (grounded). Do not use such appliances in damp conditions and, again, beware of creating a spark or applying excessive heat in the vicinity of fuel or fuel vapour.

Ignition HT voltage

A severe electric shock can result from touching certain parts of the ignition system, such as the HT leads, when the engine is running or being cranked, particularly if components are damp or the insulation is defective. Where an electronic ignition system is fitted, the HT voltage is much higher and could prove fatal.

Routine maintenance

Maintenance is essential for ensuring safety and desirable for the purpose of getting the best in terms of performance and economy from the car. Over the years the need for periodic lubrication – oiling, greasing and so on – has been drastically reduced if not totally eliminated. This has unfortunately tended to lead some owners to think that because no such action is required the items either no longer exist or will last for ever. This is a serious delusion. It follows therefore that the largest initial element of maintenance is visual examination. This may lead to repair or renewals.

The service intervals shown below are basically those recommended by the manufacturer. Service intervals have been extended considerably in recent years, partly as a result of improvements in lubricants and overall reliability, partly in an effort to reduce running costs. The DIY mechanic may prefer to reduce the service intervals for some tasks, particularly on older or high-mileage cars.

Every 250 miles (400 km) travelled or weekly, whichever comes first

Steering
Check the tyre pressures, including the spare wheel (photo)
Examine tyres for wear or damage
Is steering smooth and accurate?

Brakes
Check reservoir fluid level (photo)
Is there any fall off in braking efficiency?
Try an emergency stop. Is adjustment necessary?

Lights, wipers and horns
Do all bulbs work at the front and rear?
Are the headlamp beams aligned properly?
Do the wipers and horns work?
Check windscreen washer and tailgate washer fluid level (photos)

Engine
Check the sump oil level and top up if required (photo)
Check the coolant level and top up if required (photo)
Check the battery electrolyte level and top up to the level of the plates with distilled water as needed (photo)
Check the drivebelt tension

First 1000 miles (1600 km)

With new cars, or cars fitted with new engines, the following checks should be carried out:
Change engine oil
Check tension of alternator drivebelt
Tighten down cylinder head bolts (see Chapter 1)
Check tightness of bolts on engine and manifolds
Check valve clearances
Check engine idle speed and fuel mixture
Check cooling system hoses and fuel pipe connections for leaks and damage
Check brake system pipes and hoses for leaks and damage
Make a general check of all chassis and body components

Checking the fluid level in the brake and clutch master cylinder reservoir

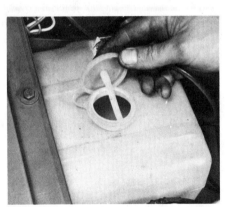
Checking the level of the windscreen washer reservoir

Checking the tyre pressures

Rear window washer reservoir is located in luggage compartment

Topping up the engine oil. Amount needed to raise level from low to high on dipstick is one litre

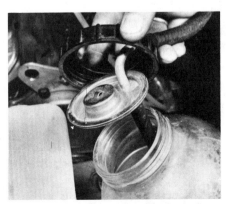
Topping up the cooling system expansion bottle

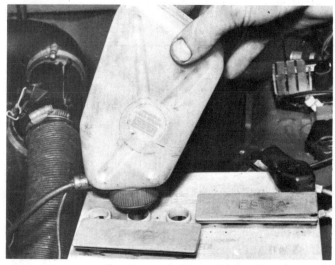

Topping up the battery

Location of gearbox filler/level and drain plugs (arrowed)

Final drive filler and drain plugs

Engine sump drain plug

Every 5000 miles (8000 km) or six months, whichever comes first

Drain engine oil when hot and refill with fresh oil (photo)
Examine spark plugs, regap or renew as necessary

Every 10 000 miles (16 000 km) or twelve months, whichever comes first

In addition to the work specified for the 5000-mile service
Renew engine oil filter when changing oil
Clean flame trap
Clean fuel pump filter
Check valve clearances and adjust if necessary
Lubricate distributor felt pad (where fitted) under rotor arm
Clean and examine HT leads and distributor cap
Renew spark plugs
Check ignition timing and adjust if necessary
Check carburettor adjustments and correct if necessary
Check brake calipers, pipes and hoses for leakage, corrosion or damage
Check disc pads for wear

Check drivebelt tension
Examine handbrake cable and check for correct operation
Check operation of brake fluid level warning light
Examine steering and suspension balljoints and gaiters
Check shock absorbers for leakage and damaged mountings
Check driveshaft gaiters for damage
Check tightness of wheel nuts
Clean battery terminals and coat with petroleum jelly
Check gearbox and final drive oil levels (photos), or automatic transmission fluid level, as appropriate, and top up if necessary
Examine exhaust system for leakage or defective mountings
Check brake pressure reducing valve lever for free operation and lubricate pivot
Examine engine/transmission, cooling system, fuel and clutch hydraulic system for leaks
Clean out door drain holes and heater intake drain
Lubricate all pivots, hinges, locks, catches etc

Every 18 months or 20 000 miles (32 000 km), whichever comes first

Renew brake fluid

Every 20 000 miles (32 000 km) or 2 years, whichever comes first

In addition to the work specified for the 10 000-mile service
Renew air cleaner element (more frequently in dusty conditions)
Renew fuel line filter (if fitted)
Check rear hubs for leakage, adjust endfloat if necessary
Remove rear brake drums and check linings for wear
Drain and renew the gearbox and final drive oils

Every 3 years or 40 000 miles (64 000 km), whichever comes first

Renew all brake rubber parts, including hoses. Inspect pads and
shoes at the same time and renew if necessary

Every 40 000 miles (64 000 km) or 4 years, whichever comes first

*In addition to, or instead of, the work specified for the 10 000-mile
and 20 000-mile services*
Repack rear hub bearings with grease and adjust

Every Autumn

Check antifreeze strength and correct if necessary
In alternate years, drain, flush and refill cooling system

Fault diagnosis

Introduction

The car owner who does his or her own maintenance according to the recommended schedules should not have to use this section of the manual very often. Modern component reliability is such that, provided those items subject to wear or deterioration are inspected or renewed at the specified intervals, sudden failure is comparatively rare. Faults do not usually just happen as a result of sudden failure, but develop over a period of time. Major mechanical failures in particular are usually preceded by characteristic symptoms over hundreds or even thousands of miles. Those components which do occasionally fail without warning are often small and easily carried in the car.

With any fault finding, the first step is to decide where to begin investigations. Sometimes this is obvious, but on other occasions a little detective work will be necessary. The owner who makes half a dozen haphazard adjustments or replacements may be successful in curing a fault (or its symptoms), but he will be none the wiser if the fault recurs and he may well have spent more time and money than was necessary. A calm and logical approach will be found to be more satisfactory in the long run. Always take into account any warning signs or abnormalities that may have been noticed in the period preceding the fault – power loss, high or low gauge readings, unusual noises or smells, etc – and remember that failure of components such as fuses or spark plugs may only be pointers to some underlying fault.

The pages which follow here are intended to help in cases of failure to start or breakdown on the road. There is also a Fault Diagnosis Section at the end of each Chapter which should be consulted if the preliminary checks prove unfruitful. Whatever the fault, certain basic principles apply. These are as follows:

Verify the fault. This is simply a matter of being sure that you know what the symptoms are before starting work. This is particularly important if you are investigating a fault for someone else who may not have described it very accurately.

Don't overlook the obvious. For example, if the car won't start, is there petrol in the tank? (Don't take anyone else's word on this particular point, and don't trust the fuel gauge either!) If an electrical fault is indicated, look for loose or broken wires before digging out the test gear.

Cure the disease, not the symptom. Substituting a flat battery with a fully charged one will get you off the hard shoulder, but if the underlying cause is not attended to, the new battery will go the same way. Similarly, changing oil-fouled spark plugs for a new set will get you moving again, but remember that the reason for the fouling (if it wasn't simply an incorrect grade of plug) will have to be established and corrected.

Don't take anything for granted. Particularly, don't forget that a 'new' component may itself be defective (especially if it's been rattling round in the boot for months), and don't leave components out of a fault diagnosis sequence just because they are new or recently fitted. When you do finally diagnose a difficult fault, you'll probably realise that all the evidence was there from the start.

Electrical faults

Electrical faults can be more puzzling than straightforward mechanical failures, but they are no less susceptible to logical analysis if the basic principles of operation are understood. Car electrical wiring exists in extremely unfavourable conditions – heat, vibration and chemical attack – and the first things to look for are loose or corroded connections and broken or chafed wires, especially where the wires pass through holes in the bodywork or are subject to vibration.

All metal-bodied cars in current production have one pole of the battery 'earthed', ie connected to the car bodywork, and in nearly all

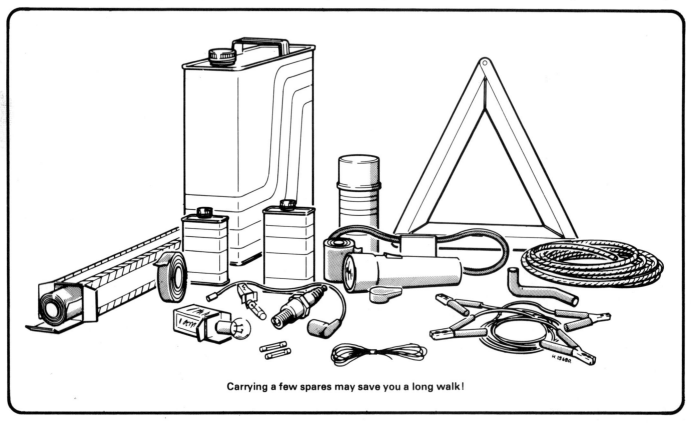

Carrying a few spares may save you a long walk!

modern cars it is the negative (–) terminal. The various electrical components' motors, bulb holders etc – are also connected to earth, either by means of a lead or directly by their mountings. Electric current flows through the component and then back to the battery via the car bodywork. If the component mounting is loose or corroded, or if a good path back to the battery is not available, the circuit will be incomplete and malfunction will result. The engine and/or gearbox are also earthed by means of flexible metal straps to the body or subframe; if these straps are loose or missing, starter motor, alternator and ignition trouble may result.

Assuming the earth return to be satisfactory, electrical faults will be due either to component malfunction or to defects in the current supply. Individual components are dealt with in Chapter 11. If supply wires are broken or cracked internally this results in an open-circuit, and the easiest way to check for this is to bypass the suspect wire temporarily with a length of wire having a crocodile clip or suitable connector at each end. Alternatively, a 12V test lamp can be used to verify the presence of supply voltage at various points along the wire and the break can be thus isolated.

If a bare portion of a live wire touches the car bodywork or other earthed metal part, the electricity will take the low-resistance path thus formed back to the battery: this is known as a short-circuit. Hopefully a short-circuit will blow a fuse, but otherwise it may cause burning of the insulation (and possibly further short-circuits) or even a fire. This is why it is inadvisable to bypass persistently blowing fuses with silver foil or wire.

Spares and tool kit

Most cars are only supplied with sufficient tools for wheel changing; the *Maintenance and minor repair* tool kit detailed in *Tools and working facilities,* with the addition of a hammer, is probably sufficient for those repairs that most motorists would consider attempting at the roadside. In addition a few items which can be fitted without too much trouble in the event of a breakdown should be carried. Experience and available space will modify the list below, but the following may save having to call on professional assistance:

Spark plugs, clean and correctly gapped
HT lead and plug cap – long enough to reach the plug furthest from the distributor
Distributor rotor
Drivebelt – emergency type may suffice
Spare fuses
Set of principal light bulbs
Tin of radiator sealer and hose bandage
Exhaust bandage
Roll of insulating tape
Length of soft iron wire
Length of electrical flex
Torch or inspection lamp (can double as test lamp)
Battery jump leads
Tow-rope
Ignition waterproofing aerosol
Litre of engine oil
Sealed can of hydraulic fluid
Emergency windscreen
Worm drive hose clips.
Tube of filler paste
Tyre valve core

If spare fuel is carried, a can designed for the purpose should be used to minimise risks of leakage and collision damage. A first aid kit and a warning triangle, whilst not at present compulsory in the UK, are obviously sensible items to carry in addition to the above.

When touring abroad it may be advisable to carry additional spares which, even if you cannot fit them yourself, could save having to wait while parts are obtained. The items below may be worth considering:

Throttle cables
Cylinder head gasket
Alternator brushes
Fuel pump repair kit (where applicable)

One of the motoring organisations will be able to advise on availability of fuel etc in foreign countries.

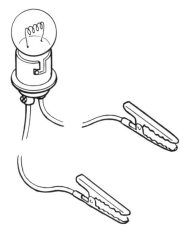

A simple test lamp is useful for diagnosing electrical faults

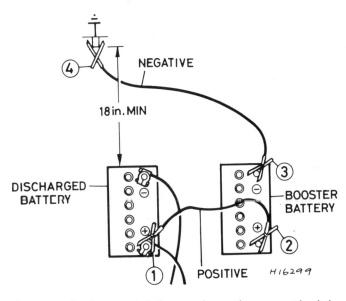

Jump start lead connections for negative earth – connect leads in order shown

Checking for a spark at the HT lead. Use an insulated tool if you need to hold the lead

Engine will not start

Engine fails to turn when starter operated
Flat battery (recharge, use jump leads, or push start)
Battery terminals loose or corroded
Battery earth to body defective
Engine earth strap loose or broken
Starter motor (or solenoid) wiring loose or broken
Automatic transmission selector in wrong position, or inhibitor switch faulty
Ignition/starter switch faulty
Major mechanical failure (seizure) or long disuse (piston rings rusted to bores)
Starter or solenoid internal fault (see Chapter 10)

Starter motor turns engine slowly
Partially discharged battery (recharge, use jump leads, or push start)
Battery terminals loose or corroded
Battery earth to body defective
Engine earth strap loose
Starter motor (or solenoid) wiring loose
Starter motor internal fault (see Chapter 10)

Starter motor spins without turning engine
Starter motor pinion sticking on sleeve
Flywheel gear teeth damaged or worn
Starter motor mounting bolts loose

Engine turns normally but fails to start
Damp or dirty HT leads and distributor cap (crank engine and check for spark) (photo)
Dirty or incorrectly gapped CB points
No fuel in tank (check for delivery at carburettor)
Excessive choke (hot engine) or insufficient choke (cold engine)
Fouled or incorrectly gapped spark plugs (remove, clean and regap)
Other ignition system fault (see Chapter 4)
Other fuel system fault (see Chapter 3)
Poor compression (see Chapter 1)
Major mechanical failure (eg camshaft drive)

Engine fires but will not run
Insufficient choke (cold engine)
Air leaks at carburettor or inlet manifold
Fuel starvation (see Chapter 3)

Engine cuts out and will not restart

Engine cuts out suddenly – ignition fault
Loose or disconnected LT wires
Wet HT leads or distributor cap (after transversing water splash)
Coil or condenser failure (check for spark)
Other ignition fault (see Chapter 4)

Engine misfires before cutting out – fuel fault
Fuel tank empty
Fuel pump defective or filter blocked (check for delivery)
Fuel tank filler vent blocked (suction will be evident on releasing cap)
Carburettor needle valve sticking
Carburettor jets blocked (fuel contaminated)
Other fuel system fault (see Chapter 3)

Engine cuts out – other causes
Serious overheating
Major mechanical failure (eg camshaft drive)

Engine overheats

Ignition (no-charge) warning light illuminated
Slack or broken drivebelt – retension or renew (Chapter 2)

Ignition warning light not illuminated
Coolant loss due to internal or external leakage (see Chapter 2)
Thermostat defective
Low oil level
Brakes binding
Radiator clogged externally or internally
Engine waterways clogged
Ignition timing incorrect or automatic advance malfunctioning
Mixture too weak

Note: *Do not add cold water to an overheated engine or damage may result*

Low engine oil pressure

Gauge reads low or warning light illuminated with engine running
Oil level low or incorrect grade
Defective gauge or sender unit
Wire to sender unit earthed
Engine overheating
Oil filter clogged or bypass valve defective

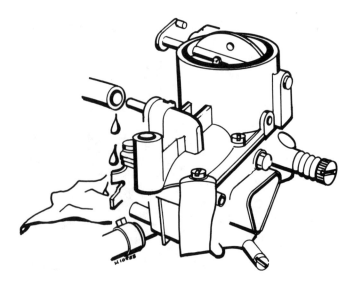

Remove fuel pipe from carburettor and check for fuel delivery

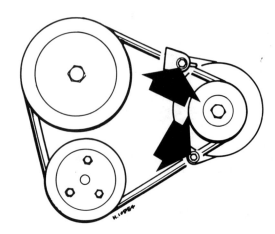

A slack drivebelt can cause overheating and battery charging problems. Slacken bolts (arrowed) to adjust

Oil pressure relief valve defective
Oil pick-up strainer clogged
Oil pump worn or mountings loose
Worn main or big-end bearings

Note: *Low oil pressure in a high-mileage engine at tickover is not ncessarily a cause for concern. Sudden pressure loss at speed is far more significant. In any event, check the gauge or warning light sender before condemning the engine.*

Engine noises

Pre-ignition (pinking) on acceleration

Incorrect grade of fuel
Ignition timing incorrect
Distributor faulty or worn
Worn or maladjusted carburettor
Excessive carbon build-up in engine

Whistling or wheezing noises

Leaking vacuum hose
Leaking carburettor or manifold gasket
Blowing head gasket

Tapping or rattling

Incorrect valve clearances
Worn valve gear
Worn timing chain
Broken piston ring (ticking noise)

Knocking or thumping

Unintentional mechanical contact (eg fan blades)
Worn drivebelt
Peripheral component fault (alternator, water pump etc)
Worn big-end bearings (regular heavy knocking, perhaps less under load)
Worn main bearings (rumbling and knocking, perhaps worsening under load)
Piston slap (most noticeable when cold)

Chapter 1 Engine

For modifications, and information applicable to later models, see Supplement at end of manual

Contents

Specifications

General

Type	Four-cylinder, ohv
Location	Transverse, inclined to rear by 41°
Firing order	1-3-4-2, No 1 at flywheel end
Direction of rotation	Clockwise viewed from timing cover

Cylinder block

	1118 cc	1294 cc and 1442 cc
Cylinder bore diameter:		
Class A	73.9920 to 73.9995 mm	76.6870 to 76.6945 mm
Class B	73.9995 to 74.0070 mm	76.6945 to 76.7020 mm
Class C	74.0070 to 74.0145 mm	76.7020 to 76.7095 mm
Class D	74.0145 to 74.0220 mm	76.7095 to 76.7170 mm
Bore oversizes	+0.1 mm, + 0.4 mm	+ 0.1 mm, + 0.4 mm
Main bearing bore diameter:		
Class A red	55.873 to 55.883 mm	
Class B blue	55.882 to 55.892 mm	
Width of centre bearing bore	26.58 to 26.62 mm	
Camshaft bore diameter (bearings fitted):		
No 1 (flywheel end)	35.484 to 35.520 mm	
No 2	40.984 to 41.020 mm	
No 3	41.484 to 41.520 mm	

Crankshaft and connecting rods

Main bearing journal diameter:	
Class A red	51.975 to 51.985 mm
Class B blue	51.966 to 51.976 mm
Undersizes for regrinding	0.1, 0.2 and 0.5 mm

1 1

1 1 1 1

Main bearing running clearance .... 0.04 to 0.078 mm (0.0015 to 0.003 in)
Big-end journal diameter:
  Class A red .... 40.957 to 40.965 mm
  Class B blue .... 40.949 to 40.957 mm
Undersizes for regrinding .... 0.1, 0.2 and 0.5 mm
Big-end running clearance .... 0.03 to 0.064 mm (0.001 to 0.0025 in)
Crankshaft stroke:
  1118 cc .... 65 mm (2.559 in)
  1294 cc .... 70 mm (2.756 in)
  1442 cc .... 78 mm (3.071 in)
Crankshaft endfloat .... 0.09 to 0.27 mm (0.003 to 0.011 in)
Thrustwasher thickness .... 2.31 to 2.36 mm

Pistons

Material .... Aluminium alloy
Number of rings .... 2 compression, 1 oil control
Maximum weight difference between any two pistons .... 3 g

	1118 cc	1294 cc and 1442 cc
Piston diameter:		
Class A	73.9625 to 73.9700 mm	76.6575 to 76.6650 mm
Class B	73.9700 to 73.9775 mm	76.6650 to 76.6725 mm
Class C	73.9775 to 73.9850 mm	76.6725 to 76.6800 mm
Class D	73.9850 to 73.9925 mm	76.6800 to 76.6875 mm
Piston oversizes	+ 0.1 mm, + 0.4 mm	+ 0.1 mm, + 0.4 mm
Piston-to-bore clearance (nominal)	0.022 to 0.042 mm	0.027 to 0.047 mm
Piston ring end gap:		
Top ring	0.35 to 0.50 mm (0.014 to 0.020 in)	0.30 to 0.45 mm (0.012 to 0.018 in)
2nd ring	0.25 to 0.40 mm (0.010 to 0.016 in)	0.30 to 0.45 mm (0.012 to 0.018 in)
Oil control ring	0.20 to 0.35 mm (0.008 to 0.014 in)	0.25 to 0.40 mm (0.010 to 0.016 in)

Gudgeon pin

Material .... Steel
Outside diameter .... 21.991 to 21.995 mm
Inside diameter .... 13 mm
Length:
  1118 cc .... 64 mm
  1294 cc and 1442 cc .... 66.7 mm

Camshaft and valve gear

Camshaft journal diameter:
  No 1 (flywheel end) .... 35.439 to 35.459 mm
  No 2 .... 40.939 to 40.959 mm
  No 3 .... 41.439 to 41.459 mm
Camshaft endfloat .... 0.10 to 0.20 mm (0.004 to 0.008 in)

	1118 cc and 1294 cc	1442 cc
Valve timing:		
Inlet opens	16° 30' BTDC	19° BTDC
Inlet closes	41° 48' ABDC	61° ABDC
Exhaust opens	52° BBDC	59° BBDC
Exhaust closes	16° 20' ATDC	21° ATDC
Inlet cam lift	5.41 mm	6.05 mm
Exhaust cam lift	5.71 mm	6.05 mm

Cam followers:
  Outside diameter .... 22.974 to 23.000 mm
  Clearance in bores .... Zero to 0.047 mm
  Length .... 39.5 to 40.5 mm

	1118 cc and 1294 cc	1442 cc
Pushrods:		
Length (to bottom of rocker arm ball seat)	201 mm	216.5 mm

Cylinder head

	1118 cc	1294 cc and 1442 cc
Maximum amount to be skimmed from gasket face	1.0 mm (0.039 in)	0.6 mm (0.024 in)
Gasket thickness for use with machined head	2.2 mm (0.086 in)	1.8 mm (0.070 in)
Standard gasket thickness	1.2 mm (0.47 in)	

Valve guides:
  Material .... Cast iron
  Inside diameter .... 8.022 to 8.040 mm
Valve seats:
  Nominal seat width .... 1.5 mm (0.059 in)
  Valve seat angle .... 46°

Valves

Valve clearances – cold:
  Inlet .... 0.25 mm (0.010 in)
  Exhaust .... 0.30 mm (0.012 in)

Valve sequence (from flywheel end)	I,E,I,E,E,I,E,I
Inlet valves:	
Stem diameter	7.970 to 7.985 mm
Stem-to-guide clearance	0.037 to 0.070 mm
Exhaust valves:	
Stem diameter	7.950 to 7.965 mm
Stem-to-guide clearance	0.057 to 0.090 mm
Valve springs free length	48.4 mm (1.905 in)

Lubrication system

Oil pump	Externally mounted gear type
Endfloat-oil pump driveshaft	0.05 to 0.50 mm (0.002 to 0.020 in)
Pump driveshaft bush diameter	12.030 to 12.055 mm
Oil pressure at 80°C and 3000 rpm	3.6 to 5.6 bar (52 to 80 lbf/in²)

Torque wrench settings

	lbf ft	Nm
Cylinder head bolts	52	70
Main bearing cap bolts	48	65
Big-end cap bolts	28	37.5
Flywheel-to-crankshaft	40	55
Crankshaft pulley bolt	110	150
Inlet manifold-to-head	11	15
Exhaust manifold-to-head	15	20
Timing cover-to-block:		
7 mm bolts	9	12.5
8 mm bolts	22	30
Sump main body-to-block	9	12.5
Bottom plate-to-sump	7	10
Oil pump-to-block	9	12.5
Camshaft sprocket-to-camshaft	11	15
Camshaft thrust plate-to-block	11	15
Crankshaft oil seal housing-to-block	9	12.5
Water inlet elbow-to-sump	9	12.5
Distributor mounting plate-to-block	15	20
Dipstick mounting-to-block	9	12.5
Sump drain plug	26	35
Engine mounting rubbers-to-supports	15	20
Right-hand mounting support-to-block	22	30
Left-hand mounting support-to-final drive	22	30
Front mounting support-to-block (10mm bolts)	44	60

1 General description

The Talbot Horizon is powered by a water-cooled, four-cylinder, four-stroke petrol engine of overhead valve configuration and of 1118cc, 1294 cc or 1442 cc capacity. The different engine capacities are obtained by using different cylinder bore diameters and lengths of piston stroke.

The engine is located in a transverse position and is inclined rearwards at an angle of 41°. This lowers the centre of gravity and also improves accessibility to the ancillary components mounted on the front of the engine.

The combined crankcase and cylinder block is of cast iron construction and houses the pistons, connecting rods, crankshaft and camshaft. The cast aluminium alloy pistons are retained on the connecting rods by gudgeon pins which are an interference fit in the connecting rod small-end bore. The connecting rods are attached to the crankshaft by renewable shell type big-end bearings.

The forged steel crankshaft is carried in five main bearings, also of the renewable shell type. Crankshaft endfloat is controlled by semi-circular thrust washers on the upper half of the centre main bearing.

The camshaft runs in three bearings recessed into bores in the cylinder block. Camshaft drive is by a double row timing chain from a sprocket on the crankshaft.

The cylinder head is an aluminium alloy die-casting of crossflow configuration. Inclined inlet and exhaust valves operate in renewable valve guides pressed into the cylinder head. Valve actuation is by rocker arms, pushrods and cam followers activated by the camshaft lobes.

An external spur gear type oil pump is bolted to the rear face of the cylinder block and is driven by a skew gear off the camshaft. Oil is pumped through a full flow filter to the crankshaft main oil gallery and then through drillings in the cylinder block to the camshaft, timing gears and valve train. The cylinder bores, gudgeon pins and valve stems are splash lubricated by oil thrown off the moving parts.

As the Horizon is of European design, all critical engine dimensions and tolerances, described in the text and given in the Specifications, are in metric units only. It is recommended that only metric measuring instruments are used to check and measure these dimensions. Where applicable, the appropriate Imperial conversion is shown against the less critical dimensions.

2 Major operations possible with the engine in the car

The Horizon engine is quite accessible and the following operations can be carried out with the engine in place:

Removal and refitting of the cylinder head, valves and rocker gear
Removal and refitting of the oil pump
Removal and refitting of the sump
Removal and refitting of the big-end bearings (after removal of the sump)
Removal and refitting of the piston/connecting rod assemblies (after removal of the cylinder head and sump)
Removal and refitting of the timing gear components
Removal and refitting of the engine mountings
Removal and refitting of the flywheel (after removal of the transmission)
Removal and refitting of the major ancillary components — inlet and exhaust manifolds, starter motor, water pump, distributor, alternator and oil filter

3 Major operations requiring engine removal

The following operations can only be carried out with the engine removed from the car:

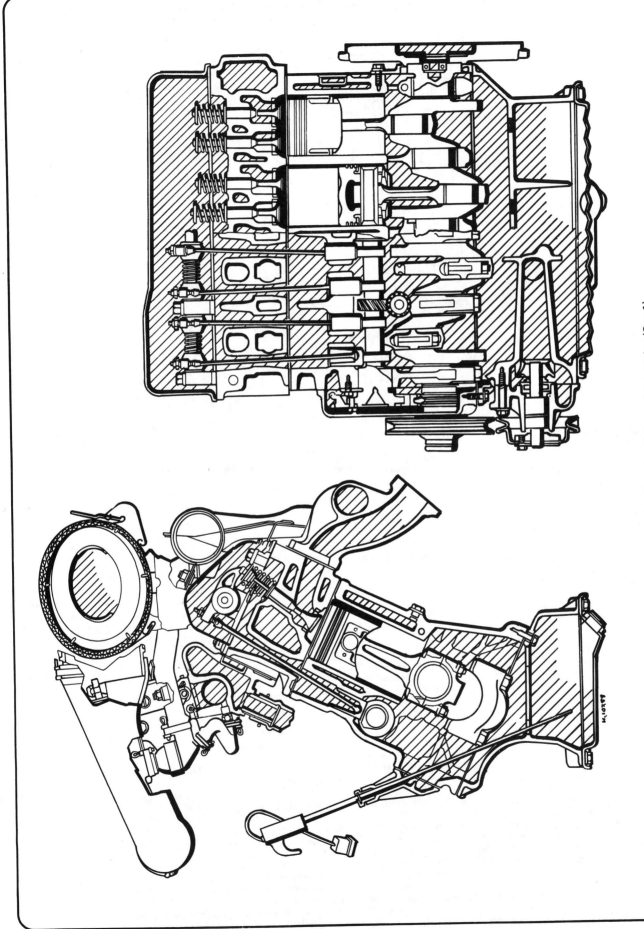

Fig. 1.1 Side and end sectional views of the engine (Sec 1)

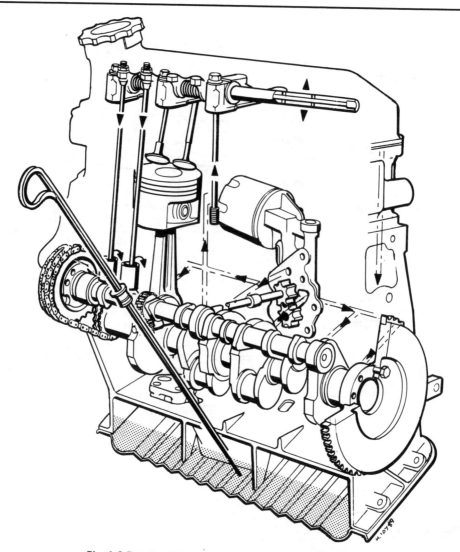

Fig. 1.2 Details of the engine lubrication system (Sec 1)

Removal and refitting of the main bearings
Removal and refitting of the crankshaft
Removal and refitting of the camshaft (but see Section 17)

4 Methods of engine removal

The engine may be removed from the car either on its own or in unit with the manual gearbox or automatic transmission. Unless attention to the transmission is also required, it is recommended that the engine be lifted out separately as this is the easier of the two methods. In both cases removal is from above.

5 Engine – removal (without gearbox or automatic transmission)

1   The removal of the engine is a fairly straightforward operation, but it is essential to have a suitable hoist, and two axle stands if an inspection pit is not available.
2   The sequence of operations listed in this Section is not critical, as the position of the person undertaking the work or the tool in his hand will determine to a certain extent the order in which the work is tackled. Obviously the engine cannot be lifted out until everything is removed from it and the following sequence will ensure that nothing is forgotten.
3   Open the bonnet and mark the position of the hinge brackets using a soft pencil.
4   Disconnect the windscreen washer hose from the outlet on the

washer pump and detach the hose from the clip on the right-hand bonnet hinge.
5   With the help of an assistant, support the bonnet, undo and remove the two bolts securing each hinge and lift the bonnet off the car. Take care to avoid scratching the paintwork.
6   Disconnect the battery terminals, remove the retaining clamp and lift out the battery.
7   Referring to Chapter 2, drain the cooling system and then remove the radiator and electric cooling fan.
8   Remove the complete air cleaner assembly using the procedure described in Chapter 3.
9   Make a careful note of the location of the electrical connections at the alternator and starter solenoid and then disconnect them.
10 Detach the brake servo vacuum hose from the inlet manifold (photo).
11 Detach the heater supply hose from the thermostat housing and the return hose from the outlet on the front of the engine (photos).
12 Make a note of their positions and disconnect the LT and HT connections at the ignition coil (photos).
13 Disconnect the distributor and dipstick multi-plug connectors (photos).
14 Disconnect the electrical leads at the temperature transmitter and oil pressure switch (photos).
15 Undo and remove the bolt securing the battery earth cable and heater hose bracket to the bellhousing. Undo and remove the nut and bolt securing the additional earth lead to the right-hand engine lifting bracket (photos).
16 Slacken the retaining clip and detach the fuel inlet pipe at the fuel pump (photo). Plug the hose after removal.

5.10 Brake vacuum hose connection on inlet manifold

5.11a Removing the heater supply ...

5.11b ... and return hoses

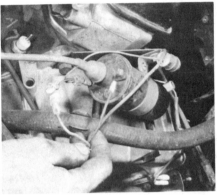
5.12a Removing the LT ...

5.12b ... and earth connections from the coil

5.13a Disconnecting the distributor ...

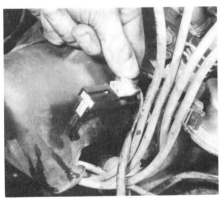
5.13b ... and dipstick connectors

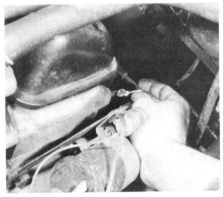
5.14a Disconnecting the temperature transmitter ...

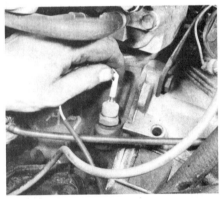
5.14b ... and oil pressure switch leads

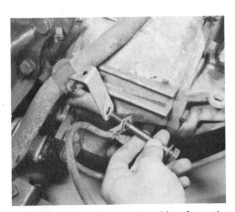
5.15a Removing the earth cables from the bellhousing ...

5.15b ... and from the engine lifting bracket

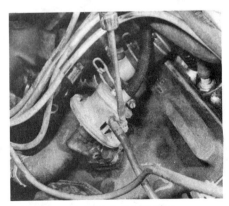
5.16 Removal of the fuel inlet pipe

17 Release the clip securing the electrical harness wiring to the front engine mounting bracket. Move the harness and heater hose toward the left side of the engine compartment, well clear of the engine.

18 Refer to Chapter 3, and disconnect the carburettor control cable(s) according to type of carburettor fitted.

19 Jack up the front of the car and support it on axle stands.

20 Working underneath the car, undo and remove the nuts securing the exhaust front pipe flange to the manifold (photo). Recover the heat shield and gasket.

21 Undo and remove the retaining bolts and lift away the alternator splash shield from under the right-hand wheel arch.

22 Undo and remove the bolts securing the starter motor flange to the bellhousing and the additional lower support bracket bolt. Withdraw the starter motor from the engine.

23 Release the securing bolt and lift off the flywheel dirt shield from the lower face of the bellhousing.

24 If automatic transmission is fitted, mark the relationship of the torque converter to the driveplate using a dab of paint. Rotate the crankshaft pulley until each of the three torque converter securing bolts becomes accessible from the dirt shield or starter motor aperture, and remove the bolts.

25 Support the engine centrally under the sump using a jack and interposed block of wood.

26 Undo and remove the bolts securing the right-hand side stiffener bracket to the body sidemember and upper suspension crossmember (photo). Lift away the stiffener bracket.

27 Undo and remove the nut and two bolts securing the right-hand rear engine mounting rubber to the engine support bracket and crossmember (photos). Now undo and remove the four bolts securing the support bracket to the engine and lift off the bracket and engine mounting rubber.

28 Undo and remove the lower bolts securing the engine to the bellhousing.

29 At the front of the engine, undo and remove the bolts securing the engine mounting rubber to the front body member and the bracket to the cylinder block. Lift off this assembly (photo).

30 Attach suitable lifting gear to the right-hand engine lifting bracket and to a home made angle bracket or similar support bolted to the upper threaded hole of the front engine mounting in the cylinder block.

31 Raise the hoist slightly to just take the weight of the engine and then transfer the jack and block of wood so that it supports the transmission/final drive assembly.

32 Undo and remove the bolts securing the clutch slave cylinder to the bellhousing and position it clear of the engine. Take care not to strain the fluid hose (photo).

33 Undo and remove the remaining engine-to-bellhousing securing bolts and the coil mounting bracket.

34 Make a final check that all cables, pipes, hoses and connections

5.20 The exhaust manifold flange nuts are accessible from beneath the car

5.26 Stiffener bracket-to-crossmember retaining bolts (arrowed)

5.27a Location of the right-hand engine mounting nut (arrowed) ...

5.27b ... and two bolts (arrowed)

5.29 Front engine mounting-to-body member retaining bolts

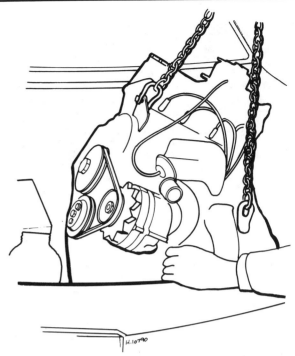

Fig. 1.3 Correct positioning of lifting gear for engine removal (Sec 5)

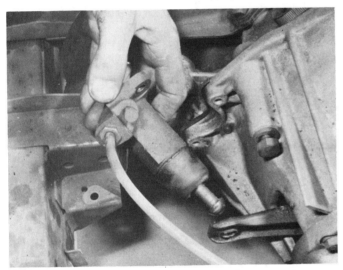

5.32 Removing the clutch slave cylinder

have been disconnected and are well clear of the engine.

35 Move the engine sideways to disengage the gearbox input shaft splines. If automatic transmission is fitted, make sure that the torque converter stays behind on the transmission.

36 Slowly raise the engine, making sure that there is sufficient clearance for the distributor at the front and for the master cylinder at the rear. When the engine is high enough to clear the front body panel, draw the hoist forwards or move the car backwards and then lower the engine to the ground.

37 If the engine is to be dismantled, the oil should now be drained and then the engine exterior thoroughly cleaned as described in Section 9.

6 Engine – removal (with manual gearbox)

1 Begin by referring to Section 5, and carrying out the operations described in paragraphs 1 to 18 inclusive.

2 Disconnect the two wires from the reversing light switch located on the gearbox top cover.

3 Undo and remove the pinch-bolt securing the gear linkage relay lever to the shift rod on the gearbox top cover. Having removed the bolt, it will be seen that the relay lever is still secured to the shift rod by a tapered cotter fitted in the pinch-bolt hole. To remove the cotter, fit a spacer of suitable length, and of larger internal diameter than that

of the cotter, over the bolt, then refit the bolt to the *back* of the cotter. If the bolt is now tightened, the cotter will be drawn into the spacer and once the taper is released can be slid out of the relay lever.

4 Undo and remove the two bolts securing the clutch slave cylinder to the bellhousing. Lift off the cylinder, leaving the hydraulic fluid hose connected, and position it out of the way. Take care not to strain the hose.

5 Jack up the front of the car and securely support it on axle stands.

6 Refer to Chapter 7, and remove both front driveshafts.

7 Working underneath the car, undo and remove the two nuts securing the gear linkage relay lever support bracket to the final drive housing (photo).

8 Slide the support bracket off the studs and withdraw the previously disconnected relay lever off the shift rod. Recover the spring, spring cup and reversing light striker plate from the shift rod, and allow the disconnected linkage to hang down out of the way.

9 Undo and remove the nuts securing the exhaust front pipe flange to the manifold. Recover the heat shield and gasket.

10 Undo and remove the retaining bolts and lift away the alternator splash shield from under the right-hand wheel arch.

11 Undo and remove the clamp bolt securing the speedometer cable to the housing on the final drive. Lift out the cable and position it well clear.

12 Disconnect the wiring at the horn(s) (photo). Undo and remove the retaining bolts and lift off the horn(s) complete with mounting brackets.

13 Disconnect the two wires at the brake master cylinder reservoir filler cap. Undo and remove the two nuts securing the master cylinder to the servo unit, ease the cylinder off its mounting studs and move it as far as possible to the right of the engine compartment without straining the hydraulic pipes or hose (photo).

14 Attach suitable lifting gear to the right and left-hand engine lifting brackets and just take the weight of the engine/transmission assembly.

15 Undo and remove the bolts securing the right-hand side stiffener bracket to the body sidemember and upper suspension crossmember. Lift away the stiffener bracket.

16 Undo and remove the nut and two bolts securing the right-hand rear engine mounting rubber to the engine support bracket and crossmember. Undo and remove the four bolts securing the support bracket to the engine and lift off the bracket and engine mounting rubber.

17 At the front of the engine, undo and remove the bolts securing the engine mounting rubber to the front body member and the mounting

6.7 Relay lever support bracket retaining nuts

6.12 Disconnecting the horn wiring

6.13 Easing the brake master cylinder off its mounting studs. Wires on cap should have been disconnected first!

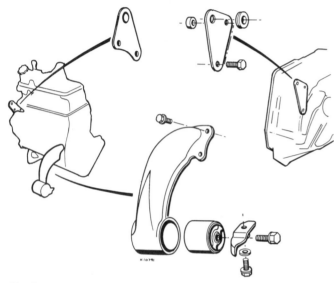

Fig. 1.4 Details of the front engine mountings and lifting brackets (Sec 6)

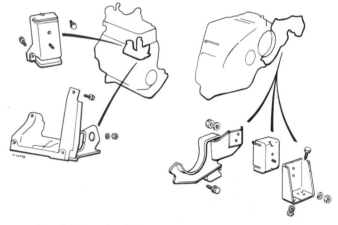

Fig. 1.5 Details of the rear engine mountings (Sec 6)

bracket to the cylinder block. Lift off this assembly.
18 Undo and remove the nut securing the left-hand rear engine mounting bracket to the mounting rubber (photo).
19 Place a jack or stand with interposed block of wood beneath the engine sump and lower the engine onto it.
20 Reposition the lifting gear so that when the engine is raised it will adopt approximately a 30° angle to the horizontal with the right side high.
21 Make a final check that all cables, pipes, hoses and connections have been disconnected and are well clear of the engine.
22 Raise the engine slowly and carefully, stopping periodically to check that nothing is trapped or caught as the unit is lifted (photo).

6.18 Left-hand rear engine mounting rubber and retaining nut

6.22 Lifting out the engine/transmission assembly

23 When sufficient height is gained, lift the transmission end over the front grille panel, draw the hoist forwards or move the car backwards and lower the engine/transmission unit to the ground.

7 Engine – removal (with automatic transmission)

1 Begin by referring to Section 5, and carrying out the operations described in paragraphs 1 to 18 inclusive.
2 Extract the retaining clips and remove the gear selector inner cable from the operating lever on the transmission. Release the outer cable from the support bracket and position the disconnected cable well clear of the engine.
3 Move the throttle valve on the transmission to the fully open position and slide the nipple of the throttle valve inner cable out of its slot. Undo and remove the securing bolts and lift off the throttle valve cable support bracket complete with cable. Position this assembly well clear also.
4 Disconnect the wires at the cruise control speed sensor, if fitted.
5 Make a note of their positions and then disconnect the wires from the starter inhibitor switch on the front face of the transmission.
6 Jack up the front of the car and securely support it on axle stands.
7 Refer to Chapter 7, and remove both front driveshafts.
8 From underneath the car, release the clips securing the fluid cooler pipes to the transmission.
9 Wipe clean the area around the fluid cooler pipe unions on the transmission. Position a suitable container beneath the unions and then unscrew them. Withdraw the pipes from the transmission and allow the fluid to drain. When the fluid has drained, plug the pipe and transmission unions.
10 Undo and remove the nuts securing the exhaust front pipe flange to the manifold. Recover the heat shield and gasket.
11 Undo and remove the retaining bolts and lift away the alternator splash shield from under the right-hand wheel arch.
12 Disconnect the wiring at the horns. Undo and remove the retaining bolts and lift off the horns complete with mounting brackets.
13 Disconnect the two wires at the brake master cylinder reservoir filler cap. Undo and remove the two nuts securing the cylinder to the servo unit, ease the cylinder off its mounting studs and move it as far as possible to the right of the engine compartment without straining the hydraulic pipes or hose.
14 Attach suitable lifting gear to the right and left-hand engine lifting brackets and just take the weight of the engine/transmission assembly.
15 At the front of the engine, undo and remove the bolts securing the engine mounting rubber to the front body member, and the mounting bracket to the cylinder block. Lift off this assembly.
16 Undo and remove the securing bolts and nuts and then lift away the right-hand rear engine mounting and the left-hand rear engine mounting complete with support bracket.
17 Place a jack or stand with interposed block of wood beneath the engine sump and lower the engine onto it.
18 Reposition the lifting gear so that when the engine/transmission assembly is raised, it will adopt approximately a 30° angle to the horizontal with the right-hand side (timing cover end) high.
19 Make a final check that all cables, pipes, hoses and connections have been disconnected and are well clear of the engine.
20 Raise the engine slowly and carefully, stopping periodically to check that nothing is trapped or caught as the assembly is lifted.
21 When sufficient height is gained, lift the automatic transmission over the front grille panel, draw the hoist forwards or move the car backwards, and lower the engine/automatic transmission unit to the ground.

8 Engine – separation from manual gearbox or automatic transmission

1 If the engine has been removed complete with transmission assembly, it is necessary to separate the two units before dismantling work on the engine can begin.
2 To do this, first undo and remove the bolts securing the starter motor flange to the bellhousing and the bolt securing the lower support bracket to the cylinder block. Lift away the starter motor.
3 Undo and remove the bolts securing the ignition coil mounting plate to the bellhousing and lift off this assembly.
4 Undo and remove the bolts securing the flywheel or torque converter dirt shield to the lower face of the bellhousing and withdraw the shield.
5 If automatic transmission is fitted, mark the relationship of the torque converter to the driveplate using a dab of paint. Rotate the crankshaft pulley until each of the three torque converter securing bolts becomes accessible from the dirt shield or starter motor aperture and remove the bolts.
6 Suitably support the gearbox or automatic transmission assembly and undo and remove the remaining bolts securing the bellhousing to the engine.
7 The bellhousing and gearbox or automatic transmission assembly can now be withdrawn from the engine. If a manual gearbox is fitted, take care not to allow any excessive side loads to be imposed on the input shaft as it is drawn out of the clutch disc, otherwise the shaft and disc may be damaged. If automatic tranmmission is fitted, make sure that the torque converter stays on the transmission assembly as it is withdrawn.
8 If the engine is to be dismantled, the oil should now be drained and then the engine exterior thoroughly cleaned as described in the following Section.

9 Engine – dismantling (general)

1 Ideally, the engine is mounted on a proper stand for overhaul but it is anticipated that most owners will have a strong bench on which to place it. If a sufficiently large strong bench is not available then the work can be done at ground level. It is essential, however, that some form of substantial wooden surface is available. Timber should be at least ¾ inch thick, otherwise the weight of the engine will cause projections to punch holes straight through it.
2 It will save a great deal of time later if the engine is thoroughly cleaned down on the exterior before any dismantling begins. This can be done by using paraffin and a stiff brush or more easily, probably, by the use of a water soluble solvent which can be brushed on and then the dirt swilled off with a water jet. This will dispose of all the heavy grease and grit once and for all so that later cleaning of individual components will be a relatively clean process and the paraffin bath will not become contaminated with abrasive metal.
3 As the engine is stripped down, clean each part as it comes off. Try to avoid immersing parts with oilways in paraffin as pockets of liquid could remain and cause oil dilution in the critical first few revolutions after reassembly. Clean oilways with wire, or preferably, an air jet.
4 Where possible, avoid damaging gaskets on removal, especially if new ones have not been obtained. They can be used as patterns if new ones have to be specially cut.
5 It is helpful to obtain a few blocks of wood to support the engine while it is in the process of dismantling. Start dismantling at the top of the engine and then turn the block over and deal with the sump and crankshaft etc, afterwards.
6 Nuts and bolts should be refitted in their locations where possible to avoid confusion later. As an alternative keep each group of nuts and bolts together in a jar or tin.
7 Many items which are removed must be refitted in the same position, if they are not being renewed. These include valves, rocker arms, tappets, pistons, pushrods, bearings and connecting rods. Some of these are marked on assembly to avoid any possibility of mixing them up during overhaul. Others are not, and it is a great help if adequate preparation is made in advance to classify these parts. Suitably labelled tins or jars and, for small items, egg trays, tobacco tins and so on, can be used. The time spent in this operation will be amply repaid later.
8 Other items which will be useful are a notebook and pencil, masking tape (for labelling components) and a good supply of plastic bags. Do make notes of the positions of washers, shims etc – you may think you will remember as you are dismantling but it can be a different story when the time comes for reassembly!

10 Engine ancillary components – removal

1 Before basic engine dismantling begins it is necessary to remove the engine ancillary components as follows:

(a) Distributor cap and HT leads
(b) Rocker cover

(c) Exhaust manifold
(d) Thermostat housing
(e) Inlet manifold and carburettor
(f) Water inlet elbow and hose assembly
(g) Alternator
(h) Distributor
(j) Oil filter and housing (with pump unit)
(k) Fuel pump
(m) Water pump
(n) Clutch assembly

2   It is possible to remove any of these components with the engine in place in the car, if it is merely the individual items which require attention. Assuming the engine to be out of the car and on a bench, and that the items mentioned are still on the engine, follow the procedures described below.

3   *Distributor cap and HT leads:* Mark the HT leads one to four with a dab of paint, noting that No 1 cylinder is next to the flywheel, and then pull the leads off the spark plugs. Lift up the protective cover over the distributor cap and spring back the clips or unscrew the two screws. Detach the HT leads from the support clip and lift off the cap and lead.

4   *Rocker cover:* First undo and remove the nuts and bolt securing the hot air box to the rocker cover and lift off the box. The remaining rocker cover nuts can now be removed and the cover lifted away complete with gasket.

5   *Exhaust manifold:* Undo and remove the five nuts, lift the manifold off the studs and recover the gasket.

6   *Thermostat housing:* Compress and slide the water hose securing clip away from the end of the hose nearest the thermostat housing. Undo and remove the two housing retaining bolts, disengage the housing outlet from the hose and lift off.

7   *Inlet manifold and carburettor:* Compress and slide the clip, securing the water hose to the outlet beneath the manifold, away from the hose end. Detach the water hoses from the carburettor flange (where applicable), the vacuum pipe and fuel inlet hose from the carburettor and then undo and remove the manifold securing nuts. Lift off the manifold complete with carburettor and disengage the lower water hose.

8   *Water inlet elbow and hose assembly:* Undo and remove the adjusting bolt at the base of the alternator. Next undo and remove the inlet elbow retaining bolts and HT lead support bracket retaining bolt. Lift off the alternator lower support bracket, followed by the inlet elbow and hose assembly.

9   *Alternator:* Undo and remove the upper retaining bolt, lift off the drivebelt and withdraw the alternator.

10 *Distributor:* Before removing the distributor carefully scribe an alignment mark between the distributor body and its mounting bracket using a small sharp screwdriver or similar tool. The distributor clamp retaining bolt can now be removed, the clamp lifted away and the distributor withdrawn.

11 *Oil filter, pump and housing:* Remove the filter cartridge first by unscrewing it from the housing. If it is tight, use a strap or chain wrench to turn it the first half a turn. The housing (which is also the oil pump) can be withdrawn after undoing the retaining bolts.

12 *Fuel pump:* Undo and remove the two bolts and lift off the pump. Recover the insulator block and gaskets.

13 *Water pump:* Ease back the hose clips and remove the water hose from pump to timing cover. Undo and remove the three pulley bolts and take off the pulley. Now undo and remove the five water pump retaining bolts and remove the pump.

14 *Clutch assembly:* Slacken the clutch cover retaining bolts in a diagonal and progressive sequence. Mark the position of the cover relative to the flywheel, remove the bolts and ease the cover off its locating dowels. Recover the clutch disc, noting which way round it is fitted.

15 With all the ancillary components removed, the major engine components can now be dismantled as described in the following Sections

11 Cylinder head – removal (engine in car)

1   Disconnect the battery earth terminal and then drain the cooling system as described in Chapter 2.
2   Remove the complete air cleaner assembly as described in Chapter 3.

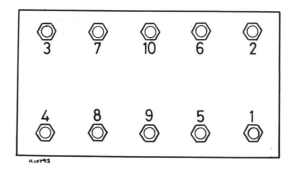

Fig. 1.6 Sequence of slackening the cylinder head bolts (Sec 11)

3   Undo and remove the nuts securing the exhaust front pipe to the manifold flange and recover the heat shield and gasket. If it is necessary to jack up the car for this operation, make sure that it is well supported on axle stands.

4   Slacken the retaining clip and remove the brake servo vacuum hose from the inlet manifold.

5   Undo and remove the two nuts and one bolt securing the air cleaner hot air box to the rocker cover. Lift off the air box.

6   Slacken the retaining clips and withdraw the radiator top hose and heater hose from their outlets on the thermostat housing.

7   Slacken the hose clips and detach the water hose from the bottom of the inlet manifold, and the two carburettor flange or automatic choke water hoses from the carburettor.

8   Mark the positions of the HT leads and then pull them off the spark plugs. Note that No 1 cylinder is nearest to the flywheel.

9   Detach fuel inlet pipe and distributor vacuum advance pipe from the carburettor.

10 Refer to Chapter 3, and disconnect the accelerator cable and choke cable (where applicable) from the carburettor.

11 Detach the electrical lead from the temperature gauge transmitter at the rear of the cylinder head.

12 Undo and remove the remaining securing nuts and lift off the rocker cover complete with breather hose. Recover the rocker cover gasket. The engine must be cold before proceeding any further to avoid distortion of the cylinder head.

13 Slacken all the cylinder head bolts one turn at a time in the order shown in Fig. 1.6, and then undo and remove them completely.

14 Lift off the rocker shaft assembly, holding it at both ends to prevent it springing apart. After removal secure the assembly with wire to keep it together.

15 Lift out each pushrod in turn, using a twisting motion to release them from the cam followers. Punch eight holes in a stiff piece of cardboard, number them one to eight and place the pushrods in order of removal through the cardboard.

16 The cylinder head, complete with manifolds and carburettor, can now be removed by lifting it upwards. If the head is stuck, try to rock it to break the seal or strike it sharply with a hide or plastic mallet. Under no circumstances should the head be struck directly with a metal hammer, nor should any attempt be made to prise it apart from the cylinder block using a screwdriver or cold chisel. Cranking the engine on the starter motor may be effective in breaking the seal of a stubborn gasket.

17 Having removed the cylinder head, lift out the cam followers. Withdraw them one at a time, keeping each follower in its correct order of removal so that it can be refitted in its original bore.

18 If further work is to be carried out on the cylinder head, remove the thermostat housing and manifolds as described in Section 10, before proceeding.

12 Cylinder head – removal (engine out of car)

Remove the engine ancillary components as described in Section 10, and then proceed as directed in paragraphs 13 to 17 inclusive, of the previous Section.

13 Valves – removal

With the cylinder head removed from the engine, the valves can be removed as follows.

1   First remove the spark plugs.

2   Using a conventional valve spring compressor, compress each valve spring in turn until the two halves of the collets can be removed. Release the compressor and remove the spring and spring cup, valve oil seal, spring seat and the valve itself.

3   As before, identify all the parts so that they may be refitted into the same positions from which they were taken.

4   If when the valve spring compressor is screwed down, the valve spring cup refuses to free and expose the split collets, do not screw the compressor further down in an effort to force the cup free. Gently tap the top of the tool directly over the spring cup with a light hammer. This will usually free the cup. Whilst tapping the tool, hold the compressor firmly with your other hand to prevent the tool jumping off the cup when it is released.

14 Sump – removal

1   The sump consists of two parts: a lower pressed steel baseplate, containing the drain plug, and a light alloy main body incorporating anti-surge baffles. A separate compartment on the front face of the main body houses the water pump and water inlet elbow.

2   If the sump is to be removed with the engine in the car it is first necessary to drain the engine oil and the cooling system, and then remove the starter motor, alternator dirt shield, alternator and water pump hoses. Full information covering these operations will be found in the relevant Sections and Chapters of this manual.

3   If the engine is out of the car and on the bench, turn it over on its side so that the sump bolts are accessible.

4   Undo and remove the fourteen baseplate retaining bolts and lift off the plate.

5   Undo and remove the three retaining bolts and withdraw the oil pick-up and strainer assembly.

6   Undo and remove the bolts inside and along the outer edge of the main body and lift off this assembly. If it is stuck, tap it free using a hide or plastic mallet. Recover the cork and paper gaskets from the baseplate, main body and strainer mating faces.

15 Flywheel – removal

1   If this component is to be removed with the engine in the car, it will first be necessary to remove the bellhousing and gearbox assembly and then the clutch as described in Chapter 6 and Chapter 5 respectively.

2   If the engine is on the bench, turn it the right way up and stand it on wooden blocks positioned beneath the crankcase.

3   Lock the flywheel to prevent it turning by engaging a strip of angle iron with the ring gear teeth and resting it against a bar inserted through the rear engine-to-bellhousing retaining bolt hole.

4   Undo and remove the flywheel retaining bolts in a progressive, diagonal sequence, recover the seating plate, and lift off the flywheel. Be careful not to drop it, it is heavy.

16 Timing cover, gears and chain – removal

1   Remove the sump as described in Section 14.

2   Place a block of wood between the crankshaft and the side of the crankcase to prevent rotation of the crankshaft.

3   Using a socket and extension bar, undo and remove the crankshaft pulley retaining bolt and then lever off the pulley using two screwdrivers. The retaining bolt is very tight.

4   Undo and remove the timing cover retaining bolts, ease the cover off its locating dowels and remove it from the front face of the engine.

5   Undo and remove the three bolts securing the camshaft sprocket to the camshaft. On early models these bolts are secured with lockwashers whose tabs must be relieved first.

6   Lift off the camshaft sprocket complete with chain and then using two screwdrivers, lever off the crankshaft sprocket. Recover the Woodruff key from the end of the crankshaft.

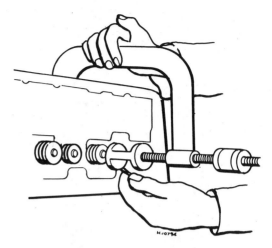

Fig. 1.7 Using a valve spring compressor to remove the valves (Sec 13)

17 Camshaft and oil pump driveshaft – removal

It is theoretically possible to remove the camshaft with the engine in the car. However, the preliminary work is so extensive – removal of cylinder head, sump, starter motor and fuel pump, followed by the lowering of the front of the engine – that the procedure is not recommended. With the engine on the bench and the camshaft sprocket removed as described in Section 16, proceed as follows.

1   Undo and remove the two bolts that secure the distributor mounting plate to the side of the cylinder block and lift off the plate.

2   Withdraw the distributor driving dog from the splined end of the oil pump driveshaft.

3   Using a pair of pliers, extract the small circlip from the end of the shaft, lift out the driven gear and then slide out the driveshaft from the oil pump side of the cylinder block.

4   Rotate the camshaft until the cut-outs on the front flange are aligned with the thrust plate retaining bolts. Relieve the locktabs (if applicable), then undo and remove the thrust plate retaining bolts.

5   Lift off the thrust plate and then carefully withdraw the camshaft from the front of the engine. Take care to avoid scratching the soft bearing surfaces with the camshaft lobes.

18 Piston and connecting rod assemblies – removal

1   This operation may be carried out with the engine in the car after removal of the cylinder head, described in Section 11, and the sump, described in Section 14.

2   Before removing the piston and connecting rod assemblies, clean off all traces of carbon from the top of the cylinder bores. If a wear ridge can be felt, reduce this as much as possible, using a suitable scraper, to avoid damaging the pistons and rings during removal.

3   Rotate the crankshaft in the normal direction of rotation until No 1 piston is at the bottom of its stroke.

4   Undo and remove the big-end bearing nuts on No 1 connecting rod and take off the cap and lower bearing shell. If the cap is tight, tap it gently from side to side using a hammer.

5   Push the piston and connecting rod assembly up through the bore and withdraw it from the top of the cylinder block. Take care not to score the crankshaft journal with the big-end bolts.

6   Refit the bearing cap and lower shell to the connecting rod and secure with the nuts finger tight. Make sure that the upper and lower bearing shells are not interchanged if they are to be re-used. Identification numbers may be stamped on the connecting rod and big-end cap to indicate the cylinder to which they are fitted (photo). If numbers are not visible, suitably mark the cap and rod using a centre punch.

7   Repeat the above procedure for the remaining three piston and connecting rod assemblies, turning the crankshaft as necessary to gain access to the big-end nuts.

18.6 Identification numbers stamped on connecting rod and cap

23.2 Checking crankshaft journal wear with a micrometer

19 Crankshaft and main bearings – removal

1   In order to be able to remove the crankshaft it will be necessary to have completed the following tasks:

   (a) Removal of engine
   (b) Separation of engine from transmission
   (c) Removal of cylinder head
   (d) Removal of sump and flywheel
   (e) Removal of timing cover, gears and chain
   (f) Removal of big-end bearings

2   It is not essential to have extracted the pistons and connecting rods, but it makes for a less cluttered engine block during crankshaft removal.
3   Begin by removing the five retaining bolts and lifting off the oil seal housing at the rear of the crankshaft and cylinder block.
4   Check that the main bearing caps have identification numbers marked on them; No 1 should be at the flywheel end and No 5 at the timing gear end. If identification is not visible, use a centre punch to mark the caps. Also note the direction of fitting of the caps.
5   Slacken the main bearing cap retaining bolts by one turn only to begin with. Once all have been loosened, proceed to unscrew and remove them.
6   The bearing caps can now be lifted away, together with the shells inside them. Finally the crankshaft can be removed, followed by the upper shells seated in the crankcase.

20 Gudgeon pins – removal

The pistons are retained on the connecting rods by gudgeon pins, which are an interference fit in the connecting rod small-end bore. If new pistons are to be fitted, it is strongly recommended that you take the assemblies to your Talbot dealer or motor engineering specialist to have this done, otherwise damage to the piston or distortion of the connecting rod may result.

21 Piston rings – removal

1   To remove the piston rings, slide them carefully over the top of the piston, taking care not to scratch the aluminium alloy; never slide them off the bottom of the piston skirt. It is very easy to break the cast iron piston rings if they are pulled off roughly, so this operation should be done with extreme care. It is helpful to make use of an old 0.5 mm (0.020 in) feeler gauge.
2   Lift one end of the piston ring to be removed out of this groove and insert under it the end of the feeler gauge.
3   Turn the feeler gauge slowly round the piston and, as the ring

comes out of its groove, apply slight upward pressure so it rests on the land above. It can then be eased off the piston with the feeler gauge stopping it from slipping into an empty groove if it is any but the top piston ring that is being removed.
4   Repeat the procedure on the remaining piston rings. Keep the rings with their pistons if they are to be re-used.

22 Engine components – examination for wear

When the engine has been stripped down and all parts properly cleaned, decisions have to be made as to what needs renewal. The following Sections tell the examiner what to look for. In any border-line case it is always best to decide in favour of a new part. Even if a part may still be serviceable, its life will have to be reduced by wear and the degree of trouble needed to renew it in the future must be taken into consideration. However, these things are relative and it depends on whether a quick 'survival' job is being done or whether the car as a whole is being regarded as having many thousands of miles of useful and economical life remaining.

23 Crankshaft – examination and renovation

1   Look at the main bearing journals and the crankpins. If there are any deep scratches or score marks, the shaft will need regrinding. Such conditions will nearly always be accompanied by similar deterioration in the matching bearing shells.
2   Each bearing journal must also be perfectly round and can be checked with a micrometer (photo) or caliper gauge around the periphery at several points. If there is more than 0.02 mm (0.001 in) of ovality, regrinding is necessary.
3   A main Talbot agent or motor engineering specialist will be able to decide to what extent regrinding is necessary and also supply the special oversize shell bearings to match whatever may need grinding off.
4   Before taking the crankshaft for regrinding, check also the cylinder bore and pistons as it may be advantageous to have the whole engine done at the same time.
5   Check the spigot bearing or bush in the end of the crankshaft for wear, and if necessary renew it.

24 Crankshaft main and big-end bearings – examination and renovation

1   With careful servicing and regular oil and filter changes, bearings will last for a very long time. But they can still fail for unforeseen reasons. With big-end bearings, an indication is a regular rhythmic loud knocking from the crankcase. The frequency depends on engine

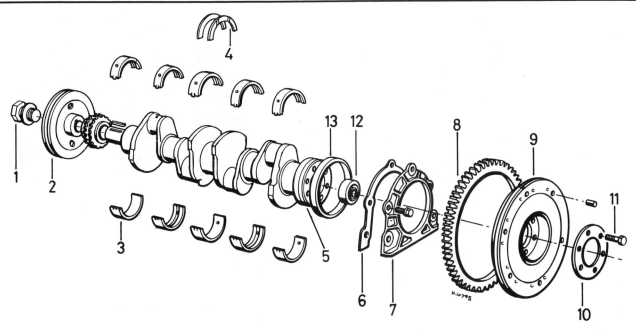

Fig. 1.8 Crankshaft and flywheel assembly (Sec 24)

1 Pulley retaining bolt	5 Crankshaft	8 Starter ring gear	11 Flywheel bolt
2 Pulley	6 Gasket	9 Flywheel	12 Spigot bush
3 Shell bearing	7 Oil seal cover	10 Locking plate	13 Crankshaft rear flange seal
4 Thrust washers			

speed and is particularly noticeable when the engine is under load. This symptom is accompanied by a fall in oil pressure although this is not normally noticeable unless an oil pressure gauge is fitted. Main bearing failure is usually indicated by serious vibration, particularly at higher engine revolutions, accompanied by a more significant drop in oil pressure and a 'rumbling' noise.

2   Big-end bearings can be removed with the engine still in the car. If the failure is sudden and the engine has a low mileage since new or overhaul, this is possibly worth doing. Bearing shells in good condition have bearing surfaces with a smooth, even matt silver/grey colour all over. Worn bearings will show patches of a different colour when the bearing metal has worn away and exposed the underlay. Damaged bearings will be pitted or scored. It is always well worthwhile fitting new shells as their cost is relatively low. If the crankshaft is in good condition, it is merely a question of obtaining another set of standard size shells (but see below). A reground crankshaft will need new bearing shells as a matter of course.

3   During production, engines may be fitted with crankshafts having their main bearing journals, or crankpin journals, or both, 0.20 mm undersize. Additionally, the width of the centre main bearing journal may be 0.20 mm oversize. These crankshafts are identified by the letters Ab stamped on the flywheel end balance weight if the crankpins are undersize, and/or Bb if the main journals are undersize. Similarly, Cb is stamped on the centre balance weight if the centre main journal is oversize. There is also a blue paint mark on the timing cover end balance weight on all crankshafts which are not standard size in all respects.

4   To maintain the specified bearing running clearances, main and big-end bearing shells are available in two thicknesses for the standard size and each undersize. The colour coding is red for the larger size and blue for the smaller size, and can be seen along the circumferential edge of each bearing shell. The paint colour on the main bearing cap and connecting rod cap indicates the colour of shell that must be fitted to the crankcase upper half and connecting rod upper half respectively. The paint colour on the crankshaft web adjacent to each journal indicates the colour of shell that must be fitted to the main bearing cap or connecting rod cap. Thus the half shells in any one journal may be the same or different colours. To maintain the correct running clearances they must not be interchanged.

5   If the crankshaft is not being reground, but the bearings are to be renewed, take the old shells along to your supplier and check that you are getting the correct size bearings.

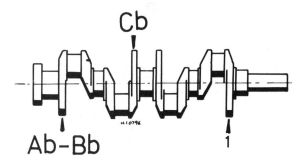

Fig. 1.9 Crankshaft identification markings (Sec 24)

Ab Crankpin journals 0.20 mm undersize
Bb Main journals 0.20 mm undersize
Cb Centre journal 0.20 mm oversize width
1   Blue paint mark

25 Cylinder bores – examination and renovation

1   A new cylinder is perfectly round and the walls parallel throughout its length. The action of the piston tends to wear the walls at right-angles to the gudgeon pin due to side thrust. This wear takes place principally on that section of the cylinder swept by the piston rings.

2   It is possible to get an indication of bore wear by removing the cylinder head with the engine still in the car. With the piston down in the bore, first signs of wear can be seen and felt just below the top of the bore where the top piston ring reaches and there will be a noticeable lip. If there is no lip it is fairly reasonable to expect that bore wear is not severe and any lack of compression or excessive oil comsumption is due to worn or broken piston rings or pistons.

3   If it is possible to obtain a bore measuring micrometer, measure the bore in the thrust plane below the lip and again at the bottom of

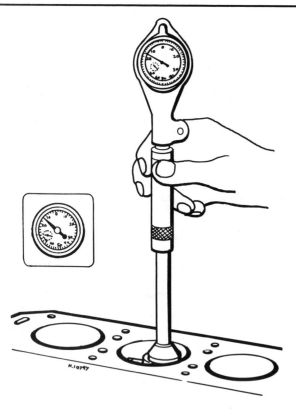

Fig. 1.10 Measuring cylinder bore wear with a bore gauge (Sec 25)

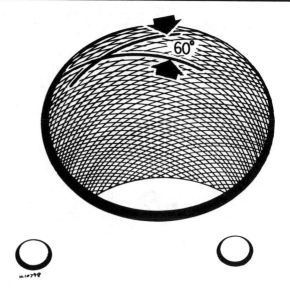

Fig. 1.11 Desired cross-hatch pattern in cylinder bore after deglazing (Sec 25)

Fig. 1.12 Checking the piston ring gap with feeler gauges (Sec 26)

the cylinder in the same plane. If the difference is more than 0.15 mm (0.006 in), a rebore is necessary. SImilarly, a difference of 0.08 mm (0.003 in) or more between two measurements of the bore diameter taken at right angles to each other is a sign of ovality, calling for a rebore.

4   Any bore which is significantly scratched or scored will need reboring. This sympton usually indicates that the piston or rings are damaged also. In the event of only one cylinder being in need of reboring it will still be necessary for all four to be bored and fitted with new oversize pistons and rings. Your Talbot agent or local motor engineering specialist will be able to rebore and obtain the necessary matched pistons. If the crankshaft is undergoing regrinding also, it is a good idea to let the same firm renovate and reassemble the crankshaft and pistons to the block. A reputable firm normally gives a guarantee for such work.

5   If the cylinders are in a satisfactory condition and a rebore is not necessary but new pistons and/or rings are to be fitted, the cylinder bores must be deglazed. This entails removing the high surface polish or glaze on the cylinder walls which will otherwise prevent the new rings from properly bedding in, with resultant high oil consumption.

6   Deglazing can be carried out using a fine grade emery cloth wrapped around a suitable former. Use liberal amounts of paraffin to keep the emery unclogged and use a criss-cross action so that the resulting finish is of a cross-hatch pattern. On completion thoroughly wash the block and remove all traces of emery grit.

26 Pistons and piston rings – examination and renovation

1   Worn pistons and rings can usually be diagnosed when the symptoms of excessive oil consumption and low compression occur and are sometimes, though not always, associated with worn cylinder bores. Compression testers that fit into the spark plug hole are available and these can indicate where low compression is occurring. Wear usually accelerates the more it is left so when the symptoms occur, early action can possibly save the expense of a rebore.

2   Another sympton of piston wear is piston slap – a knocking noise from the crankcase not to be confused with big-end bearing failure. It can be heard clearly at low engine speed when there is no load (idling

for example) especially when the engine is cold and is much less audible when the engine speed increases. Piston wear usually occurs in the skirt or lower end of the piston and is indicated by vertical streaks in the worn area which is always on the thrust side. It can also be seen where the skirt thickness is different.

3   Piston ring wear can be checked by first removing the rings from the pistons as described in Section 21. Then place the rings in the cylinder bores from the top, pushing them down about 38 mm (1.5 in) with the head of a piston (from which the rings have been removed) so that they rest square in the cylinder. Now measure the gap at the ends of the rings with a feeler gauge and compare the dimension obtained with the figures given in Specifications. It the gaps are excessive the rings must be renewed.

4   The grooves in which the rings locate in the pistons can also become enlarged in use. These clearances can be measured with the rings in position on the piston. Excessive clearances will require renewal of the piston and rings as an assembly.

27 Connecting rods – examination and renovation

1   The connecting rods are not subject to wear but can, in the case of engine seizure, become bent or twisted. If any distortion is visible or even suspected, the rod must be renewed,

2   The rods should also be checked for hairline cracks or deep nicks and if in evidence, the rod discarded and a new one fitted.

28 Camshaft and camshaft bearings – examination and renovation

1   The camshaft lobes and bearing journals should be carefully examined for any indications of flat spots, deep scoring, pitting or breakdown of the surface hardening. If any of these conditions exist the camshaft must be renewed, together with a complete set of cam followers.

2   If only very slight scoring marks on the lobes are noticed, these can be removed by a very gentle rubbing down with fine emery cloth or an oil stone. The greatest care should be taken to keep the cam profiles smooth.

3   Removal of the camshaft bearings in the cylinder block can be carried out using the following method.

4   First drive out the camshaft bearing sealing plug from the flywheel end bearing, using a long tubular drift.

5   Removal of the front, rear and centre camshaft bushes is best accomplished by the use of a length of threaded rod and nuts with suitable tubular distance pieces.

6   Note the precise positioning of each bearing bush before removal and ensure that the bearing seats are not damaged during the removal operation.

7   Fit the new bearing bushes using the same method as for removal, starting with the centre one. It is essential that the bearing oil hole is in exact alignment with the one drilled in the bearing seat and marks should be made on the edge of the bearing bush and seat before pulling into position.

8   Fit a new camshaft front bearing sealing cap.

29 Cam followers and pushrods – examination and renovation

1   The cam followers (tappets) should be checked in their respective bores in the crankcase and no excessive side play should be apparent. The faces of the followers which bear against the camshaft lobes should also have a clear smooth shiny surface. If they show signs of pitting or serious wear they should be renewed.

2   The pushrods should be checked for straightness by rolling them along a flat surface. Also check for wear of the ball end which locates in the cam follower, and the cup end that accepts the rocker adjusting ball. Renew as necessary.

30 Cylinder head, valves and piston crowns – decarbonising

1   When the cylinder head is removed, either in the course of an overhaul or for inspection of bores or valve condition when the engine is in the car, it is normal to remove all carbon deposits from the piston crowns, cylinder head and valves.

2   This is best done using a scraper, but when working on the cylinder head and piston crowns, take care not to damage the relatively soft alloy in any way.

3   When the engine is in the car, certain precautions must be taken when decarbonising the piston crowns in order to prevent dislodged pieces of carbon falling into the interior of the engine which could cause damage to the cylinder bores, piston and rings, or if allowed into the water passages, damage to the water pump. Turn the engine so that the piston being worked on is at the top of its stroke and then mask off the adjacent cylinder bores and all surrounding orifices with paper and adhesive tape. Press grease into the gap all round the piston to keep the carbon particles out and then scrape all carbon away. When completed, carefully clear out the grease around the rim of the piston with a matchstick or something similar – bringing any carbon particles with it. Repeat the process on the other piston crown. It is not recommended that a ring of carbon is left round the edge of the piston on the theory that it will aid oil consumption. This was valid in the earlier days of long stroke, low revving engines but modern engines, fuels and lubricants cause less carbon deposits anyway, and any left behind tends merely to cause hot spots.

31 Cylinder head, valves and rocker gear – examination and renovation

1   Examine the cylinder head for signs of cracks around the valve

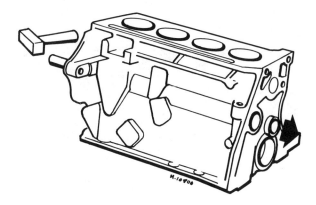

Fig. 1.13 Removing the camshaft sealing plug (Sec 28)

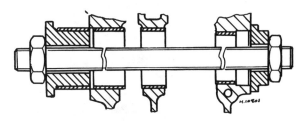

Fig. 1.14 Removing the camshaft bushes using a threaded rod, nuts and distance pieces (Sec 28)

seats or spark plug holes and for water erosion around the passages and outlets in the cylinder head face. Also check for distortion of the cylinder head face using a straight-edge. If any cracks are apparent the head must be renewed. Minor erosion or distortion of the cylinder head face can be rectified by having the face skimmed by a motor engineering specialist or machine shop. If this work is carried out, refer to the Specifications for the maximum amount of metal that can be removed from the head face and note also that a thicker gasket must be used on reassembly.

2   The valve seats should be examined for signs of pitting or ridging. Slight pitting can be ground away using carborundum paste and an *old* valve. New valves are specially plated and **must not** be used to grind in the seats. If the valve faces are burnt or cracked, new valves must be obtained. If the valve seats require re-cutting ensure that the seat width and seat angle are maintained to the dimensions shown in the Specifications.

3   The rocker gear should be dismantled and thoroughly cleaned of the sludge deposits which normally tend to accumulate on it. The gear is dismantled by simply sliding the pedestals, springs and rockets off the shafts (photo). The shafts may be removed from the centre pedestal after drifting out the retaining roll pin.

4   The rocker arms should be a slide fit over the shaft with very little play. If play is excessive, or if ridges are apparent in the shaft, renew these components. Also check the domed ends of the rocker adjusting screws for wear and renew any that are deformed. The pad of the rocker that bears against the valve stem should also be examined. It is normal to detect a slight wear ridge using the edge of your fingernail. If the ridge is visibly apparent then it has penetrated the surface hardening of the pad and the rocker arm should be renewed. A very slight ridge can be dressed with an oilstone.

5   Refit the valve into its guide in the head and note if there is any sideways movement which denotes wear between the stem and guide. Here again the degree of wear can vary. If excessive, the performance of the engine can be noticeably affected and oil consumption increased. Wear is normally in the guide rather than on the valve stem but check a new valve in the guide if possible first. Valve guide renewal is a tricky operation and should be left to a Talbot dealer.

6   Check that the end face of the valve stem is not 'hammered' or ridged by the action of the rocker arm. If it is, dress it square and smooth with an oilstone.

31.3 Rocker gear dismantled for cleaning and inspection

32.1a Separate the two halves of the oil pump ...

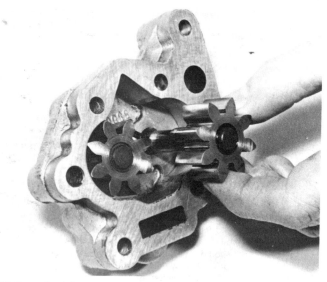

32.1b ... check for wear of the internal components ...

32.1c ... and measure the endfloat of the shaft using feeler gauges and a straight-edge

32.2a Unscrew the pressure relief valve plunger ...

32.2b ... and carefully examine the relief valve components

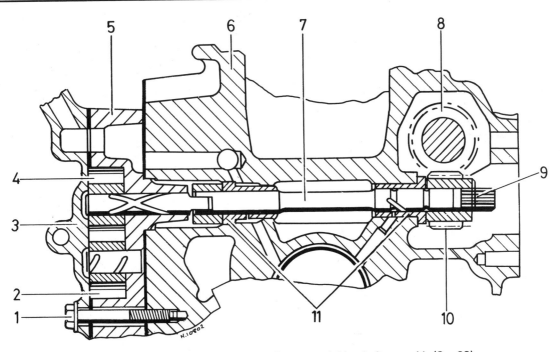

Fig. 1.15 Sectional view of the oil pump and driveshaft assembly (Sec 32)

1 Fixing bolt	4 Driven gear	7 Driveshaft	10 Drivegear
2 Idler gear	5 Body	8 Camshaft	11 Driveshaft bushes
3 Cover	6 Crankcase	9 Circlip	

32 Oil pump – examination and renovation

1 Separate the two halves of the oil pump body and examine the gears and internal walls of the housing for scoring pitting or wear ridges. Check the endfloat of the gears using a straight-edge and feeler gauges, and compare the dimensions with those given in the Specifications (photos).

2 Remove the domed nut and sealing washer and then using an Allen key, unscrew the pressure relief valve plunger. Take out the plunger, spring and ball. Thoroughly clean away any sludge deposits from the relief valve and then check the ball and housing for pitting or ridging (photos).

3 If the oil pump or pressure relief valve are worn or in any way suspect, the pump will have to be renewed as parts are not available separately. It is always a good idea to renew the pump if the engine is being overhauled or reconditioned, particularly if it has covered a high mileage.

33 Oil pump driveshaft bushes – examination and renovation

1 The two bushes in the cylinder block in which the oil pump/dipstick driveshaft runs should be examined for wear by refitting the shaft and checking for excessive side play.

2 If wear has taken place the bushes should be renewed. To remove them, draw each one out using a threaded rod, nuts, and distance piece as shown in Fig. 1.16.

3 New bushes can be fitted using the following procedure.

4 Fit the shorter bush to the distributor side, pulling it in tight to the machined surface of the cylinder block. It is vital that the oil hole in the bush aligns with the crankshaft bearing oil passage.

5 Fit the bush to the oil pump side, again using the threaded rod and nut method and avoid damage to the bush just fitted. There is no need to align the oil hole on this bush as it opens into a circular oil chamber in the cylinder block.

6 Test the driveshaft in the bushes for ease of rotation. A hard spot

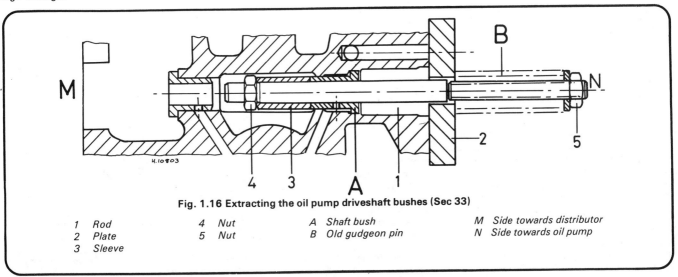

Fig. 1.16 Extracting the oil pump driveshaft bushes (Sec 33)

1 Rod	4 Nut	A Shaft bush	M Side towards distributor
2 Plate	5 Nut	B Old gudgeon pin	N Side towards oil pump
3 Sleeve			

will indicate mis-alignment or distortion.

34 Flywheel – examination and renovation

1 The clutch friction disc mating surface of the flywheel should be examined for scoring. If this is apparent then it should either be exchanged for a new unit or if the scoring is very light it may be skimmed.
2 The starter ring gear should be examined and if the teeth are worn or chipped it must be renewed.
3 To remove the ring, support the flywheel and drive off the ring gear using a bronze or steel bar.
4 Take care not to damage the flywheel locating dowels during this operation or they will have to be renewed.
5 To fit a new ring gear requires heating the ring to 220°C (430°F). This can be done by polishing four equal spaced sections of the gear, placing it on a suitable heat resistant surface (such as fire bricks) and heating it evenly with a blow lamp or torch until the polished areas turn a light yellow tinge. Do not overheat, or the hard wearing properties will be lost. The gear has a chamfered inner edge which should go against the shoulder when put on the flywheel. When hot enough, place the gear in position quickly, tapping it home if necessary, and let it cool naturally without quenching in any way.

35 Timing gears, chain and cover – examination and renovation

1 Carefully examine the teeth of the timing gears and the links of the chain for wear. Place the chain over the gears and ensure that it is a snug fit without slackness. Renew any of the components where necessary.
2 The crankshaft front oil seal in the timing cover should be renewed as a matter of course. The old seal may be drifted out using a hammer and a suitable tube, or levered out with a screwdriver or stout bar. Tap a new seal into position using a hammer and a block of wood. The lips of the seal must face toward the engine when installed (photo).

36 Engine – reassembly (general)

Ensure absolute cleanliness during assembly operations and lubricate each component with clean engine oil before fitting.
Renew all lockwashers, gaskets and seals as a matter of course. Also renew the big-end nuts; these nuts are of the self-locking type and must not be re-used.
Take care to tighten nuts and bolts to the torque specified in the Specifications and watch out for any differences in bolt lengths which might mean attempting to screw a long bolt into a short hole with subsequent fracturing of a casting.
Follow the sequence of reassembly given in the following Sections and do not skip any adjustment procedure essential at each fitting stage.
In addition to the normal range of socket spanners and general tools which are essential, the following must be available before reassembling begins:

Complete set of new gaskets and seals
Supply of clean rags
Clean oil can full of clean engine oil
Torque wrench
All new parts as necessary

37 Crankshaft and main bearings – refitting

1 Ensure that the crankcase is thoroughly clean and all oilways are clear. A thin twist drill is useful for clearing the oilways, or if possible, they may be blown out with compressed air. Treat the crankshaft in the same fashion, then inject engine oil into the oilways.
2 Wipe the bearing shell seats in the crankcase clean, then fit the upper halves of the new main bearing shells into their seats (photo).
3 Note that there is a tab on the back of each bearing shell which engages with a groove in the seating.
4 Wipe the seats in the main bearing caps clean and fit the remaining shells to their seats. Note that the shells in caps 2 and 4

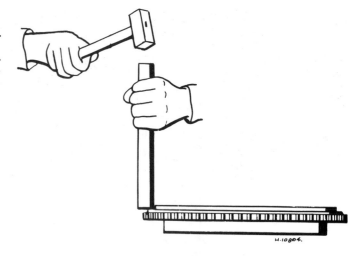

Fig. 1.17 Drifting off the flywheel ring gear (Sec 34)

35.2 Correct installation of timing cover oil seal

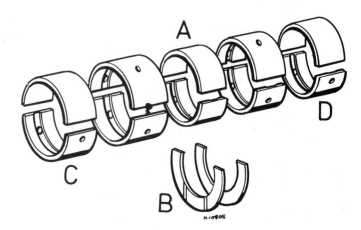

Fig. 1.18 Position of grooved and plain main bearing shells (Sec 37)

A Lower (cap) shells
B Upper (cylinder block) shells
C Timing cover end
D Flywheel end

37.2 Fit the main bearing upper shells in the crankcase ...

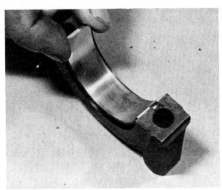

37.4 ... and the lower shells in the caps

37.5 Fit the thrust washers with the oil grooves facing outwards

37.6a Liberally lubricate the main bearing shells ...

37.6b ... and lower the crankshaft into place

37.7a Refit the caps having plain ...

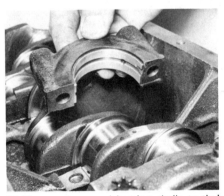

37.7b ... and grooved bearing shells to their correct locations in the crankcase

37.8 Tighten the retaining bolts progressively to the specified torque

37.11 Position a new gasket on the rear face of the crankcase ...

have oil grooves, the shells in caps 1, 3 and 5 do not (photo).

5   Fit the semi-circular thrust washers to each side of the centre main bearingin the crankcase. Retain the thrust washers with a smear of grease and position them with the oil grooves facing outwards (photo).

6   Liberally lubricate the main bearing shells in the crankcase and then carefully lower the crankshaft into position (photos).

7   Lubricate the bearing shells in the caps and then refit the caps and retaining bolts to their correct locations in the crankcase (photos).

8   With all the caps in place, tighten the retaining bolts progressively to the specified torque wrench setting (photo). Check the crankshaft for ease of rotation. If new bearing shells have been fitted, it may be fairly stiff to turn, but there should be no high spots.

9   Should the crankshaft be very stiff to turn or possess high spots, a most careful inspection should be made – preferably by a skilled mechanic – to trace the cause of the trouble. It is very seldom that trouble of this nature will be experienced when fitting the crankshaft.

10   Using a screwdriver, ease the crankshaft fully forward and measure the endfloat, with feeler gauges, between the side of the crankshaft centre journal and the thrust washers. Ensure that the clearance is within the limits given in the Specifications. Oversize thrust washers are available.

11   Position a new oil seal housing gasket, lightly smeared with jointing compound, on the rear face of the crankcase (photo).

12   Lubricate the lips of the oil seal and then carefully ease it over the crankshaft flange using a twisting action (photo).

13   Refit the oil seal housing retaining bolts finger tight, rotate the crankshaft one full turn to centralise the seal and then progressively tighten the bolts to the specified torque wrench setting.

38 Gudgeon pins – refitting

As interference fit gudgeon pins are used (see Section 20), this operation must be carried out by your Talbot dealer or motor engineering specialists.

37.12 ... and carefully fit the oil seal and housing

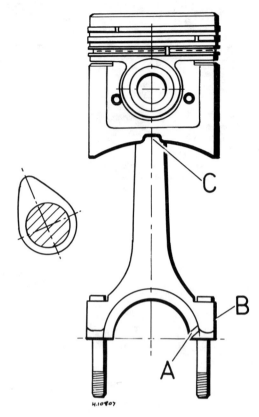

Fig. 1.20 Correct assembly of piston and connecting rod (Sec 40)

A Lubrication slot
B Production markings
C Notch must face timing cover

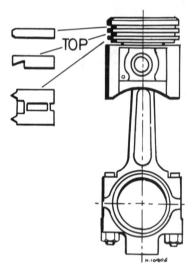

Fig. 1.19 Piston ring identification (Sec 39)

39 Piston rings – refitting

1   Check that the piston ring grooves and oilways are thoroughly clean and unblocked. Piston rings must always be fitted over the head of the piston and never from the bottom.
2   The easiest method to use when fitting rings is to wrap a 0.38 mm (0.015 in) feeler gauge round the top of the piston and place the rings one at a time, starting with the bottom oil control ring, over the feeler gauge.
3   The feeler gauge, complete with ring, can then be slid down the piston over the other piston ring grooves until the correct groove is reached. The piston ring is then slid gently off the feeler gauge into the groove.
4   An alternative method is to fit the rings by holding them slightly open with the thumbs and both of the index fingers. This method requires a steady hand and great care, as it is easy to open the ring too much and break it.
5   The top compression ring and oil control ring may be fitted either way up; however the second ring must be fitted with the word TOP uppermost.
6   When all the rings are in position on the pistons, move them around to bring each ring gap approximately 120° away from the adjacent ring.
7   If special oil control rings are being fitted, follow the maker's instructions closely.

40 Piston and connecting rod assemblies – refitting

1   Clean the cylinder bores with a non-fluffy rag and then liberally lubricate them with engine oil.
2   Apply clean engine oil to the piston rings of No 1 piston and insert this piston connecting rod assembly into No 1 cylinder bore.
3   Turn the piston round until the notch on the piston skirt (photo) is facing the timing cover end of the engine and the oil squirt hole in the connecting rod is toward the camshaft side of the engine.
4   Make sure that the piston ring gaps are still correctly staggered and then compress the rings using a piston ring compressing tool. A large diameter worm drive hose clip will serve as a ring compressor if a proper tool is not available.
5   Now tap the top of the piston down through the ring compressor and into the cylinder using a block of wood or hammer handle (photo). Guide the big-end of the connecting rod near to its position on the crankshaft, taking care not to scratch the crankpin with the big-end bolts.
6   Wipe the shell seat in the big-end of the connecting rod clean, and the underside of the new shell bearing. Fit the shell into position in the connecting rod with its locating tongue engaged with the appropriate groove in the big-end.
7   Generously lubricate the crankpin journals with engine oil and turn the crankshaft so that it is in its most advantageous position for the rod to be drawn onto it.
8   Wipe the bearing shell seat in the bearing cap clean, and then the underside of the new shell. Fit the shell into the cap, engaging the shell tongue with the groove in the cap (photo).
9   Draw the big-end of the connecting rod onto the crankpin, then fit the cap into position (photo). Make sure it is the correct way around, then fit new nuts.
10 Tighten the nuts progressively to the specified torque wrench

40.3 Refit the piston/connecting rod assemblies with the notch on the skirt toward the timing cover

40.5 With a ring compressor in place, tap the pistons into the cylinders

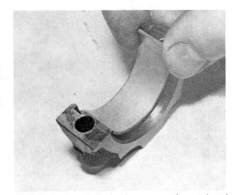

40.8 Refit the shells in the connecting rod and bearing cap ...

40.9 ... assemble the cap onto the connecting rod ...

40.10 ... fit new nuts and tighten to the specified torque

41.1a Lubricate the camshaft bearings ...

41.1b ... and carefully insert the camshaft

41.2a Position the camshaft thrust plate in the groove in the camshaft flange ...

41.2b ... and refit the retaining bolts

setting (photo) and then check that the crankshaft is still free to rotate without tight spots. (A certain additional amount of resistance is to be expected from the friction between piston rings and cylinder bore).

11 Repeat this procedure for the remaining piston/connecting rod assemblies.

41 Camshaft, timing gears, chain and cover – refitting

1 Liberally lubricate the camshaft bearings and insert the camshaft, taking care not to damage the bearings as the cam lobes pass through them (photos).

2 Engage the camshaft thrust plate with the groove behind the camshaft flange (photo), and refit the retaining bolts, tightened to the specified torque wrench setting (photo). Knock up the lockwasher tabs (if fitted).

3 Pull the camshaft fully forward and check the endfloat using feeler gauges inserted between the thrust plate and flange (photo). If the

endfloat is outside the specified tolerance, various sizes of thrust plate are available.

4 Rotate the crankshaft until Nos 1 and 4 pistons are at TDC.

5 Refit the Woodruff key to the slot in the crankshaft and slide on the crankshaft sprocket (photo).

6 Temporarily position the camshaft sprocket on the camshaft and align the bolt holes.

7 Rotate the camshaft and sprocket until the dot on the edge of the sprocket is aligned between the two lines on the crankshaft sprocket.

8 Remove the camshaft sprocket without rotating the camshaft and lift the timing chain over both sprockets. Refit the camshaft sprocket and check that the timing marks are still in alignment, using a straight-edge if necessary (photos).

9 Refit the three camshaft sprocket retaining bolts and tighten to the specified torque wrench setting (photo). Knock up the tabs of the lockwashers (if used).

10 Lightly smear a new timing cover gasket with jointing compound and position it on the cylinder block. Refit the timing cover and

41.3 Using feeler gauges, check the camshaft endfloat

41.5 Refit the Woodruff key and crankshaft sprocket

41.8a Position the camshaft sprocket and chain on the camshaft ...

41.8b ... with the timing marks on the sprockets aligned

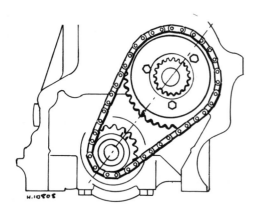

Fig. 1.21 Alignment of timing marks on sprockets (Sec 41)

41.9 Refit and tighten the camshaft sprocket retaining bolts

41.10a Position a new gasket on the cylinder block ...

41.10b ... and refit the timing cover

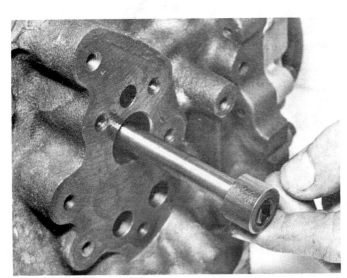
42.2 Insert the oil pump driveshaft

retaining bolts and then tighten the bolts to the specified torque. Note that the front engine lifting bracket is also retained by the two upper bolts (photos).

42 Oil pump driveshaft – refitting

1 Temporarily refit the crankshaft pulley and then rotate the crankshaft until the notch on the pulley is aligned with the specified BTDC mark on the timing scale of the timing cover. No 1 cylinder must be on its compression stroke, ie the cam lobes for No 1 cylinder will point downwards.
2 Smear the oil pump driveshaft with engine oil and insert it into its bushes from the oil pump side of the cylinder block (photo).
3 With the shaft in place, slide on the driven gear from the distributor side of the cylinder block, ensuring that the flanged side of the gear faces outward (photo).
4 Secure the gear and shaft with the circlip (photo).
5 With the crankshaft positioned as described above, slide the distributor driving dog onto the end of the shaft. When installed the slot in the dog must be at approximately 45° with the larger segment uppermost (photo).
6 Refit the distributor mounting plate so that its boss is towards the timing cover and secure with the retaining bolts (photo).

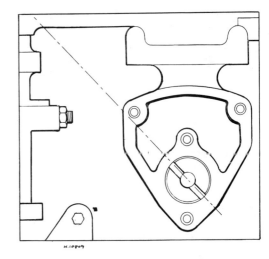
Fig. 1.22 Correct position of distributor driving dog, engine at specified BTDC, No 1 piston on compression stroke (Sec 42)

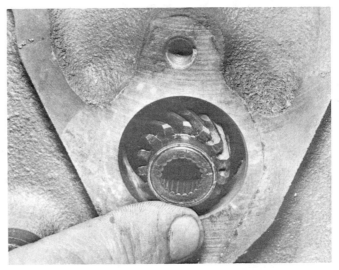
42.3 ... slide on the driven gear ...

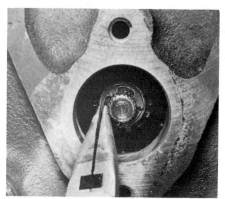
42.4 ... secure the gear with the circlip ...

42.5 ... and then refit the distributor driving dog with the slot in this position

42.6 Refit the distributor mounting plate with its boss toward the timing cover

43.1 Place the flywheel on the crankshaft and align the bolt holes

43.2 Apply thread locking compound to the retaining bolt threads and refit them

43.4 Tighten the bolts to the specified torque. Note flywheel locking device

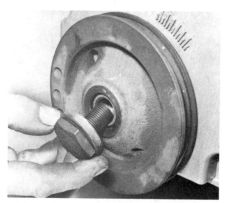
43.6a Refit the crankshaft pulley and retaining bolt ...

43.6b ... and tighten to the correct torque wrench setting

44.2a Place the sump on the crankcase ...

44.2b ... and secure with the retaining bolts

44.3a With a new gasket in position ...

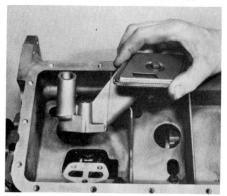
44.3b ... install the oil pick-up/strainer assembly

43 Flywheel and crankshaft pulley – refitting

1   Place the flywheel in position on the crankshaft flange and turn it as necessary until all the offset bolt holes are aligned (photo).
2   Apply a drop of thread locking compound to the retaining bolts and then refit the bolts and seating plate (photo).
3   Lock the flywheel using a piece of angle iron and bar engaged in the ring gear, or a block of wood between the crankshaft and crankcase.
4   Tighten the flywheel retaining bolts in a diagonal sequence to the specified torque wrench setting (photo).
5   Lubricate the lips of the timing cover oil seal and slide on the crankshaft pulley.
6   Refit the retaining bolt and tighten to the specified torque wrench setting (photos).

44 Sump – refitting

1   Ensure that the mating surfaces of the sump and crankcase are clean, smear both sides of a new gasket with jointing compound and position it on the crankcase.
2   Place the sump main body over the gasket and secure with the internal and external retaining bolts (photos), using thread locking compound.
3   Smear the oil pick-up/strainer assembly gasket with jointing compound, position it on the sump and refit the pick-up/strainer assembly (photos).
4   Finally refit the baseplate, again using a new gasket with jointing compound, and secure with the retaining bolts, correctly tightened (photo).

45 Valves – refitting

1   Place the lower valve spring seat in position and then install a new oil seal over the valve guide (photos).
2   Liberally lubricate the valve stems and then insert them into the valve guides from which they were removed (photo).
3   Refit the valve spring and spring cup over the valve stem and then position the spring compressor over the assembly (photo).
4   Compress the spring sufficiently to allow the cotters to be slipped into place in the groove machined in the top of the valve stem (photo). Now release the spring compressor.
5   Repeat this operation until all eight valves have been assembled into the cylinder head.
6   With all the valves installed, gently tap the top of the valve stems once or twice, using a soft-faced mallet, to seat the cotters and centralise the components.

46 Cylinder head – refitting

1   Before refitting the cylinder head, insert the cam followers, liberally lubricated, into their original bores in the cylinder block (photo).
2   Make sure that the two alignment dowels are in position on the cylinder block face and then wipe the block and cylinder head faces with a petrol-moistened rag. Allow time to air dry.
3   Make sure that the head gasket being fitted is of the correct type for Horizon engines. Similar gaskets are used on other Talbot models, but these do not have the triangular identification holes shown in Fig. 1.23. Also ensure that if any machining operations have been carried out on the cylinder head face, a gasket of the correct thickness is being used (see Specifications).
4   Locate the new cylinder head gasket in position on the block, ensuring that the word DESSUS is visible on the upper surface (photo). The gasket should normally be fitted dry, but if there has been evidence of water leaks from the previous head gasket, or if there is slight eroding of the aluminium face around the water passages, then a thin film of 'Hylomar' should be applied to both sides of the gasket. This is a non-setting jointing compound, particularly resistant to oil, water and heat, and will also provide protection against further erosion

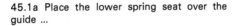

44.4 The baseplate can now be refitted

45.1a Place the lower spring seat over the guide ...

45.1b ... followed by a new valve stem oil seal

45.2 Insert the valves into their correct guides

45.3 Place the spring and spring cup over the valve stem ...

45.4 ... and then compress the spring and fit the collets

46.1 Insert the cam followers into their original bores

of the head.

5   Lower the cylinder head gently into position on the cylinder block and engage the locating dowels (photo).

6   Fit the pushrods in their correct locations, carefully engaging their lower ends in the cam followers (photo).

7   If the rocker shaft has been dismantled for removal of worn components, it should be reassembled with the parts fitted in the sequence shown in Fig. 1.24. Note that the shafts are assembled with their plugged ends facing outward.

8   Make sure that the rocker pillar alignment dowels are in position (photo), and lower the rocker gear into place over the dowels (photo). Make sure that the adjusting screw ball on each rocker arm engages with its respective pushrod.

9   Refit the cylinder head retaining bolts, having first cleaned their threads with a wire brush. Oil the threads also.

10   Using a torque wrench, tighten the cylinder head bolts progressively and evenly, in the sequence shown in Fig. 1.25, to the torque wrench setting given in the Specifications (photo).

11   Now adjust the valve clearances as described in the following Section.

47 Valve clearances – checking and adjusting

1   The importance of correct rocker arm/valve stem clearance cannot be over-stressed as it vitally affects the performance of the engine. If

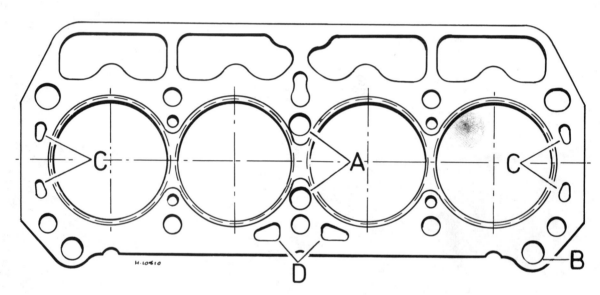

Fig. 1.23 Cylinder head gasket identification (Sec 46)

A Holes for main coolant passages
B Oil drain passage hole
C Triangular identification holes
D Triangular identification holes

46.4 Position the gasket on the cylinder block with the word DESSUS uppermost

46.5 Carefully lower the head into position ...

46.6 ... and refit the pushrods

46.8a With the alignment dowels in place ...

46.8b ... refit the rocker gear ...

46.10 ... followed by the cylinder head bolts, tightened to the specified torque in the correct sequence

Fig. 1.24 Correct reassembly of the rocker gear (Sec 46)

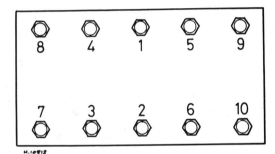

Fig. 1.25 Cylinder head bolt tightening sequence (Sec 46)

the clearances are set too wide, the efficiency of the engine is reduced as the valves open later and close earlier than intended. If, however, the clearances are too tight, there is a danger that as the valve stems expand with heat there will be insufficient clearance to allow the valves to close properly. This will cause loss of compression and possible burning of the valve head and seat.

2   Valve clearances must only be adjusted with the engine cold. With the engine in the car, access to the rockers is gained after removing the air cleaner, as described in Chapter 3, and the rocker cover as described in Section 10 of this Chapter. The crankshaft can be rotated for adjustment of the clearances by engaging a socket on the crankshaft pulley bolt, accessible through a hole in the splash guard under the right-hand wheel arch.

3   It is important that the clearances are adjusted only when the appropriate piston is at TDC on the compression stroke. The following table shows the order in which the valves should be adjusted (which also avoids turning the crankshaft more than necessary):

Valves rocking on cylinder No	Adjust valves on cylinder No
4	1
2	3
1	4
3	2

4   Turn the crankshaft in the normal direction of rotation and observe the movement of the exhaust valves. (Counting from the flywheel end, exhaust valves are Nos 2, 4, 5 and 7). When one is moving upward to its closed position, continue turning slowly until the inlet valve on the same cylinder just starts to open. This is the 'valves rocking' position. The piston in the appropriate cylinder shown in the table is now at TDC

on the compression stroke and its valve clearances can be checked and if necessary adjusted.

5   Insert a feeler blade of the specified thickness into the gap between the valve stem and the rocker arm. The blade should be a firm sliding fit. Note that the clearances specified for inlet and exhaust valves differ slightly.

6   If adjustment is necessary, slacken the hexagon locknut on the rocker arm, then screw the adjusting screw in or out as necessary until the feeler blade is a firm sliding fit (photo). Hold the adjusting screw to prevent it turning further and tighten the locknut, then recheck the clearance. Repeat the operation if necessary.

7   Check the adjacent valve of that cylinder in the same way and then repeat the procedure until all eight valves have been adjusted.

8   If the engine is in the car, refit the rocker cover on completion, using a new gasket if the old one was damaged during removal, and then the air cleaner assembly.

48 Ancillary components – refitting

1   Begin by refitting the clutch assembly to the flywheel. Full details of the fitting procedure and centralisation of the clutch disc are given in Chapter 5.

2   Place a new gasket, lightly coated with jointing compound, in position on the water pump housing and then refit the pump and retaining bolts. With the pump in position refit the pulley, and the pump-to-timing cover water hose (photos).

3   Position new gaskets on both sides of the fuel pump insulator block. Hold the block in place on the engine and refit the fuel pump, ensuring that the operating arm goes over the camshaft eccentric, not under it. Secure the pump with the two bolts (photo).

4   Liberally lubricate the oil pump gears and the inside of the housing. Place a new gasket between the two halves of the pump body and join them together. Using another new gasket refit the pump to the cylinder block and secure with the retaining bolts (photo).

5   Smear clean engine oil onto the rubber seal of a new oil filter and screw the filter onto its housing on the oil pump (photo). Tighten the

filter by hand only. Do not use any tools.

6   Refit the distributor to the engine, using the procedure described in Chapter 4 to ensure that the ignition timing is correct.

7   Position the alternator on the engine and refit the upper retaining bolt finger tight only at this stage (photo).

8   Place a new water inlet elbow gasket in position on the cylinder block. Refit the inlet elbow and hose assembly and the alternator adjusting bracket and secure with the two bolts (photos). Attach the HT lead support bracket and retaining bolt. Slip the alternator drivebelt over the pulleys, refit the lower adjusting bolt and adjust the belt tension to 12 mm (0.5 in) deflection at its longest run (photo). Now fully tighten the alternator upper retaining bolt.

9   Refit the inlet manifold using a new gasket. Secure the lower water hose with its retaining clip and attach the carburettor water hoses, the vacuum pipe, and the fuel inlet pipe (photos).

10 Stick a new gasket onto the thermostat housing, engage the housing with the hose from the inlet manifold and refit the bolts. Secure the hose clip in position (photos).

11 Refit the exhaust manifold and retaining bolts, again using a new gasket (photos).

12 Apply jointing compound to the rocker cover gasket face and position a new gasket on it. Fit the cover to the cylinder head and then position the air cleaner hot air box over the rocker cover. Note which nuts also secure the hot air box and then refit and progressively tighten all the rest. Now fit the hot air box and remaining securing nuts (photos).

13 Refit the spark plugs, distrtributor cap and HT leads.

49 Engine – reconnecting to manual gearbox on automatic transmission

1   If the engine and transmission were removed from the car as a unit, the two assemblies must now be reconnected before being refitted to the car.

2   The reconnecting procedure is a straightforward reverse of the removal sequence, bearing in mind the following points:

47.6 Adjusting the valve clearances

48.2a Refit the water pump ...

48.2b ... and pulley

48.3 Refit the fuel pump ...

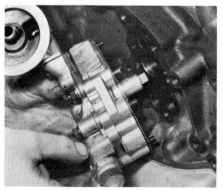
48.4 ... and the oil pump ...

48.5 ... and then the filter after lubricating its seal

48.7 Install the alternator upper retaining bolt ...

48.8a ... water inlet elbow and hose assembly ...

48.8b ... and alternator support bracket

48.8c Refit the HT lead support bracket retaining bolt ...

48.8d ... the alternator lower adjusting bolt ...

48.8e ... slip on the drivebelt and adjust it to the correct tension

48.9a Fit a new inlet manifold gasket ...

48.9b ... followed by the manifold, after engaging the lower water hose

48.10a Refit the thermostat housing ...

48.10b ... and secure the hose clips

48.11a With a new gasket in place ...

48.11b ... refit the exhaust manifold

48.12a Install the rocker cover ...

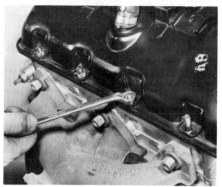

48.12b ... secured with the retaining nuts

48.12c ... and finally refit the hot air box

(a) If difficulty is experienced engaging the manual gearbox input shaft splines, engage a gear by moving the shift rod and then rotate the crankshaft slightly. This should align the clutch disc and input shaft splines and allow the shaft to enter the disc. On no account allow the weight of the gearbox to hang unsupported on the input shaft

(b) If automatic transmission is being refitted, ensure that the torque converter is in position on the transmission before reconnecting to the engine

(c) With the transmission in position, align the previously made marks between the torque converter and driveplate before refitting the retaining bolts

50 Engine – refitting

1   Refitting the engine is a reversal of the removal procedure. A little trouble taken in getting the engine properly slung (so it takes up a suspended angle similar to its final position) will pay off when it comes to locating the engine mountings.

2   Ensure that all loose leads, cables, hoses, etc are tucked out of the way. If not, it is easy to trap one and cause additional work after the engine is refitted in the car.

3   Carefully lower the engine while an assistant guides it into position. If the gearbox is still in place in the car, it may be necessary to turn the crankshaft slightly to engage the splines of the gearbox input shaft.

4   The engine is likely to be stiff to turn over initially if new bearings or pistons and rings have been fitted, and it will save a lot of frustration if the battery is well charged. After a rebore the stiffness may initially be more than the battery can cope with, so be prepared to connect another battery in parallel with jump leads.

5   The following check list should ensure the engine starts safely and with the minimum of delay:

(a) Fuel lines connected and tightened
(b) Water hoses connected and secured with clips
(c) Coolant drain plug fitted and tightened
(d) Cooling system replenished
(e) Sump drain plug fitted and tight
(f) Oil in engine
(g) LT wiring connected to distributor and coil
(h) Oil pressure and water temperatre sender wire connected
(j) Spark plugs tight
(k) Rotor arm fitted in distributor
(l) Distributor cap and HT leads correctly fitted

(m) Throttle linkage connected
(n) Earth strap connected
(p) Starter motor leads connected
(q) Alternator leads connected
(r) Battery fully charged and leads connected
(s) Oil or fluid in gearbox or transmission

51 Engine – initial start-up after major repair or overhaul

1   Make sure that the battery is fully charged and that all lubricants, coolant and fuel are replenished.

2   If the fuel system has been dismantled, it will require several revolutions of the engine on the starter motor to pump petrol to the carburettor. It will help to remove the spark plugs, which will enable the engine to turn over much easier, and enable oil to be pumped around the engine before starting it.

3   Refit the spark plugs and as soon as the engine fires and runs, keep it going at a fast tickover only (no faster) and bring it up to normal working temperature.

4   As the engine warms up, there will be odd smells and some smoke from parts getting hot and burning off oil deposits. Look for water or oil leaks which will be obvious if serious. Check also the clamp connection of the exhaust pipe to the manifold as these do not always find their exact gastight position until the warmth and vibration have acted on them, and it is almost certain that they will need tightening further. This should be done, of course, with the engine stationary.

5   When the engine running temperature has been reached, adjust the idling speed as described in Chapter 3.

6   Stop the engine and wait a few minutes to see if any lubricant or coolant leaks.

7   Road test the car to check that the timing is correct and that the engine is giving the necessary smoothness and power. Do not race the engine. If new bearings and or pistons and rings have been fitted, it should be treated as a new engine and run in at reduced revolutions for 500 miles (800 km).

8   Re-tighten the cylinder head bolts, with the engine cold, after the first 1000 miles have been covered. It is best to slacken each bolt $\frac{1}{4}$ turn to break the 'stiction' before tightening. Follow the tightening sequence shown in Fig. 1.25, and check the valve clearances on completion.

9   Also after the first 1000 miles, it is a good idea to change the engine oil and filter if many new engine parts have been fitted. This is because the small metal particles produced by new components bedding in to each other will be circulating in the oil, or trapped in the filter.

52 Fault diagnosis – engine

Symptom	Reason(s)
Engine fails to turn over when starter operated No current at starter motor	Flat or defective battery Loose battery leads Defective starter solenoid switch or broken wiring Engine earth strap disconnected
Current at starter motor	Jammed starter motor drive pinion Defective starter motor or solenoid
Engine turns over but will not start No spark at spark plug	Ignition damp or wet Ignition leads to spark plugs loose Shortened or disconnected low tension leads Fault in electronic ignition system Defective ignition switch Ignition leads connected wrong way round Faulty coil
Excess of petrol in cylinder, or carburettor flooding	Too much choke allowing too rich a mixture to wet plugs Float damaged or leaking or needle not seating Float lever incorrectly adjusted
Engine stalls and will not start No spark at spark plug	Ignition failure
No fuel getting to engine	No petrol in petrol tank Petrol tank breather choked Obstruction in carburettor Water in fuel system Vapour lock in fuel line (in hot conditions or at high altitude) Blocked float chamber needle valve Fuel pump filter blocked Choked or blocked carburettor jets Faulty fuel pump
Engine misfires or idles unevenly Intermittent spark at spark plugs	Ignition leads loose Battery leads loose on terminals Battery earth strap loose on body attachment point Engine earth lead loose Low tension leads on coil loose Dirty, or incorrectly gapped plugs Fault in electronic ignition system Tracking across inside of distributor cover Ignition too retarded Faulty coil
Fuel shortage at engine	Mixture too weak Air leak in carburettor Air leak at inlet manifold to cylinder head, or inlet manifold to carburettor Fuel pump filter blocked Blocked carburettor jets Faulty fuel pump
Mechanical wear	Incorrect valve clearances Burnt out exhaust valves Sticking or leaking valves Weak or broken valve springs Worn valve guides or stems Worn pistons and piston rings
Lack of power and poor compression Fuel/air mixture leaking from cylinder	Burnt out exhaust valves Sticking or leaking valves Worn valve guides and stems Weak or broken valve springs Blown cylinder head gasket (accompanied by increase in noise) Worn pistons and piston rings Worn or scored cylinder bores

Symptom	Reason(s)
Incorrect adjustments	Ignition timing wrongly set Incorrect valve clearances Incorrectly set spark plugs
Carburation and ignition faults	Distributor automatic balance weights or vacuum advance and retard mechanism not functioning correctly Faulty fuel pump giving top end fuel starvation

Excessive oil consumption

Oil being burnt by engine	Badly worn, perished or missing valve stem oil seals Excessively worn valve stems and valve guides Worn piston rings Worn pistons and cylinder bores Excessive piston ring gap allowing blow-by Piston oil return holes choked
Oil being lost due to leaks	Leaking oil filter gasket Leaking sump gasket Loose sump plug Leaking oil seals

Unusual noises from engine

Excessive clearances due to mechanical wear	Worn valve gear (noisy tapping from rocker box) Worn big-end bearing (regular heavy knocking) Worn timing chain or gears (rattling from front of engine) Worn main bearings (rumbling and vibration) Worn crankshaft (knocking rumbling and vibration)

Chapter 2 Cooling system

Contents

Specifications

General
System type ....

Semi-sealed, thermo-syphon, water pump assisted with electric cooling fan

Water pump type ....

Centrifugal, belt-driven

Thermostat
Location ....

Right-hand side of cylinder head

Opening temperature:
Up to May 1979 ....

83°C (181°F)

From May 1979 ....

89°C (192°F)

Expansion bottle
Expansion cap relief valve pressure ....

9 lbf/in² (0.6 bar)

Volume between 'mini' and 'maxi' marks on expansion bottle ....

0.75 pints (0.45 litres)

Electric fan
Motor rating ....

60 watts

Fan temperature sensing unit:
Cut-in temperature ....

95°C (203°F)

Cut-out temperature ....

86°C (187°F)

Antifreeze
Type ....

Universal antifreeze conforming to British Standard 3151 or 3152

Torque wrench settings

	lbf ft	Nm
Cylinder block drain plug	13	17.5
Water pump drain plug	13	17.5
Fan cowl-to-radiator	13	17.5
Fan motor-to-cowl	7	10
Fan-to-motor	4	5
Outlet pipe-to-inlet manifold	9	12.5
Temperature sensing unit-to-radiator	26	35
Water elbow-to-sump	9	12.5
Water pump pulley-to-hub	11	15
Water pump-to-sump	9	12.5

1 General description

The cooling system is of conventional type and operates by means of thermo-syphon action with the assistance of a belt-driven water pump.

The coolant in the radiator flows from side to side instead of the more common downward direction and the 'header' tanks are situated on either side of the radiator matrix.

Coolant heated in the cylinder jackets is cooled by the ram effect of air passing through the radiator matrix when the car is in motion and assisted by a thermostatic, electrically-operated fan which operates within a pre-determined temperature range.

Coolant from the system also circulates through the vehicle heater and is used to pre-heat the inlet manifold.

The system is semi-pressurized and incorporates an expansion bottle to accept coolant displaced when the engine is hot and to act as a reservoir when the system cools down or in the event of minor leakage.

A thermostat is fitted in the system to restrict coolant circulation until the normal operating temperature has been reached.

The original coolant is effective indefinitely, but where a loss has

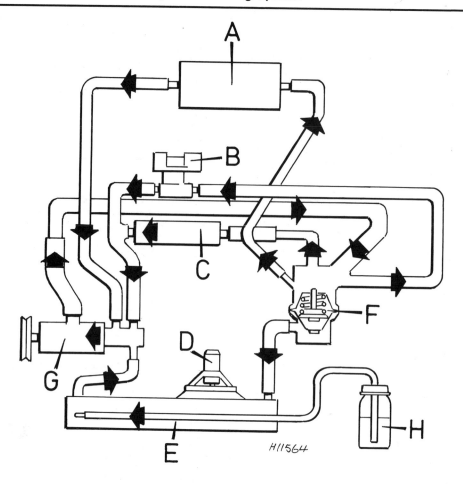

Fig. 2.1 Layout of the cooling and interior heating system (Sec 1)

A Heater matrix
B Heated carburettor flange
C Heated inlet manifold
D Electric fan

E Radiator
F Thermostat
G Water pump
H Expansion bottle

occured or the strength of the coolant (antifreeze mixture) is suspect, then the system should be drained, flushed and refilled as described in later Sections of this Chapter.

When working on the cooling system, take care to keep hands and loose clothing clear of the electric fan at all times. On a hot engine, with the ignition switched on, the fan may come into operation at any time, even if the engine is not running.

2   Cooling system – draining

1   If it is wished to retain the coolant for further use, place a clean receptacle beneath the engine and then set the vehicle interior heater to the full on (hot) position.

2   Unscrew and remove the lid from the expansion bottle and the filler cap from the radiator **Caution:** *If the system is to be drained while hot, unscrew the expansion bottle lid very slowly to allow the pressure in the system to vent gradually.*

3   Unscrew and remove the plug and sealing washer from the base of the water pump (photo) and allow the coolant to drain into the receptacle.

4   Do not allow the coolant to come into contact with the vehicle paintwork as its antifreeze content will damage the surface of the finish.

5   The coolant should be retained in a covered vessel pending return to the system and any sediment which precipitates should be discarded.

2.3 The cooling system drain plug (arrowed)

3 Cooling system – flushing

1   Providing the cooling system is maintained in good order, flushing will only be necesssary once every two years. Where the coolant has become discoloured or become contaminated with oil due to gasket failure, then the system should be thoroughly cleansed.

2   To do this, remove the radiator filler cap and insert a hose in the filler neck, then, with the water pump drain plug removed and the heater control full on, allow the water to flow until it is quite clear when emerging from the water pump drain plug.

3   If the radiator appears blocked then it should be removed as described in Section 6 and reverse flushed. This is carried out by placing the hose in the right-hand radiator outlet so that the water flow is in the opposite direction to normal.

4   The removal of scale from the system should not normally be a problem as, with a semi-sealed circuit, only initial scaling occurs unless, due to leaks, continual topping up is required.

5   The use of chemical de-scalers and cleansers is not recommended as, unless specifically formulated, damage to the aluminium cylinder head, water pump and thermostat housings may occur.

6   Never flush a hot engine cooling system with cold water, or cracks or distortion of the block or head may be caused.

7   In the event of blockages in the heater matrix then this should be removed as described in Chapter 12 and serviced as previously described for the radiator.

4 Cooling system – filling

1   The best water to use in the cooling system is rain water and this should be used whenever possible with the addition of the correct quantity of antifreeze (see Section 5).

2   Ensure that the drain plug is refitted to the base of the water pump and that the vehicle interior heater is set to the full position.

3   Unscrew and remove the lid from the expansion bottle and the filler cap from the radiator.

4   Unscrew and remove the bleed plug from the thermostat housing (photo) and then carefully fill the system with coolant, through the radiator filler, until coolant runs from the bleed hole. Now refit the bleed plug.

5   Top up the radiator to the filler neck with the coolant.

6   Refit the radiator filler cap securely, but without overtightening it and deforming the filler back flange.

7   Top up the expansion bottle to the 'maxi' mark and then refit the expansion bottle.

8   Start the engine and allow it to warm up until the electric fan cuts in. This will ensure that the thermostat has opened. With the engine still running, *slowly* unscrew the expansion bottle lid and if necessary add coolant to maintain the level between the 'mini' and 'maxi' marks.

9   With the electric fan in operation, accelerate the engine several times to approximately 5000 rpm to complete the bleeding of air from the system. This will be indicated by the absence of air bubbles from the hose in the expansion tank.

10 Stop the engine and allow it to cool. When cool top up the expansion bottle to the 'maxi' mark.

5 Antifreeze mixture

1   The use of antifreeze mixture in the cooling system fulfils two purposes: to protect the engine and heater components against fracture during periods of low ambient temperature and to utilise the effects of the rust and corrosion inhibitors incorporated in the antifreeze product.

2   A 'long-life' type of antifreeze may be used, but where a normal commercial type is used it is wise to renew it or at least check its strength with a hydrometer every year.

3   Ensure that the mixture is of a type compatible with aluminium components and refer to the following table for strength recommendations.

Quantity of antifreeze	Gives protection to
25%	−12°C (10°F)
33⅓%	−19°C (−3°)
40%	−23°C (−10°F)
50%	−37°C (−35°F)

4   Due to the searching action of antifreeze mixture, always check the security of hose clips and gasket joints before filling.

6 Radiator – removal, inspection, cleaning and refitting

1   Drain the cooling system as described in Section 2.

2   Disconnect the battery earth terminal.

3   Disconnect the two wires from the temperature sensing unit located on the rear left-hand side of the radiator (photo) and the wires to the electric fan at the connector.

4   Disconnect the top and bottom radiator hoses.

5   Disconnect the expansion bottle hose from the top of the radiator.

6   If automatic transmission is fitted, undo and remove the fluid cooler pipe unions at the radiator. Plug the pipe ends and radiator connections to prevent dirt ingress.

7   Remove the nuts and washers from both the lower radiator mountings and the top mounting (photos).

8   Tilt the radiator assembly towards the engine and then lift it clear of the lower mounting plates (photo).

9   The radiator matrix should be cleaned internally as described in

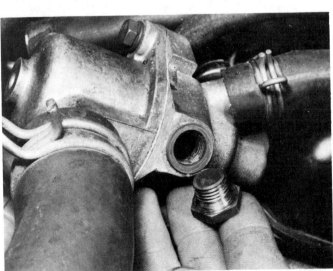

4.4 Bleed plug removed from thermostat housing

6.3 Electrical connections at the radiator temperature sensing unit

6.7a Radiator lower ...

6.7b ... and upper mountings

6.8 Removing the radiator

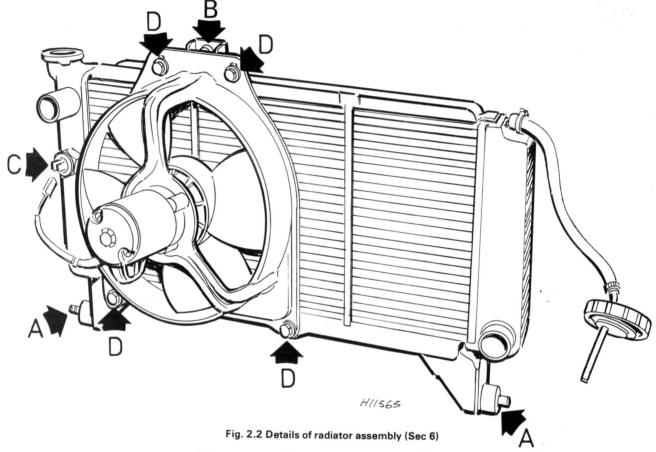

Fig. 2.2 Details of radiator assembly (Sec 6)

A Lower mountings   C Temperature sensing unit
B Top mounting   D Fan cowl attachments

Section 3. Any accumulation of flies on the radiator fins should be removed by lightly brushing or blowing out with compressed air.

10 If the radiator is leaking, do not attempt to repair it yourself as the heat used for soldering must be carefully localised if further leaks are not to be created. Take the unit to a specialist repairer or exchange the unit for a factory reconditioned one. The use of any type of leak sealant is at its best, a temporary cure and its use may clog the fine tubes of the heater matrix and damage the water pump seals.

11 Refitting the radiator is a reversal of removal. Refill the system as described in Section 4.

12 If automatic transmission is fitted, check and if necessary top up the fluid level as described in Chapter 6.

7 Thermostat – removal, testing and refitting

1 Drain the cooling system as previously described.

2 Unscrew and remove the two bolts which secure the thermostat housing cover in position.

3 Remove the cover and gasket and withdraw the thermostat. If it is stuck in its seat do not try to lever it out but cut round its seat joint with a pointed blade to break the seal (photo).

4 To test whether the thermostat is serviceable, suspend it in a pan of water into which a thermometer has been placed. Heat the water and check that the thermostat begins to open when the water temperature reaches that at which the thermostat is rated (see Specifications).

5 Similarly, when the thermostat is fully open, place it into cooler water and observe its closure. Any failure in the opening or closing actions of the unit will necessitate renewal. Fit one with the specified temperature marked on it, nothing is to be gained by fitting one having a different operating temperature range and could cause cool running or overheating of the engine and heater inefficiency.

6 Refitting is a reversal of removal but ensure that the locating tab

7.3 Removing the thermostat cover

on the thermostat is correctly aligned and use a new cover gasket. Do not overtighten the cover securing bolts.
7   Refill the system as described in Section 4.

8 Water pump – removal and refitting

1   Drain the cooling system as described in Section 2.
2   Jack up the front of the car and support it securely on axle stands.
3   From underneath the right-hand side of the car, undo and remove the five securing bolts and lift off the engine splash shield.
4   Slacken the alternator mounting and adjusting arm bolts, move

the alternator towards the engine and lift off the drivebelt.
5   Undo and remove the three retaining bolts and withdraw the water pump pulley from the pump flange.
6   Disconnect the water hose from the outlet on the side of the pump.
7   Undo and remove the four retaining bolts and withdraw the water pump assembly from its location in the sump casting.
8   Refitting the water pump is the reverse sequence to removal, bearing in mind the following points:

   (a) Ensure that the sump face and water pump mating surfaces are thoroughly clean and free from any traces of old gasket
   (b) Use a new gasket lightly smeared on both sides with sealing compound
   (c) Tighten the pulley and water pump retaining bolts to the torque settings shown in the Specifications
   (d) Adjust the drivebelt tension as described in Section 11

9 Water pump – dismantling and reassembly

1   The water pump is designed for long trouble-free service and if it has been in operation for a considerable mileage then it will probably be more realistic to exchange the complete unit for one which has been factory reconditioned, rather than attempt to repair a pump without the necessary experience and tools.
2   Check the condition of the impeller for corrosion. Other than this, any fault will lie with a worn shaft seal.
3   Press off the hub from the shaft. To achieve this, support the rear face of the hub and exert pressure on the end of the shaft. (If only the seal is to be renewed, do not remove the hub).
4   Turn the pump over and again, adequately supporting the rear face of the impeller, press the end of the shaft to expel it from the impeller bore.
5   Now immerse the pump body in boiling water for two or three minutes. Remove the pump quickly and drive out the shaft/bearing assembly by driving it out from the seal end with a copper or plastic-faced hammer.

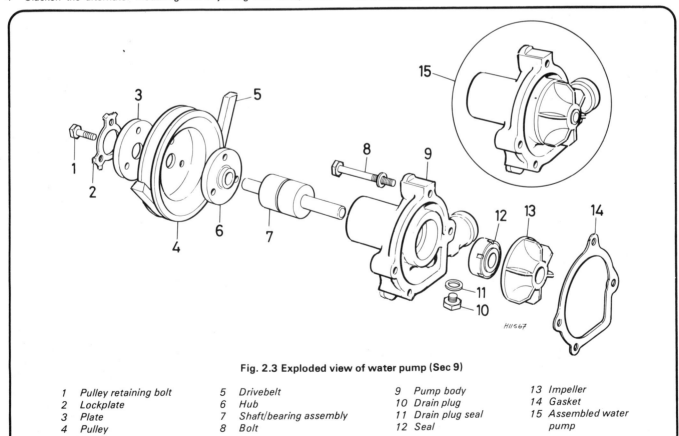

Fig. 2.3 Exploded view of water pump (Sec 9)

1 Pulley retaining bolt
2 Lockplate
3 Plate
4 Pulley
5 Drivebelt
6 Hub
7 Shaft/bearing assembly
8 Bolt
9 Pump body
10 Drain plug
11 Drain plug seal
12 Seal
13 Impeller
14 Gasket
15 Assembled water pump

6   Drive the seal from the water pump body by means of a drift inserted from the front end of the pump.

7   The shaft/bearing assembly cannot be separated, and if necessary, must be renewed as a single component.

8   Check the condition of the seal and shaft bearing mating surfaces of the pump body. Where necessary, these may be improved with grade '600' abrasive paper.

9   Press the water pump seal into its seating in the body.

10 Again heat the pump body in boiling water and then press the shaft bearing assembly into the body ensuring that the bearing seats securely against the bore inner shoulder. Note that the longer end of the shaft is at the seal end.

11 Supporting the end face of the shaft at the seal end, press on the flanged hub so that its boss is towards the shaft bearing. The hub is correctly positioned on the shaft when there is a clearance of 0.050 in (1.270 mm) between the pump and hub faces measured with feeler gauges.

12 Support the front end face of the shaft and press on the impeller (vanes outwards) until there is again a clearance of 0.050 in (1.270 mm) between the pump and impeller faces.

13 Check for free rotation by turning the vanes of the impeller.

10 Radiator cooling fan – description and servicing

1   The assembly comprises a four-bladed fan attached to the driving spindle of an electric motor.

2   The fan motor is controlled by a temperature sensing unit that is screwed into the rear left-hand side of the radiator.

3   When the coolant temperature reaches 95°C (203°F) the temperature sensor contacts close and energise the fan. When the water temperature falls to between 86 and 88°C (187 and 191°F) the contacts open and the fan is de-energised.

Warning: *It must be realised that during adjustments within the engine compartment, with the engine at operating temperature, the fan blades may turn unexpectedly if the ignition is switched on. From the point of view of safety, disconnect the fan motor leads before carrying out adjustments in close proximity to the radiator, but watch the coolant temperature if the engine is running!*

4   If the operation of the temperature sensing unit is suspect it should be removed for testing.

5   Disconnect the battery earth terminal, drain the cooling system as described in Section 2 and unscrew the sensor unit from the radiator.

6   Suspend the sensor unit in a water filled container with a thermometer of a suitable temperature range and connect up a 12V battery and test lamp as shown in Fig. 2.4.

7   Heat the water on a stove and check that the lamp lights at a temperature of 95°C (203°C) and extinguishes when the water is allowed to cool to 86°C (187°C).

8   If the lamp does not light, or lights and extinguishes at a different temperature than that specified, the sensor unit is faulty and must be renewed.

9   Should the sensor unit function correctly then the fault must be in the fan motor itself.

10 Remove the fan motor and base assembly after disconnecting the electrical leads and withdrawing the four securing bolts.

11 Unscrew and remove the nut and spring washer which secure the fan blades to the motor shaft. *This has a left-hand thread and the nut must therefore be unscrewed in a clockwise direction.*

12 Unscrew and remove the three bolts which secure the motor to the fan assembly outer frame. Renew the motor on an exchange basis.

13 Reassembly and refitting of the fan cooling unit is a reversal of removal and dismantling.

11 Drivebelt – adjustment, removal and refitting

1   To adjust the alternator drivebelt, slacken the pivot bolt and locking bolt and move the alternator in the necessary direction.

2   The correct tension for the belt is ½ in (12 mm) of free movement on the longest run of the belt. When correctly adjusted tighten the pivot and locking bolts.

3   To remove the belt, slacken the bolts and push the alternator in towards the engine as far as possible. Ease the belt off the pulleys, rotating the alternator if necessary.

4   Fit the new belt using the reverse procedure to removal and adjust

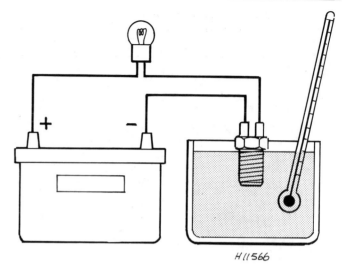

Fig. 2.4 Method of testing the temperature sensing unit (Sec 10)

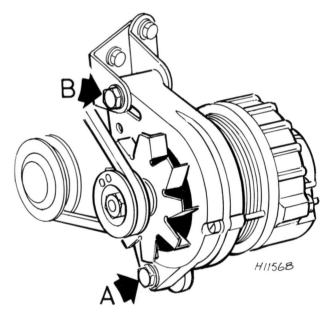

Fig. 2.5 Alternator mounting bolts for drivebelt adjustment (Sec 11)

A *Locking bolt*
B *Pivot bolt*

the tension as described previously. Do not lever against the body of the alternator or damage may result.

12 Water temperature gauge – fault finding

1   Correct operation of the water temperature gauge is important as the engine could attain a considerable degree of overheating, unnoticed, if giving false readings.

2   To check the correct operation of the gauge, first disconnect the connector from the sender unit plug screwed into the side of the inlet manifold. With the ignition on, the gauge should be at the cold mark. Then earth the lead to the engine block when the needle should indicate hot, at the opposite end of the scale. This test shows that the gauge on the dash is functioning properly. If it is not then it will need renewal. If there is still a fault in the system with this check completed satisfactorily, there will be a fault in the sender unit or the wire leading from it to the gauge. Renew these as necessary.

13 Fault diagnosis – cooling system

Symptom	Reason(s)
Overheating	Insufficient water in cooling system Cooling fan inoperative Drivebelt slipping Thermostat faulty or incorrect type fitted Radiator core blocked or radiator grille restricted Expansion bottle valve faulty Ignition timing incorrect Blown cylinder head gasket Brakes binding Restriction in exhaust system
Overcooling	Thermostat faulty or not fitted Incorrect type of thermostat fitted Inaccurate temperature gauge
Water loss	Overfilling of system Water boiling due to overheating Internal or external leakage Inoperative thermostat or blocked radiator Expansion bottle valve faulty
External leakage	Leakage at hoses or joint faces Water pump seal faulty Leakage from core plugs Leakage from heater matrix Leakage from radiator core or header tanks
Internal leakage	Faulty cylinder head gasket Loose cylinder head bolts Cracked cylinder bore Cracked or excessively corroded cylinder head Cracked or corroded inlet manifold or carburettor flange (if applicable)

Chapter 3 Fuel and exhaust systems

For modifications, and information applicable to later models, see Supplement at end of manual

Contents

Specifications

Fuel pump
Type .... Mechanical, driven from eccentric on camshaft
Mean operating pressure .... 133 mbar (1.9 lbf/in²)

Fuel filters
Type .... Nylon or wire mesh, and disposable cartridge
Location .... Fuel pump cover, fuel pump outlet hose and carburettor inlet (where applicable)

Air cleaner
Filter type .... Disposable paper element

Carburettor application
9 Series (1978/79)
1118 cc .... Solex 32 BISA 6A, Weber 31 IBSA or Bressel 31 IBSA
1294 cc .... Solex 32 BISA 6A, Weber 32 IBSA or Bressel 32 IBSA
1442 cc:
    Single choke carburettor .... Solex 32 BISA 7
    Twin choke carburettor (automatic transmission) .... Weber 36 DCA
    Twin choke carburettor (manual transmission) .... Weber 36 DCNV or Bressel 36 DCNV

A Series (1979/80)
1118 cc .... Solex 32 BISA 7, Weber 32 IBSH or Bressel 32 IBSH
1294 cc .... Solex 32 BISA 7, Weber 32 IBSH or Bressel 32 IBSH
1442 cc:
    Single choke carburettor .... Solex 32 BISA 7
    Twin choke carburettor (automatic transmission) .... Weber 36 DCA or Bressel 36 DCA
    Twin choke carburettor (manual transmission) .... Weber 36 DCNVH or Bressel 36 DCNVH

Carburettor data
Solex 32 BISA 6A

	1118 cc (9 Series)*	**1294 cc (9 Series)**
Engine type		
Choke tube	25	27
Secondary venturi	2 mm	2 mm
Main jet	127.5 ± 2.5	135 ± 2.5
Air correction jet	160 ± 5	165 ± 5
Emulsion tube	E7	E7
Econostat fuel jet	50 ± 10	60 ± 10
Econostat air jet	3 mm	3 mm
Idling fuel jet	39 to 45	39 to 45
Idling air jet	130	130
Pump injector	40	40
Pump stroke	3 mm	3 mm

* 9 Series – 1978 to 1979 models

Float needle	1.5 with ball	1.5 with ball	
Float weight	5.7 g	5.7g	
Fast idle gap	0.95 ± 0.05	0.95 ± 0.05	
Constant CO circuit:			
Air intake aperture	500	500	
Fuel calibration	30	30	
Air calibration	100	150	

Solex 32 BISA 7

	1118 cc** (A Series)	1294 cc (A Series)	1442 cc (9 and A Series)
Engine type			
Choke tube	25	27	27
Main jet	122.5 ± 2.5	135 ± 2.5	135 ± 2.5
Air correction jet	175 ± 5	170 ± 5	155 ± 5
Emulsion tube	EC	EC	EC
Fuel enricher	50 ± 10	50 ± 10	50 ± 10
Econostat fuel jet	50 ± 10	50 ± 10	55 ± 10
Econostat air jet	300	300	300
Idling fuel jet	39 to 43	39 to 45	36 to 42
Idling air jet	130	130	130
Pump injector	40	40	40
Float needle	1.5	1.5	1.5
Float weight	5.7g	5.7g	5.7g
Fast idle gap	0.9 ± 0.05 mm	0.9 ± 0.05 mm	0.9 ± 0.05 mm
Constant CO circuit:			
Air calibration	5.8	5.8	5.8
Fuel calibration	35	35	35
Emulsion aerator	160	160	140

Weber or Bressel 31 IBSA

	1118 cc (9 Series)
Engine type	
Choke tube	24.5
Main jet	127^{+3}_{-2}
Air correction jet	160
Emulsion tube	F56
Idling fuel jet	39 to 45
Pump injector	45
Float needle	150
Fast idle gap	0.9 ± 0.05 mm
Float level	6 mm $\pm$ 0.25 mm (gasket in position)

Weber or Bressel 32 IBSA

	1294 cc (9 Series)
Engine type	
Choke tube	26
Main jet	145^{+2}_{-3}
Air correction jet	175 ± 5
Emulsion tube	F57
Idling fuel jet	39 to 45
Pump injector	45
Float needle	150
Fast idle gap	1.05 ± 0.05 mm
Float level	6 mm $\pm$ 0.25 mm (gasket in position)

Weber or Bressel 32 IBSH

	1118 cc (A Series)	1294 cc (A Series)
Engine type		
Choke tube	26	26
Main jet	140^{+2}_{-3}	135^{+2}_{-3}
Air correction jet	180 ± 5	175 ± 5
Emulsion tube	F56	F6
Fuel enricher	80 ± 10	130
Idling fuel jet	37 to 42	40 to 45
Idling air jet	160	200 ± 5
Progression	70, 70, 70	100, 100, 70
Pump injector	45	45
Float needle	150	150
Float weight	11g	11g
Float level (gasket in position)	6 mm $\pm$ 0.25 mm	6 mm $\pm$ 0.25 mm
Fast idle gap	1.05 ± 0.05 mm	1.05 ± 0.05 mm
Vacuum enricher	40^{+10}_{-0}	55 ± 10

** A Series – 1979 to 1980 models

Weber or Bressel 36 DCA

Engine type	
Choke tube	28
Main jet	127^{+3}_{-2}
Air correction jet	170 ± 5
Emulsion tube	F46
Idling fuel jet	37 to 42
Pump stroke	No 2
Pump injector	40 long
Pump cam	No 42
Float needle	175
Float level	41 mm $\pm$ 0.25 mm (without gasket)
Automatic choke:	
Vacuum opening	4 to 4.5 mm
Modulated opening	6 to 7 mm
Opening on cocking	0.50 to 0.60 mm

1442 cc – automatic transmission (9 and A Series)

Weber or Bressel 36 DCNV

Engine type	
Choke tube	28
Main jet	132 ± 2.5
Air correction jet	175 ± 5
Emulsion tube	F36
Idling fuel jet	40 to 42
Pump stroke	No 2
Pump injector	50
Pump cam	No 42
Float needle	175
Fast idle gap	0.40 to 0.45 mm
Float level	52 mm $\pm$ 0.25 mm (without gasket)

1442 cc – manual transmission (9 Series)

Weber or Bressel 36 DCNVH

Engine type	
Choke tube	28
Main jet	127^{+3}_{-2}
Air correction jet	170 ± 5
Emulsion tube	F46
Idling fuel jet	40 to 42
Idling air jet	160 ± 5
Progression	90, 90, 90, 100
Pump injector	50 long
Float needle	175
Float weight	14.5g
Float level	42.55 mm $\pm$ 0.25 mm (without gasket)
Fast idle gap	0.4 ± 0.05 mm
Vacuum enricher	50 ± 10

1442 cc – manual transmission (A Series)

Idling speeds

1118 cc and 1294 cc	850 rpm
1442 cc single choke carburettor	900 rpm
1442 cc twin choke carburettor:	
Automatic transmission	950 rpm
Manual transmission	900 rpm

Torque wrench settings

	lbf ft	Nm
Inlet manifold-to-cylinder head	11	15
Exhaust manifold-to-cylinder head	15	20
Fuel pump-to-cylinder block	15	20
Exhaust front pipe-to-manifold	15	20
Carburettor-to-inlet manifold	15	20

1 General description

The fuel system comprises a fuel tank, a mechanically operated fuel pump and either a single or twin choke downdraught carburettor, with associated fuel pipes and controls. The fuel tank is positioned below the rear luggage compartment and is bolted to the vehicle underbody. The tank incorporates a fill limiting device that reduces the risk of overfilling the tank, with consequent danger of fuel spilling from the vent due to expansion. The tank also houses the fuel gauge sender unit, located on the tank top face.

The fuel pump is located on the front of the engine and is driven by an eccentric on the camshaft. Located in the pump is a small filter to which access is gained by removing the pump top cover. On some models a disposable in-line filter is fitted in the output fuel pipe to the carburettor.

Carburettors may be of Solex, Weber or Bressel manufacture. The Bressel unit is made under licence from both Solex and Weber and is virtually identical to the parent instrument. A water-heated inlet manifold is used on all models to improve fuel atomization and on some models the carburettor flange is also water-heated. Mixture enrichment for cold starting is by a manually operated choke control, or (on some models) an automatic choke sensitive to the engine cooling water temperature.

2 Air cleaner – description and servicing

1   All models are fitted with a renewable paper element air filter housed in a plastic casing on top of the engine which is retained by a quick-release strap. The filter element must be renewed at the specified intervals if engine efficiency and fuel economy are to be maintained.

2   The temperature of the air entering the air cleaner can be controlled by means of a selector lever on the intake duct. In the 'summer' position cold air is drawn into the air cleaner assembly via a hose leading in from the front wing, while the 'winter' position allows air to be drawn in through a hot air duct fitted over the exhaust manifold. An intermediate position provides mixed hot and cold air.

3   To renew the filter element, disconnect the inlet hose from the end cover, release the spring clips and withdraw the end cover complete with filter element.

4   The end cover is integral with the filter element and the complete assembly must be discarded.

5   When fitting the new filter and end cover, ensure that the arrows on top of the cover and filter housing are in alignment before fastening the clips and refitting the intake hose. Also ensure that the new filter is of the same make as the old; several different types have been fitted and not all are interchangeable.

6   To remove the complete air cleaner assembly first, in the case of the 1118 cc and 1294 cc engines, undo and remove the two nuts securing the air cleaner adaptor to the top of the carburettor (photo). On the 1442 cc engines, release the seven clips securing the two halves of the adaptor together. Lift off the top half, using a thin blade if necessary to prise it up, and then undo and remove the nuts securing the lower half to the carburettor.

7   Release the strap securing the air cleaner body, disengage the locating peg from its grommet and lift off the air cleaner assembly.

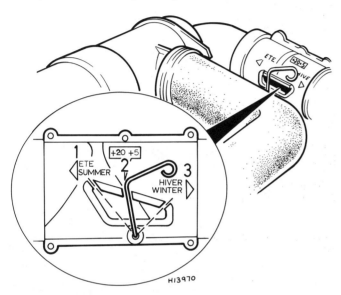

Fig. 3.1 Air cleaner inlet temperature control lever (Sec 2)

1   Summer (Ete) position
2   Mid position
3   Winter (Hiver) position

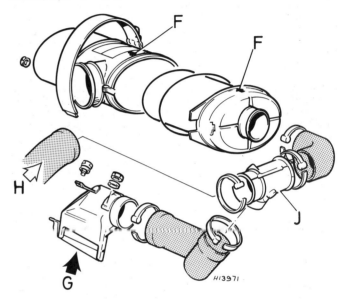

Fig. 3.2 Air cleaner components (Sec 2)

F   Alignment marks, end   H   Cold air intake
     cover and body   J   Air temperature control
G   Hot air pick-up

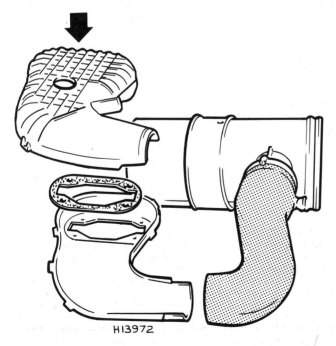

Fig. 3.3 Air cleaner adaptor assembly (arrowed) fitted to the 1442 cc engine (Sec 2)

2.6 With the nuts removed, lift off the air cleaner adaptor ...

2.7a ... release the strap ...

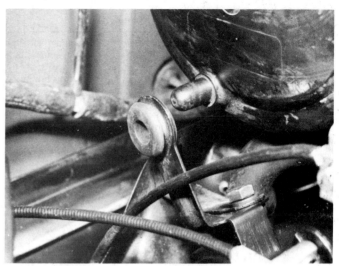

2.7b ... disengage the locating peg and lift off the air cleaner

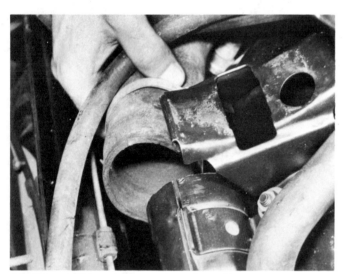

2.7c When sufficient clearance exists, release the hot air duct ...

2.7d ... and detach the fume extractor hose

When sufficient clearance exists, release the hot air inlet duct from the heat box on the exhaust manifold and detach the fume extractor hose (photos).

8   With the air cleaner removed, the flame trap in the fume extractor hose should be detached and cleaned.

9   Separate the two halves using a thin-bladed tool and lift out the filter discs.

10   Clean the discs in paraffin and wipe them dry.

11   Place the discs in the flame trap body and press the two halves together. Refit the flame trap to the hoses.

12   Refitting the air cleaner is the reverse sequence to removal.

3   Carburettors – general

As can be seen from the Specifications at the beginning of this Chapter, a wide range of carburettors is fitted to Horizon models, all being of Solex, Weber or Bressel manufacture. The Bressel unit is manufactured under licence from both Solex and Weber, shares the same type number, and is identical to its equivalent Solex or Weber counterpart.

During manufacture, the sizes of certain jets are selected by flow testing each carburettor to determine the fuel delivery in relation to the airflow. When dismantling carburettors it is therefore possible to find

two identical instruments, or the twin chokes of one instrument (Weber), with different jet settings within the tolerances shown in the Specifications. It is therefore essential that when removing jets from twin choke carburettors, the jets are identified with the choke from which they were removed to avoid interchanging them. Similarly, if the jets are renewed they must be the same size as the original.

4   Solex carburettors – description and operation

1   The Solex 32 BISA 6A and 32 BISA 7 are downdraught single choke carburettors and both are similar in design and construction. The main differences between the two instruments are the jet sizes and the diameter of the internal drillings in the carburettor body.

2   These carburettors comprise three main assemblies, namely the throttle block, the main body and the top cover. The throttle block embodies the throttle plate and control linkages and incorporates a water-heated jacket connected to the engine cooling system to provide pre-heating of the carburettor.

3   The main body incorporates the choke tube (sometimes known as the venturi or throttle barrel), the float chamber, accelerator pump and the jets, also the distributor vacuum and crankcase breather connections.

4   The top cover carries the choke plate, fuel inlet connection and

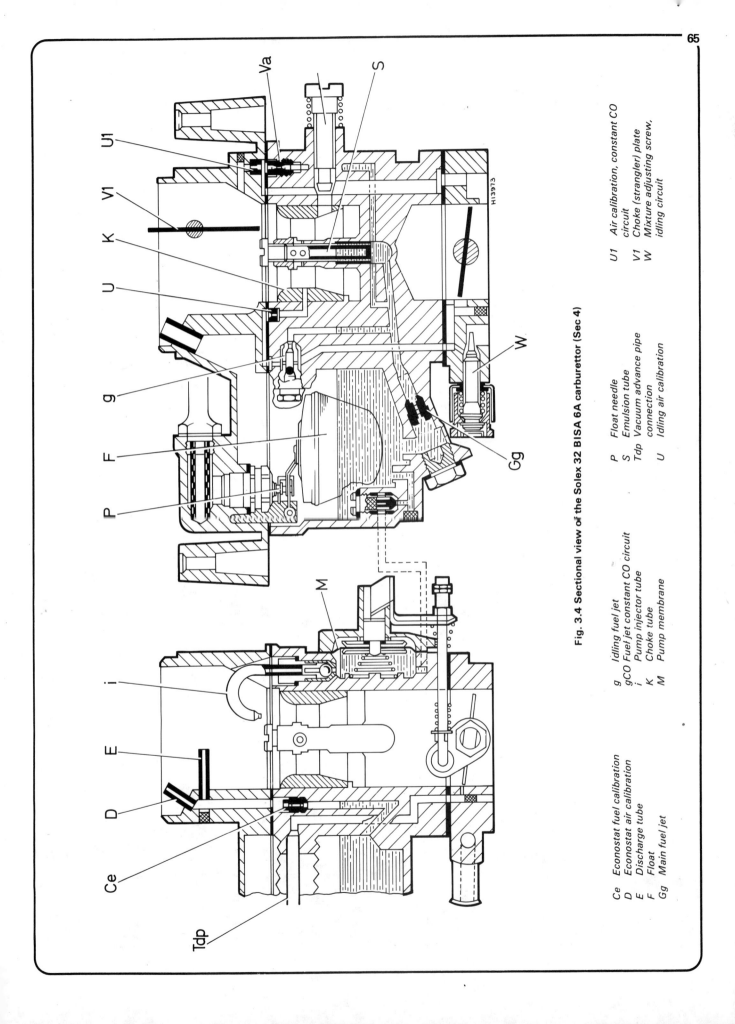

Fig. 3.4 Sectional view of the Solex 32 BISA 6A carburettor (Sec 4)

Ce Econostat fuel calibration
D   Econostat air calibration
E   Discharge tube
F   Float
Gg Main fuel jet

g   Idling fuel jet
gCO Fuel jet constant CO circuit
i   Pump injector tube
K   Choke tube
M   Pump membrane

P   Float needle
S   Emulsion tube
Tdp Vacuum advance pipe
    connection
U   Idling air calibration

U1 Air calibration, constant CO
    circuit
V1 Choke (strangler) plate
W   Mixture adjusting screw,
    idling circuit

needle valve and the Econostat discharge nozzle.

5   The cold start enrichment device comprises a strangler type choke, which is operated manually by the driver. The choke plate is held open by a linkage when the control is pushed in; however, when the control is pulled out the linkage is released and the choke plate is closed by a spring. When the engine starts, the depression in the carburettor overcomes the spring tension and automatically opens the choke plate slightly. Thus once the engine is running the mixture will be weakened by the additional air past the choke plate.

6   The accelerator pedal is connected via a cable to the linkage of the carburettor and operates the throttle plate. The depression created in the carburettor choke tube causes fuel to be drawn from the jets and out through the various drillings in the carburettor body. The fuel mixes with the incoming air to form a combustible mixture, the strength of which is controlled by the jet diameter.

7   When the accelerator is depressed quickly, a spring-loaded rod attached to the throttle spindle operates an accelerator pump which provides a jet of neat fuel into the choke tube. This creates the slightly richer mixture demanded by the engine during initial acceleration and eliminates flat spots.

8   An Econostat device is incorporated to provide additional emulsified mixture into the choke tube at high engine rpm.

9   Two idling mixture circuits are provided, each being adjustable by means of a control screw. The principal circuit discharges the idling mixture from a small orifice in the throttle block. This circuit is adjustable by the mixture screw, but is preset during manufacture and does not normally require further adjustment. The additional 'constant CO' (carbon monoxide) circuit discharges through a larger orifice and is adjustable by means of the volume screw. Adjustment of engine idling is normally made using this screw only.

5 Solex carburettors – removal and refitting

1   Unscrew the filler cap from the radiator expansion bottle slowly, to release pressure in the cooling system.

2   Remove the complete air cleaner assembly as described in Section 2.

3   Slacken the retaining clips and detach the two water hoses from the carburettor throttle block. Plug the hoses quickly to avoid loss of coolant.

4   Slacken the retaining bolt securing the accelerator inner cable to the throttle linkage and slide the inner cable out of the linkage connector (photos).

5   Using a pair of pliers, detach the hooked end of the throttle return spring guide rod from the linkage (photo). Slide the other end of the guide rod out of the nylon bracket and recover the spring.

6   Rotate the bracket until the flats are aligned with those on the mounting and slide out the bracket complete with accelerator cable (photo).

7   Now slacken the choke inner and outer cable fixing bolts and detach the cable (photos).

8   Slacken the hose clip and remove the fuel supply hose from the carburettor. Plug the hose after removal.

9   Detach the distributor vacuum advance pipe from the carburettor body.

10   Finally undo and remove the nuts securing the carburettor to the inlet manifold and lift the unit off.

11   Refitting the carburettor is the reverse sequence to removal, bearing in mind the following points:

   (a) Ensure that the mating faces of the carburettor and manifold are clean, and use a new gasket
   (b) Check for full and correct operation of the throttle and choke after reconnecting the cables
   (c) Top up the cooling system if any coolant was lost when the hoses were removed
   (d) Adjust the carburettor idling settings as described in Section 14, if necessary

6 Solex carburettors – setting and adjustment of components

Accelerator pump stroke

1   Remove the carburettor from the engine as described in Section 5.

2   Turn the carburettor over and open the throttle plate approximately halfway.

5.4b ... and slide out the inner cable

5.5 Detach the guide rod from the linkage ...

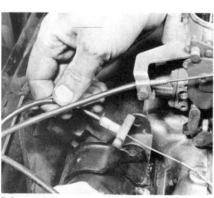

5.4a Slacken the accelerator cable retaining bolt ...

5.6 ... and then remove the cable assembly

5.7a Slacken the choke cable retaining bolts ...

5.7b ... and withdraw the cable

3   Close the throttle plate slowly until the nut on the end of the accelerator pump operating rod just contacts the pump lever. With the throttle plate held in this position, a 3 mm diameter drill or rod should just fit between the open throttle plate and the side of the choke tube.

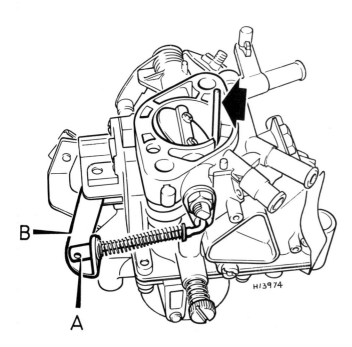

Fig. 3.5 Accelerator pump stroke adjustment – Solex carburettors. Arrow shows 3 mm dia rod (Sec 6)

A   Adjustment nut
B   Pump lever

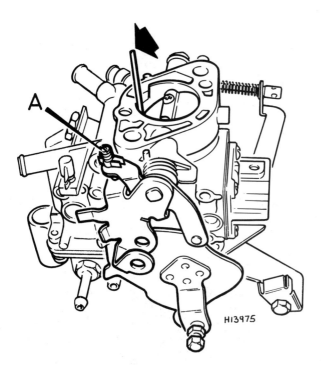

Fig. 3.6 Fast idle gap adjustment – Solex carburettors. Arrow shows 1 mm dia rod (Sec 6)

A   Fast idle gap adjusting screw

4   If necessary screw the nut in or out to alter the gap as required. **Note:** *The operating rod is crimped in the nut and if adjustment is necessary new parts may have to be obtained.*

Fast idle gap
5   This adjustment also requires removal of the carburettor from the engine.
6   Invert the carburettor and move the choke operating lever to fully close the choke plates.
7   With the choke plates closed, it will be seen that the throttle plates have opened slightly. The amount by which they have opened is the fast idle gap.
8   To check the gap insert a 1 mm diameter rod between the edge of the throttle plate and the side of the choke tube.
9   Adjust the fast idle screw as necessary until the rod will just slide up and down in the gap.

7   Solex carburettors – dismantling, servicing and reassembly

1   Remove the carburettor from the car as described in Section 5, and thoroughly clean the exterior with petrol. Wipe dry with a lint-free cloth or use an air-line.
2   Extract the small circlips and lift off the fast idle link.
3   Undo and remove the retaining screws and lift off the top cover and gasket.
4   Undo and remove the fuel inlet union and slide out the small filter.
5   Withdraw the retaining/pivot pin and take off the float.
6   Undo and remove the fuel inlet needle valve and retain the sealing washer.
7   Disconnect the accelerator pump operating rod.
8   Undo and remove the screws securing the throttle block to the carburettor body. Separate the two parts and recover the gasket and spacer (if fitted).
9   Undo and remove the securing screws and withdraw the accelerator pump cover. Take out the diaphragm and spring.
10   Make a careful note of their locations and then unscrew the various jets from their locations in the housings. Store the jets safely as they are easily lost.
11   With the carburettors now dismantled, clean the components in petrol and dry with a lint-free cloth. Blow out all the jets and carburettor drillings using air from a tyre pump; never probe with wire.
12   Examine the choke and throttle spindles and plates for wear or excessive side play of the spindles in their bearings. If wear is apparent in these areas it is advisable to obtain an exchange carburettor.
13   If the spindles and plates are satisfactory, check the accelerator pump diaphragm and renew it if it is punctured or shows signs of deterioration.
14   Examine the float for signs of deterioration and shake it, listening for fuel inside. If so, renew it as it is leaking and will give an incorrect float level height or cause flooding.
15   Blow through the float needle valve while holding it closed and then open. Renew if faulty, or as a matter of course if high mileages have been covered.
16   Obtain the new parts as necessary and also a repair kit which will contain a complete set of new gaskets, washers and other essentials.
17   Reassemble the carburettors using the reverse of the dismantling procedure, and when assembled carry out the adjustment of components described in Section 6.
18   After refitting the carburettor to the car, adjust the idling settings as described in Section 14.

8   Weber carburettors – description and operation

1   Six types of Weber carburettors are fitted to Horizon models and they can be classified into two groups. The 31 IBSA, 32 IBSA are all single choke downdraught types of similar design and construction. The 36 DCNV, 36 DCNVH and 36 DCA are all twin choke downdraught types, similar in design but having one or two significant differences.
2   Brief descriptions and the general principles of operation of these instruments are given below.

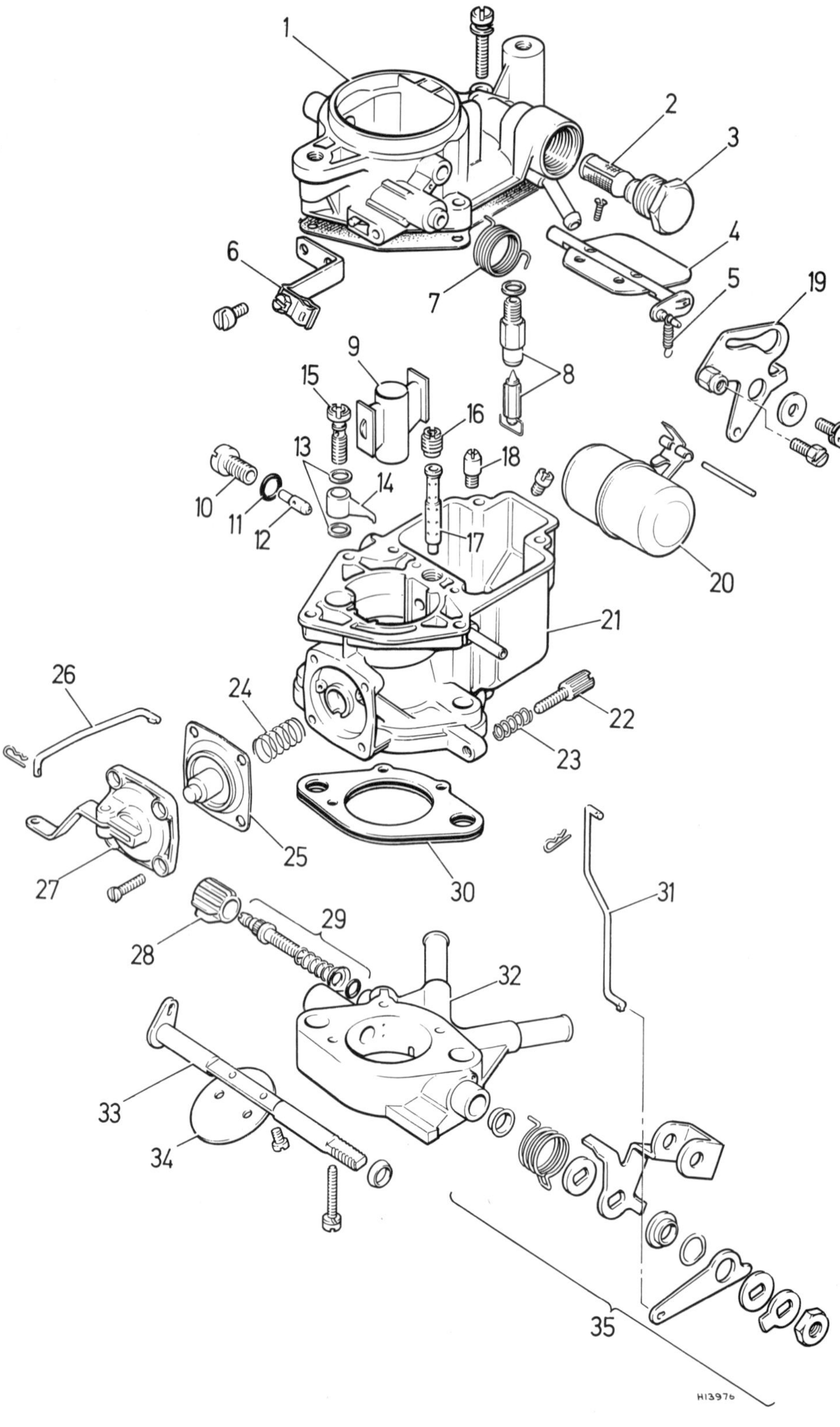

68

Fig. 3.7 Exploded view of the
Weber 32 IBSA carburettor
(Sec 8)

1 Top cover
2 Fuel filter
3 Filter plug
4 Choke plate
5 Pull-off spring
6 Cable bracket
7 Tension spring
8 Float needle valve
9 Venturi
10 Screw
11 Seal
12 Idling jet
13 Seals
14 Accelerator pump
    discharge
15 Accelerator pump
    jet
16 Main jet
17 Emulsion tube
18 Progression jet
19 Choke linkage
20 Float
21 Main body
22 Idle speed (throttle
    stop) screw
23 Screw tension
    spring
24 Pump diaphragm
    spring
25 Accelerator pump
    diaphragm
26 Accelerator pump
    linkage
27 Accelerator pump
    cover
28 Tamperproof cap
29 Mixture control
    screw
30 Gasket
31 Choke operating
    rod
32 Throttle block
33 Throttle spindle
34 Throttle plate
35 Throttle linkage

31 IBSA, 32 IBSA and 32 IBSH

3 As with the Solex units described previously, these carburettors also comprise three main assemblies, namely the throttle block, the main body and the top cover. The throttle block embodies the throttle plate and control linkages, the mixture control screw and a water-heated jacket connected to the engine cooling system.

4 The main body incorporates the choke tube, float chamber, accelerator pump, the jets and the distributor vacuum pipe connection.

5 The top cover contains the choke plate, fuel inlet connection, filter and needle valve.

6 The operation of the carburettor is also the same as the Solex units described in detail in Section 4, with the exception of the Econostat device and the twin idling mixture circuits which are not used on these carburettors.

7 Control of the idling mixture strength is by a single adjustment screw located in the throttle block. Engine rpm at tickover is adjustable by an idling speed control screw acting directly on the carburettor throttle linkage.

36 DCNV

8 This instrument comprises two main assemblies, the main body and the top cover. Housed within the main body are the float chamber and float, the choke tubes and secondary venturi, the accelerator pump, the cold start vacuum kick diaphragm, the throttle plates and linkages, the mixture control and idle speed screws, and the various jets and drillings.

9 The top cover contains the fuel inlet connection, the needle valve and float chamber, and the choke (strangler) plates and linkages.

10 The carburettor circuits as duplicated in each choke tube and both choke tubes operate simultaneously, supplying two adjacent engine cylinders. The effect is therefore the same as a twin carburettor installation.

11 Cold start enrichment is by a manually operated choke control assisted by a vacuum kick diaphragm. When the manual choke control is pulled out, the choke plates in the top cover are closed by a spring-loaded rod connected to the choke linkage. As the engine starts, the depression in the carburettor acts on the vacuum kick diaphragm. The diaphragm is connected to the choke plate spindle and allows the plates to open by a predetermined amount. Thus as soon as the engine fires, the rich cold starting mixture is weakened slightly by the air entering past the partially open choke plates. When the choke control is pushed in, the choke plates will open under the influence of the spring.

12 The accelerator pedal is connected via a cable to the linkage on the carburettor and operates the throttle plates. According to the depression in the choke tubes, governed by the position of the throttle plates, fuel will be supplied as an emulsified mixture from the progression and main jet orifices into the choke tube. The fuel mixes with the incoming air through the choke tube and secondary venturi to form a combustible mixture, the strength of which is controlled by the jet diameters.

13 A conventional accelerator pump is fitted to provide the richer mixture demanded by the engine during initial periods of acceleration.

14 When the engine is idling the mixture is discharged through two small orifices, one in each choke tube, located below the throttle plates. The fuel is supplied by the idling fuel jets and mixes with air from the idling air calibrations. The resulting mixture passes out of the orifices below the throttle plates to be further diluted by air passing around the plates. The amount of mixture entering the air stream is controlled by the two mixture screws. The position of the throttle plates at tickover is controlled by the throttle stop screw.

36 DCNVH

15 This instrument is identical to the 36 DCNV, with the addition of a vacuum-operated enriching device.

16 The enriching device is a vacuum-operated diaphragm, the vacuum being created by the depression in the carburettor choke tube. The enriching device enables the main jets to be smaller in diameter,

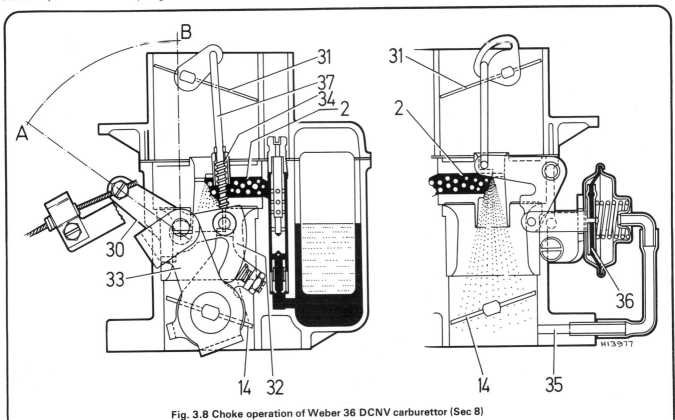

Fig. 3.8 Choke operation of Weber 36 DCNV carburettor (Sec 8)

2 Main discharge passages	32 Fast idle cam	35 Vacuum kick passage	A Choke lever, closed position
14 Throttle plates	33 Throttle lever	36 Vacuum kick membrane	B Choke lever, open position
30 Choke operating lever	34 Spring	37 Spring-loaded rod	
31 Choke plates			

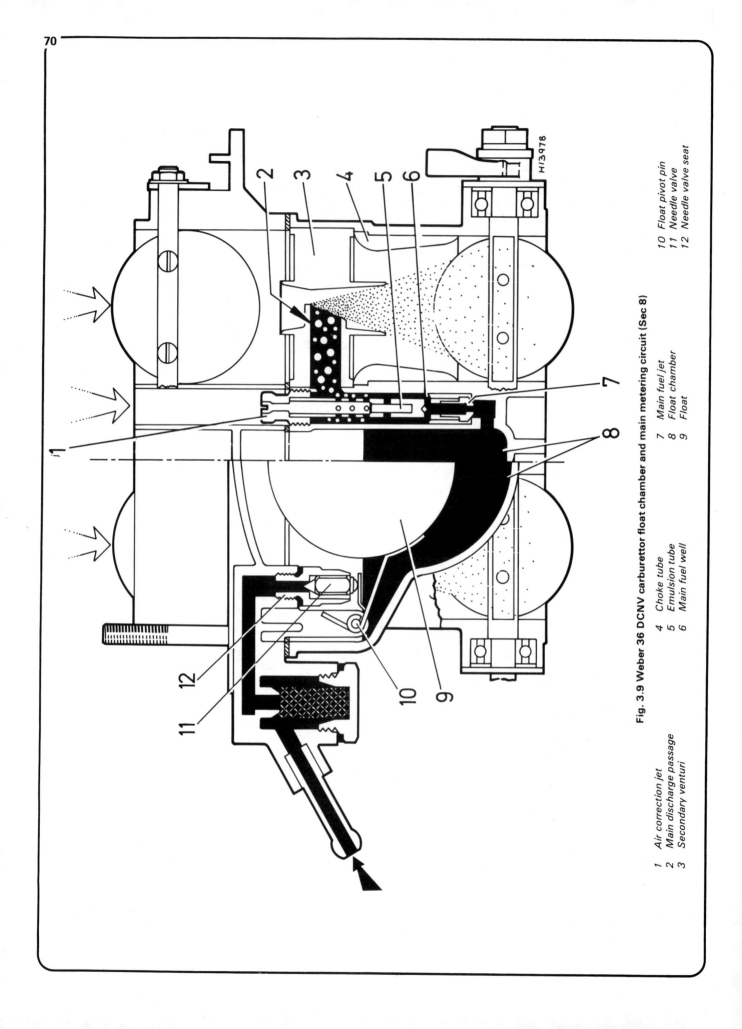

HI3978

Fig. 3.9 Weber 36 DCNV carburettor float chamber and main metering circuit (Sec 8)

1 Air correction jet
2 Main discharge passage
3 Secondary venturi

4 Choke tube
5 Emulsion tube
6 Main fuel well

7 Main fuel jet
8 Float chamber
9 Float

10 Float pivot pin
11 Needle valve
12 Needle valve seat

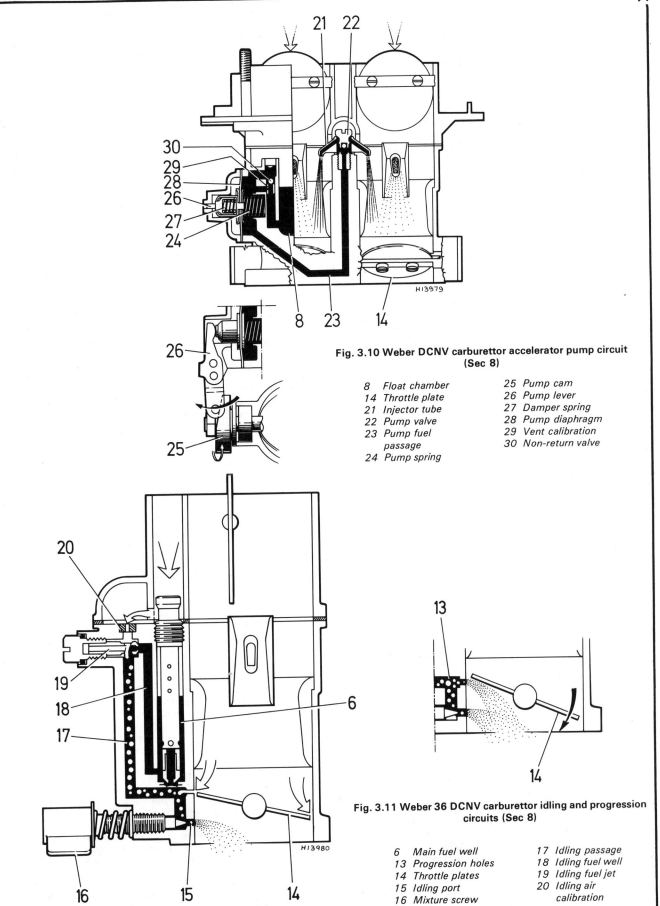

Fig. 3.10 Weber DCNV carburettor accelerator pump circuit (Sec 8)

8	Float chamber	25 Pump cam
14	Throttle plate	26 Pump lever
21	Injector tube	27 Damper spring
22	Pump valve	28 Pump diaphragm
23	Pump fuel passage	29 Vent calibration
24	Pump spring	30 Non-return valve

Fig. 3.11 Weber 36 DCNV carburettor idling and progression circuits (Sec 8)

6	Main fuel well	17 Idling passage
13	Progression holes	18 Idling fuel well
14	Throttle plates	19 Idling fuel jet
15	Idling port	20 Idling air calibration
16	Mixture screw	

giving greater fuel economy at low speeds. To prevent the mixture from becoming too weak at higher engine speeds, due to the reduced main jet size, the enrichment device opens an additional fuel circuit, supplying additional fuel for full power operation.

36 DCA
17 This carburettor is also virtually identical to the 36 DCNV, but with the addition of the depression-operated enriching device, as fitted to the 36 DCNVH, and also a fully automatic choke.
18 The choke is controlled by a water-heated, bi-metallic, thermostatic spring, which will fully close the choke plates at temperatures below 68°F (20°C).
19 When the engine is stopped, a spring-loaded plunger acts directly on the throttle linkage, opening it slightly and therefore keeping the fast idle adjustment screw clear of the stepped fast idle cam. This allows the choke plates to automatically adopt the correct position, according to temperature, and obviates the need for depressing the accelerator pedal, to 'cock' the carburettor, before a cold start.
20 When the engine has started, the spring-loaded plunger is withdrawn by manifold vacuum. Engine fast idle during warm-up is controlled by the fast idle adjustment screw, on the appropriate step of the fast idle cam.
21 As the engine warms up, coolant circulating through the choke housing heats the thermostatic spring. The spring expands, causing the choke plates to open, and releases the stepped cam fully. The throttle linkage when at idle will now rest on the throttle stop screw until the engine is switched off. Then the spring-loaded plunger will open the linkage and the cycle will be repeated.

---

9 Weber carburettors – removal and refitting
---

31 IBSA, 32 IBSA and 32 IBSH
1 The removal and refitting of these carburettors is the same as described for the Solex units, and full information will be found in Section 5.

36 DCNV and 36 DCNVH
2 Begin by removing the air cleaner assembly from the car as described in Section 2.
3 Slacken the retaining clip and remove the fuel inlet hose from the carburettor top cover. Plug the hose after removal.
4 Detach the distributor vacuum advance pipe from the carburettor body.
5 Disconnect the accelerator cable from the throttle linkage and mounting bracket. Similarly detach the choke cable from the retaining bracket and linkage.
6 Undo and remove the four bolts securing the carburettor flange to the inlet manifold and lift off the unit.
7 Refitting the carburettor is the reverse sequence to removal, bearing in mind the following points:

   (a) Ensure that the mating faces of the carburettor and inlet manifold are clean, and use a new gasket
   (b) Check for correct operation of the throttle and choke after reconnecting the cables
   (c) Adjust the carburettor idling settings as described in Section 14, if necessary

36 DCA
8 Unscrew the cap on the radiator expansion bottle slowly to relieve pressure in the system.
9 Remove the air cleaner assembly as described in Section 2.
10 Slacken the hose clips and remove the two water hoses from the automatic choke housing. Make a note of the correct locations of the hoses and plug their ends to prevent coolant loss.
11 Disconnect the throttle cable from the linkage on the carburettor and remove the outer cable from the support bracket.
12 Slacken the hose clips and pull off the fuel supply hose from the carburettor top cover.
13 Detach the distributor vacuum advance pipe connection from the carburettor body.
14 Undo and remove the four nuts securing the carburettor flange to the inlet manifold and lift the unit off.
15 Refitting is the reverse sequence to removal, bearing in mind the following points:

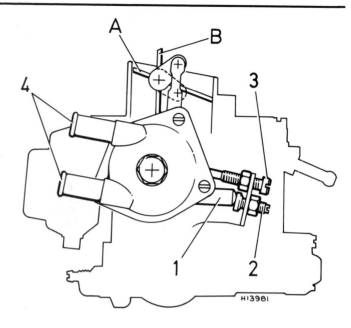

Fig. 3.12 Details of the automatic choke controls – Weber 36 DCA carburettor (Sec 8)

   1 Spring-loaded   A Choke plate - closed
      pushrod   position
   2 Stop screw   B Choke plate - open
   3 Fast idle screw   position
   4 Water hose outlets

   (a) Ensure that the mating faces of the carburettor and inlet manifold are clean, and use a new gasket
   (b) Adjust the throttle cable and the other automatic transmission control cables using the procedure described in Chapter 6, Section 19
   (c) Top up the cooling system if coolant was lost during hose removal
   (d) Adjust the carburettor idling settings as described in Section 14, if necessary

---

10 Weber carburettors – setting and adjustment of components

Float level
1 With the carburettor top cover removed, hold the cover vertically on its side with the float hanging down. With the tongue of the float arm in light contact with the ball of the needle valve, the dimension from the bottom face of the cover to the lower part of the float is the float level. The correct dimension for the various carburettor types is given in the Specifications. Note that on single choke carburettors the measurement must be taken with the cover gasket in position, and on twin choke carburettors, with the gasket removed.
2 To alter the setting, carefully bend the float arm slightly.

Fast idle gap
3 For carburettors having a manually operated choke control, the fast idle gap is set as follows.
4 Invert the carburettor and fully close the choke plates by moving the linkage. This will cause the throttle plates to open slightly; the amount by which they open is the fast idle gap.
5 To adjust the gap, refer to the Specifications for the correct setting for the carburettor being worked on and then insert a drill shank or rod, having a diameter equal to the setting, between the throttle plate and choke tube bore. Slacken the fast idle adjusting screw locknut and turn the adjusting screw until the throttle plate just touches the drill shank or rod. Now tighten the locknut. On the single choke types, adjustment is made by bending the operating link rod slightly.

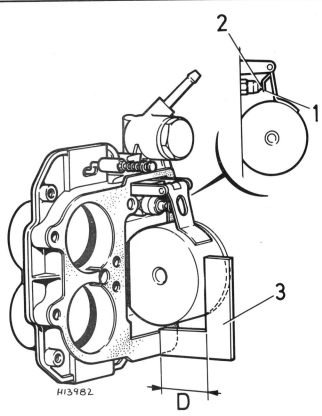

Fig. 3.13 Float level adjustment – Weber 36 DCNV carburettor (Sec 10)

1   Float arm tongue
2   Float needle ball
3   Float setting gauge
D   Float level dimension

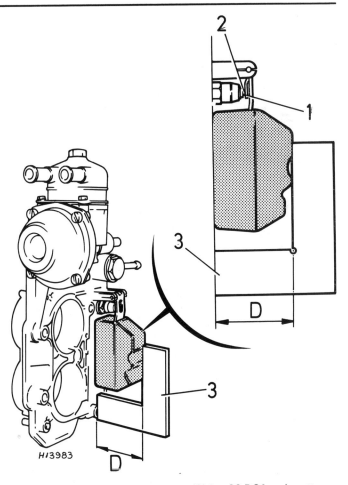

Fig. 3.14 Float level adjustment – Weber 36 DCA carburettor (Sec 10)

1   Float arm tongue   3   Float setting gauge
2   Float needle ball   D   Float level dimension

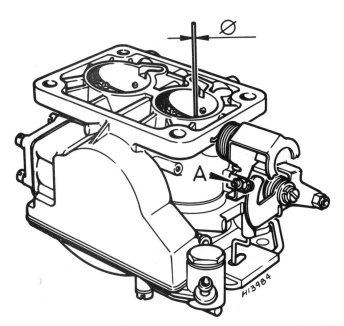

Fig. 3.15 Checking the fast idle gap – Weber carburettors (Sec 10)

A   Fast idle adjustment
     screw
Ø   Gauge rod

Vacuum kick opening

6   The vacuum kick opening on twin choke carburettors is adjusted as follows.

7   Hold the choke plates lightly in the closed position. Move the vacuum kick lever into contact with its adjusting screw. The gap between the choke plates and the choke tube bore, on the float chamber side, should now be 6.0 to 6.5 mm. This can be checked using a drill shank or rod of the specified diameter. To alter the setting, turn the vacuum kick lever adjusting screw in the desired direction.

---

11   Weber carburettors – dismantling, servicing and reassembly

31 IBSA, 32 IBSA and 32 IBSH

1   Remove the carburettor from the car as described in Section 9, and thoroughly clean the exterior with petrol. Wipe dry with a lint-free cloth or use an air line.

2   Extract the small circlip and disengage the fast idle link from the choke plate linkage.

3   Undo and remove the retaining screws and lift off the top cover and gasket.

4   Undo and remove the retaining bolt and slide the filter out of the top cover.

5   Withdraw the retaining/pivot pin and take off the float. As the float is removed, recover the fuel inlet needle valve which is attached to a tag on the float by a wire clip.

6   Undo and remove the fuel inlet needle valve seat from its location in the top cover.

7   Extract the small circlip and lift the accelerator pump operating rod

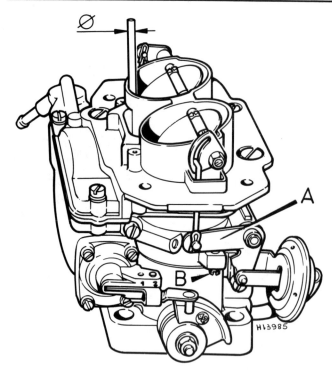

Fig. 3.16 Checking the vacuum kick opening – Weber carburettors (Sec 10)

A Vacuum kick lever
B Adjustment screw
Ø Gauge rod

out of the pump lever.
8 Undo and remove the screws securing the throttle block to the carburettor body. Separate the two parts and recover the gasket.
9 Undo and remove the securing screws and take off the accelerator pump cover. Carefully lift out the diaphragm and spring.
10 The remainder of the dismantling, servicing and reassembly is the same as described for the Solex units in Section 7, paragraphs 10 to 17 inclusive. Before refitting the top cover, check and if necessary reset the float level as described in Section 10. After refitting the carburettor to the engine, adjust the idling settings as described in Section 14.

36 DCNV, 36 DCNVH and 36 DCA

11 Remove the carburettor from the car as described in Section 9, and then thoroughly clean the exterior in petrol. Wipe dry with a lint-free cloth or use an air line.
12 Extract the small circlip securing the choke flap operating rod to the vacuum kick lever and detach the rod from the lever (not 36 DCA).
13 Undo and remove the screws securing the top cover to the carburettor body and separate the two units. Recover the gasket.
14 Withdraw the float hinge/pivot pin and lift off the float. Unscrew the fuel inlet needle valve seat and recover the washer.
15 Undo and remove the securing screws, lift off the accelerator pump cover and take out the diaphragm and spring. Take care not to lose the small non-return ball valve from the passages behind the accelerator pump.
16 Undo and remove the filter retaining plug from the top cover and withdraw the filter.
17 Lift out the secondary venturi from the choke tube bores.
18 Unscrew the jets from their locations in the carburettor body, making a careful note of their positions as each one is removed.
19 On the 36 DCNVH and 36 DCA units, undo and remove the securing screws and lift off the enriching device cover. Lift out the diaphragm, spring and ball valve assembly.
20 The automatic choke assembly fitted to the 36 DCA carburettor may be removed if necessary as described in Section 12. However, unless this unit has been giving trouble or its operation is suspect, it is advisable not to disturb it.
21 With the carburettors now dismantled, clean the components in

petrol and dry with a lint-free cloth. Blow out all the jets and carburettor drillings using air from a tyre pump; never probe with wire.
22 Examine the choke and throttle spindles and plates for wear or excessive side play of the spindles in their bearings. If wear is apparent in these areas it is advisable to obtain an exchange carburettor.
23 If the spindles and plates are satisfactory, check the accelerator pump and enriching device diaphragms and renew them if they show signs of deterioration.
24 Examine the float for signs of deformation and shake it, listening for any signs of fuel inside. If so renew it, as it is leaking and will give an inaccurate float level height or cause flooding.
25 Blow through the float needle valve while holding it closed and then open. Renew if faulty, or as a matter of course if high mileages have been covered.
26 Obtain the new parts as necessary and also a repair kit which will contain a complete set of new gaskets, washers and other essentials.
27 Reassemble the carburettors using the reverse of the dismantling sequence. Before refitting the top cover to the carburettor, check and if necessary reset the float level as described in Section 10. After reassembly carry out the remaining component adjustment also described in Section 10.
28 After refitting the carburettors to the car, adjust the idling settings as described in Section 14.

12 Weber 36 DCA carburettor – automatic choke removal and refitting

1 With the carburettor removed from the engine, undo and remove the three choke housing cover securing screws. Lift off the cover complete with thermostat spring and retrieve the plastic separator plate, noting its relative position.
2 Extract the small circlip and detach the link rod from the choke plate operating lever.
3 Undo and remove the two securing screws and lift off the complete automatic choke assembly.
4 To refit the automatic choke, first ensure that the small O-ring seal is in position on the choke vacuum pipe.
5 Refit the assembly to the carburettor and secure with the two screws, evenly tightened. Connect the link rod to the operating lever and refit the circlips.
6 Position the separator plate on the choke assembly, engage the hooked end of the thermostat spring with the fork of the operating mechanism and then refit the cover. Refit the three retaining screws finger tight only at this stage.
7 Rotate the cover back and forth and check that the choke plates open and close smoothly without jerks or hesitation. If the action is not smooth, remove the cover and check the alignment of the fork, bending it slightly if necessary.
8 When satisfactory movement of the choke plates has been achieved, carry out the automatic choke adjustments described in the following Section before refitting the carburettor to the car.

13 Weber 36 DCA carburettor – automatic choke adjustments

1 With the carburettor removed from the car, it is first necessary to establish the choke thermostat reference marks. This is particularly important if a new automatic choke assembly has been fitted, as the original reference marks that may be visible on the housing will not be accurate for the new unit.
2 Take the carburettor into a warm room or somewhere where the ambient temperature is 68°F (20°C).
3 Slacken the three screws securing the choke housing cover and then turn the cover anti-clockwise until the choke plates just close, but without compressing the thermostat spring in the choke housing.
4 Make a pencil mark on the choke housing opposite the scribed line on the cover.
5 Turn the cover clockwise until the choke plates just start to re-open. Make a second pencil mark on the housing opposite the line on the cover.
6 Turn the cover back so that the scribed line is midway between the two pencil marks. This is the choke thermostat reference point. Providing these checks have been carried out at 68°F (20°C), a more permanent mark can be made on the housing to make subsequent setting easier.

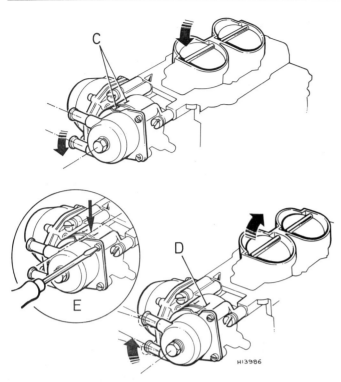

Fig. 3.17 Setting the choke thermostat reference mark – Weber 36 DCA carburettor (Sec 13)

C   Pencil mark, choke plates just closed
D   Pencil mark, choke plates just opening
E   Final setting, midway between C and D

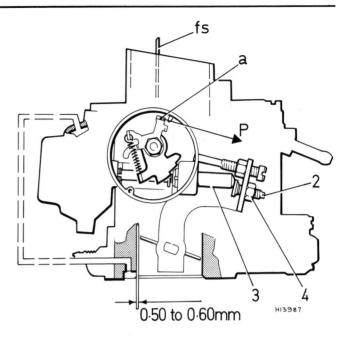

Fig. 3.18 Setting the throttle plates – Weber 36 DCA carburettor (Sec 13)

a	Fork	2	Stop screw
fs	Choke plate	3	Pushrod
P	Direction to move the fork	4	Locknut

7   Now unscrew the three screws carefully and take off the choke housing cover complete with thermostat spring. Recover the plastic separator plate noting its relative position.

8   Referring to Fig. 3.18, depress the pushrod against its spring and release it slowly until it contacts the stop screw. Pull the stop screw away from the pushrod while carefully observing its action. If it moves out a fraction more when the stop screw is pulled away, there is excessive friction between the pushrod and stop screw which must be eliminated before making further adjustments. Polish and lubricate the stop screw head and the end of the pushrod until correct operation is achieved.

9   With the mechanism working smoothly, push the fork in the direction of the arrow (Fig. 3.18) to fully open the choke plates and move the fast idle cam clear of the fast idle screw. The opening of the throttle plates in this position should be 0.50 to 0.60 mm, measured between the edge of the choke plate and choke tube wall. If necessary slacken the locknut and adjust the stop screw to obtain the correct setting.

10   Having done that, release the choke mechanism and the choke plates should move to the closed position and the fast idle cam should move towards its stop.

11   Refer to Fig. 3.19, and push the stop screw (arrowed) until the end of the fast idle screw contacts the first (highest) step of the cam.

12   Hold the mechanism in this position, turn the carburettor over and note the position of the edge of the throttle plates in relation to the small progression orifices in the choke tube wall.

13   The throttle plates should uncover at least the first hole, or the first hole and no more than $\frac{1}{3}$ of the second hole.

14   If necessary slacken the locknut and alter the position of the fast idle screw to achieve the correct throttle plate positions. Tighten the locknut when satisfactory.

15   With the fast idle screw adjustment completed, release the throttle lever and turn the fork to position the second (middle) step of the cam opposite the fast idle screw.

16   Refer to Fig. 3.20, and push the stop screw (arrowed) until the fast idle screw contacts the second step of the cam.

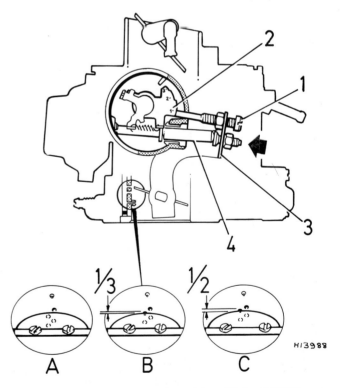

Fig. 3.19 Setting the fast idle position – Weber 36 DCA carburettor. Stop screw is arrowed (Sec 13)

1	Fast idle screw	A	First hole uncovered
2	Fast idle cam	B	Second hole $\frac{1}{3}$ uncovered
3	Throttle lever		
4	Pushrod	C	Second hole $\frac{1}{2}$ uncovered

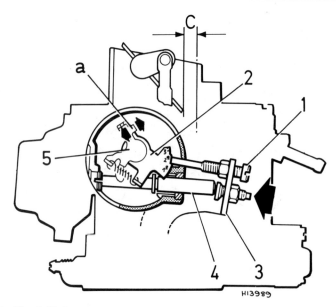

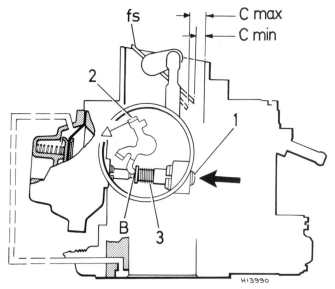

Fig. 3.20 Setting the fast idle cam – Weber 36 DCA carburettor.
Stop screw is arrowed (Sec 13)

1	Fast idle screw	5	Fork lever
2	Fast idle cam	a	Drive lug
3	Throttle lever	C	Choke plate opening
4	Pushrod		

Fig. 3.21 Setting the vacuum opening – Weber 36 DCA
carburettor. Fast idle cam and screw are omitted for clarity
(Sec 13)

1	Pushrod fully	B	Adjusting tang
	depressed	C	Choke plate
2	Fork		opening
3	Pushrod spring	fs	Choke plate

17 In this position the opening of the choke plates should be 6 to 6.5 mm. If necessary bend the drive lug of the fork lever to obtain the correct opening of the choke plates.

18 Referring to Fig. 3.21, open the throttle plates, place your thumb over the pushrod and hold it in the fully depressed position. Push on the fork in the direction of the arrow until the pushrod spring is fully compressed. In this position the choke plate opening should be 4 to 4.5 mm. If the fork is now released, the spring should move the mechanism until the choke plate opening is 6 to 7 mm. Bend the tang of the fork lever if necessary to obtain these choke plate settings.

19 Having completed all the adjustments, make sure that all linkages move freely without binding or fouling. This is particularly important at the point where the link rod to the choke plates passes through the aperture in the top cover. Bend or straighten the link rod slightly if it touches the sides of the housing.

20 Finally refit the separator plate, the choke cover and the three retaining screws. Rotate the cover back and forth, checking for smooth operation of the choke plates and if satisfactory, line up the previously made reference marks and tighten the retaining screw.

14 Carburettors – tuning and idling adjustments

1 Adjustment of the carburettor should always be the last step in a complete engine tuning operation. Altering any of the carburettor settings will have little or no effect if any of the engine, ignition, fuel or exhaust system components are worn or incorrectly adjusted. These should all be checked first before making any carburettor adjustments.

2 Make sure that the engine is at normal working temperature, that the manual choke control (where applicable) is pushed fully in, and that the air cleaner assembly is in position on the carburettor. Adjustment of the various carburettors is as follows.

Solex 32 BISA 6A and 32 BISA 7

3 If a tachometer is available, connect it to the engine following its manufacturer's instructions, then start the engine and allow it to idle.

4 Adjust the volume control screw (photo) until the correct engine rpm, as shown in the Specifications, is obtained.

5 This is normally the only adjustment necessary on these carburettors. However, if the idling is unsatisfactory and all other engine variables as described above are in order, then adjustment of the mixture screw may be carried out as follows.

6 If a tamperproof cap is fitted over the mixture screw (photo) this

14.4 Adjusting the carburettor volume control screw

must be first removed. Prise off the end of the cap and then unscrew the mixture screw and steel sleeve assembly, counting the number of turns taken to remove the screw. Separate the screw and spring from the sleeve, discard the remainder of the plastic tamperproof seal and reassemble the screw, spring, sleeve retainer and sleeve. Refit the assembly, ensuring that the stop on the sleeve retainer is correctly positioned in the end of the sleeve, and set the mixture screw in its original position.

7 Start the engine and if necessary reset the idling speed by means of the volume screw.

8 Turn the mixture screw in or out to obtain the highest possible idling speed.

9 Return the idling speed to the correct setting again by means of the volume screw.

10 Reduce the idling speed very slightly by screwing the mixture screw in, but without going so far as to cause uneven running.

11 Reset the idling speed to the correct figure by final adjustment of

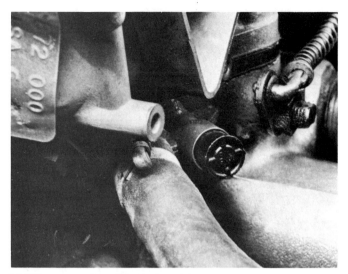

14.6 Tamperproof cap fitted to the mixture screw

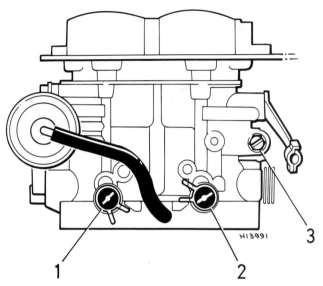

Fig. 3.22 Idling adjustment screws – Weber twin choke carburettors (Sec 14)

1   Mixture screw, left-hand choke
2   Mixture screw, right-hand choke
3   Throttle stop screw

the volume screw. Switch off the engine and disconnect the tachometer.

Weber 31 IBSA, 32 IBSA and 32 IBSH

12 Connect a tachometer to the engine, following its manufacturer's instructions, then start the engine and allow it to idle.
13 Adjust the throttle stop screw until the correct engine rpm, as shown in the Specifications, is obtained. Refer to Fig. 3.7 for the location of the throttle stop screw.
14 Normally this is the only adjustment required. The mixture screw is set on production and should not need altering. If however the idling is unsatisfactory, and all other engine variables described at the beginning of this Section are in order, the mixture may be adjusted as follows.
15 First break off the tamperproof cap on the end of the mixture screw, taking care not to bend the screw.
16 Start the engine and check that the idling speed is still at the specified rpm. Adjust the throttle stop screw if necessary.
17 Turn the mixture screw in or out until the highest possible idling speed is obtained.
18 Bring the idling speed back to the specified setting by adjusting the throttle stop screw.
19 Reduce the idling speed very slightly by screwing in the mixture screw, but without going so far as to cause uneven running.
20 Finally reset the idling speed again by altering the throttle stop screw. Switch off the engine and disconnect the tachometer.

Weber 36 DCNV, 36 DCNVH and 36 DCA

21 Connect a tachometer to the engine, following its manufacturer's instructions, then start the engine and allow it to idle.
22 Adjust the throttle stop screw, until the correct engine rpm is obtained. Refer to Fig. 3.22 if necessary.
23 The mixture screws should only be adjusted if the idling is still unsatisfactory, and after ensuring that all other engine variables described at the beginniing of this Section are in order.
24 To adjust the mixture settings, first break off the tamperproof caps on the mixture screws using a pair of pliers. Take care not to bend or damage the screws.
25 Start the engine and check that the idling speed is still at the specified rpm. Adjust the throttle stop screw as necessary.
26 Now adjust the mixture screws alternately, by small amounts, until the highest possible rpm is obtained.
27 Bring the idling speed back to the specified setting by readjusting the throttle stop screw.
28 Turn one of the mixture screws inwards very slightly, but not so far as to cause uneven running. Repeat this on the other mixture screw.
29 Finally readjust the idling speed by means of the throttle stop screw to the correct setting.
30 Switch off the engine and disconnect the tachometer.

15 Fuel pump – routine maintenance

1   Detach the fuel supply hose from the pump and plug the hose to prevent loss of fluid.
2   Unscrew the top cover retaining screw(s) and carefully lift the cover off the pump.
3   Withdraw the filter gauze and wash it thoroughly in petrol. If it is badly contaminated it is best to renew it.
4   Remove all traces of dirt and sediment from the interior of the pump chamber.
5   Refit the filter to the pump body, place the cover gasket in position and refit the cover. Tighten but do not use excessive force on the retaining screw(s).
6   Reconnect the fuel hose, start the engine and check for leaks.

16 Fuel pump – removal and refitting

1   Disconnect the fuel supply inlet and outlet hoses from the pump and plug their ends to prevent fuel loss.
2   Undo and remove the two bolts securing the pump to the cylinder block and lift off the pump and heat insulator block.
3   To refit the pump, first ensure that the mating faces of the cylinder block and pump are clean and free from traces of old gasket.
4   Fit new gaskets to each side of the insulator block and smear them with a trace of jointing compound.
5   Position the insulator block on the pump, tilt the top of the pump back and enter the operating lever into the aperture. Ensure that the operating lever contacts the side of the eccentric and does not go underneath the camshaft.
6   Push the pump fully into place and refit the retaining bolts.
7   Reconnect the fuel hoses, start the engine and check for leaks.

17 Fuel pump (Sofabex) – diaphragm renewal

1   Fuel pumps from several manufacturers are fitted to Horizon models. All are sealed assemblies, and cannot be dismantled, with the exception of the Sofabex pump. The two halves of this unit may be separated to allow renewal of a faulty diaphragm.
2   First remove the fuel pump from the car as described in the previous Section.
3   Scribe a line on the upper and lower pump bodies to ensure correct refitment.

4   Support the pump in a vice with protected jaws and using a hammer and drift, drive out the operating lever pivot pin. Withdraw the lever from the pump.

5   Undo and remove the screws securing the upper and lower pump bodies together and separate the two. Lift out the diaphragm.

6   Examine the diaphragm for signs of deterioration or excessive deformation and renew if suspect.

7   Begin reassembly by ensuring that the mating faces of the upper and lower body are clean and free from burrs.

8   Place the diaphragm in position on the lower body and then refit the upper half, aligning the previously made marks. Do not use jointing compound.

9   Refit the securing screws finger tight only at this stage.

10 Ensure that the plastic washer is at the bottom of the pull-rod, engage the fork of the operating lever over the pull-rod and refit the

pivot pin and spring.

11 Operate the lever several times to flex the diaphragm and then with the operating lever pushed fully in towards the pump, tighten the body retaining screws fully and evenly in a diagonal sequence.

12 Release the lever and recheck the pump action.

18 Fuel tank and transmitter unit – removal, servicing and refitting

1   Petrol is a highly volatile and dangerous liquid, and certain precautions must be observed when working with it or near it (as will be the case during removal of the fuel tank):

(a) *Always work in an open or well ventilated area, never over a pit. Petrol vapour is heavier than air and will gather in a pit or confined space creating a highly explosive environment*

(b) *Ensure that the tank is less than quarter full before removal. This will reduce the risk of spillage and make the tank more manoeuverable. If necessary, syphon off a quantity of petrol into suitably marked sealed metal containers before removing the tank*

(c) *When the fuel tank is removed seal off the filler neck to prevent evaporation*

2   The pressed steel fuel tank is located beneath the rear floor section of the vehicle.

3   The air vent pipe is fitted with an expansion device to reduce the possibility of fuel blowback if the tank is filled too quickly.

4   The fuel gauge transmitter unit is fitted to the top of the tank and can be detached without having to remove the fuel tank from the car.

5   To remove the complete fuel tank assembly, first disconnect the battery earth terminal and remove the spare wheel from beneath the vehicle.

6   Pull back the luggage compartment mat, remove the fuel tank access cover securing screws and lift away the cover (photo).

7   Make a note of the colour and position of the two wires and disconnect them from the transmitter unit.

8   Place a clean container beneath the fuel tank outlet pipe (photo), disconnect the pipe and drain the tank. Note that on some models there is a fuel return pipe from the pump and this must also be disconnected.

9   Remove the clip and disconnect the tank filler hose from beneath the rear right-hand wing.

10 Support the weight of tha tank and remove the four securing bolts. Lower the tank sufficiently to disconnect the top vent pipe and then withdraw the tank from beneath the vehicle.

11 If the tank is dirty or contains sediment, use two or three lots of clean paraffin to wash it out and then let it drain thoroughly. Do not shake the tank too vigorously, or use a stick to probe the interior, or damage may be caused to the transmitter float and arm.

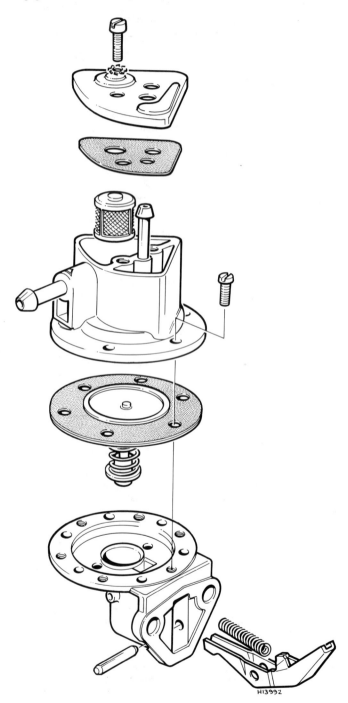

Fig. 3.23 Exploded view of the Sofabex fuel pump (Sec 17)

18.6 Fuel tank transmitter unit located under luggage compartment floor

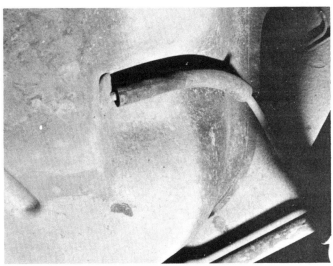

18.8 Fuel pipe connection at base of tank

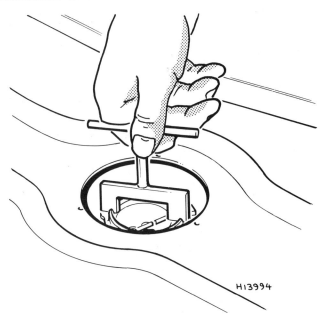

Fig. 3.25 Removing the fuel gauge transmitter locking ring (Sec 18)

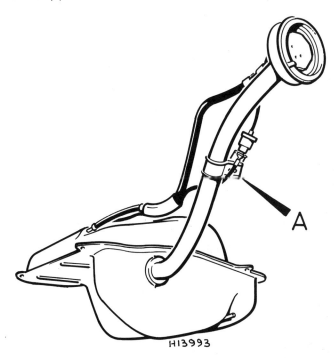

Fig. 3.24 Fuel tank filler tube details (Sec 18)

A Support clip under right-hand rear wing

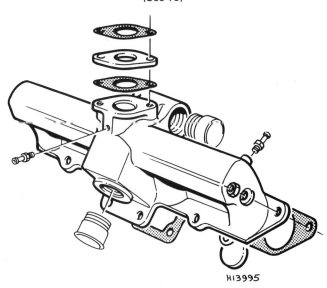

Fig. 3.26 Inlet manifold assembly – 1118 cc and 1294 cc engines (Sec 19)

12 Do not try to solder a leak in a fuel tank. This is a specialised job. If the leak cannot be repaired with a cold setting compound then the tank should be renewed.
13 The fuel gauge transmitter unit can be unscrewed from the tank using a tool similar to that shown in Fig. 3.25. It is not necessary to remove the tank from the car. The unit is not repairable and if faulty must be renewed.
14 Refit the fuel tank and transmitter unit using the reverse procedure to that of removal.

19 Inlet manifold – removal and refitting

1 Open the bonnet and disconnect the battery earth terminal.
2 Remove the complete air cleaner from the engine as described in Section 2, and then remove the carburettor as described in Section 5 or 9 according to type.
3 Refer to Chapter 2 and drain the cooling system.
4 Release the steady bracket and retaining clip from the hose at the base of the inlet manifold.
5 Release the hose clips and securing bolts and lift off the thermostat housing adaptor assembly from the side of the cylinder head.
6 Disconnect the brake servo vacuum hose connection and the oil separator/breather hose from the inlet manifold.
7 Undo and remove the manifold securing nuts and washers, lift the manifold off the studs, disengage the lower hose and lift off.
8 Refitting is the reverse sequence to removal, ensuring that all joint faces are clean and that new gaskets are used. Refill the cooling system as described in Chapter 2, on completion of reassembly.

20 Exhaust system – general

1 The exhaust system consists of a cast iron manifold, twin front pipes incorporating flexible ball and socket joints, and a main pipe with twin silencers. The complete system is suspended from beneath the

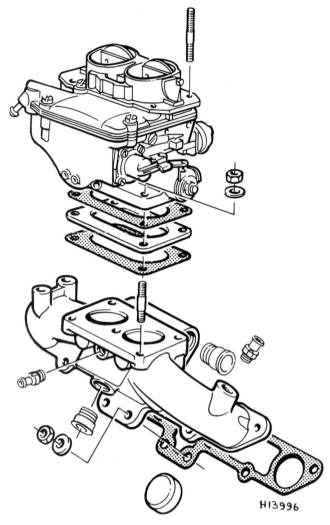

H13996

Fig. 3.27 Inlet manifold assembly – 1442 cc engines (Sec 19)

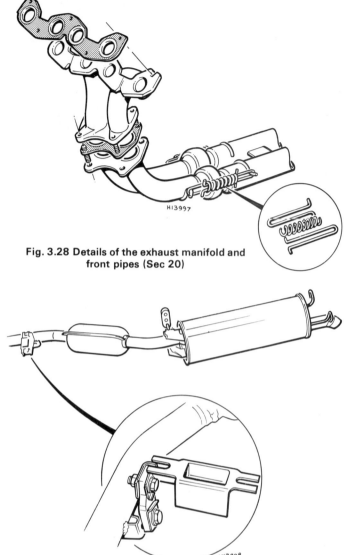

H13997

Fig. 3.28 Details of the exhaust manifold and front pipes (Sec 20)

H13998

Fig. 3.29 Details of the exhaust rear section and mounting (Sec 20)

car on rubber mounting blocks and rubber O-ring straps.

2   The flexible ball and socket joints cater for movement of the engine/transmission assembly and are held together by springs (photo). These joints cannot be separated.

3   The front pipes are bolted to the exhaust manifold flange, while the remainder of the system joints are of the overlap type, secured by a clamp (photo).

4   Periodically the complete system should be inspected for corrosion and for leaks at the joints.

5   Renewal of the individual pipes or of the complete system is straightforward, requiring only the slackening of the clamps or removal of the manifold flange bolts. The O-ring mountings can then be slipped off or the mounting block removed and the system lowered to the ground (photos).

6   Removal of the manifold is eqully straightforward. With the flange bolts undone, remove the air cleaner heat box nuts at the rocker cover and manifold, remove the remaining manifold bolts, lift up the heat box and withdraw the manifold off the studs.

7   Always use a new gasket whenever the front pipe flange or the manifold-to-cylinder head joints are separated. Make sure also that the joint faces are clean and free from burrs.

21 In-line fuel filter – general

1   On some models a filter is fitted in the fuel line between the fuel pump and the carburettor.

2   This filter cannot be cleaned and should be renewed at the recommended service intervals.

20.2 Exhaust system flexible ball and socket joints

20.3 Front pipe to rear section overlap joint and clamp

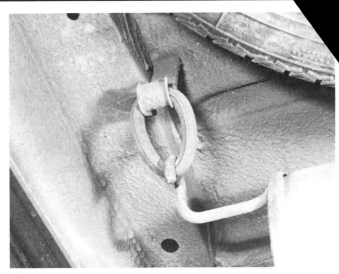

20.5a Exhaust system rear O-ring ...

20.5b ... and rubber block mountings

20.5c Exhaust centre mounting block and strap

3   Note that an arrow stamped on the side of the filter indicates the direction of fuel flow, and when installed this arrow must always point towards the carburettor.

22 Accelerator and choke controls – general

1   A typical layout of the carburettor controls is shown in Fig. 3.31.
2   Ensure that the accelerator cable has enough slack in the idling position for correct closure of the throttle plates to occur when the accelerator pedal is released.
3   On carburettors having a manual choke control, check that the choke plate is fully open when the control is pushed in and closes completely when the knob is pulled right out. Adjust the cable at the carburettor if necessary.
4   Where automatic transmission is fitted, the cable from the accelerator pedal operates a series of cams in a cam box, which in turn operate the carburettor and control valves in the transmission. The cable from the cruise control servo (where this unit is fitted) also terminates in the cam box. Adjustment of all these cables must be done in a certain sequence and full information will be found in Chapter 6.
5   On all models, lightly oil the moving levers and swivels of the controls and linkages at regular intervals and keep them free of dirt and grit.

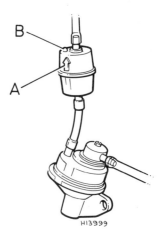

H13999

Fig. 3.30 Fuel pump and in-line filter (Sec 21)

A Fuel flow direction arrow
B Lug identifying the outlet end

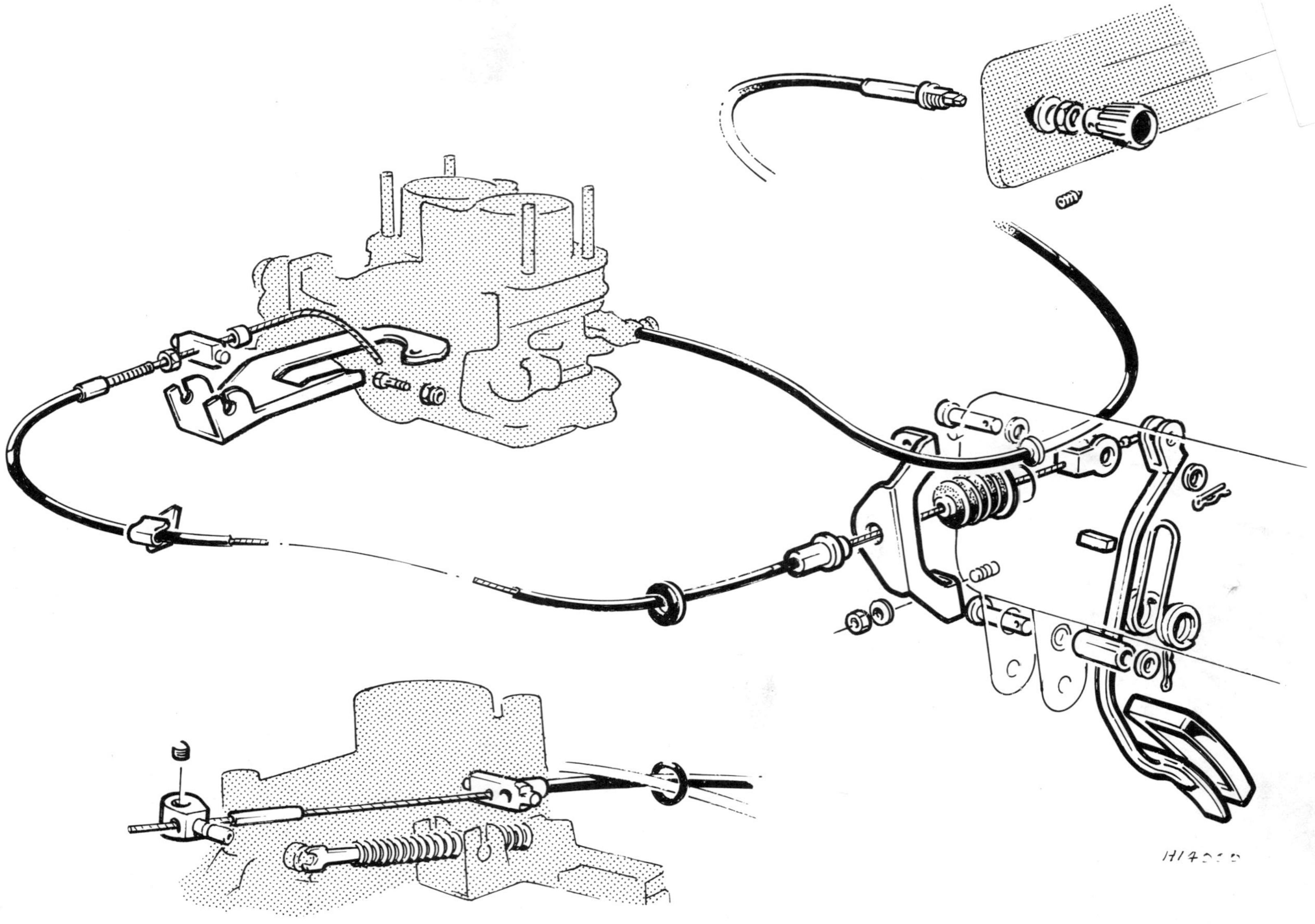

H14908

Fig. 3.31 Typical layout of accelerator and choke controls (Sec 22)

23 Fault diagnosis – fuel and exhaust systems

Symptom	Reason(s)
Engine difficult to start when cold	Manual choke incorrectly adjusted (choke plate not closing)
	Automatic choke incorrectly adjusted
	Automatic choke inoperative
	Insufficient fuel in float chamber
	See also 'Fault diagnosis – ignition system'
Engine difficult to start when hot	Manual choke incorrectly adjusted (choke plate not fully opening)
	Automatic choke incorrectly adjusted
	Air cleaner dirty or choked
	Insufficient fuel in float chamber
	See also 'Fault diagnosis – ignition system'
Engine will not idle, or idles erratically	Air cleaner dirty or choked
	Carburettor idling adjustments incorrectly set
	Blocked carburettor jets or internal passages
	Air leaks at carburettor or manifold joint faces
	Automatic choke or fast idle adjustments incorrect
	Generally worn carburettor
	Engine or ignition system defect
Engine performance poor accompanied by hesitation, missing or cutting out	Blocked carburettor jets or internal passages
	Accelerator pump diaphragm punctured
	Float level incorrect
	Fuel filter choked
	Fuel pump faulty or delivery pressure low
	Fuel tank vent blocked
	Fuel lines restricted
	Air leaks at carburettor or manifold joint faces
	Engine internal components worn or out of adjustment
	See also 'Fault diagnosis – engine' and 'Fault diagnosis – ignition system'
Fuel consumption excessive	Air cleaner dirty or choked
	Fluid leaking from carburettor, fuel pump, fuel tank or fuel lines
	Float chamber flooding
	Ignition system out of adjustment
	Tyres under-inflated
	Brakes binding
	Engine internal components worn or out of adjustment
Excessive noise or fumes from exhaust system	Leaking pipe or manifold joints
	Leaking, corroded or damaged silencers or pipe
	System in contact with body or suspension due to broken mounting

Chapter 4 Ignition system

Contents

Specifications

General
System type .... Electronic (breakerless)
Firing order .... 1, 3, 4, 2 (No 1 at flywheel end)

Distributor
Make .... Bosch, Talbot (Chrysler) or Ducellier
Direction of rotation .... Clockwise

Coil
Primary resistance .... 1.4 to 1.6 ohms at 20°C (68°F)
Secondary resistance .... 8000 to 12 000 ohms at 20°C (68°F)

Spark plugs
Type .... Champion N79Y, Bosch W 175 T 301, Marchal GT 34 5HA, Chrysler A 75 P, or equivalent
Electrode gap .... 0.025 in (0.6 mm)

Ignition timing (dynamic)

	Degrees BTDC*	Engine rpm
1118 cc engines:		
Standard models	10^{+2}_{-0}	850
Low compression (A Series)	8^{+0}_{-2}	850
1294 cc engines	8^{+2}_{-0}	850
1442 cc engines:		
Twin choke carburettor	12^{+2}_{-0}	950
Single choke carburettor models:		
9 and A Series (code 2Y1)	8^{+2}_{-0}	900
B Series (code 2Y1B)	4^{+2}_{-0}	650

*Vacuum pipe disconnected

Torque wrench settings

	lbf ft	Nm
Distributor mounting bracket-to-block	15	20
Distributor-to-mounting bracket	7	10
Spark plugs	22	30

1 General description

In order that the engine can run correctly it is necessary for an electrical spark to ignite the fuel/air mixture in the combustion chamber and at exactly the right moment in relation to engine speed and load. The ignition system is based on feeding low tension voltage from the battery to the coil where it is converted to high tension voltage. The high tension voltage is powerful enough to jump the spark plug gap in the cylinders many times a second under high compression pressures providing that the system is in good condition and that all adjustments are correct.

The Horizon models are fitted with an electronic ignition system which provides a high degree of reliability with virtually no servicing requirements apart from periodically checking the HT (high tension) and LT (low tension) lead connections.

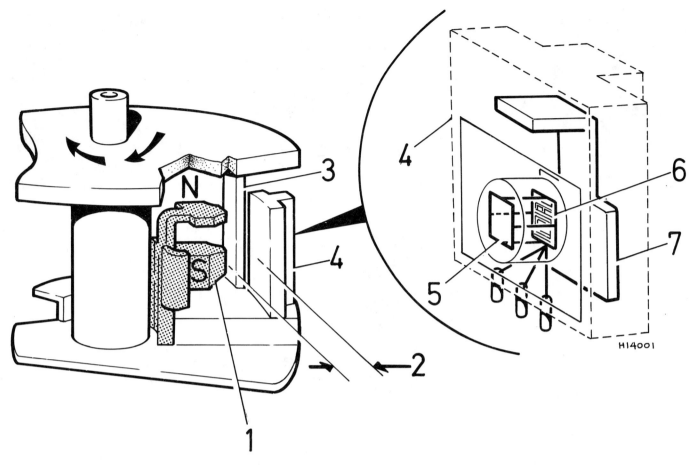

Fig. 4.1 Details of the distributor pick-up assembly (Sec 1)

1 Magnet	3 Vane	5 Detector plate	7 Armature
2 Air gap	4 Detector/amplifier	6 Printed circuit amplifier	

This new system retains the normal ignition coil, distributor advance mechanism and distributor cap, but replaces the conventional contact breaker points and condenser with a vane and pick-up unit operating in conjunction with a control unit.

The vane unit is a four-toothed wheel, (one for each cylinder) that is fitted to the distributor shaft in place of the conventional contact breaker operating cam.

The pick-up unit is also located in the distributor and comprises basically a coil and permanent magnet.

The control unit is a transistorised amplifier that is used to boost the voltage induced by the pick-up coil.

When the ignition switch is ON, the ignition primary circuit is energised. When the distributor vane 'teeth' or 'spokes' approach the magnetic coil assembly, a voltage is induced which signals the amplifier to turn off the coil primary current. A timing circuit in the amplifier module turns on the coil current again after the coil field has collapsed.

When switched on, current flows from the battery through the ignition switch, through the coil primary winding, through the amplifier module and then to ground. When the current is off, the magnetic field in the ignition coil collapses, inducing a high voltage in the coil secondary winding. This is conducted to the distributor cap where the rotor directs it to the appropriate spark plug. This process is repeated for each power stroke of the car engine.

The distributor is fitted with devices to control the actual point of ignition according to the engine speed and load. As the engine speed increases, two centrifugal weights move outwards and alter the position of the armature in relation to the distributor shaft to advance the spark slightly. As the engine load increases (for example when climbing hills or accelerating), a reduction in intake manifold depression causes the base plate assembly to move slightly in the opposite direction (clockwise) under the action of the spring in the vacuum unit, this retarding the spark slightly and tending to counteract the centrifugal advance. Under light loading conditions (for example at moderate steady speeds) the comparatively high intake manifold depression on the vacuum advance diaphragm causes the baseplate assembly to move in a counterclockwise direction to give a larger amount of spark advance.

2 Distributor – servicing

1   Periodically the condition of the distributor cap and rotor should be checked.
2   Remove the protective boot from around the distributor cap, release the two spring clips or unscrew the two retaining screws and lift off the cap.
3   Clean the inside and outside of the cap with a clean cloth and check the centre contact and four segments on the inside of the cap for excessive wear or burning. If evident the cap should be renewed.
4   Carefully lift the rotor off the distributor shaft and check the end of the brass segment for burning. Renew if necessary.
5   The air gap between the vane tips and the magnetic pick-up point is preset. It cannot be adjusted and requires no maintenance.
6   Apply a few drops of clean engine oil to the felt pad in the top of the distributor shaft.
7   Refit the rotor and distributor cap followed by the protective boot.

3 Distributor – removal and refitting

1   Disconnect the vacuum pipe from the vacuum unit on the side of

3.1 Distributor vacuum advance pipe connection

3.3 Removing the protective boot from the distributor cap

3.4 Alignment marks scribed on distributor body and mounting bracket

3.12 Flywheel timing mark and timing scale on clutch housing

3.15 Correct position of rotor vane prior to fitting distributor

the distributor (photo).

2   Disconnect the wires from the distributor to the control unit at the multi-plug connector.

3   Remove the protective boot from around the distributor cap (photo), release the two spring clips or unscrew the two retaining screws, lift off the cap and move it to one side.

4   Using a small sharp screwdriver or similar instrument, carefully scribe an alignment mark between the distributor body and the crankcase mounting bracket (photo).

5   Undo the distributor clamp bolt, remove the clamp and lift out the distributor from the engine.

6   To refit the distributor, enter it into the crankcase mounting bracket and then turn the distributor rotor until the tongue on the distributor shaft engages with the slot in the driveshaft.

7   Rotate the distributor body to line up the previously made scribe marks, refit the clamp and tighten the securing bolt.

8   Refit the remaining distributor components using the reverse sequence to removal. After completing the installation it is advisable to check the ignition timing as described in Section 7.

9   If a new distributor is being fitted or if for any reason the alignment marks scribed between the distributor body and mounting bracket have been lost, it will be necessary to time the distributor to the engine, before fitting, as described below.

10 Pull off the HT lead and remove No 1 spark plug (nearest the flywheel end of the engine).

11 Place a finger over the spark plug hole and rotate the engine until pressure is felt, indicating that the piston is on the compression stroke. (Rotate the engine by means of a large socket on the crankshaft pulley bolt, or put the car in gear and move it forwards – except automatic). The direction of engine rotation is clockwise viewed from the timing cover end.

12 Continue turning the engine slowly until the mark on the flywheel (seen through the clutch housing aperture) (photo) is opposite the correct degree mark given for dynamic timing in the Specifications. The TDC mark on the flywheel or driveplate (automatic transmission) takes the form of a dimple. The slots are for triggering the timing sensor and are positioned 20° ATDC.

13 Temporarily place the distributor cap in position on the distributor and make a mark on the distributor body, with pencil or crayon

adjacent to the No 1 HT lead segment of the cap.

14 Remove the cap and turn the distributor rotor so that it is pointing toward the mark.

15 If the distributor vane unit is now observed it will be seen that the vane for No 1 cylinder will be approximately adjacent to the magnet of the pick-up assembly. Turn the rotor slightly, if necessary, so that the trailing edge (rear edge assuming clockwise rotation) of the vane is just in line with the magnet (photo).

16 Enter the distributor into the crankcase mounting bracket and engage the tongue on the distributor shaft with the slot in the driveshaft.

17 Refit the clamp and securing bolt, check that the trailing edge of the vane is still correctly positioned and tighten the securing bolt.

18 Refit No 1 spark plug, the distributor cap, HT leads and the protective boot.

19 Refer to Section 7, and reset the ignition timing.

4   Distributor – dismantling

1   Horizon models covered by this manual may be equipped with either a Bosch, Talbot (Chrysler) or Ducellier distributor. The Ducellier distributor cannot be dismantled and if it is known to be faulty (see Section 10), it must be renewed. Dismantling of the Bosch and Talbot units is limited to removal of the vacuum unit, pick-up and baseplate assembly as described below.

Bosch distributor

2   Remove the distributor from the car as described in the previous Section.

3   Withdraw the rotor arm from the distributor shaft. Remove the dust shield.

4   Undo and remove the screws securing the distributor cap clips. Note that the longer clip is fitted under the screw that also secures the vacuum unit.

5   Undo and remove the remaining vacuum unit retaining screw, unhook the pull-rod from the baseplate and lift off the vacuum unit. Recover the pull-rod guide.

6   Undo and remove the two screws securing the baseplate to the

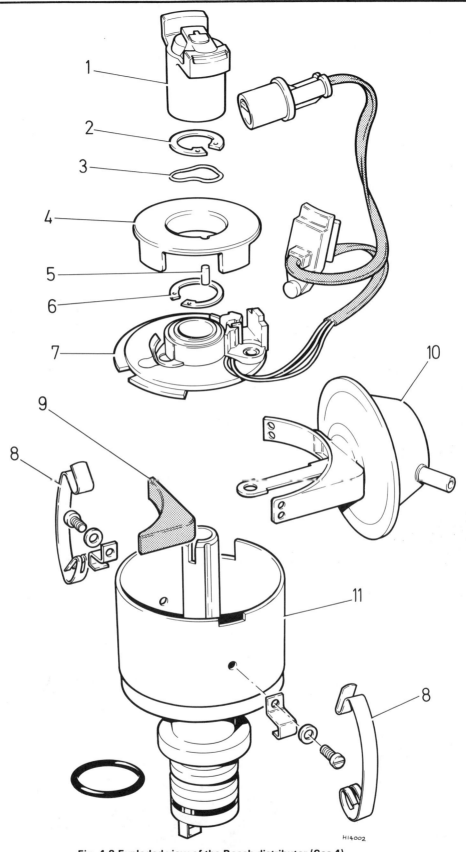

Fig. 4.2 Exploded view of the Bosch distributor (Sec 4)

1	Rotor	4	Vanes	7	Baseplate and pick-up	9	Pull-rod guide
2	Circlip	5	Locking pin		assembly	10	Vacuum capsule
3	Wavy washer	6	Circlip	8	Distributor cap clips	11	Distributor body

distributor body.

7   Using circlip pliers, extract the vane retaining circlip and lift off the wavy washer.

8   Carefully prise the vanes off the distributor shaft using two thin screwdrivers positioned opposite each other under the vane centre boss. Recover the locking pin.

9   Extract the second circlip that retains the baseplate assembly.

10   Withdraw the plastic pin securing the wiring harness insulator to the distributor body and lift off the insulator and harness.

11   Carefully prise the baseplate assembly out of the distributor body.

Talbot (Chrysler) distributor

12   Remove the distributor from the car as described in the previous Section.

13   Withdraw the rotor from the distributor shaft, taking care not to bend the vanes beneath the rotor.

14   Undo and remove the two vacuum unit securing screws, disengage the pull-rod from the baseplate and lift off the vacuum unit.

15   Disengage the two spring clips securing the baseplate to the distributor body and lift off the baseplate complete with pick-up assembly.

5   Distributor – inspection and repair

1   Inspect the metal portion of the rotor arm for pitting or burning and check the fit of the rotor arm on the distributor shaft. If the arm is badly burned or if it is a slack fit on the shaft it must be renewed. If only slightly burned or pitted, clean the end with a fine file. On Talbot units check that the contact spring has adequate pressure and that the bearing surface is clean and in good condition.

2   Examine the distributor advance weights for free movement and the springs for slackness. Also check the distributor shaft for excessive side play or endfloat. If any of these components require renewal it will be necessary to obtain a complete distributor as only the vacuum unit, rotor, baseplate and pick-up assembly are available separately.

6   Distributor – reassembly

Bosch distributor

1   Begin reassembly by securing the wires from the pick-up unit under the small tag on the baseplate. Turn the insulator block clockwise two turns to twist the wires together. This will help to keep them in place under the tag and also prevent them from fouling the vanes.

2   Place the baseplate assembly in position in the distributor body, press it down lightly and refit two of the shorter screws opposite the vacuum unit aperture, finger tight only at this stage. Note that the baseplate securing holes are offset so it can only be fitted one way.

3   Refit the pull-rod guide to the vacuum unit, move the baseplate to the fully retarded position and engage the pull-rod with its peg. Loosely refit the two securing screws and distributor cap clips. Note that the longer screw and longer clip go together.

4   Evenly tighten all the securing screws and then check that the baseplate moves freely by sucking the vacuum unit outlet. If satisfactory, refit the baseplate retaining circlip.

5   Align the slot on the vanes with the groove in the distributor shaft and carefully tap the vanes into position. Refit the locating peg.

6   Refit the wavy washer and vane retaining circlip.

7   Slide the wiring harness insulator into its slot and refit the locating peg. Refit the dust shield engaging its lug in the notch in the rim of the distributor body.

8   Refit the rotor arm.

Talbot (Chrysler) distributor

9   Place the baseplate and pick-up assembly in position on the distributor body and secure with the two spring clips (photos).

10   Engage the pull-rod of the vacuum unit with the peg on the baseplate, position the vacuum unit over the lug on the baseplate and refit the two securing screws (photo).

11   Check that the pick-up wires are positioned as shown in Fig. 4.3. If necessary, remove the insulator from the baseplate and turn it anticlockwise to twist the wires (photo). This is necessary to ensure that the wires are kept clear of the vanes.

12   Finally refit the rotor and vane assembly (photo).

7   Ignition timing

1   Because the distributor only gives a timing signal when the shaft is rotating, a stroboscopic timing light must be used with the engine running at idling speed. The timing light must be suitable for use with electronic ignition systems.

2   First disconnect the vacuum advance pipe from the distributor and connect the timing light between No 1 spark plug (nearest the flywheel end of the engine) and its associated HT lead, or as instructed by the maker of the timing light.

3   Remove the rubber plug from the clutch housing aperture (where fitted). Clean the flywheel and housing timing marks with a piece of rag and mark them with a spot of white paint. For the correct degree mark, refer to the Specifications at the beginning of this Chapter.

4   Start the engine and adjust the engine idling speed (refer to Chapter 3 if necessary) to the correct setting as shown in the Specifications. If a tachometer is not fitted to the car, it will be necessary to obtain a unit that is suitable for use on electronic ignition systems. Some timing lights have a tachometer incorporated.

5   Aim the timing light at the clutch housing aperture and observe the timing marks. They will appear stationary, and if the timing is correct the mark on the flywheel will be adjacent to the appropriate degree mark on the scale. If this is not the case, slacken the clamp bolt at the base of the distributor and then turn the distributor slowly in the desired direction (clockwise to retard the timing, anti-clockwise to advance it) until the mark on the flywheel is in line with the appropriate mark on the scale. Tighten the clamp bolt and recheck that the marks are still in alignment.

6   To check the centrifugal advance, increase the engine speed and note whether the white mark on the flywheel moves away from the mark on the scale. If it does, the centrifugal advance is functioning.

7   To check the vacuum advance, reconnect the vacuum pipe to the distributor. If the unit is functioning, this should also cause the timing marks to move away from each other slightly.

8   When all checks are completed, readjust the engine idling speed if necessary and then switch off and disconnect the timing light and tachometer (where applicable).

6.9a Place the baseplate in position ...

6.9b and secure with the wire clips

6.10 Then refit the vacuum unit and retaining screws

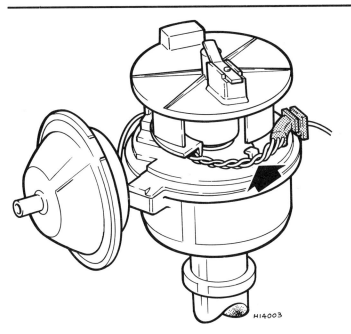

Fig. 4.3 Pick-up wires (arrowed) twisted and correctly positioned (Talbot distributor) (Sec 6)

6.11 Twist the pick-up wires to keep them clear of the rotor vanes ...

6.12 ... and finally refit the rotor and vane assembly

8 Coil – general

The two LT wire connections on top of the coil should be periodically checked for security. Remove the rubber sleeve from the centre HT lead and make sure that the end of the wire is clean and making good contact with the coil.

A possible source of arcing is between the top of the coil or sleeve and the LT terminals. To avoid this, keep the top of the coil clean and renew the rubber sleeve if cracked or perished.

The coil cannot be repaired and if suspect should be taken to an electrical specialist for testing and if unsatisfactory, renewed.

As the coil operates in conjunction with the ignition control unit, it must be replaced with one of the same specifications.

9 Spark plugs and HT leads

1   The correct functioning of the spark plugs is vital for the correct running and efficiency of the engine.

2   At intervals of 6000 miles (9500 km) the plugs should be removed examined, cleaned, and if worn excessively, renewed. The condition of the spark plugs will also tell much about the overall condition of the engine.

3   If the insulator nose of the spark plug is clean and white, with no deposits, this is indicative of a weak mixture, or too hot a plug. (A hot plug transfers heat away from the electrode slowly – a cold plug transfers it away quickly).

4   If the tip and insulator nose is covered with hard, black looking deposits, then this is indicative that the mixture is too rich. Should the plug be black and oily, then it is likely that the engine is fairly worn, as well as the mixture being too rich.

5   If the insulator nose is covered with light tan to greyish brown deposits, then the mixture is correct and it is likely that the engine is in good condition.

6   If there are any traces of long brown tapering stains on the outside of the white portion of the plug, then the plug will have to be renewed, as this shows that there is a faulty joint between the plug body and the insulator, and compression is being allowed to leak away.

7   Plugs should be cleaned by a sand blasting machine, which will free them from carbon more thoroughly than cleaning by hand. The machine will also test the condition of the plugs under compression. Any plug that fails to spark at the recommended pressure should be renewed.

8   The spark plug gap is of considerable importance as, if it is too

large or too small, the size of the spark and its efficiency will be seriously impaired. The spark plug gap should be set to the figure given in the Specifications at the beginning of this Chapter.

9   To set it, measure the gap with a feeler gauge, and then bend open, or close, the outer plug electrode until the correct gap is achieved. The centre electrode should never be bent as this may crack the insulation and cause plug failure if nothing worse.

10   When refitting the plugs, refit the leads from the distributor in the correct firing order, which is 1-3-4-2, No 1 cylinder being the one nearest the flywheel.

11   The plug leads require no routine attention other than being wiped over regularly and kept clean. At intervals of 6000 miles (9500 km) however, pull the leads off the plugs and distributor one at a time and make sure no water has found its way onto the connections. Remove any corrosion from the ends, wipe out the sockets on top of the distributor cap and refit the leads.

10 Fault diagnosis – ignition system

By far the majority of breakdown and running troubles are caused by faults in the ignition system, either in the low tension or high tension circuits.

There are two main symptoms indicating faults. Either the engine will not start or fire, or the engine is difficult to start and misfires. If it is a regular misfire (ie, the engine is running on only two or three cylinders), the fault is almost sure to be in the secondary or high tension circuit. If the misfiring is intermittent the fault could be in either the high or low tension circuits. If the car stops suddenly, or will not start at all, it is likely that the fault is in the low tension circuit. Loss of power and overheating, apart from faulty carburation settings, are normally due to faults in the distributor or to incorrect ignition timing.

By eliminating the conventional (and troublesome) contact breaker points and condenser the electronic ignition system fitted to the Horizon is extremely reliable.

If a fault does develop in the system it will usually result in complete engine stoppage or failure to start. Misfiring is unlikely to be caused by the electronic side of the ignition system.

Specialised electrical equipment is required to test the electronic ignition components and this task should be entrusted with your nearest Talbot dealer.

Before assuming however, that the electronic side of the ignition system has failed, the following basic ignition system checks should be carried out.

Engine fails to start

1   If the engine fails to start and the car was running normally when it was last used, first check there is fuel in the petrol tank. If the engine turns over normally on the starter motor and the battery is evidently well charged, then the fault may be in either the high or low tension circuits. First check the HT circuit. **Note:** If the battery is known to be fully charged, the ignition light comes on, and the starter motor fails to turn the engine **check the tightness of the leads on the battery terminals and also the secureness of the earth lead to its connection to the body.** It is quite common for the leads to have worked loose, even if they look and feel secure. If one of the battery terminal posts gets very hot when trying to work the starter motor this is a sure indication of a faulty connection to that terminal.

2   One of the commonest reasons for bad starting is wet or damp spark plug leads and distributor. Remove the distributor cap. If condensation is visible internally, dry the cap with a rag and also wipe over the leads. Refit the cap.

3   If the engine still fails to start, check that voltage is reaching the plugs by disconnecting each plug lead in turn at the spark plug end, and holding the end of the cable with an insulated tool about $\frac{1}{4}$ in (6 mm) away from the cylinder block. Spin the engine on the starter motor.

4   Sparking between the end of the cable and the block should be fairly strong with a strong regular blue spark. If voltage is reaching the

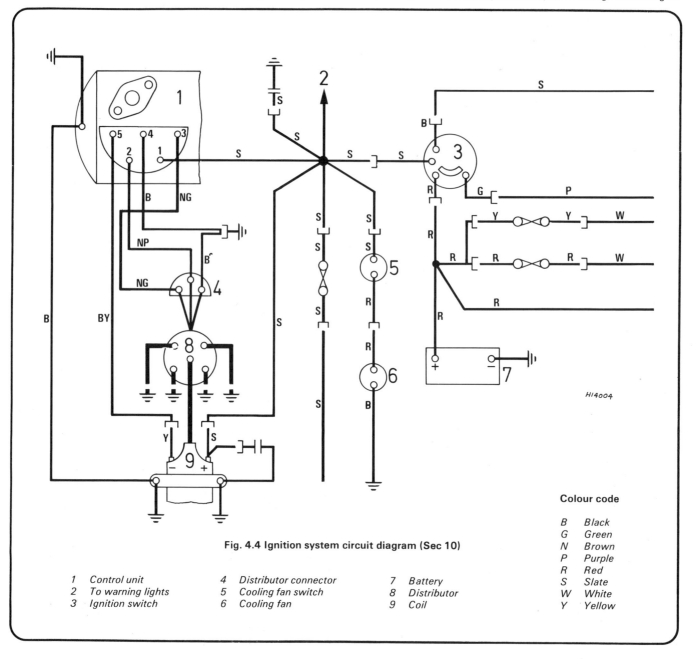

Fig. 4.4 Ignition system circuit diagram (Sec 10)

1	Control unit	4	Distributor connector
2	To warning lights	5	Cooling fan switch
3	Ignition switch	6	Cooling fan

7	Battery
8	Distributor
9	Coil

Colour code

B	Black
G	Green
N	Brown
P	Purple
R	Red
S	Slate
W	White
Y	Yellow

Measuring plug gap. A feeler gauge of the correct size (see ignition system specifications) should have a slight 'drag' when slid between the electrodes. Adjust gap if necessary

Adjusting plug gap. The plug gap is adjusted by bending the earth electrode inwards, or outwards, as necessary until the correct clearance is obtained. Note the use of the correct tool

Normal. Grey-brown deposits, lightly coated core nose. Gap increasing by around 0.001 in (0.025 mm) per 1000 miles (1600 km). Plugs ideally suited to engine, and engine in good condition

Carbon fouling. Dry, black, sooty deposits. Will cause weak spark and eventually misfire. Fault: over-rich fuel mixture. Check: carburettor mixture settings, float level and jet sizes; choke operation and cleanliness of air filter. Plugs can be re-used after cleaning

Oil fouling. Wet, oily deposits. Will cause weak spark and eventually misfire. Fault: worn bores/piston rings or valve guides; sometimes occurs (temporarily) during running-in period. Plugs can be re-used after thorough cleaning

Overheating. Electrodes have glazed appearance, core nose very white – few deposits. Fault: plug overheating. Check: plug value, ignition timing, fuel octane rating (too low) and fuel mixture (too weak). Discard plugs and cure fault immediately

Electrode damage. Electrodes burned away; core nose has burned, glazed appearance. Fault: pre-ignition. Check: as for 'Overheating' but may be more severe. Discard plugs and remedy fault before piston or valve damage occurs

Split core nose (may appear initially as a crack). Damage is self-evident, but cracks will only show after cleaning. Fault: pre-ignition or wrong gap-setting technique. Check: ignition timing, cooling system, fuel octane rating (too low) and fuel mixture (too weak). Discard plugs, rectify fault immediately

plugs, then remove them and clean and regap them. The engine should now start.

5   If there is no spark at the plug leads, take off the HT lead from the centre of the distributor cap and hold it to the block as before. Spin the engine on the starter once more. A rapid succession of blue sparks between the end of the lead and the block indicates that the coil is in order and that the distributor cap is cracked, and the rotor arm is faulty, or the carbon brush in the top of the distributor cap is not making good contact with the rotor arm.

6   If there are no sparks from the end of the lead from the coil, check the connection at the coil end of the lead. If it is in order start checking the low tension circuit.

7   Before checking the low tension circuit reference should be made to Fig. 4.4 which shows the ignition wiring diagram and the colour coding of each wire.

8   Using a voltmeter or test bulb, first check that current is reaching the coil. Switch on the ignition and connect the test wires between the (+) terminal on the coil and earth. No reading indicates a break in the supply from the ignition switch to the coil. Check the ignition switch connections and test the input wire (coloured slate) for continuity.

9   With the ignition switch still on, check that a voltage reading can be obtained at the (-) terminal on the coil and the No 5 terminal on the electronic control box.

10 If no voltage reading can be obtained, check the wires for breaks and the terminal connections for security. If a positive voltage reading is obtained but the engine still refuses to start it is possible that some part of the electronic circuitry is at fault and the assistance of a Talbot dealer will be required to check it out.

Engine misfires

11 If the engine misfires regularly run it at a fast idling speed. Pull off each of the plug caps in turn and listen to the note of the engine. Hold the plug cap in a dry cloth or with a rubber glove as additional protection against a shock from the HT supply.

12 No difference in engine running will be noticed when the lead from the defective circuit is removed. Removing the lead from one of the good cylinders will accentuate the misfire.

13 Remove the plug lead from the end of the defective plug and hold it about $\frac{1}{4}$ in (6 mm) away from the block. Restart the engine. If the sparking is strong and regular the fault must lie in the spark plug.

14 The plug may be loose, the insulation may be cracked, or the points may have burnt away giving too wide a gap for the spark to jump. Worse still, one of the points may have broken off. Either renew the plug, or clean it, reset the gap, and then test it.

15 If there is no spark at the end of the plug lead, or, if it is weak and intermittent, check the ignition lead from the distributor to the plug. If the insulation is cracked or perished, renew the lead. Check the connections at the distributor cap.

16 If there is still no spark, examine the distributor cap carefully for tracking. This can be recognised by a very thin black line running between two or more electrodes, or between an electrode and some other part of the distributor. These lines are paths which now conduct electricity across the cap thus letting it run to earth. The only answer is a new distributor cap. Scraping or filing the track may give temporary relief.

17 Apart from the ignition timing being incorrect, other causes of misfiring have already been dealt with under the section dealing with the failure of the engine to start. To recap – these are that:

  (a)   *The coil may be faulty giving an intermittent misfire*
  (b)   *There may be a damaged wire or loose connection in the low tension circuit*
  (c)   *There may be a mechanical fault in the distributor*

18 If the ignition timing is too far retarded, it should be noted that the engine will tend to overheat, and there will be a quite noticeable drop in power. If the engine is overheating and the power is down, and the ignition timing is correct, then the carburettor should be checked, as it is likely that this is where the fault lies.

Chapter 5 Clutch

Contents

Specifications

General
Clutch type .... Single dry plate, diaphragm spring, hydraulically operated

Clutch assembly
Make .... Borg and Beck or Verto
Driven plate diameter:
    1118 cc and 1294 cc engines .... 7 in (180 mm)
    1442 cc engines .... 7.5 in (190 mm)

Master cylinder
Make .... Lockheed
Bore diameter .... 0.87 In (22.2 mmm)
Stroke .... 0.68 in (17.4 mm)

Slave cylinder
Bore diameter .... 1.0 in (25.4 mm)
Stroke .... 0.62 in (15.8 mm)

Hydraulic fluid
Type .... Universal brake and clutch fluid to specification SAE J1703C

Torque wrench settings

	lbf ft	Nm
Clutch cover-to-flywheel	11	15
Master cylinder-to-pedal bracket	7	10
Slave cylinder-to-clutch housing	16	22.5

1 General description

The clutch assembly comprises a single (dry) driven plate, a pressure plate, release bearing and mechanism. The driven plate (friction disc) is free to slide along the gearbox primary shaft and is held in position between the flywheel and pressure plate faces by the pressure exerted by the diaphragm spring of the pressure plate. The friction linings are riveted to the driven plate which incorporates a spring cushioned hub to absorb transmission shocks and to assist smooth take-up of the drive.

The diaphragm spring is mounted on shouldered pins and is held in place in the cover by fulcrum rings. The clutch is actuated by a pendant type foot pedal which operates a hydraulic master and slave cylinder. Depressing the clutch pedal pushes the release bearing, mounted on its hub, forward to bear against the spring fingers of the diaphragm. This action causes the diaphragm spring outer edge to deflect and move the pressure plate rearwards to disengage the pressure plate face from the driven plate linings. When the clutch pedal is released, the diaphragm spring forces the pressure plate into contact with the friction linings and sandwiches the driven plate between it and the flywheel so taking up the drive.

As the friction linings wear, the pressure plate automatically moves closer to the driven plate to compensate.

The release bearing is a ball race type, grease packed and sealed for life. The slave cylinder is the hydrostatic type that automatically compensates for clutch lining wear. No clutch adjustment is required or provided.

2 Clutch hydraulic system – bleeding

Bleeding the hydraulic system is necessary whenever air has entered the system, ie after disconnecting any component or as a result of leakage (which should first be rectified!)

1   Gather together a clean glass jar, a length of rubber or plastic tubing which fits tightly over the bleed nipple on the slave cylinder and a tin of hydraulic fluid. An assistant will also be required to operate the clutch pedal and to keep the fluid level in the master cylinder topped up.

2   Check that the master cylinder resevoir is full – if not, fill it – and also cover the bottom inch of the glass jar with hydraulic fluid.

3   Remove the rubber dust cap (if present) from the bleed nipple on the slave cylinder and place one end of the tube securely over it. Place

engine may be left in the car and the transmission unit removed independently as described in Chapter 6, Section 8.

2   Having separated the transmission from the engine, the clutch assembly can be removed. Note that on original assembly the flywheel and clutch cover were marked with dabs of paint to indicate their light and heavy points respectively. The mark on the flywheel will be obscured by the clutch cover but note its position as the cover is removed, to aid refitment.

3   Undo and remove the six clutch cover securing bolts, working in a diagonal sequence and slackening the bolts only a few turns at a time.

4   Ease the clutch cover off its locating dowels and be prepared to catch the driven plate which will drop out as the cover is removed. Note which way round the driven plate is fitted.

5   It is important that no oil or grease is allowed to come into contact with the friction material of the driven plate or the pressure plate and flywheel faces. It is advisable to refit the clutch assembly with clean hands and to wipe down the pressure plate and flywheel faces with a clean dry rag before assembly begins.

6   Place the driven plate against the flywheel with the longer end of the hub facing the flywheel. In most cases the words 'flywheel side' will be stamped near the centre of the hub. If the driven plate is fitted the wrong way round it will be found on reassembly to be quite impossible to operate the clutch (photo).

7   Refit the clutch cover loosely on the dowels, making sure that the painted balance marks on the flywheel and cover are as nearly adjacent to each other as the dowel locations will allow. Refit the six retaining bolts and spring washers and tighten them finger tight so that the driven plate is gripped but can still be moved.

8   The driven plate must now be centralised so that when the engine and gearbox are mated the gearbox input shaft splines will pass through the splines in the centre of the driven plate hub.

9   Centralisation can be carried out quite easily by inserting a round bar or long screwdriver through the hole in the centre of the driven plate so that the end of the bar rests in the hole in the end of the crankshaft containing the input shaft support bearing.

10   Using the input shaft bearing as a fulcrum, moving the bar sideways or up and down will move the driven plate in whichever direction is necessary to achieve centralisation (photo).

11   Centralisation is easily judged by removing the bar and viewing the driven plate hub in relation to the input shaft bearing. When the hub appears exactly in the centre of the input bearing hole, all is correct (photo).

12   An alternative and more accurate method of centralisation is to use an old gearbox input shaft, or a commercially available clutch aligning tool obtainable from most accessory shops (photo).

13   Once the clutch is centralised, progressively tighten the cover bolts in a diagonal sequence to the torque wrench setting shown in the Specifications.

14   The transmission can now be refitted to the engine as described in the relevant Chapters of this manual.

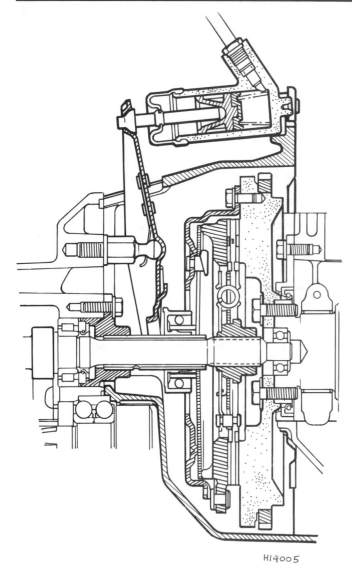

H14005

Fig. 5.1 Sectional view of the clutch assembly (Sec 1)

the other end of the tube in the glass jar, ensuring that the tube orifice is below the level of the fluid.

4   Using a suitable open-ended spanner, unscrew the bleed nipple approximately one turn and then have your assistant slowly depress the clutch pedal.

5   Tighten the bleed nipple while the pedal is held in the fully depressed position.

6   Have your assistant release the clutch pedal slowly, allowing it to return fully. After waiting four seconds to allow the master cylinder to recoup, repeat the above procedure.

7   Keep the master cylinder reservoir topped up throughout the bleeding operation, otherwise further air will be introduced into the system.

8   When clean hydraulic fluid free from air bubbles can be seen coming from the end of the tube, tighten the bleed nipple, remove the rubber tube and refit the dust cap.

9   Finally top up the master cylinder reservoir and refit the cap. Discard the old hydraulic fluid as it is contaminated and must not be re-used in the system.

3   Clutch – removal and refitting

1   Access to the clutch may be gained in one of two ways. Either the engine, or engine/transmission unit, can be removed as described in Chapter 1, and the transmission separated from the engine, or the

4   Clutch – inspection

1   Examine the driven plate friction linings for wear and loose rivets and also for rim distortion, cracks, broken hub springs and worn splines. The surface of the friction linings may be highly glazed but as long as the friction material can be clearly seen this is satisfactory. If the friction material is dark in appearance, further investigation is necessary as it is a sign of oil contamination caused by a leaking crankshaft rear oil seal or gearbox input shaft oil seal.

2   Compare the amount of lining wear with a new driven plate at the stores in your local garage, and if the linings are more than three quarters worn, renew the driven plate. Renew the plate regardless of wear if it is badly contaminated or mechanically damaged.

3   Check the machined faces of the flywheel and pressure plate. If deep grooves or heavy scoring are apparent the units must be renewed. It will also be necessary to renew the pressure plate and cover assembly if it is cracked or split or if the pressure of the diaphragm spring is suspect.

4   If either the driven plate or cover assembly require renewal, practical experience has shown that it is always advisable to renew both components and the release bearing at the same time. Renewal of the driven plate or cover assembly individually can often cause clutch judder or vibration as new components do not easily bed in to old ones. Bear in mind also that clutch assemblies of various

3.6 Refitting the clutch driven plate and cover assembly

3.10 Using a screwdriver to centralise the clutch

3.11 Clutch driven plate correctly centralised

3.12 Clutch aligning tool in position

5.3 Detach the wire clip ...

5.4 ... slide off the release bearing ...

5.5 ... and then withdraw the release fork

5.7 Forked spring of release fork engaged behind pivot stud

manufacture are available for the Horizon, and when obtaining new units the driven plate and cover assembly should always be of the same make.

5 Clutch release bearing – removal, inspection and refitting

1 With the engine and gearbox separated to provide access to the clutch, attention can be given to the release bearing located in the bellhousing, over the input shaft.
2 The release bearing is a relatively inexpensive but important component and unless it is nearly new it is a mistake not to renew it during an overhaul of the clutch.
3 To remove the release bearing, detach and remove the spring wire clip securing the bearing to the release fork (photo).
4 Disengage the bearing from the fork and slide it off the end of the input shaft (photo).
5 The release fork can be removed by pulling it out slightly to

disengage the forked spring from the mounting pivot stud and then removing it from the bellhousing (photo).
6 Check the release bearing for wear by spinning it and listening for any roughness or harshness of the bearing race and balls. Renew the bearing if this is the case.
7 Refitting is the reverse sequence to removal. Make sure that the forked spring of the release fork locates behind the pivot stud (photo) and that the bearing retaining wire clip is properly in position when fitted.

6 Clutch master cylinder – removal and refitting

1 The clutch master cylinder is located inside the car above the pedal assembly and is supplied with hydraulic fluid from the brake master cylinder reservoir via a flexible hydraulic hose.
2 To minimise fluid leakage when the hose is disconnected, carefully crimp it at a point midway along its length using a brake hose clamp

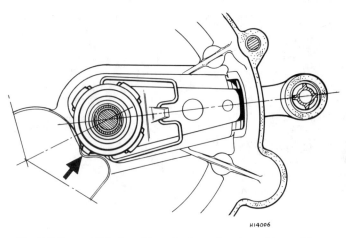

Fig. 5.2 Correct fitted position of release bearing with small lug (arrowed) between the bosses (Sec 5)

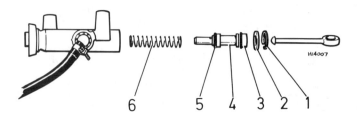

Fig. 5.3 Details of clutch master cylinder (Sec 7)

1	Circlip	4	Piston
2	Stop washer	5	Primary cup
3	Secondary cup	6	Spring

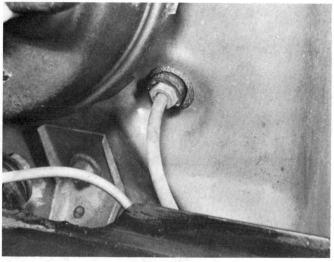

6.4 Clutch master cylinder outlet pipe union

or a self-grip wrench with its jaws suitably protected.

3   From inside the car slacken the hose clip and detach the rubber supply hose from the inlet union on the master cylinder.

4   Now undo and remove the outlet pipe from the end of the master cylinder, accessible from inside the engine compartment (photo).

5   Remove the spring clip, disengage the master cylinder pushrod from the pedal and withdraw it from the master cylinder.

6   Undo and remove the securing nuts and bolts and lift the cylinder away. Take care to avoid dripping hydraulic fluid on the vehicle paintwork.

7   Refitting is the reverse sequence to removal. On completion bleed the clutch hydraulic system as described in Section 2.

7   Clutch master cylinder – dismantling, inspection and reassembly

1   Having removed the master cylinder from the car as described in the previous Section, begin dismantling by wiping away any traces of dirt or foreign material with a clean cloth.

2   Using a thin screwdriver or metal rod, depress the piston slightly and remove the retaining circlip and stop washer.

3   Release the piston slowly and withdraw it from the cylinder bore complete with seals and return spring. If the piston sticks in the cylinder, gently tap the body of the master cylinder on a block of wood until the piston emerges.

4   Note the location of the primary and secondary cup seals on the piston, paying particular attention to the way the lips are facing, and then remove them from the piston.

5   If required the inlet union can be removed from the side of the master cylinder by prising out the retaining ring with a small screwdriver. Mark the angular position of the union in relation to the cylinder body so that it can be refitted in the same way.

6   Wash all the dismantled parts and the interior of the cylinder body in clean hydraulic fluid and dry with a lint-free rag.

7   Carefully inspect the piston and master cylinder bore for signs of scoring, ridges or corrosion and if evident renew the master cylinder as a complete assembly.

8   If the piston and cylinder bore are satisfactory, a new set of seals should be obtained and the cylinder reassembled as described in the following paragraphs. Never re-use the old seals. If the inlet union has been removed, a new retaining ring will also be required as the old ring will have been deformed and weakened during removal.

9   Lubricate the seals and piston in clean hydraulic fluid and carefully slide the seals into place using the fingers only. The lip or larger diameter of the seals must be toward the return spring end of the piston.

10   Locate the return spring in the cylinder bore and then lubricate the bore liberally with clean hydraulic fluid. Insert the piston assembly using a twisting motion and ensuring that the lips of the seals are not trapped or pinched during this operation.

11   Push the piston down the bore using a thin screwdriver and refit the stop washer and retaining circlip.

12   Refit the inlet union (if previously removed) and ensure that it is angled in the same direction as was marked during removal. Place a new retaining ring over the union and carefully push it down into position using a small screwdriver or similar instrument. Check that the union is secure by trying to rock it vertically.

13   The master cylinder is now ready for refitting to the car.

8   Clutch slave cylinder – removal and refitting

1   Working in the engine compartment, undo and remove the supply pipe union from the slave cylinder and then plug or tape over the end of the pipe to prevent loss of fluid and dirt ingress.

2   Undo and remove the bolts securing the slave cylinder to the clutch housing, push the outer end of the clutch release fork toward the front (timing cover end) of the engine and lift off the complete slave cylinder assembly.

3   Refitting is the reverse sequence to removal. Smear a trace of medium grease to the pushrod and clutch release fork friction surfaces before refitting and bleed the clutch hydraulic system as described in Section 2, on completion of the installation.

9   Clutch slave cylinder – dismantling, inspection and reassembly

1   With the slave cylinder removed from the car as described in the previous Section, wipe off the outside of the cylinder body and remove all dirt and foreign material before dismantling.

2   Remove the rubber boot and pushrod from the end of the cylinder and then withdraw the piston complete with cup seal and return spring. If necessary tap the cylinder body on a block of wood to release the piston assembly.

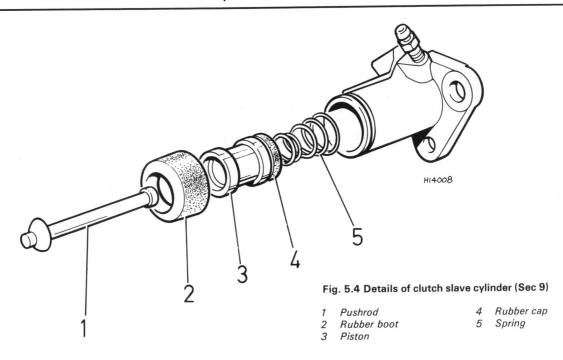

Fig. 5.4 Details of clutch slave cylinder (Sec 9)

HI4008

1	Pushrod	4	Rubber cap
2	Rubber boot	5	Spring
3	Piston		

3   Inspection and reassembly of the slave cylinder is straightforward and follows the procedures described for the master cylinder in Section 7.

10 Clutch pedal – removal and refitting

1   Disconnect the clutch master cylinder pushrod from the clutch pedal by removing the pin and cotter.
2   Remove the pin from the pedal cross-shaft.
3   Detach the pedal return spring (if fitted).
4   Withdraw the cross-shaft sufficiently far to enable the clutch pedal to be removed downwards. Take care to note the sequence of the various cross-shaft washers, spacers and springs.
5   Refitting is a reversal of removal, but grease the cross-shaft and use new pins.

11 Fault diagnosis – clutch

There are four main faults to which the clutch and release mechanism are prone. They may occur by themselves or in conjunction with any of the other faults. They are squeal, slip, spin and judder.

Clutch squeal – diagnosis and cure
1   If on taking up the drive or when changing gear, the clutch squeals, this is a sure indication of a badly worn clutch release bearing.
2   As well as regular wear due to normal use, wear of the clutch release bearing is much accentuated if the clutch is ridden, or held down for long periods in gear, with the engine running. To minimise wear of this component the car should always be taken out of gear at traffic lights and for similar holdups.

Clutch slip – diagnosis and cure
3   Clutch slip is a self evident condition which occurs when the clutch driven plate is badly worn, when oil or grease have got onto the flywheel or pressure plate faces, or when the pressure plate itself is faulty.
4   The reason for clutch slip is that, due to one of the faults listed above, there is either insufficient pressure from the pressure plate, or insufficient friction from the driven plate to ensure solid drive.
5   If small amounts of oil get into the clutch, they will be burnt off under the heat of clutch engagement, and in the process, gradually darken the linings. Excessive oil on the clutch will burn off leaving a carbon deposit which can cause quite bad slip, or fierceness, spin and judder.

6   If clutch slip is suspected, and confirmation of this condition is required, there are several tests which can be made.
7   With the engine in top gear and pulling lightly up a moderate incline sudden depression of the accelerator pedal may cause the engine to increase its speed without any increase in road speed.
8   In extreme cases of clutch slip the engine will race under normal acceleration conditions.
9   If slip is due to oil or grease on the linings a temporary cure can sometimes be effected by squirting carbon tetrachloride into the clutch. The permanent cure is, of course, to renew the clutch driven plate and trace and rectify the oil leak.

Clutch spin – diagnosis and cure
10   Clutch spin is a condition which occurs when there is a leak in the clutch hydraulic actuating mechanism; the release arm free travel is excessive; there is an obstruction in the clutch either on the primary gear splines, or in the operating lever itself; or the oil may have partially burnt off the clutch linings and have left a resinous deposit which is causing the clutch driven plate to stick to the pressure plate or flywheel.
11   The reason for clutch spin is that due to any, or a combination of, the faults just listed, the clutch pressure plate is not being completely freed from the driven plate even with the clutch pedal fully depressed.
12   If clutch spin is suspected, the condition is confirmed by extreme difficulty in changing gear, and very sudden take-up of the clutch drive at the fully depressed end of the clutch pedal travel as the clutch is released.
13   Check the clutch master and slave cylinders and the connecting hydraulic pipe for leaks. Fluid in one of the rubber boots fitted over the end of either the master or slave cylinders is a sure sign of a leaking piston seal.
14   If these points are checked and found to be in order then the fault lies internally in the clutch, and it will be necessary to remove the clutch for examination.

Clutch judder – diagnosis and cure
15   Clutch judder is a self-evident condition which occurs when the gearbox or engine mountings are loose or too flexible, when there is oil on the faces of the clutch friction plate, or when the clutch diaphragm spring is broken or distorted.
16   The reason for clutch judder is that due to one of the faults just listed, the clutch pressure plate is not freeing smoothly from the driven plate, and is snatching.
17   Clutch judder normally occurs when the clutch pedal is released in first or reverse gears, and the whole car shudders as it moves backwards or forwards.

Chapter 6 Manual gearbox, automatic transmission and final drive

For modifications, and information applicable to later models, see Supplement at end of manual

Contents

Specifications

Manual gearbox

Number of gears	4 forward, 1 reverse
Type of gears (forward)	Helical, constant mesh
Synchromesh	All forward gears
Gear ratios:	
First	3.90 : 1
Second	2.31 : 1
Third	1.52 : 1
Fourth:	
1118 cc and 1294 cc engines	1.08 : 1
1442 cc engine	1.04 : 1
Reverse	3.77 : 1
Output shaft (final drive pinion):	
Number of teeth:	
1118 cc engines	16
1294 cc and 1442 cc engines	17
Endfloat	Zero (no endfloat, no preload)

Final drive (manual gearbox)

Type of gears	Helical spur
Final drive ratio:	
1118 cc engine	3.71 : 1
1294 cc engine	3.59 : 1
1442 cc:	
Single choke carburettor	3.47 : 1
Twin choke carburettor	3.59 : 1
Crownwheel teeth:	
1118 cc engine	63
1294 cc engine	61
1442 cc engine:	
Single choke carburettor	59
Twin choke carburettor	61
Differential carrier bearing preload	0.004 in (0.10 mm)

Automatic transmission

Number of gears	3 forward, 1 reverse
Gear ratios:	
First	2.48 : 1
Second	1.48 : 1
Third	1.00 : 1
Reverse	2.10 : 1
Torque converter ratio	Variable between 2 : 1 and 1 : 1
Final drive ratio	3.67 : 1

Torque wrench settings

	lbf ft	Nm
Manual gearbox		
Release bearing guide tube	11	15
Drain and filler plugs	26	35
Gearbox-to-bellhousing	18	25
Output shaft locknut	107	145
Rear cover-to-gearbox	9	12
Selector finger-to-shaft	18	25
Selector forks-to-shift rods	12	17
Shift rod end cover-to-gearbox	9	12
Top cover-to-gearbox	9	12
Final drive half housing	16	22
Gearshift lever-to-floor	7	10
Relay lever support bracket-to-final drive	20	27.5
Reverse switch bracket-to-top cover	11	15
Linkage support bracket-to-steering rack housing	11	15
Final drive carrier bearing flange-to-housing	16	22
Bellhousing-to-engine	33	45
Crownwheel-to-carrier	40	55
Speedometer drivegear housing	16	22
Automatic transmission		
Torque converter-to-driveplate	40	55
Fluid cooler pipes-to-transmission	30	40
Fluid cooler pipes-to-radiator	16	22.5
Sump-to-transmission	21	28
Throttle valve cable bracket-to-housing	7	10
Selector cable bracket-to-plate	11	15
Front engine mounting bracket-to-cylinder block	44	60
Front engine mounting-to-crossmember	16	22.5
Front engine mounting bracket-to-mounting	33	45
Left-hand engine mounting-to-support	16	22.5
Left-hand engine support-to-converter housing	22	30
Right-hand engine mounting-to-cylinder block	22	30

1 General description

The manual transmission fitted to all Horizon models except the SX, comprises four forward gears and one reverse gear. All forward gears are engaged through baulk ring synchromesh units to obtain smooth silent gear changes.

The transmssion comprises four main assemblies, namely a detachable clutch bellhousing, the main gearbox assembly, the final drive assembly and a remote control gear linkage.

Housed within the gearbox are the input shaft, the output shaft, gear clusters and synchronizer units, the reverse idle pinion and the selector forks and shafts. The input shaft gear cluster is in constant mesh with the corresponding gears on the output shaft and all are helically cut to achieve quiet running.

Movement of the gear lever is transmitted to the selector forks via the remote control linkage. The forks act on the sliding synchronizing sleeves of two hubs splined to the output shaft. The sleeves are moved forward or rearward against the gear to be engaged. As the sleeves move toward the selected gears, the internal surface of the sleeve will contact a baulk ring on the gear to be engaged. The friction between the sleeve and baulk ring serves to bring the gear train speed to that of the sliding sleeve on the output shaft. Once the speeds are synchronized, the sleeve can pass further to fully engage the gear. A locking panel and drive spring in the synchro hub offer additional friction and assist the baulk ring when the speed difference between sleeve and gear is excessive.

When reverse gear is selected, an idler gear is moved into mesh by the reverse selection fork with the toothed first/second sliding sleeve and the reverse gear teeth on the input shaft. The reverse idler gear, the toothed first/second sleeve and the reverse gear teeth on the input shaft all have straight cut spur teeth: synchromesh action is not provided.

A helical pinion on the gearbox output shaft transmits the drive to a matching helical crownwheel in the differential. The crownwheel is bolted to the differential carrier that houses the conventional level pinions and gears. The differential gears are internally splined to accept the front wheel driveshafts.

Horizon SX models are equipped with a threespeed automatic transmission as standard equipment. Further information regarding this unit will be found in Section 14.

2 Gearbox – removal

1 The gearbox may be removed in either of two ways. It can be removed complete with the engine and final drive as described in Chapter 1, or it can be removed separately without disturbing the engine, final drive or driveshafts using the following method.
2 Open the bonnet and disconnect the battery earth terminal.
3 Working in the engine compartment, disconnect the two wires at the reversing light switch (photo).
4 Undo and remove the pinch-bolt securing the gear linkage relay lever to the shift rod on the gearbox top cover (photo). Having removed the bolt, it will be seen that the relay lever is still secured to the shift rod by a tapered cotter fitted in the pinch-bolt hole. To remove the cotter, fit a spacer of suitable length and of larger internal diameter than that of the cotter, over the bolt, and then refit the bolt to the *back* of the cotter. If the bolt is now tightened, the cotter will be drawn into the spacer and once the taper is released can be slid out of the relay lever.
5 Undo and remove the upper bolts securing the gearbox to the bellhousing, and the bolts securing the left-hand engine lifting bracket. Recover the spacer from behind the lifting bracket and then position the bracket and fuel pipe clear of the gearbox.
6 Undo and remove the two bolts securing the clutch slave cylinder to the bellhousing. Lift off the cylinder, leaving the hydraulic fluid hose connected, and position it out of the way. Take care not to strain the hose.
7 Jack up the front of the car and securely support it on axle stands. Remove the left-hand front roadwheel.
8 Undo and remove the securing bolts and lift off the splash shield from underneath the left-hand wheel arch (photo).
9 Working underneath the car, undo and remove the two nuts securing the gear linkages relay lever support bracket to the final drive housing (photo).
10 Slide the support bracket off the studs and then withdraw the relay lever off the shift rod. Recover the spring, spring cup and reversing light striker plate from the shift rod and allow the disconnected linkage to hang down out of the way (photos).
11 Undo and remove the gearbox drain plug and allow the oil to drain into a suitable container. Refit the plug after all the oil has drained.
12 Undo and remove the remaining gearbox-to-bellhousing securing

Fig. 6.1 Sectional view of the manual gearbox and final drive assembly (Sec 1)

H14009

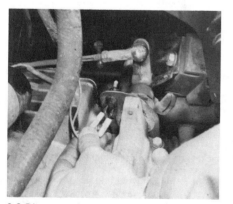

2.3 Disconnecting the reversing light switch leads

2.4 Gear linkage relay lever pinch-bolt (ar-rowed)

2.8 Left-hand splash shield retaining bolts (arrowed)

2.9 Removal of the relay lever support bracket retaining nuts

2.10a Slide the support bracket off the studs ...

2.10b ... withdraw the relay lever and reversing light striker ...

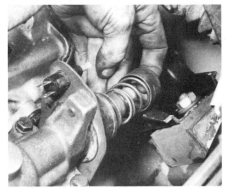

2.10c ... followed by the spring and cup from the shift rod

3.6 Solder wire (arrowed) positioned in bellhousing pinion bearing recess

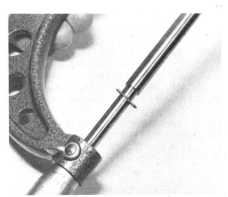

3.10 Measuring the compressed solder wire with a micrometer

bolts and carefully withdraw the gearbox from the bellhousing. Recover and carefully store the final drive pinion shims, but discard the O-ring oil seals as these must be renewed when the gearbox is refitted.

3 Final drive pinion shims – thickness calculation

1   When the gearbox is in position on the bellhousing, the clearance between the double row bearing that supports the final drive pinion

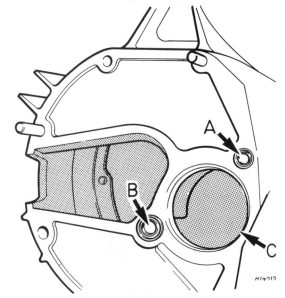

Fig. 6.2 O-ring and shim location in bellhousing (Sec 3)

A   O-ring   B   O-ring   C   Pinion shims

and the bellhousing must be zero, ie no preload and no endfloat. If the bearing is preloaded the gearbox and bellhousing faces will not seal and oil leaks around the O-rings will occur. If there is bearing endfloat, gear chatter may be experienced when the engine is idling.
2   The correct shim sizes can be determined as follows. First remove the original shims from the recess in the bellhousing (if not already done).
3   Remove the two small O-ring seals from their recesses in the bellhousing and the larger O-ring from its aperture over the pinion bearing.
4   Thoroughly clean the mating faces of the bellhousing and gearbox and make sure that they are free from burrs.
5   Place the gearbox on the bench with the mating face uppermost and tap the pinion firmly with a soft-faced mallet. This will ensure that the bearing is fully seated in its recess.
6   Position four pieces of soft solder wire, each approximately 0.040 in (1 mm) in diameter and $\frac{3}{8}$ in (10 mm) long, equally spaced within the pinion bearing recess in the bellhousing. Use a thin smear of grease to hold them in place (photo).
7   Now very carefully fit the gearbox to the bellhousing without disturbing the solder.
8   Refit the securing bolts and evenly tighten them to a torque of 18 lbf ft (25 Nm). Do not exceed this setting.
9   Release the securing bolts evenly, withdraw the gearbox and recover the solder wires.
10 Using a micrometer, measure the thickness of the four solder wires which will have been compressed by the pinion bearing (photo). Take an average of the measured thickness. This average figure will represent the total thickness of shims that must be fitted between the bearing and bellhousing.
11 Shims are available in the following thicknesses:

0.10 mm ± 0.01 mm
0.15 mm ± 0.01 mm
0.20 mm ± 0.015 mm
0.50 mm ± 0.025 mm

12 Having selected the required shims, measure the total shim pack

thickness with a micrometer to include the tolerances. Under no circumstances should the shim pack be thicker than the average measured thickness of the compressed solder wires.

13 The gearbox and shim pack can now be refitted to the car as described in the next Section.

4 Gearbox – refitting

1 If a new or reconditioned gearbox is being fitted, or if the output shaft of the existing gearbox has been renewed, a new crownwheel, supplied with these units, must be fitted to the final drive (see Section 10). Also if any of the following gearbox components have been renewed it will be necessary to recalculate the final drive pinion shim thickness, as described in the previous Section, before refitting the gearbox:

Complete gearbox assembly
Gearbox case
Output shaft
Final drive pinion bearing
Bellhousing

If the original gearbox and components are being refitted, the existing shims may be re-used and the gearbox installed as follows.

2 Clean out all traces of oil or grease from the oil transfer apertures in the bellhousing, lightly smear two new O-ring oil seals with clean grease and place them in position in the apertures.

3 Smear the final drive shim pack with grease and insert the pack into the recess in the bellhousing.

4 Install a new O-ring over the final drive pinion, ensuring that it is properly seated in its groove.

5 Very carefully, without dislodging the shims or O-rings, refit the gearbox to the bellhousing. Have an assistant turn the crankshaft pulley slightly if necessary, to facilitate engagement of the gearbox input shaft splines with those on the clutch driven plate.

6 Refit the securing bolts and engine lifting bracket, and then tighten the bolts evenly to the specified torque wrench setting.

7 Refit the clutch slave cylinder, securing it with the two retaining bolts.

8 Position the reverse bias spring cup and reversing light striker plate over the gearbox shift rod and then slide on the relay lever. Align the groove in the shift rod with the pinch-bolt hole in the relay lever, and then refit the tapered cotter and pinch-bolt.

9 Reconnect the two reversing light switch wires.

10 From underneath the car refit the relay lever support bracket to the studs on the final drive housing and secure with the two nuts.

11 Undo the filler plug and refill the gearbox with the recommended grade and quantity of oil.

12 Refit the left-hand splash shield, followed by the roadwheel. Finally lower the car to the ground and reconnect the battery terminals.

5 Gearbox – dismantling

1 With the engine removed from the car, lift up the ends of the spring wire clip securing the clutch release bearing to the release fork. Lift away the clip and slide the release bearing off the guide tube and input shaft. Pull the release fork outward to disengage the retaining spring fingers from the rear of the ball pivot stud and then take out the fork from the front of the bellhousing.

2 Before carrying out any further dismantling, clean the external surfaces of the gearbox thoroughly with a non-fluffy cloth.

3 Place the gearbox on a clean uncluttered work surface and have a selection of containers handy to store the small easily lost parts in.

4 Begin dismantling by removing the nine securing bolts and lifting off the gearbox top cover. Tilt the cover as it is withdrawn to disengage the selector forks.

5 Undo and remove the seven securing bolts and take off the rear cover.

6 Engage reverse and one forward gear simultaneously by moving into mesh the reverse pinion and the sliding sleeve of one of the synchro hubs.

7 Using a small chisel, tap up the staking on the retaining nut at the rear of the output shaft and then remove the nut. Unscrew the nut

clockwise as it has a left-hand thread.

8 Position two flat strips of metal or two small screwdrivers between the front face of the 1st speed gear and the gearbox casing.

9 Using a hammer and soft metal drift, tap the rear of the output shaft through the gear train. When the pinion bearing is free, withdraw the shaft complete with bearing from the bellhousing end of the gearbox. Don't worry if the pinion bearing comes apart as the output shaft is removed, leaving the outer race and possibly the rear inner race still in the casing. These can be removed at a later stage in the dismantling sequence.

10 Remove the metal strips or screwdrivers used when removing the output shaft and then lift out the 1st and 2nd speed gears with the synchronizer assemblies from the gearbox casing. Note that there is a spacer and needle roller thrust bearing located in front of the 1st speed gear.

11 Now take out the 3rd and 4th speed gears and synchronizer assemblies from the casing.

12 Using a screwdriver, extract the circlip from the front of the reverse idler gear shaft.

13 Lift out the locking pin from the hole directly above the shaft and then drift out the shaft towards the bellhousing end of the gearbox. The reverse idler gear can now be removed.

14 Undo and remove the single retaining screw and lift off the release bearing guide tube from the front of the input shaft.

15 Using a hammer and a suitable tube bearing against the oil seal at the front of the input shaft, drift the shaft complete with bearings and oil seal rearwards and then when the bearings are free lift the assembly out of the rear of the casing. Discard the oil seal and recover the spacer.

16 If the pinion bearing outer race is still in position in the casing, this can now be removed by drifting it out towards the front of the casing using a suitable tube.

17 The output shaft rear bearing can be removed if necessary in the same manner, drifting the bearing inwards into the casing.

18 The bearings on the input shaft and the pinion bearing on the output shaft can be removed using suitable two or three-legged pullers, or by supporting the underside of the bearings and drifting the shafts through. If removing the input shaft bearings the circlips must be removed first.

19 To dismantle the gearbox top cover and gain access to the selector forks and shift rods, first undo and remove the two securing bolts and take off the reversing light switch bracket and dust cover.

20 Undo and remove the four bolts and lift off the end cover.

21 Position the shift rods so that the selector forks are all in neutral and then unscrew the 3rd/4th slector fork locking bolt. (Refer to Fig. 6.7 to identify the shift rods and selector forks).

22 Push the shift rod out until the end is flush with the detent spring housing in the centre of the cover. Place your finger and thumb on the end of the rod and over the ball aperture and then pull the rod through a little more. Retrieve the ball when it is released, pull the rod out the rest of the way and remove the fork. Recover the interlock plunger from the end of the shift rod.

23 Unscrew the 1st/2nd selector fork locking bolt, push the shift rod out just enough to allow the fork to be removed and then lift out the fork.

24 Now rotate the shift rod through 90° so that the locking bolt does not engage the detent ball. Push the rod out until it is flush with the detent housing, place finger and thumb over the end of the rod and ball aperture, and slide the rod out of the cover. Recover the detent ball and also the interlock ball between 3rd/4th and 1st/2nd rods.

25 Rotate the reverse shaft to gain access to the fork locking bolt and unscrew the bolt. Push the shaft out until the fork can be removed and then withdraw the rod and detent ball using the same procedure as for the other two rods. Retrieve the interlock ball between 3rd/4th and reverse shift rods.

26 Using an Allen key, unscrew the socket-headed bolt securing the selector finger to the longitudinal shift rod. The bolt is assembled with thread locking compound and may prove difficult to remove. If this is the case heat the screw using a butane gas torch or similar equipment until the screw is red hot. This will burn out the Locktite and allow it to be removed. Discard the bolt after removal.

27 Slide out the shift rod and remove the finger and rubber ring. Prise out the shift rod oil seal using a screwdriver.

28 Insert the gearbox cover, tap it lightly and recover the three detent springs as they fall out. Also retrieve the washers over the springs (if fitted).

6 Gearbox – examination

1   Examine each component for wear, distortion, chipping or scoring and renew if apparent.

2   Examine the gear wheels, particularly for wear and chipping or teeth, and renew as necessary.

3   Check all ball and roller bearings for play. If even the slightest wear is evident then they must be withdrawn from their shafts and renewed.

4   The condition of the synchromesh units will be known from previous driving experience. The units can be dismantled for inspection and renewal of components using the following method.

5   Using a strong pair of circlip pliers, carefully remove the large circlip from the synchro unit.

6   With the clip removed, make a careful note of the position of the baulk ring, the two curved springs and pawls.

7   Lift out the components and check the ends of the springs for burrs and ensure the edges of the spring stop and locking pawl are smooth and square.

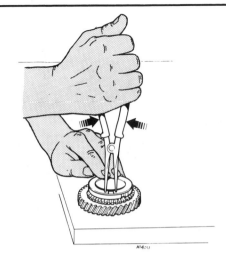

Fig. 6.3 Removing the synchro unit retaining circlip (Sec 6)

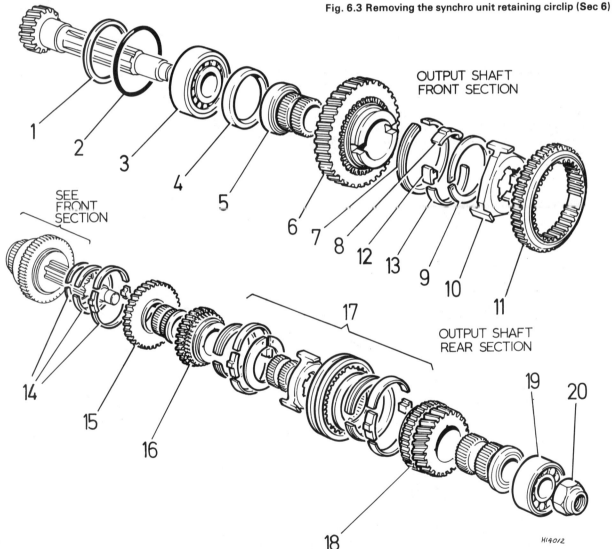

Fig. 6.4 Exploded view of the gearbox output shaft components
(Sec 6)

1 Spacer	7 Synchroniser ring	12 Spring stop	16 3rd gear
2 O-ring seal	8 Synchro locking piece	13 Stop	17 3rd/4th synchro unit
3 Double ball race	9 Synchro circlip	14 1st/2nd synchro assembly	18 4th gear
4 Oil seal	10 Synchro hub	(part)	19 Bearing
5 Bush	11 1st/2nd synchro sleeve	15 2nd gear	20 Locking nut
6 1st gear	(reverse on periphery)		

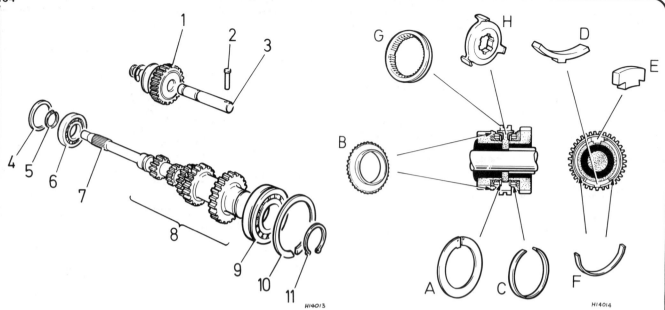

Fig. 6.5 Exploded view of the reverse gear and input shaft assembly (Sec 6)

1	Reverse gear	7	Input shaft
2	Pin	8	Gear assembly
3	Reverse idler shaft	9	Bearing
4	Spacer	10	Bearing snap-ring
5	Circlip	11	Circlip
6	Bearing		

Fig. 6.6 Exploded view of the synchromesh assembly (Sec 6)

A	Circlip	E	Spring stop
B	Dog tooth ring, driven gear	F	Drive springs
C	Baulk ring	G	Sliding sleeve
D	Locking pawl	H	Driving hub

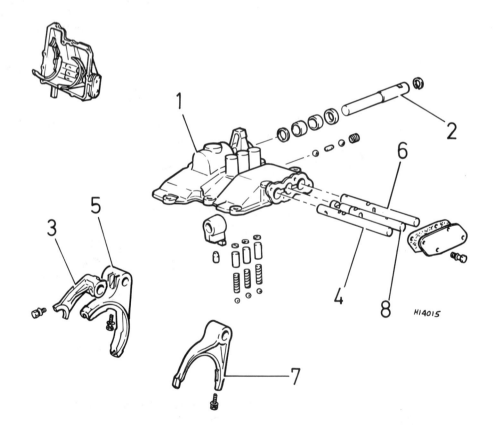

Fig. 6.7 Exploded view of the top cover and selector forks (Sec 6)

1	Cover	3	Reverse selector fork	5	3rd/4th selector fork	7	1st/2nd selector fork
2	Transverse shift rod	4	Reverse shift rod	6	3rd/4th shift rod	8	1st/2nd shift rod

8   Check the small internal teeth for wear and breakage. The sliding sleeve and hub are meant to be a fairly loose fit, and this should not be mistaken for wear.

9   If difficult gearchanging has been experienced or if any doubts exist about the synchro units, the best policy is to obtain complete new units.

10   To reassemble the synchromesh units, first refit the spring stop followed by the locking pawl (photos).

11   Place the drive springs in position, followed by the baulk ring, and then secure the unit with the circlip (photos).

12   Now refit the hub and sliding sleeve (photo).

13   Examine the ends of the selector forks at their points of contact. Comparison of their profiles with new components will give a guide to the actual wear that has taken place.

14   Check the gearbox casing for cracks, particularly around the shaft bearing and bolt holes.

15   Renew all gearbox gaskets and oil seals as a matter of course.

7   Gearbox – reassembly

1   Begin reassembly by installing a new input shaft oil seal in the gearbox casing. Coat the outer diameter of the seal with jointing compound and then insert the seal into the casing with the lip facing inwards. Tap it in carefully, using a tube of suitable diameter, and use the release bearing guide tube as a depth gauge (photos).

2   Again using a suitable tube, drift the output shaft rear bearing into position until it is flush with the rear face of the casing.

3   Refit the pinion bearing rear inner race and outer race to the output shaft if this bearing came apart during dismantling (photo). Also refit the two input shaft bearings if this has not already been done (photos).

4   From the rear of the gearbox insert the input shaft into the casing and engage the bearings in their locations (photo). Tap the shaft fully home, using a soft-faced mallet, until the circlip on the rear bearing

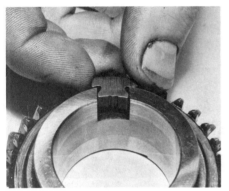
6.10a Refit the spring stop ...

6.10b ... and locking pawl ...

6.11a Position the drive springs ...

6.11b ... and baulk ring on the synchromesh unit ...

6.11c ... and secure with the circlip

6.12 Finally refit the hub and sliding sleeve

7.1a Fit a new input shaft oil seal to the casing ...

7.1b ... and use the release bearing guide tube as a depth gauge

7.3a Using a tube to drift on the pinion bearing inner and outer races

7.3b Input shaft front ...

7.3c ... and rear bearings in position

7.4 Refitting the input shaft

7.5 Refitting the reverse idler shaft and pinion

7.6a With the shaft in place refit the retaining circlip ...

7.6b ... and the locking pin

7.8a The shoulder of the 4th gear bush ...

7.8b ... must be against the bearing when installed in the casing

7.9 Assembled 1st/2nd gear train positioned in the casing

7.10a Place the needle roller bearing on the 1st gear bush ...

7.10b ... and position the spacer over the bearing

7.11 Inserting the output shaft into the gear assemblies

contacts the casing.

5   Slide the reverse idler shaft into the gearbox and engage the pinion. The selector fork groove on the pinion must be toward the front of the casing (photo).

6   Push the idler shaft fully through and then locate the retaining circlip into its groove (photo). Align the locking pin hole in the shaft with the one in the casing and insert the pin (photo).

7   Position the gearbox on end with the bellhousing end uppermost. The geartrain components can now be installed in the following order, starting at the lower rear end.

8   Place the assembled 3rd/4th gears and synchro unit into the casing with the shoulder of the 4th gear bush against the bearing (photos). Note that on later type synchro units there is a groove machined in the outer circumference on one side of the sliding sleeve. This groove must be toward 3rd gear (uppermost).

9   Now place the assembled 1st/2nd gears and synchro unit in position with the shoulder of the 2nd bush against 3rd gear (photo)..

10   Centralize the needle roller bearing on the 1st gear bush (photo) and then place the spacer over the bearing (photo). If the spacer has a groove machined in one side, the groove must be away from the bearing.

11   Insert the output shaft into the gear assemblies (photo), rotating them as necessary to align the splines. Enter the pinion bearing into its location and then tap the shaft fully home using a hide or plastic mallet.

12   Engage reverse gear and one forward gear to lock the output shaft and then fit a new retaining nut to the end of the shaft (photo). Tighten the nut to the specified torque, but do not peen the nut over at this stage.

13   Return the gears to neutral and rotate the input and output shafts. Check that there is no bindingg of the bearings and that the shafts are both free to turn. There may be a little roughness from the bearings but this should disappear when the gearbox is filled with oil. Engage and disengage each gear several times, checking for correct action of the synchro units. If anything is amiss go back and recheck now before carrying on with the reassembly.

14   If everything is satisfactory, peen the output shaft retaining nut into the groove in the shaft using a hammer and small punch (photo).

15   The gearbox top cover can now be reassembled as follows.

16   Position a new transverse shift rod oil seal in the aperture in the cover with the lip towards the cover. Tap it fully into place using a suitable drift.

17   Lubricate the shift rod and carefully insert it through the seal. Install a new O-ring on the end of the rod and then enter the rod into the selector finger, finger end first. Apply thread locking compound to a new socket-headed locking bolt, align the bolt holes in finger and rod, and then refit and fully tighten the bolt (photo).

18   Install the washers where fitted and then the detent springs into their recesses in the housing (photo).

19   Place a detent ball on the centre spring (photo) and then slide the 3rd/4th shift rod into the cover with the notch uppermost so that it does not engage the ball.

20   Engage the 3rd/4th selector fork with the rod (photo), push the detent ball down with a screwdriver or thin flat rod, and push the shift rod in until it just covers the ball (photo).

21   Place the interlock plunger in the shift rod, push the rod fully into the cover and then align the locking bolt holes. Apply thread locking compound to the locking bolt and then refit and fully tighten the bolt (photo).

22   Position the detent plunger on the detent spring (the one nearest to the selector finger) and place an interlock ball between 3rd/4th shift rod and reverse.

23   Slide the reverse shift rod into the cover with the locking bolt hole horizontal.

24   Depress the detent plunger and push the shift rod through. Engage the reverse selector fork, turn the shift rod to align the locking bolt holes and refit the bolt after applying thread locking compound to the threads (photo).

25   Position a detent ball over the remaining spring and an interlock ball between 3rd/4th and 1st/2nd shift rods. Make sure that the two shift rods already installed are in their neutral positions, otherwise it will be impossible to install the remaining rod.

7.12 Output shaft retaining nut in position ...

7.14 ... and peened to the groove in the shaft

7.17 Tightening the selector finger locking bolt

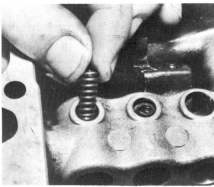
7.18 Fit the three detent springs into the housing ...

7.19 ... and then place a ball over the centre spring

7.20a Engage the 3rd/4th selector fork with the rod ...

7.20b ... push the detent ball down and push the rod in until the ball is covered

7.21 With the rod in position align the holes and refit the locking bolt

7.24 Refitting the locking bolt to the reverse selector fork

7.26 Refitting the 1st/2nd selector fork

7.27 Use a new gasket when refitting the end cover

7.28 Ensure that the selector forks engage the synchro sliding sleeves when refitting the top cover

7.29a Finally refit the rear cover ...

7.29b ... and release bearing guide tube

8.20 Speedometer cable and adaptor housing on final drive

26 Insert the shift rod with the locking bolt hole horizontal, depress the detent ball and push the rod through. Engage the 1st/2nd selector fork, turn the shift rod to align the locking bolt holes and refit the bolt after applying thread locking compound to the threads (photo).

27 Check the action of the shift rods and if satisfactory refit the end cover using a new gasket (photo).

28 Position a new gasket on the top cover joint face of the gearbox casing and lower the top cover into place, making sure the selector forks engage their grooves on the synchro unit sliding sleeves. Refit and fully tighten the retaining bolts after applying a little jointing compound to their threads (photo).

29 Refit the gearbox rear cover using a new gasket. Refit the release bearing guide tube (photos).

30 Refit the clutch release bearing and fork and the reversing light switch bracket.

31 The gearbox can now be refitted to the bellhousing as described in Section 4.

8 Bellhousing assembly (manual gearbox) – removal and refitting

1 In order to gain access to the clutch components or to enable the final drive to be dismantled it is first necessary to remove the bellhousing assembly complete with gearbox and final drive as follows.

2 Open the bonnet and disconnect the battery earth terminal.

3 Refer to Chapter 3 if necessary and remove the air cleaner assembly.

4 Undo and remove the two bolts securing the left-hand engine lifting bracket to the gearbox flange. Recover the spacer and lift off the bracket after detaching the various cable and pipe clips.

5 Disconnect the two leads to the reversing light switch on the gearbox top cover.

6 Undo and remove the bolts securing the coil bracket to the bellhousing flange. Without disconnecting the wires, position the coil

clear of the bellhousing.

7 Position all disconnected wires and unsupported pipes, hoses etc well clear of the bellhousing, noting and disconnecting any other wiring, according to model, that may be likely to interfere with bellhousing removal.

8 Refer to Chapter 11, and remove the starter motor.

9 Undo and remove the pinch-bolt securing the gear linkage relay lever to the shift rod on the gearbox top cover. Having removed the bolt it will be seen that the relay lever is still secured to the shift rod by a tapered cotter fitted in the pinch-bolt hole. Remove the cotter as described in Section 2, paragraph 4.

10 Remove the left-hand front hub cap and then using a hammer and small chisel, tap up the staking on the driveshaft hub nut.

11 Slacken the nut using a large socket and extension bar.

12 Jack up the front of the car and securely support it on axle stands. Remove both front roadwheels.

13 Undo and remove the drain plug from the final drive and allow the oil to drain into a suitable container. Refit the plug when the oil has drained.

14 Refer to Chapter 7, and remove the left-hand driveshaft.

15 Undo and remove the nut securing the right-hand lower balljoint to the suspension arm. Release the balljoint taper, lift the suspension assembly upwards until the inner end of the driveshaft can be withdrawn from the final drive.

16 Undo and remove the clutch slave cylinder securing bolts, lift off the cylinder and position it well clear without straining the hydraulic fluid pipe.

17 Undo and remove the securing bolts and lift off the splash shield from under the left-hand front wheelarch.

18 Undo and remove the two nuts and lift off the gear linkage relay lever support bracket from the studs on the final drive housing.

19 Now slide the relay lever off the shift rod on the gearbox top cover and recover the spring, spring cup and reversing light striker plate from the shift rod. Allow the disconnected linkage to hang down out of the way.

20 Undo and remove the securing bolt and withdraw the speedometer cable and housing as an assembly (photo). Remove the driven gear and position the cable clear of the final drive housing.

21 Place a jack beneath the final drive housing and take the weight of the engine.

22 Undo and remove the bolts securing the left-hand engine support bracket to the final drive housing and to the rubber mounting block. Lift off the support bracket.

23 Lower the jack slowly until the full weight of the engine is taken by the remaining two engine mountings. Leave the jack in contact with the final drive housing and just taking its weight.

24 Undo and remove the bellhousing-to-engine securing bolts and the additional bolt securing the dirt shield over the flywheel aperture.

25 Slide the bellhousing off the engine, using the jack to steady it and keeping it absolutely straight until the gearbox input shaft is clear of the clutch unit. Lower the jack and withdraw the assembly from under the car.

26 Refitting the bellhousing/gearbox/final drive assembly is the direct reversal of the foregoing sequence. Don't forget to refill the final drive, and gearbox if applicable, with the recommended grade and quantity of oil after refitting.

9 Final drive (manual gearbox) – dismantling

1 Begin by removing the bellhousing assembly from the car as described in the previous Section.

2 Undo and remove the gearbox drain plug and allow the oil to drain into a suitable container. Refit the plug when all the oil has drained.

3 Place the bellhousing assembly face downwards on the bench and undo and remove the gear-to-bellhousing retaining bolts.

4 Separate the gearbox from the bellhousing and recover the pinion bearing shims and the two small O-ring oil seals.

5 If still in position, undo and remove the retaining bolt and take off the speedometer pinion gear housing and gear.

6 Undo and remove the four retaining bolts and lift the carrier bearing flange off the side having the large bearing. Discard the O-ring but retain the bearing preload shims.

7 Undo and remove the nuts and bolts securing the two halves of the final drive casing together. Lift off the outer casing and the oil seal from the small bearing end.

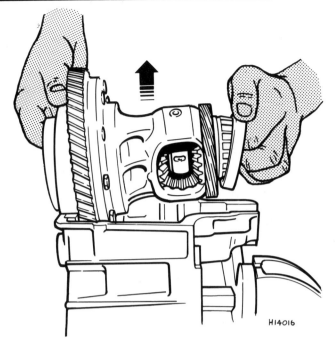

Fig. 6.8 Lifting out the differential assembly (Sec 9)

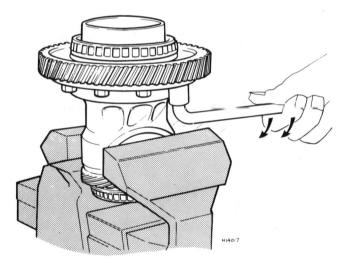

Fig. 6.9 Removing the crownwheel retaining bolts (Sec 10)

8 Carefully withdraw the differential assembly and the bearing outer tracks from the casing.

10 Final drive (manual gearbox) – inspection and servicing

1 Examine each component for wear, scoring and damage. Inspect the teeth of the crownwheel for chipping and also the gearwheels in the differential cage.

2 Examine the roller bearings for wear and for cracks in the inner and outer tracks.

3 To remove the crownwheel, support the differential unit in a vice and undo and remove the crownwheel securing bolts. Now lift off the wheel. **Note**: *If this component is renewed, the gearbox output shaft with matching pinion will also have to be renewed (and vice versa).*

4 The differential bearings may be removed with a suitable puller and then refitted using a press. If these facilities are not available it is advisable to entrust this work to a Talbot dealer.

5 Renewal of the speedometer drivegear also calls for the use of a puller and press. If this component is renewed the speedometer pinion gear must be renewed also.

6 It is not recommended that any attempt be made to dismantle the

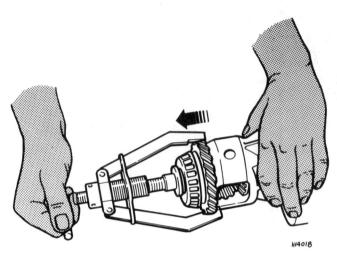

Fig. 6.10 Extracting the speedometer drivegear (Sec 10)

11 Final drive (manual gearbox) – reassembly

1 Ensure that the surfaces of the two half casings and the bearing flange are absolutely clean and free from any burrs. The two casings are a 'faced joint' and no gasket or sealing compound is used.
2 Lubricate the differential rollers and position the outer races over them (photo).
3 Now carefully lower the differential assembly into the half casing (photo), and then refit the outer half casing (photo). Wire brush the threads of the securing nuts and bolts, apply thread locking compound sparingly and tighten them to just over finger tight at this stage.
4 Using a hammer and block of wood, give the outer race of the large bearing a few gentle taps while at the same time rotating the crownwheel. This will seat the bearings fully into the housing.
5 The casing retaining nuts and bolts can now be tightened to the specified torque wrench setting.
6 If the differential carrier, carrier bearing flange, the differential bearings or either of the casings have been renewed, refer to Section 12, and recalculate the carrier bearing preload. If the original components are being re-used, the existing shims can be refitted as follows.
7 Position the pre-load shims over the bearing outer race in the bellhousing (photo).
8 Fit a new seal and O-ring to the carrier bearing flange, lubricate the lips of the seal and carefully install the flange onto the housing (photos).
9 Refit the securing bolts and tighten them to the specified torque wrench setting.
10 Fit a new small end oil seal to the housing, lip facing inward, and tap it into position using a hammer and block of wood (photos).
11 Refit the speedometer driven gear pinion and housing (photo).
12 Install two new O-rings into the gearbox joint face apertures in the bellhousing.
13 Refit the final drive pinion shims into their recess in the bellhousing and carefully lower the gearbox into position (photo). Tighten the securing bolts to the specified torque wrench setting.
14 The complete bellhousing, gearbox and final drive assembly can

differential sun and planet bevel gears. If replacement is necessary it is advisable to obtain a factory reconditioned differential assembly.
7 The three oil seals and O-ring should be renewed as a matter of course.
8 The O-ring, the large seal in the carrier bearing flange and the small oil seal located by the two half housings are installed during reassembly. The remaining oil seal in the differential can be removed by prising it out with a suitable lever and a new seal fitted using a hammer and block of wood. The lip of the seal must face inward (photo).

10.8 Driveshaft oil seal in position in the differential

11.2 Position the differential bearing outer races over the rollers ...

11.3a ... carefully lower the differential into the housing ...

11.3b ... and reassemble the half housings

11.7 Place the preload shims in position ...

11.8a ... ease a new O-ring onto the carrier bearing flange ...

11.8b ... and carefully install the flange onto the housing

11.10a Position a new small end oil seal on the housing ...

11.10b ... and tap it in place with a block of wood

11.11 Refitting the speedometer gear and housing

11.13 Refitting the gearbox to the bellhousing

now be refitted to the engine as described in Section 8.

12 Carrier bearing preload shims – thickness calculation

1   As stated previously, the carrier bearing preload must be re-calculated when any of the components in the final drive that affect it are renewed.

2   Begin by reassembling the final drive as described in Section 11, paragraphs 1 to 5 inclusive.

3   Using a micrometer, measure the thickness of the existing preload shims. If their total thickness is greater than 0.5 mm, fit a 0.5 mm shim on the carrier bearing outer race and carry out the following calculations with this shim in place. If their total thickness is less than 0.5 mm, do not fit a shim at this stage.

4   Cut four pieces of soft solder wire approximately 1 mm (0.040 in) in diameter and 10 mm ($\frac{3}{8}$ in) in length. Place the solder in the bearing recess adjacent to each bolt hole.

5   Fit the carrier bearing flange, without the O-ring, to the final drive housing. Tighten the four retaining bolts to the specified torque wrench setting.

6   Undo the bolts, remove the flange and carefully remove the four lengths of compressed solder.

7   Measure the thickness of the four lengths of solder and take an average of the four measurements.

8   The thickness of the preload shims to be fitted will be the total of the average thickness of the compressed solder, plus the specified preload, plus the 0.5 mm shim if this was fitted. For example:

Average thickness of solder	*0.35 mm*
Preload	*0.10 mm*
Thickness of shim (if fitted)	*0.50 mm*
Total preload shims required	*0.95 mm*

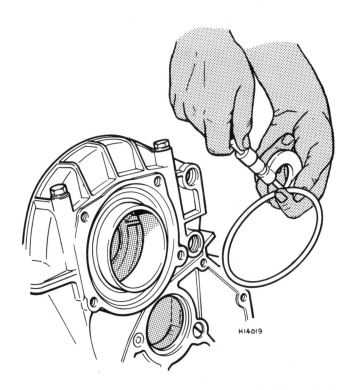

Fig. 6.11 Measuring the thickness of the carrier bearing preload shims (Sec 12)

9   Shims are available in the following sizes:

  0.1 ± 0.01 mm
  0.15 ± 0.01 mm
  0.2 ± 0.015 mm
  0.5 ± 0.025 mm
  1.0 ± 0.03 mm

Having selected the required shims, measure the total shim pack thickness with a micrometer to include the tolerances. If measurements fall between an available shim size, the measurement should be rounded up to the next available size.

10   After obtaining the necessary shims reassembly can now continue as described in Section 11, paragraph 7 onwards.

13 Gearshift lever and mechanism (manual gearbox) – adjustment

1   The gearshift lever is mounted in a ball housing bolted to the car floor and transmits its movement to the gearbox through a longitudinal control rod and a series of relay levers and rods.
2   The system should be periodically checked for wear in the balljoints of the control rods or for excess play in the relay levers. It is also a good idea to slide back the rubber boot around the gearshift lever ball housing and lubricate the ball with medium grease (photo).

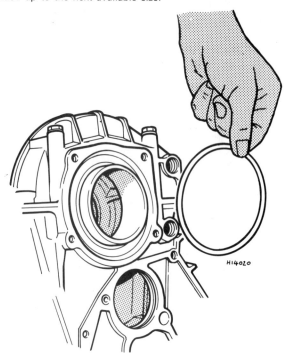

Fig. 6.12 Fitting a preload shim (if necessary) (Sec 12)

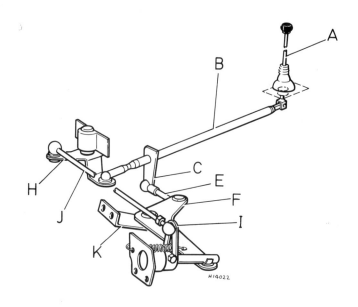

Fig. 6.14 Layout of the gearshift linkage (Sec 13)

A   Gear lever
B   Control tube
C   Operating arm
E   Adjustable rod
F   Relay lever, gear selection
H   Relay lever, gear engagement
I   Relay lever
J   Adjustable rod
K   Relay lever support

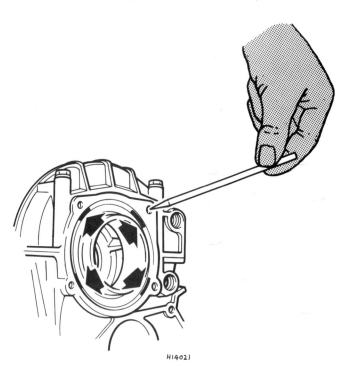

Fig. 6.13 Soft solder (arrowed) in place adjacent to the bolt holes (Sec 12)

13.2 Gearshift lever lower ball housing

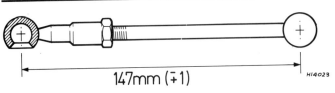

Fig. 6.15 Dimension of adjustable rod (in mm) – control tube-to-relay lever (Sec 13)

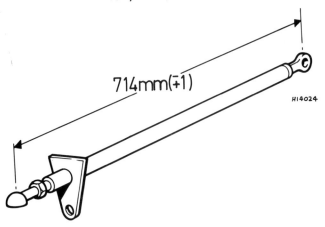

Fig. 6.16 Dimension of control tube (in mm) (Sec 13)

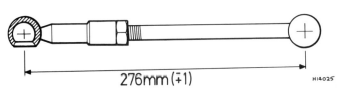

Fig. 6.17 Dimension of adjustable rod (in mm) – relay lever-to-relay lever (Sec 13)

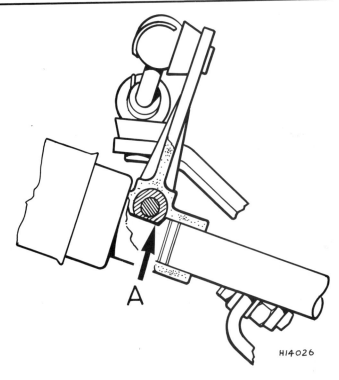

Fig. 6.18 Relay lever-to-shift rod cotter pin location (A) (Sec 13)

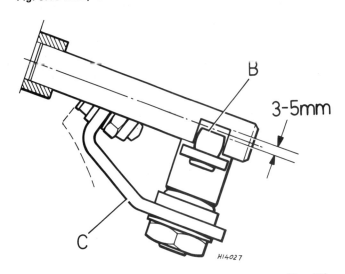

Fig 6.19 Correct shift rod-to-relay lever pin clearance (Sec 13)

B   Lever pin
C   Relay lever

3   The balljoints have nylon inserts and can be prised apart after first removing the wire clip (where fitted).
4   If gearchanging is difficult and the angle of the gearshift lever appears to be incorrect, or new linkage components are being fitted, check the length of the adjustable rods as shown in Figs. 6.15, 6.16 and 6.17.
5   If necessary remove the rod(s) and adjust the length by slackening the locknut and turning the balljoint in the required direction, then tighten the locknut.
6   Check that the tapered cotter securing the relay lever to the gearbox shift rod is tight and that there is no lost movement between lever and rod.
7   Set the lever in the neutral position and check that the correct clearance exists between the slot in the end of the shift rod and the pin on the lower relay lever (Fig. 6.19).
8   If necessary, obtain the correct clearances by slackening the nuts securing the support bracket to the final drive housing and moving the bracket up or down. Tighten the nuts when the adjustment is correct.

14 Automatic transmission – general description

Horizon SX models are equipped with a three-speed fully automatic transmission as standard equipment in place of the manual gearbox fitted to other Horizon models.
The transmission comprises two basic systems: the torque converter, which takes the place of the conventional clutch, and a torque/speed responsive hydraulically operated epicyclic gearbox. A transmission fluid cooler, incorporated in the radiator, is also fitted to maintain the transmission at the correct operating temperature.
Due to the complexity of the automatic transmission unit, any adjustments (made necessary by sub-standard performance) or overhaul work should be left to a Talbot dealer or automatic transmission

specialist, who will have the special equipment for fault diagnosis and rectification. The contents of the following Sections are therefore confined to supplying general information and any service information and instruction that can be used by the owner.

15 Automatic transmission – fluid level checking

1   Every 12 000 miles or 12 months, whichever occurs first, the automatic transmission fluid level should be checked with the engine and transmission at normal operating temperatures. A road journey of approximately 5 miles minimum will achieve this.
2   With the vehicle standing on level ground and the brake applied, leave the engine running and move the selector lever through all the gear positions in turn, pausing 5 seconds at each position. This will ensure proper filling of all hydraulic circuits in the transmission.

3   Leave the selector lever in the N position and open the bonnet.

4   Wipe off all the dirt from the dipstick, located on the front left-hand side of the engine compartment, and with the engine still running, remove the dipstick and wipe it on a clean cloth.

5   Insert the dipstick again, remove it, check the height of the fluid against the marks.

6   The level of the properly filled transmission will be near the MIN (low) mark when the fluid temperature is 68°F (20°C) and near but not above the MAX (high) mark when the fluid temperature is 176°F (80°C), which is the normal operating temperature.

7   If the fluid level is low, top it up through the dipstick filler tube using the recommended fluid.

8   After filling refit the dipstick, ensuring that it is fully seated in the filler tube to prevent dirt ingress.

16 Automatic transmission – fluid draining and refilling

1   The automatic transmission fluid does not normally need changing; this will only be necessary for the following reasons:

    (a) To facilitate removal of the transmission assembly
    (b) If the car is being used extensively in heavy traffic conditions at temperatures above 90°F (33°C)
    (c) If the car is being used mainly for short journeys

2   If the above operating conditions apply, the fluid should be drained and the transmission refilled with fresh fluid every 30 000 miles.

3   To drain the fluid it is first necessary to remove the transmission sump as a drain is not provided.

4   Clean the transmission sump and the area immediately above the sump joint face.

5   Place a suitable container beneath the transmission, and then slacken the sump securing bolts. Give the sump a tap at one corner with a mallet to break the seal and allow the fluid to drain. **Caution:** *If the fluid is at normal operating temperature, take care to avoid scalding.*

6   When all the fluid has drained, remove the sump securing bolts and lift off the sump. Scrape off all the old sealer from the joint faces of the sump and transmission, taking great care not to allow any old sealer to enter the transmission.

7   It is a good idea at this stage to remove the transmission filter, which is easily accessible, for cleaning. The filter is secured by three 'Torx' drive screws requiring a Torx drive screwdriver or adaptor to remove them.

8   With the filter removed, wash it thoroughly in clean transmission fluid and dry with compressed air or use a tyre foot pump. If the filter is heavily impregnated it should be renewed.

9   Pull down the magnet from the rear corner of the valve block, wipe it clean and refit it.

10   Place the filter in position and refit the Torx securing screws.

11   Ensure that the mating faces of the sump and transmission are clean and dry, apply a ribbon of RTV jointing compound to the sump and secure it in place with the retaining bolts, tightened to the correct torque.

12   To refill the transmission, pour approximately 5 pints (3.0 litres) of the specified transmission fluid through the dipstick filler tube.

13   Start the engine and allow it to idle for 2 minutes. Move the selector lever into each gear position, pausing each time, and then leave it in P or N position.

14   Check the fluid level with the engine running and top up as necessary until the level reaches the MIN mark on the dipstick.

15   After driving the car approximately 5 miles, recheck and if necessary top up the fluid using the procedure described in Section 15.

17 Automatic transmission – removal and refitting

1   The automatic transmission can be removed with the engine as a complete assembly using the procedure described in Chapter 1; or it can be removed separately, leaving the engine still in place, as described below. Note that any suspected faults must be referred to a Talbot main dealer or automatic transmission specialist *before* unit removal, as with this type of transmission the fault must be confirmed using specialist equipment before the transmission is removed from the car.

2   Open the bonnet and disconnect the battery earth terminal.

3   Place a suitable container beneath the transmission sump, wipe clean the sump and surrounding area and then slacken the sump securing bolts. Give the sump a sharp tap in one corner with a hide or plastic mallet to break the seal and allow the fluid to drain. After draining tighten the bolts. Take care to avoid scalding if the fluid is hot.

4   Position another container beneath the final drive, undo and remove the drain plug and allow the oil to drain. Refit the plug after draining.

5   Make a note of the electrical connections at the ignition coil and disconnect them. Undo and remove the bolts securing the coil mounting bracket to the converter housing and lift off the coil.

6   Undo and remove the bolts securing the left-hand engine lifting engine bracket to the transmission and lift away the bracket.

7   Extract the retaining clips and remove the gear selector inner cable from the operating lever on the transmission. Release the outer cable from the support bracket and position the disconnected cable well clear of the engine.

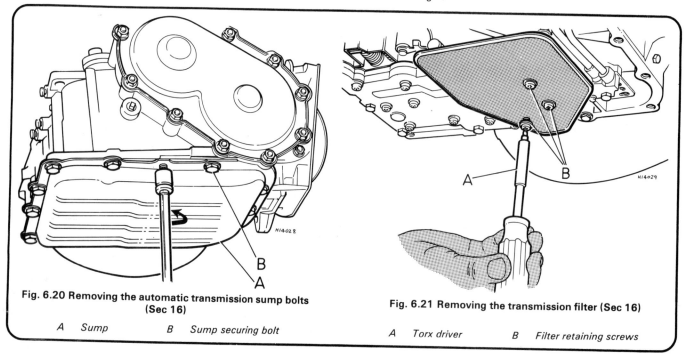

Fig. 6.20 Removing the automatic transmission sump bolts (Sec 16)

    A   Sump   B   Sump securing bolt

Fig. 6.21 Removing the transmission filter (Sec 16)

    A   Torx driver   B   Filter retaining screws

8 Move the throttle valve on the transmission to the fully open position and slide the nipple of the throttle valve inner cable out of its slot. Undo and remove the securing bolts and lift off the throttle valve cable support bracket, complete with cable. Position the bracket well clear of the engine.

9 Disconnect the electrical leads at the temperature gauge transmitter and radiator from sensor switch. Release the front wiring harness retaining clips and lift the harness and heater hose above the fan motor.

10 Open the fuel tank filler cap to release any pressure and then remove the fuel supply pipe from the fuel pump. Slide the pipe out of the grommet, plug the pipe end and position it out of the way.

11 Withdraw the transmission dipstick and plug the aperture to prevent dirt ingress.

12 Release the clips securing the fluid cooler pipes to the transmission.

13 Jack up the front of the car and securely support it on axle stands. Remove both front roadwheels.

14 From underneath the car, undo and remove the retaining bolt and lift off the speedometer cable housing and gear.

15 Disconnect the wires at the cruise control speed sensor, if fitted.

16 Refer to Chapter 7, and remove both front driveshafts.

17 Make a note of the electrical connections at the starter motor and disconnect them. Undo and remove the securing bolts and lift off the starter motor.

18 Undo and remove the securing bolts and lift off the torque converter dirt shield.

19 Wipe clean the area around the fluid cooler pipe unions on the transmission. Unscrew the unions and withdraw the pipes from the transmission. Plug or tape over the pipe ends and unions to prevent dirt ingress.

20 Disconnect the wires from the starter inhibitor switch on the front face of the transmission.

21 Place a sturdy plank of wood, or similar support, transversly across the engine bay and resting on the front wings. Make sure that the wings are well protected with old blankets and that the support is of sufficient strength to carry the full weight of the engine. Secure the engine to the support using ropes or chains at the right-hand engine lifting bracket and at the thermostat water outlet elbow.

22 Undo and remove the bolts securing the front engine mounting support bracket to the front crossmember and to the cylinder block. Withdraw the support bracket.

23 Undo and remove the securing bolts and lift off the right-hand rear engine mounting and the left-hand rear engine mounting, complete with support bracket.

24 Mark the relationship of the torque converter to the drive plate using a dab of paint. Rotate the crankshaft pulley until each of the three torque converter securing bolts become accessible from the dirt shield aperture and then undo and remove the bolts.

25 Place a jack beneath the transmission and take the weight of the unit.

26 Make a final check that all the cables and connections have been removed from the transmission and that all disconnected components are well clear.

27 Undo and remove the bolts securing the transmission to the engine, withdraw the transmission slightly and lower the unit and remove it from under the car. *It is most important to make sure that*

the torque converter stays on the transmission as it is removed. If necessary push it onto the transmission using a block of wood inserted through the starter motor aperture as the transmission is withdrawn.

28 Refitting the automatic transmission is the reverse sequence to removal, but paying particular attention to the following points:

(a) *When refitting the original torque converter, ensure that the alignment marks made during removal are adjacent before refitting the securing bolts*

(b) *If a new torque converter is being fitted, first position the engine at TDC Nos 1 and 4 pistons. Turn the converter so that the long timing slot on the periphery is adjacent to the O-mark on the converter housing timing scale. In this position one of the converter securing bolt holes will be uppermost*

(c) *The bolts securing the engine rear support to the cylinder block must be assembled with thread locking compound*

(d) *On completion of the installation check the adjustment of the selector and throttle valve cables as described in Sections 18 and 19 respectively*

(e) *Top up the transmission fluid level as described in Section 15. If the unit has been completely drained, refill as described in Section 16*

(f) *Refill the final drive with the recommended grade of automatic transmission fluid via the filler/level plug on the final drive casing.*

---

18 Selector cable (automatic transmission) – adjustment

1 Working in the engine compartment, slacken the bolt securing the selector cable support bracket to the plate bolted to the transmission. Make sure that the support bracket is free to slide on the plate and to turn on the cable.

2 Position the gear selector lever in P (park).

3 Move the selector lever on the transmission fully forward toward the front of the car, to the P position.

4 With the selector lever held in this position, tighten the support bracket retaining bolt.

5 Move the gear selector lever slowly towards the N position until it clicks into the N stop in the selector gate. Check that this is equal movement from the detent position to the front and rear selector lever gate stops. Check that this is also the case in the remaining selector lever positions.

6 Ensure that the engine will only start in the P and N selector lever positions and that the reversing lights are illuminated in the R position only.

7 Slight repositioning of the cable support bracket may be made, if necessary, until all the above checks are satisfactory.

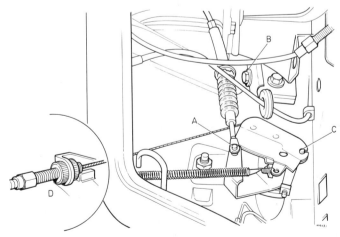

Fig. 6.23 Details of the automatic transmission selector and throttle valve cables (Sec 18)

A *Selector cable clevis pin*   C *Cable nipple*
B *Support bracket securing*   D *Throttle valve adjuster*
   bolt

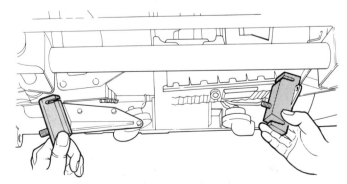

Fig. 6.22 Removing the automatic transmission rear mountings and supports (Sec 17)

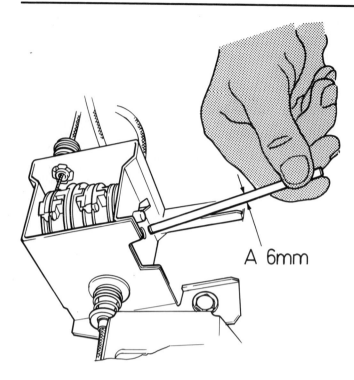

A 6mm

19 Carburettor and throttle valve cables – adjustment

1   A cable relay cam box is used to interconnect the accelerator cable with the carburettor, throttle valve, and (where fitted) cruise control servo cables. The cam box consists of three cams (four if a speed control is fitted), all of different diameters. Movement of the accelerator pedal moves the accelerator cam which in turn moves the other cams and their cables by different amounts according to cam diameter.

2   Fig. 6.24 shows the layout of the cams and their cables which must always be adjusted in the order: accelerator pedal, carburettor, throttle valve, and cruise control (if fitted) as follows.

3   Remove the cover from the cam box and place a 6 mm diameter drill shank or rod through the hole in the side of the cam box and through the cams.

4   Slacken the locknut on the accelerator cable adjuster at the cam box. Screw the adjuster outwards to take up all free play and to lightly trap the 6 mm diameter rod. Now tighten the locknut and remove the rod.

5   Loosen the carburettor cable adjuster locknut at the support bracket beneath the carburettor.

6   Release the clips securing the halves of the air cleaner adaptor above the carburettor, prise the upper half carefully upward and hold the choke plates in the open position.

7   With the choke plates held in position, push the fast idle adjusting screw fully toward the choke housing. This will position the choke and fast idle linkage in the normal (hot) idle position.

8   Keep the fast idle screw pushed in and adjust the carburettor

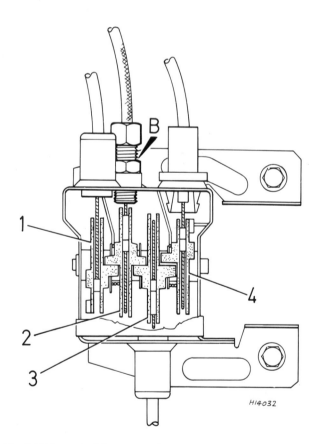

Fig. 6.24 Layout of the automatic transmission cable relay cam box (Sec 19)

1	Throttle valve cam	A 6 mm diameter rod
2	Accelerator pedal cam	B Accelerator pedal cable
3	Carburettor cam	adjuster
4	Cruise control servo cam	
	(where fitted)	

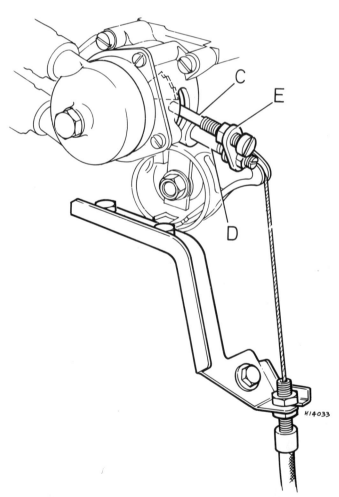

Fig. 6.25 Carburettor cable adjustment – automatic transmission models (Sec 19)

C   Fast idle screw   E   Throttle lever
D   Pushrod

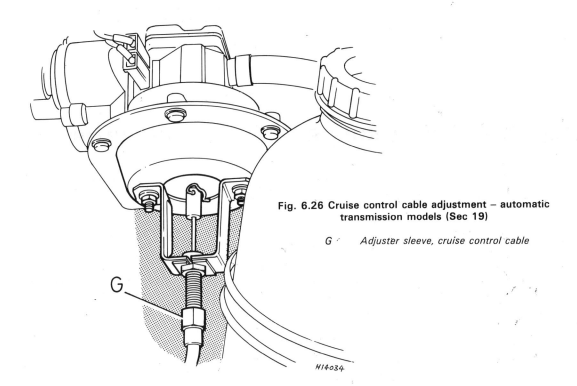

Fig. 6.26 Cruise control cable adjustment – automatic
transmission models (Sec 19)

G   Adjuster sleeve, cruise control cable

H14034

cable so that the stops of the accelerator pedal and carburettor cams in the cam box are just in contact, or so that the cable has a minimum free movement of 2 mm. Tighten the cable adjuster locknut.

9   Refit the top of the air cleaner adaptor and the retaining clips.

10 Next slacken the locknut of the throttle valve cable adjusters at the support bracket on the transmission housing.

11 Hold the transmission throttle valve lever back against its internal stop, and with the stops of the throttle valve and accelerator cams in the cam box in contact, take up all the slack in the cable. Tighten the adjuster locknuts when all free play is eliminated.

12 If a cruise control cable is fitted, slacken the adjuster locknuts of the cruise control cable at the servo end.

13 Alter the position of the adjuster and locknuts, to shorten the cable, until the cruise control cable cam in the cambox just moves away from its stop. In this position there should now also be 2 mm clearance between the stops of the cruise control cable cam and carburettor cam.

14 The cable should now be lengthened by one and a half turns of the adjuster to obtain a clearance at the servo end. Having done that, tighten the locknuts.

20 Fault diagnosis – manual gearbox and automatic transmission

Symptom	Reason(s)
Manual gearbox	
Weak or ineffective synchromesh	Worn synchromesh baulk rings or drive springs
Gearbox jumps out of gear	Selector detent balls and springs badly worn
	Excessive wear of selector forks
	Worn synchromesh units
Excessive noise	Incorrect grade of oil in gearbox or level too low
	Worn gearbox bearing
	Chipped or broken gear teeth
	Excessive output shaft endfloat
	Worn differential gears or bearings
Difficulty in engaging gears	Incorrect gear linkage adjustment
	See also Fault diagnosis – clutch (Chapter 5)

Automatic transmission

Faults in these units are nearly always the result of low fluid or incorrect adjustment of the selector, carburettor or throttle valve cables. Internal faults should be diagnosed by your Talbot main dealer or automatic transmission specialists who have the necessary equipment to carry out the work. Do not remove the transmission from the vehicle for possible repair before professional fault diagnosis has been carried out, since most tests require the transmission to be in the vehicle.

Chapter 7 Front suspension; driveshafts and hubs

Contents

Specifications

Suspension type ....   Independent with double wishbones, torsion bars, anti-roll bar and telescopic shock absorbers

Driveshafts
Type ....   Solid shaft with three-pronged sliding roller type constant velocity joint (inner) and universal joint (outer)

Torsion bar identification
Right-hand bar:
    Standard suspension ....   White-red paint mark
    Heavy duty suspension ....   Green paint mark
    Automatic transmission ....   White-orange paint mark
Left-hand bar:
    Standard suspension ....   White-blue paint mark
    Heavy duty suspension ....   Yellow-paint mark
    Automatic transmission ....   White-brown paint mark
Vehicle ride height ....   10.4 in (265 mm) + 0.39 in (10 mm) measured from centre of front jacking point recess to ground

Torque wrench settings

	lbf ft	Nm
Driveshaft retaining (hub) nut	144	195
Anti-roll bar-to-suspension arm	7	10
Anti-roll bar to frame	17	22.5
Brake caliper-to-hub carrier	46	62.5
Brake disc-to-hub	35	47.5
Shock absorber upper mounting	9	12.5
Shock absorber lower mounting	17	22.5
Lower balljoint-to-suspension arm	55	75
Lower balljoint retaining ring	250	340
Lower suspension crossmember-to-body	35	47.5
Spindle nuts, lower suspension arm	55	75
Spindle nuts, upper suspension arm	41	55
Torsion bar adjusting lever-to-crossmember	55	75
Torsion bar hub fork-to-crossmember	11	15
Upper balljoint cotter pin nut	26	35
Upper suspension arm-to-crossmember	35	47.5
Stiffening bracket-to-upper crossmember	17	22.5
Upper crossmember-to-body	17	22.5
Stiffening bracket-to-body	35	47.5

1 General description

The front suspension is of the independent double wishbone type with longitudinal torsion bars and telescopic double-acting shock absorbers.

The inner pivots of the upper suspension arms are attached to a pressed steel crossmember which is bolted to the longitudinal frame members and reinforcement brackets. Provision is made for adjust-

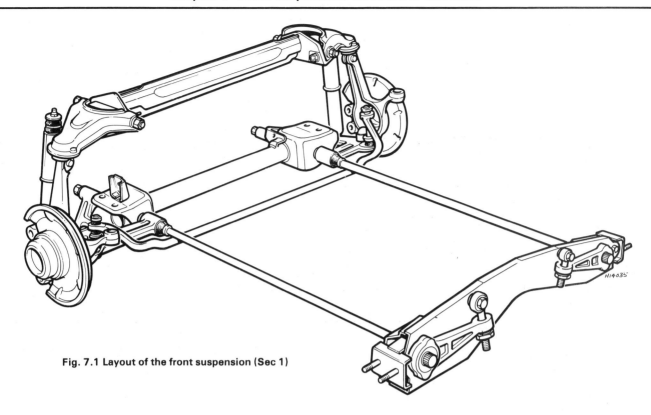

Fig. 7.1 Layout of the front suspension (Sec 1)

ment of front suspension camber and caster angles by fitting shims between the upper suspension arm pivot spindles and the crossmember.

The lower suspension arms pivot on spindles attached to a tubular steel crossmember which is also bolted to the longitudinal frame members.

The hub carriers swivel on renewable upper and lower balljoints which are lubricated and sealed for life.

The front end of each torsion bar fits into a hexagonal socket on the inner ends of the lower suspension arms while the rear ends are located in a central crossmember. Adjustable arms on the ends of each torsion bar sleeve enable the loading on the torsion bars to be altered to reset the vehicle ground clearance. The torsion bars are pre-stressed during manufacture for left-hand or right-hand fitting and must not be interchanged in service.

An anti-roll bar is attached to the frame by rubber bushes and the outer ends are connected to each lower suspension arm by tie-rods.

Each driveshaft has a constant velocity joint at the inner end and a universal joint at the outer end. Both joints are of the three-pronged sliding roller type, and are lubricated and sealed for life.

The driveshaft inner constant velocity joint is splined to the differential side gears while the outer universal joint is splined to the wheel hub which is in turn supported by a double race ball-bearing fitted to the hub carrier.

2 Driveshaft – removal and refitting

1 Jack up the front of the car and support it on axle stands positioned under the front jacking points. Remove the appropriate front roadwheel.

2 Using a small chisel or similar tool, knock back the staking on the hub nut. With an assistant firmly depressing the footbrake, undo and remove the hub nut from the end of the driveshaft (photo). This nut is very tight.

3 Undo and remove the nut securing the lower balljoint to the suspension arm and then release the taper seat of the balljoint shank using a suitable extractor. Alternatively, screw on the retaining nut two or three turns to protect the threads and then sharply strike the end of the lower suspension arm, using a medium hammer, until the shock frees the taper. Remember that the joint will separate with considerable force due to the tension of the anti-roll and torsion bars. If the nut was left on the taper pin you may have to jack up under the balljoint in order to be able to unscrew the nut.

4 Lift up the complete front hub/suspension assembly and pull it outward, pivoting it on the upper balljoint. At the same time push the driveshaft in towards the car and withdraw it from the rear of the hub carrier (photos).

5 Lower the front hub/suspension assembly and re-engage the

2.2 Removing the hub nut from the driveshaft

2.4a Disengage the lower balljoint and lift the hub assembly upwards ...

2.4b ... then withdraw the driveshaft from the hub

balljoint shank in the lower suspension arm.

6   If working on the right-hand driveshaft of models equipped with automatic transmission, it will be necessary to remove the securing screw and withdraw the speedometer cable adapter from the extension housing before removing the driveshaft inner end from the differential.

7   Pull the inner end of the driveshaft out of the differential and withdraw it from the car.

8   Refitting the driveshaft in the reverse sequence to removal. Ensure that the hub nut and lower balljoint retaining nut are tightened to the correct torque wrench settings as shown in the Specifications. The hub nut will have to be finally tightened with the weight of the car on the ground and an assistant applying the footbrake.

3   Driveshaft joints – dismantling, inspection and reassembly

Inner constant velocity joint

1   Secure the driveshaft in a vice and remove the rubber gaiter retaining ring from the tulip. On models equipped with automatic transmission a strap is used to retain the gaiter. To remove the strap, place a thin piece of steel or a flat screwdriver blade beneath the strap to protect the gaiter and cut the strap with a hammer and chisel.

2   Slide the gaiter down the driveshaft and then withdraw the tulip assembly, springs and spring seat. On automatic transmission models the right-hand driveshaft constant velocity joint is fitted with a metal plate at the rear of the tulip. This plate acts as an end stop for the rollers and must be bent up slightly with a screwdriver (Fig. 7.2) to allow the tulip to be withdrawn.

3   Wipe away as much grease as possible from the spider and roller assembly and then wrap masking or insulating tape around the rollers to retain them in place on the spider.

4   Clearly and accurately mark the relationship of the spider legs to the driveshaft using a file, centre punch or similar tool. The constant velocity joint spider is offset from the universal joint spider at the other end of the driveshaft by 57° ± 3°. This relationship must be maintained, particularly if a new spider is to be fitted, otherwise the 'constant velocity' characteristics of the joint and driveshaft will be impaired.

5   Using a press, press the splined driveshaft from the joint spider. Slide the gaiter and retaining ring up and off the end of the driveshaft.

6   With the joint now completely dismantled wipe away all traces of the old grease from the shaft, tulip and spider assembly.

7   Examine the splines on the driveshaft and spider for wear or damage. Carefully inspect the spider rollers for smoothness of operation, and the roller tracks in the tulip for wear ridges, scoring or damage. Finally check the rubber gaiter for punctures or deterioration. If the tulip spider or rubbers require renewal it will be necessary to purchase the complete joint assembly as these parts are matched and not available separately. The rubber gaiter however is obtainable in the form of a repair kit and includes the correct quantity of the special lubricating grease.

8   Commence reassembly by sliding the small retaining ring and rubber gaiter onto the driveshaft (photo).

9   Position the spider and roller assembly on the driveshaft splines using the previously made marks to accurately locate the spider. If the spider has a chamfer on one side only, this must face the universal

joint at the other end of the shaft.

10   Using a tubular drift of suitable diameter, drive the spider fully onto the shaft. Using a punch, peen the end of the shaft at three equidistant points to retain the spider.

11   Remove the tape from the spider rollers (photo), and liberally lubricate the spider, rollers, gaiter and tulip with 5 oz (145 g) of the special grease.

12   Place the spring seat and springs into the tulip and slide the tulip into position over the spider rollers (photos). If working on the right-hand joint of automatic transmission models, bend back the roller stop plate using a screwdriver.

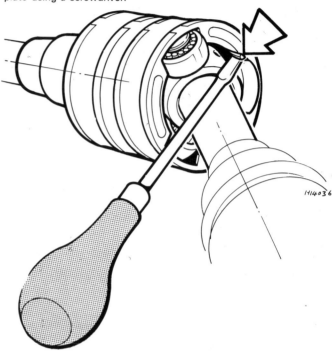

Fig. 7.2 Bending up the spider roller stops – automatic transmission models (Sec 3)

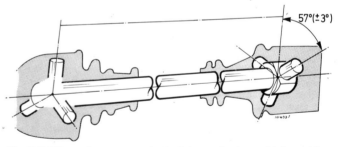

Fig. 7.3 Offset of constant velocity joint and universal joint spiders (Sec 3)

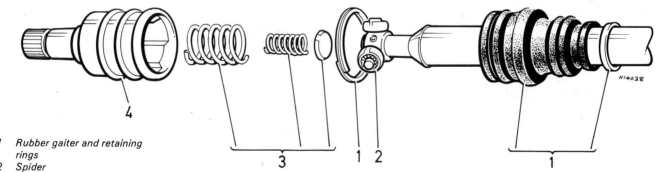

1   *Rubber gaiter and retaining rings*
2   *Spider*
3   *Springs and spring seat*
4   *Tulip*

Fig. 7.4 Constant velocity joint components (Sec 3)

3.8 Refitting the driveshaft gaiter and retaining ring

3.11 With the spider in position on the shaft ...

3.12a ... insert the springs into the tulip ...

3.12b ... and slide the tulip over the spider after applying the special grease

3.13 Refit the gaiter and retaining ring

4.8 Driveshaft outer joint gaiter repair kit. Slide gaiter onto shaft in direction of arrow to butt inner end against the location shoulder on shaft.

13 Slide the gaiter into its groove in the tulip and fit a new retaining ring to secure it (photo). Also slide the smaller retaining ring into position at the other end of the gaiter. On automatic transmission models, fit a new retaining strap to the tulip. Use the old strap as a guide to the positioning of strap and buckle and make sure that the strap is as tight as possible.

14 On completion of reassembly move the joint up and down and from side to side to distribute the grease. Make sure the operation is smooth and without tight spots or free play.

Outer universal joint

15 The outer (wheel end) universal joint is not repairable and if defective it will be necessary to obtain a complete driveshaft assembly. It is however possible to renew the rubber gaiter separately as described in Section 4.

---

4 Driveshaft joint rubber gaiters – removal and refitting

The driveshaft joint rubber gaiters can be renewed when necessary. They are supplied as a kit complete with new retaining rings and grease packs. During the gaiter removal and refitting operations it is important that the outer joint assembly must not be dismantled since reassembly is a difficult and specialised task but which if necessary, should be entrusted to your Talbot dealer.

Inner constant velocity joint gaiter

1 Remove the driveshaft from the car as described in Section 2, and then refer to Section 3, and carry out paragraphs 1, 2 and 3.

2 Remove the retaining ring from the smaller end of the gaiter and then using a sharp knife cut the gaiter in half and remove it from the driveshaft.

3 Using a round ended metal bar or similar blunt instrument carefully spread the small end of the new gaiter and ease it over the spider rollers. Take great care not to puncture the gaiter as it is stretched over the rollers.

4 Reassembly now follows the procedure described in Section 3, paragraphs 11 to 14 inclusive.

Outer universal joint gaiter

5 Remove the driveshaft from the car as described in Section 2. Refer to Section 3 and carry out paragraphs 1, 2 and 3 to remove the inner joint gaiter.

6 Prise free the inner retaining ring band and the outer retaining ring from the outer joint gaiter. Pull the gaiter back along the shaft and remove it from the inner joint end.

7 Remove all traces of old grease from the shaft, tulip and spider assembly. *This is most important as the outer universal joint lubricating grease supplied in service is not compatible with that used during manufacture.*

8 Slide the new gaiter into position on the shaft from the inner end, lubricate the joint assembly with 10 oz (280 g) of the special grease (supplied with kit), then stretch the gaiter over the joint to engage its location shoulders with the corresponding grooves of the tulip, (photo).

9 Lever the coiled spring retaining clip into position securing the gaiter outer end and secure the inner end with the new rubber ring supplied.

10 Check the joint action on completion then reassemble the inner gaiter as given in Section 3, paragraphs 11 to 14 inclusive.

---

5 Hub carrier – removal and refitting

1 Jack up the front of the car and support it on axle stands positioned under the front jacking points. Remove the appropriate front roadwheel.

2 Using a small chisel or similar tool, knock back the staking on the front driveshaft (hub) nut. Have an assistant firmly apply the footbrake and then using a large socket and bar undo and remove the nut.

3 Undo and remove the two bolts securing the brake caliper to the hub carrier. Slide the caliper, complete with pads, off the disc and suspend it from the upper suspension arm using a length of string or wire. Do not disconnect the hydraulic fluid hose when removing the caliper but take care to avoid stretching it.

4 Undo and remove the steering tie-rod balljoint retaining nut (photo) and separate the taper seat of the ball-pin shank using a suitable extractor. Alternatively, refit the nut two turns to protect the

5.4 Tie-rod balljoint retaining nut (arrowed)

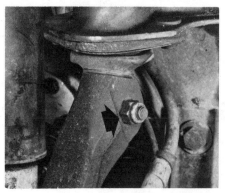

5.6 Upper suspension arm balljoint cotter pin nut (arrowed)

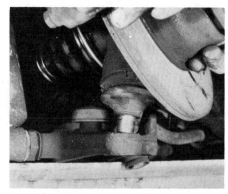

5.7 Disengaging the lower balljoint from the suspension arm

threads and strike the end of the steering arm using a medium hammer until the shock releases the taper.

5   Undo and remove the lower suspension arm balljoint retaining nut and release the ball-pin taper as described in paragraph 4.

6   Undo and remove the nut from the cotter pin that retains the shank of the upper suspension arm balljoint in the hub carrier (photo). Now drift the cotter pin out of the carrier.

7   Disengage the upper and lower balljoints from their locations (photo) and then withdraw the hub carrier assembly complete with hub and brake disc off the driveshaft. Support the driveshaft as the hub carrier is removed to avoid straining the joint rubber gaiters.

8   Refitting the hub carrier is the reverse sequence to removal, ensuring that the correct torque wrench settings are observed when tightening all nuts and bolts. Finally tighten the driveshaft nut with the weight of the car on the wheels and an assistant applying the footbrake.

6   Hub bearings – removal and refitting

1   Remove the appropriate hub carrier from the car as described in Section 5.

2   Mark the relationship of the brake disc to the hub and then undo and remove the four bolts securing the disc to the hub.

3   Rotate the brake disc just enough (approximately $\frac{1}{18}$ of a turn) so

that two suitable bolts may be screwed into the roadwheel fixing bolt holes of the hub. Tighten the two bolts evenly and progressively. The bolts will bear against the brake disc and cause the hub to be drawn out of the bearing. Once the hub is removed the brake disc can be lifted off.

4   On inspection of the hub it will be seen that the outer of the two inner bearing races will have come away with the hub. This should now be removed from the hub using a suitable puller. Alternatively drift it off with a hammer and punch.

5   Using circlip pliers extract the bearing retaining circlip from the rear (inside) of the hub carrier. With the carrier supported in a vice, drift out the bearing from front to rear using a hammer and tube of suitable diameter.

6   Thoroughly clean the hub carrier and remove any burrs from the bearing recess with a small file.

7   Before fitting a new bearing to the hub carrier there is a point worth noting. The single one-piece outer bearing casing contains two sets of balls and two separate inner races. At each end of the bearing there is a double lip oil seal which runs on the inner race. *If either of the inner races is dislodged, even partially, it cannot be refitted without damaging the seal which will render the bearing unserviceable.* New bearings are supplied with a plastic inner race retainer which should be left in position until the bearing is fitted. This will help to prevent the inner races being dislodged.

8   Smear the outer bearing casing with a trace of grease and position it against the rear of the hub carrier, either way round.

9   Using a long bolt, nut and two packing washers as shown in Fig. 7.8, carefully pull the bearing into the hub carrier. Refit the retaining circlip.

10   Make sure that the mating surfaces of the brake disc and hub are thoroughly clean and refit the disc to the hub. Line up the previously made marks and refit the four retaining bolts, tightened to the correct torque wrench setting.

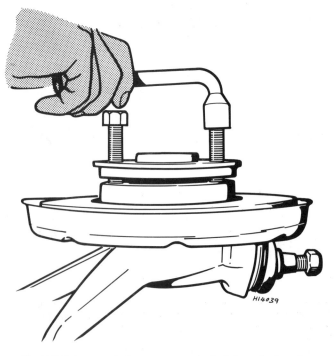

Fig. 7.5 Using two bolts to remove the hub from the bearing (Sec 6)

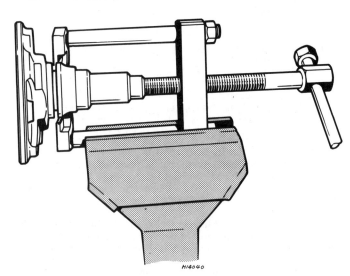

Fig 7.6 Using a puller to draw off the bearing race (Sec 6)

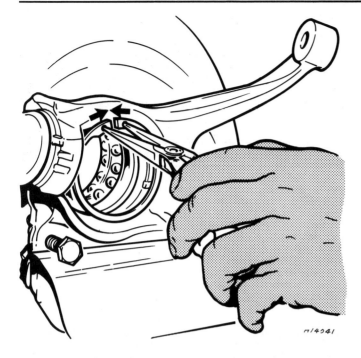

Fig. 7.7 Hub bearing retaining circlip removal (Sec 6)

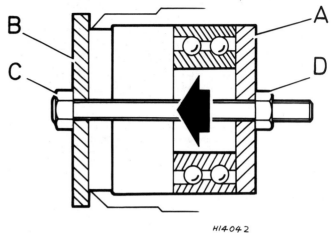

Fig. 7.8 Refitting the bearing to the hub carrier (Sec 6)

A   Suitable washer   C   Long bolt
B   Suitable washer   D   Nut

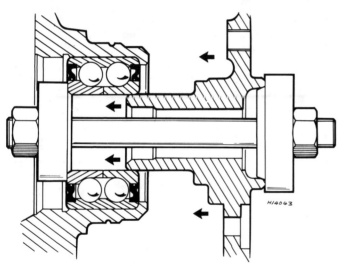

Fig. 7.9 Using a bolt, spacing washers and nut to draw the hub
into the bearing (Sec 6)

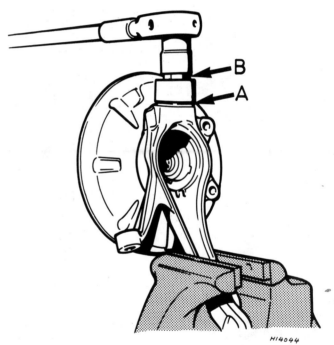

Fig. 7.10 Arrangement of special tool for balljoint nut removal
(Sec 7)

A   Tool   B   Balljoint nut

11   Smear the hub spigot lightly with grease and position the hub/disc
assembly in the bearing. Pull the hub into place using a long bolt and
suitable spacing washers. Make sure the washer bears against the
bearing inner race as shown in Fig. 7.9, to avoid the possibility of
dislodging the race.
12   The hub carrier can now be refitted as described in Section 5.

---

7   Lower suspension balljoint – removal and refitting

1   Remove the appropriate hub carrier from the car as described in
Section 5.
2   Support the hub carrier in a vice and knock back the peening
around the balljoint retaining ring nut.
3   Place Talbot tool No 21811C over the retaining ring and lock it in
place with the balljoint nut. Unless suitable facilities are available to
have a similar tool made up there is really no alternative but to use the
Talbot tool. The releasing torque of the retaining ring is likely to be in
the region of 260 lbf ft (350 Nm) and under no circumstances should
any attempt be made to undo it using a hammer and drift.

4   With the tool in position, undo and remove the retaining ring and
lift out the balljoint.
5   Place a quantity of medium grease in the balljoint dust cover and
then refit the joint and screw on the retaining ring. Place the tool in
position and tighten the ring to the specified torque wrench setting.
6   Peen the retaining ring into one of the slots in the hub carrier
casting.
7   The hub carrier can now be refitted as described in Section 5.

---

8   Upper suspension arm balljoint – removal and refitting

1   Jack up the front of the car and support it on axle stands
positioned under the front jacking points. Remove the appropriate
front roadwheel.
2   Undo and remove the nut from the cotter pin that secures the

balljoint pin to the hub carrier. Carefully tap out the cotter pin using a hammer and drift.
3   Drill out the rivets securing the balljoint to the upper suspension arm, lift up the arm and withdraw the balljoint from the hub carrier.
4   The new balljoint is supplied as a kit complete with nuts and bolts as a replacement for the rivets.
5   Refitting is a reversal of the removal sequence, ensuring that the balljoint securing nuts are located on the top surface of the upper suspension arm and are correctly locked.

9 Shock absorber – removal, testing and refitting

1   The telescopic type hydraulic shock absorbers cannot be repaired and in the event of evidence occuring of poor roadholding, steering wander or an unusually soft and bouncy ride, then the units should be removed from the car and tested.
2   Jack up the front of the car and support it on axle stands positioned under the front jacking points. Remove the appropriate front roadwheel.
3   Place another axle stand, jack or sturdy block under the lower suspension arm and in contact with it. Make sure that the stand, jack or block is taking the weight of the suspension arm and is securely positioned in such a way that there is no likelihood of it slipping.

4   Disconnect the shock absorber upper and lower mountings (photos) and withdraw the unit from under the wheel arch.
5   Secure the shock absorber by its lower mounting in a vice in the vertical position. Operate the damper plunger over the full length of its travel ten times. There should be firm resistance in both directions of travel. If the action is jerky, or if there is no resistance at all, renew the unit.
6   Refitting is a reverse of removal, but note carefully the fitting sequence of the mountings.

10 Anti-roll bar – removal, inspection and refitting

1   The anti-roll bar is connected at each end to the lower suspension arm by a long bolt, nut and bush assembly (photo).
2   It is also supported by rubber bushes retained by semicircular clamps (photo).
3   Removal of the bar is carried out by withdrawing the anchor bolts and the rubber bush clamps.
4   Inspect the bar closely for cracks and also the rubber mounting components for deterioration. Renew as appropriate.
5   Refitting the anti-roll bar is the reverse sequence to removal. Observe the correct torque wrench settings as shown in the Specifications when tightening the mountings.

9.4a Shock absorber upper ...

9.4b ... and lower mountings

10.1 Anti-roll bar suspension arm mounting assembly ...

10.2 ... and chassis attachment

11 Torsion bars – removal and refitting

1   Removal and refitting of the torsion bars is a difficult task and is considered to be beyond the scope of the average DIY owner. Before the torsion bars can be removed the tension must be released from them. This tension is in the region of 750 lbf ft (1000 Nm) and a tool having a handle approximately 63 in (1600 mm) long, to provide sufficient leverage, is necessary to release the torsion bars. It is also necessary to move this tool through an arc of 60° and this can only be done with the car on a hoist. For those who have access to the necessary tools and facilities the following procedure should be used.
2   With the car positioned on a hoist, jack up the front end and support it on stands so that the suspension is on full rebound, (no load).
3   Raise the hoist to provide sufficient working clearance under the car and release the torsion bar tension using tool No 20916Q as follows.
4   Fit the special tool on the rear end of the torsion bar sleeve located in the centre crossmember (photo) and push the tool handle upwards to release the load on the adjusting rod and remove the adjusting rod pivot bolt.
5   Slowly allow the torsion bar lever to swing down and remove the tool.
6   Remove the bolt securing the sleeve retaining fork to the rear of the crossmember and remove the fork (photo).
7   Pull the sleeve and lever assembly rearwards off the end of the torsion bar.
8   Withdraw the torsion bar from the lower suspension arm by moving it to the rear and then remove it from the car by pulling it forward out of the crossmember.
9   Refitting is the reverse sequence to removal, but make sure that the splines of the torsion bar and the hub in which it locates are well greased. Note also that the torsion bars are handed and are not interchangeable from side to side. Identification is by a paint mark; the colour code is shown in the Specifications. Never mark a torsion bar by scratching or filing as this may cause premature failure.
10   With the torsion bars correctly fitted in the vehicle, the tensioning arms should be fitted to the torsion bars at the angle shown in the diagram (Fig. 7.12).
11   A template should be used to obtain this initial setting and then the procedure described in the following Section must be carried out.

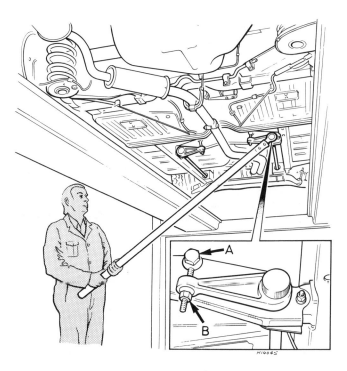

Fig. 7.11 Releasing the right-hand torsion bar (Sec 11)

A   Adjusting rod pivot bolt
B   Adjusting nut

12 Torsion bars – setting

1   Whenever a torsion bar has been removed or renewed it must be set to the correct tension which is determined by the vehicle ride height.
2   Before carrying out any adjustments ensure that the fuel tank is full and that the tyres are correctly inflated. It will also be necessary to make up two height gauges. These can easily be made from suitable lengths of dowel approximately 1 in (25 mm) in diameter, screwed or nailed to a square wooden base to keep them vertical. The gauges must be exactly 10.43 in (265 mm) measured from the top of the dowel to the ground.
3   With the car standing on level ground, disconnect the front and rear shock absorber lower mountings.
4   Remove any road dirt or excessively thick underseal from the space within the front jacking points.
5   Stand the height gauges on the ground, one each side of the car, directly beneath the jacking points and with the top of the dowel in the jacking point recess (photo).

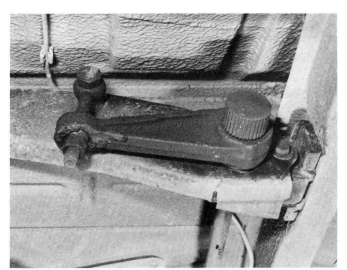

11.4 Torsion bar anchor lever, adjusting rod and pivot bolt

11.6 Torsion bar sleeve retaining fork mounting bolt (arrowed)

6   The vehicle ride height, and therefore torsion bar tension, is correct if the car is just touching the dowel of the height gauge. The permitted tolerance is for the ride height to be up to 0.39 in (10 mm) higher.

7   If the car is too high or too low the side height should be adjusted as follows.

8   Remove the height gauges from under the jacking points.

9   Loosen the pivot bolts of the torsion bar anchor lever adjusting rods. Turn both torsion bar anchor adjusting nuts anti-clockwise until they are flush with the ends of the adjusting rods.

10   Measure the height of each front jacking point from the ground. If one side is lower, turn the adjusting nut for that torsion bar clockwise until the height is the same on both sides.

11   Now turn both adjusting nuts clockwise alternately two turns at a time to raise the car until the height gauges can just be inserted. Do not turn one adjusting nut to lower the car during the adjustment. If the car is inadvertently raised too high on one side, release both nuts and start again.

12   If there is insufficient adjustment on an adjusting rod to achieve the correct ride height, reposition the anchor lever on the torsion bar splines as described in Section 11.

13   Having completed the adjustment, tighten the adjusting rod pivot bolts to the correct torque wrench setting and then reconnect the shock absorber lower mountings.

14   If the ride height has been altered appreciably, the brake pressure reducing valve should be adjusted as described in Chapter 10.

13 Lower suspension arm – removal and refitting

1   If wear is evident in the lower suspension arm bushes or spindle then the assembly must be removed and the worn components renewed as necessary.

2   Begin by removing the appropriate torsion bar as described in Section 11.

3   Disconnect the shock absorber lower mounting from the suspension arm.

4   Detach the lower suspension arm balljoint using the procedure described in Section 5.

5   Disconnect the anti-roll bar at its attachment to the lower suspension arm.

6   Remove the torsion bar thrust washer from the rear of the lower suspension arm. Hold the spindle with a screwdriver and undo the spindle retaining nut (photo).

7   Push the spindle out towards the rear and lift off the lower arm.

8   Refitting is the reverse sequence to removal, bearing in mind the following points:

(a)   Before fully tightening the spindle retaining nut, reconnect the shock absorber lower mounting and position the suspension arm at mid-stroke of the shock absorber. Tighten the spindle nut with the arm in this position

(b)   Ensure that the spacer plate is fitted above each anti-roll bar bush

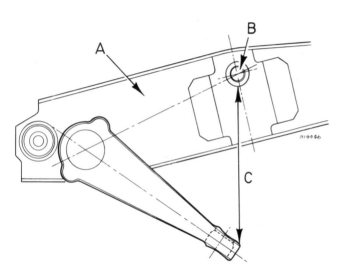

Fig. 7.12 Torsion bar lever setting position, suspension unloaded (Sec 11)

A   Crossmember
B   Adjusting rod pivot bolt hole

C   Setting dimension = 7.5 in (190 mm)

12.5 Height gauge in position beneath the front jacking point

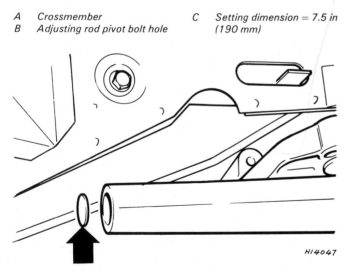

Fig. 7.13 Removing the torsion bar thrust washer from the lower suspension arm (Sec 13)

13.6 Lower suspension arm spindle retaining nut (arrowed)

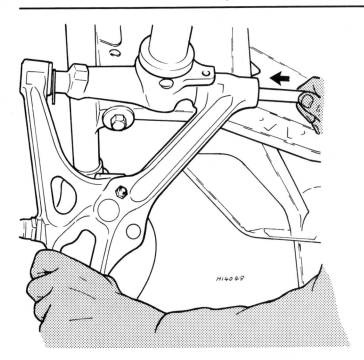

Fig. 7.14 Pushing out the lower arm spindle (Sec 13)

(c) *Make sure the thrust washer is in place in the rear of the suspension arm before fitting the torsion bar*

(d) *Adjust the torsion bar setting on completion as described in Section 12*

14 Upper suspension arm – removal and refitting

1   It will be necessary to remove the upper suspension arm when there is evidence of wear in the bushes or spindle. Its removal will also greatly ease the task of upper balljoint renewal described in Section 8.
2   Jack up the front of the car and support it on axle stands positioned under the front jacking points. Remove the appropriate front roadwheel.
3   Undo and remove the nut securing the upper balljoint retaining cotter pin to the hub carrier. Drive out the cotter pin using a hammer and drift and lift the balljoint shank out of the hub carrier.
4   Undo and remove the two bolts securing the upper suspension arm spindle to the upper crossmember (photo). As the bolts are removed, note the position and number of shims fitted between the spindle and crossmember. It is most important that these shims are refitted in exactly the same position during reassembly, otherwise the camber and caster angles of the front suspension will be incorrect.
5   Having removed the bolts and recovered the shims, withdraw the upper arm out from under the wheel arch.
6   With the upper arm removed, the spindle can be removed by undoing the two end retaining nuts, lifting out the bushes and sliding the spindle out to one side.
7   Inspect the bushes and spindle for wear or deformation and renew as necessary.
8   Refitting is the reverse sequence to removal. Observe the correct torque wrench settings when tightening all mountings. If the spindle retaining nuts have been slackened, do not fully tighten them until the car is resting on its wheels.

15 Upper suspension crossmember – removal and refitting

1   Jack up the front of the car and support it on axle stands positioned under the front jacking points. Remove both front roadwheels.
2   Undo and remove the nut from the cotter pin securing the upper suspension arm balljoint to the hub carrier. Drive out the cotter pin

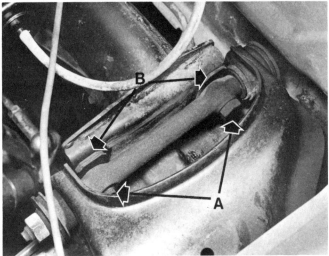

14.4 Upper suspension arm spindle retaining bolts (A) and shims (B)

using a hammer and drift and then lift the balljoint shank out of the hub carrier. Repeat this procedure on the other side of the car.
3   Referring to Chapter 3 if necessary, remove the complete air cleaner assembly, including the hot air intake hose and stove from the exhaust manifold.
4   Detach the clips securing cables and pipes to the crossmember and surrounding bodywork.
5   Undo and remove the two bolts securing the right-hand upper suspension arm to the crossmember. As the bolts are undone, note the position and quantity of shims located between spindle and crossmember. The shims must be refitted in their original positions on reassembly, otherwise the front suspension camber and caster angles will be incorrect.
6   Having removed the bolts and recovered the shims, lift out the suspension arm and spindle assembly.
7   Undo and remove the bolts securing the crossmember to the two reinforcement brackets and to the longitudinal members.
8   Carefully manoeuvre the crossmember, complete with left-hand upper suspension arm, to the left and out from under the left-hand front wing.
9   If necessary the left-hand upper suspension arm can be removed from the crossmember using the same procedure as for the right-hand arm.
10 Refitting the crossmember is the reverse sequence to removal. Make sure that the upper suspension arm shims are refitted in the same positions as noted during removal and observe the correct torque wrench settings for all mountings.

16 Lower suspension crossmember – removal and refitting

1   Remove both front torsion bars as described in Section 11.
2   Disconnect the shock absorber lower mountings from the suspension arms.
3   Detach the lower suspension arm balljoints using the procedure described in Section 5.
4   Undo and remove the bolts securing the anti-roll bar bushes to the frame.
5   Working in the engine compartment, disconnect and remove the cold air intake hose.
6   Place a sturdy length of wood, steel tube or similar support transversely across the car and resting on the front wings. Make sure the wings are well protected with blankets before placing the support in position.
7   Place chains or ropes around each end of the engine and attach them to the transverse support, making sure that the support is taking the full weight of the engine and transmission.
8   Undo and remove the bolts securing the right-hand engine mounting rubber to the crossmember.
9   Undo and remove the bolts securing the left-hand engine support

Fig. 7.15 Removing the left-hand engine support-to-crossmember mounting (Sec 16)

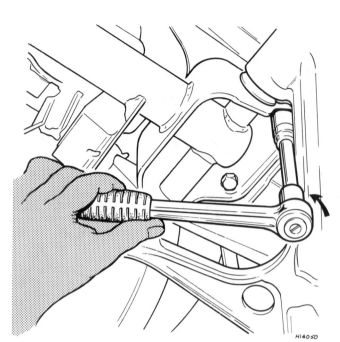

Fig. 7.16 Removing the lower crossmember retaining bolts (Sec 16)

to the crossmember.

10 Position a jack beneath the crossmember and in contact with it.

11 Undo and remove the crossmember mounting bolts. Lower the jack slowly and withdraw the crossmember, complete with lower suspension arms and anti-roll bar, from under the car.

12 Refitting is the reverse sequence to removal, bearing in mind the

following points:

(a) Ensure that the thrust washers are in position in the rear of the lower suspension arms before refitting the torsion bars

(b) On completion of reassembly adjust the torsion bar setting as described in Section 12

17 Fault diagnosis – front suspension, driveshafts and hubs

Symptom	Reason(s)
Excessive pitching and rolling on corners and during braking	Excessive wear in suspension balljoints or components Weak or ineffective shock absorbers Incorrect torsion bar settings See also Chapter 8
Wheel wobble and vibration	Excessive wear in suspension balljoints or components Weak or ineffective shock absorbers Excessive wear in wheel bearings Worn or distorted driveshaft or driveshaft joint See also Chapter 8
Knock or clunk when taking up drive	Loose driveshaft retaining (hub) nut Wear in driveshaft joints

Chapter 8 Steering, wheels and tyres

For modifications, and information applicable to later models, see Supplement at end of manual

Contents

Specifications

General
Steering type .... Rack-and-pinion
Steering wheel turns (lock-to-lock) 4.15
Turning circle:
   Cars with steel wheels .... 33.53 ft (10.22 metres)
   Cars with alloy wheels .... 34.31 ft (10.46 metres)

Steering geometry
Front wheel alignment (at kerb weight, fuel tank full) .... 0.04 in (1.2 mm) toe-in to 0.03 in (0.8 mm) toe-out – Zero setting preferred
Camber .... 0° ± 30'
Caster .... 2° ± 30'
Steering axis inclination .... 12° 50'

Steering gear
Pinion end clearance .... 0 to 0.004 in (0 to 0.01 mm)
Lubricant type:
   Up to steering rack No 1423226 .... Molybdenum disulphide grease
   From steering rack No 1423226 .... Semi-fluid EP grease
Lubricant quantity .... 2.75 oz (80 cc)

Wheels
Type .... $4\frac{1}{2}$ J x 13 or 5J x 13 with 36 or 45 mm offset, steel or alloy construction

Tyres
Type .... Radial, tubeless SR
Size (according to model) .... 145 SR 13, 155 SR 13 or 175/70 SR 13

Tyre pressures (cold)

	Front	Rear
Up to four occupants with no luggage – all sizes	26 lbf/in^2 (1.8 bar)	26 lbf/in^2 (1.8 bar)
Four occupants with luggage or sustained high speed driving:		
145 SR 13 tyres	30 lbf/in^2 (2.1 bar)	32 lbf/in^2 (2.2 bar)
155 or 175/70 SR 13 tyres	29 lbf/in^2 (2.0 bar)	29 lbf/in^2 (2.0 bar)

Torque wrench settings

	lbf ft	Nm
Track rod end balljoint nut	22	30
Steering gear-to-support bracket	15	20
Support bracket-to-frame	15	20
Cotter pin retaining nut	7	10
Steering column-to-support bracket	18	25
Universal joint pinch-bolt	11	15
Steering wheel nut	40	55
Track rod inner balljoint to rack	33	45
Pinion locknut	18	25
Rack damper locknut	44	60
Roadwheel bolts	46	63

1 General description

The steering gear is of the conventional rack-and-pinion type and is bolted to brackets which are attached to the longitudinal body members. The steering gear is adjustable for height and lateral position by the fitting of shims between the rack housing and mounting brackets.

The rack is supported within an aluminium alloy housing by a rubber-mounted bush at the end furthest from the pinion. A spring-loaded damper supports the other end of the rack and maintains the mesh of the rack teeth with the pinion. The pinion is carried within the housing by a plain bush and ball-bearing and is connected to the lower steering shaft by a rubberized coupling containing a splined collar and clamp bolt. Above the coupling the shaft is split by a Hooke's joint, designed to deflect on impact, thus minimising driver injury in the event of an accident. The upper shaft is supported by two bearings in the steering column which is in turn bolted to the dash panel. The column also contains a combined ignition switch and steering lock.

Turning the steering wheel causes the rack to move in a lateral direction and the track rods at either end of the rack pass this movement to the steering arms on the hub carrier assemblies, thereby moving the roadwheels.

The two track rods are adjustable in length to allow alteration of the front wheel alignment.

Wheels are either of pressed steel or alloy construction, with radial ply tyres as standard fitment. Due to the different wheel offset according to model type and tyre size, it is important that if a wheel is damaged it is replaced with a wheel having the same offset, otherwise the steering characteristics will be impaired.

2 Maintenance

1　No routine maintenance is required, but periodically check the condition of the rubber gaiters at each end of the rack housing and on the track rod end balljoints. If the gaiters are split or show signs of deterioration they must be renewed.

2　The gaiters at each end of the rack housing can be renewed with the steering gear in situ. However, the gaiters on the track rod end balljoints cannot be renewed separately and if damaged the complete balljoint must be obtained.

3　The steering gear is filled with molybdenum disulphide grease (or semi-fluid EP grease on later units) and is sealed for life. Replenishment of the lubricant will only be necessary if the gaiters are being renewed or if the steering gear is being overhauled.

3 Steering gear – adjustment

1　The rack-and-pinion steering gear is extremely reliable and it is unlikely that adjustment will be necessary in service. If however the car has covered a high mileage, or has been used over rough ground, an excessive amount of free play may be felt at the steering wheel, accompanied by a knocking noise from beneath the front of the car. Assuming the suspension linkages and balljoints to be in good order,

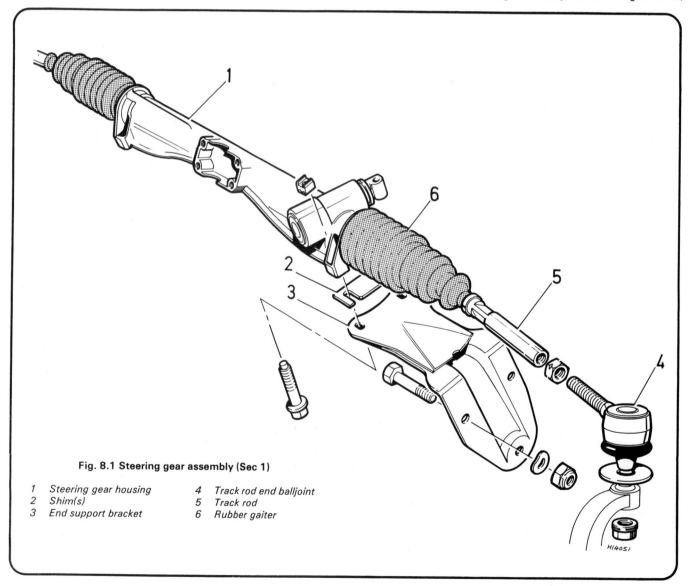

Fig. 8.1 Steering gear assembly (Sec 1)

1　Steering gear housing	4　Track rod end balljoint
2　Shim(s)	5　Track rod
3　End support bracket	6　Rubber gaiter

it is possible that adjustment of the rack damper assembly is required. This adjustment may be carried out with the steering gear in position on the car as follows.

2   Jack up the front of the car and support it on axle stands. Remove both front roadwheels.

3   Undo and remove the nuts securing each track rod end balljoint to the steering arms on the hub carriers. Extract the tapered ball-pins from the steering arms using a universal balljoint separator, or by striking the end of the steering arms with a few sharp hammer blows until the taper is released.

4   From underneath the car release the steering rack damper plug locknut.

5   Now tighten the damper plug until it can be just felt to be making contact with the damper plunger. Do not tighten the plug beyond this point.

6   From inside the car turn the steering wheel slowly from lock to lock. If a tight spot is felt, leave the steering wheel in that position and readjust the damper at that point. If more than one tight spot can be felt, readjust the damper at the tightest spot.

7   When the steering can be turned from lock to lock without feeling any tight spots the adjustment is correct.

8   Draw a pencil line across the damper plug onto the edge of the rack housing. Unscrew the plug so that the lines are separated by 0.125 in (3 mm).

9   Refit the locknut and tighten it to the specified torque wrench setting while holding the damper plug with a spanner to stop it turning. Recheck the adjustment by again turning the steering from lock to lock before refitting the track rod ends and lowering the car to the ground.

4.3 Removing the gearchange relay bracket from the rack housing

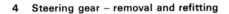

4   Steering gear – removal and refitting

1   Jack up the front of the car and support it on axle stands. Remove both front roadwheels.

2   Undo and remove the nuts securing the track rod end balljoints to the steering arms on the hub carriers. Extract the tapered ball-pins from the steering arms using a universal balljoint separator or by striking the ends of the steering arms with a few sharp hammer blows until the taper is released.

3   Undo and remove the four bolts securing the gearchange relay lever bracket to the rack housing and allow it to hang down without disconnecting the linkage (photo).

4   Undo and remove the locknut on the cotter pin that secures the steering column shaft to the rubberized coupling. Screw a nut onto the threads protruding from the other end of the cotter and tighten the nut to draw out the pin (photo).

5   Undo and remove the four bolts securing the rack housing to its mounting brackets. As the bolts are removed note the number and position of any shims that may be fitted between the rack housing and mounting brackets.

6   Undo and remove the three bolts and lift off the left-hand rack housing mounting bracket.

7   Now carefully slide the steering gear assembly to the left, through the wing valance aperture, taking care not to foul the speedometer cable. Pass the right-hand end of the rack over the anti-roll bar and towards the centre of the car to withdraw it.

8   Refitting the steering gear is the reverse sequence to removal, ensuring that any adjustment shims are refitted in the same place as noted during removal.

9   If the original steering gear is being refitted, and providing that the adjustment shims have been installed in their original locations, the steering rack height should be correct. It is advisable however to have the steering rack height checked and if necessary adjusted by your Talbot dealer as any variation from the original factory setting will affect the steering characteristics of the car.

10 If new or reconditioned steering gear is being fitted the above checks *must* be carried out as the existing shims will be incorrect for the new unit.

4.4 Steering column shaft retaining cotter pin

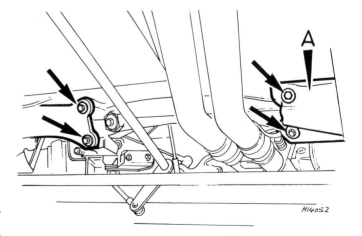

Fig. 8.2 Steering rack mounting bolts (arrowed) (Sec 4)

A   *Right-hand mounting bracket*

5   Steering gear – dismantling, inspection and reassembly

1   Remove the steering gear from the car as described in the previous Section and mount the unit in a vice with suitably protected jaws. Do not overtighten the vice.

2   Remove the spring clips and carefully pull back both rubber

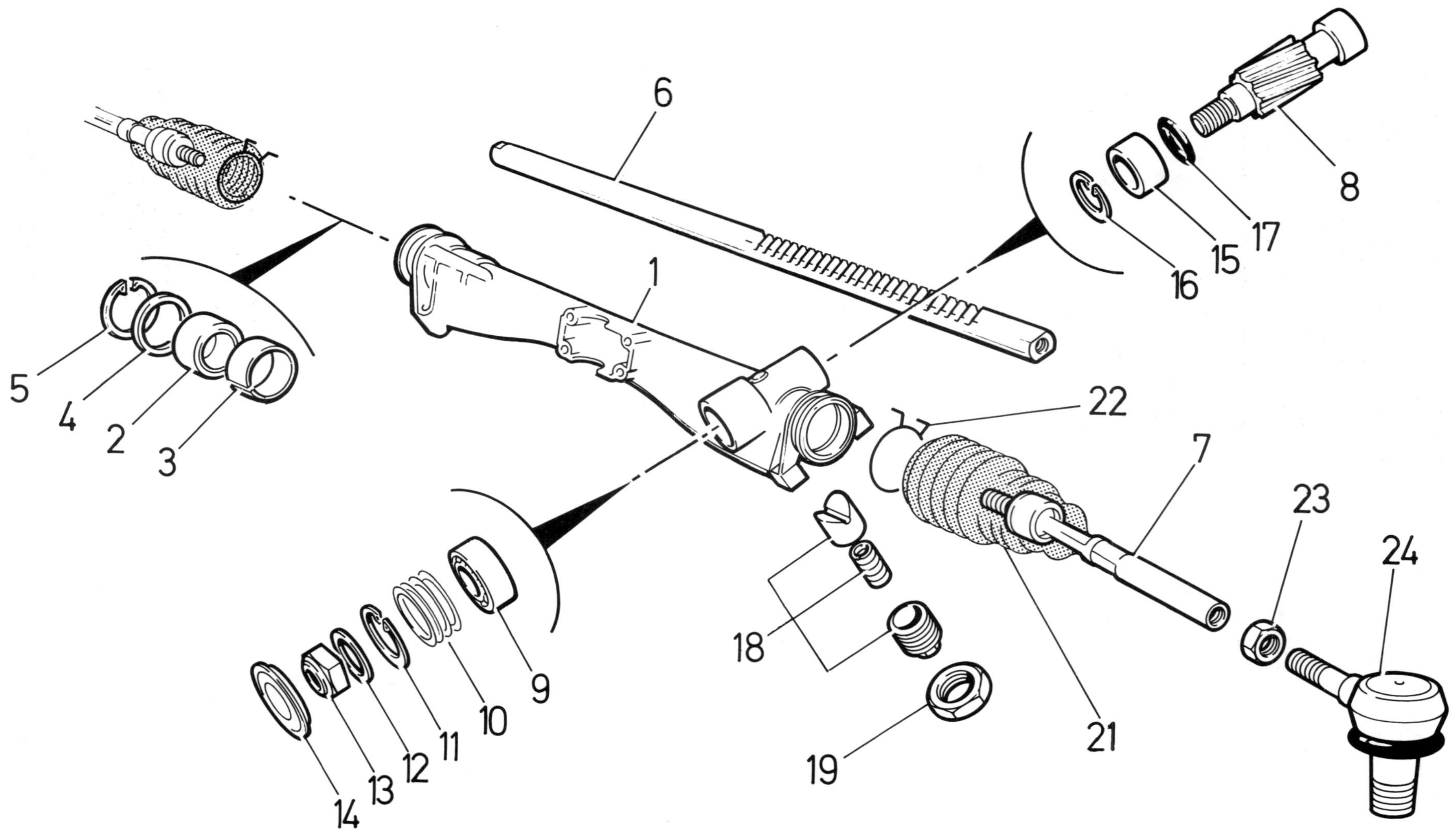

Fig. 8.3 Exploded view of the steering gear – LHD illustrated (Sec 5)

H14053

1 Rack housing
2 Rubber bush
3 Outer track
4 Washer
5 Circlip

6 Rack
7 Track rod
8 Pinion
9 Bearing
10 Shims

11 Circlip
12 Washer
13 Nut
14 Sealing cap
15 Bush

16 Circlip
17 Oil seal
18 Damper assembly
19 Locknut

21 Gaiter
22 Clip
23 Locknut
24 Balljoint

gaiters, sliding them down the track rods as far as possible.

3   Position the steering gear in approximately the straight-ahead position by turning the pinion from lock to lock, then stopping halfway.

4   Accurately measure and record the distance between the flange on the track rod inner balljoint and the edge of the rack housing nearest the pinion.

5   Without moving the rack, scribe a line on the pinion shaft and rack housing. This will enable the pinion to be refitted in the correct position relative to the rack.

6   Slacken the rack damper assembly locknut, undo and remove the

damper plug and lift out the spring and damper plunger.

7   Using a screwdriver or suitable drift, tap out the sealing cap from the rack housing at the base of the pinion assembly.

8   With the sealing cap removed, undo the locknut from the pinion shaft. Hold the pinion with a screwdriver inserted through the cotter pin hole to prevent it turning. With the nut undone, recover the washer.

9   Drive the pinion out of the housing, using a hammer and suitable soft metal drift of approximately 0.5 in (14 mm) diameter.

10   Undo and remove the track rod inner end balljoints from each end of the rack using two spanners, one to hold the rack and the other to

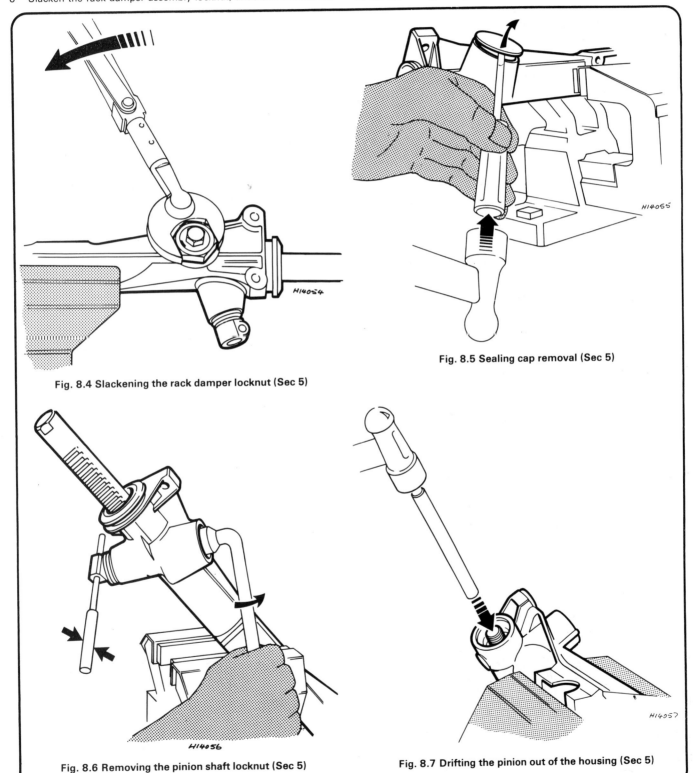

Fig. 8.4 Slackening the rack damper locknut (Sec 5)

Fig. 8.5 Sealing cap removal (Sec 5)

Fig. 8.6 Removing the pinion shaft locknut (Sec 5)

Fig. 8.7 Drifting the pinion out of the housing (Sec 5)

unscrew the balljoint. Note that the balljoints are peened onto the rack and once removed must not be re-used.

11 Carefully slide the rack out of the housing from the pinion end.
12 Extract the pinion bearing retaining circlip from the pinion housing, recover the shims and then drive out the bearing using a hammer and a suitable drift.

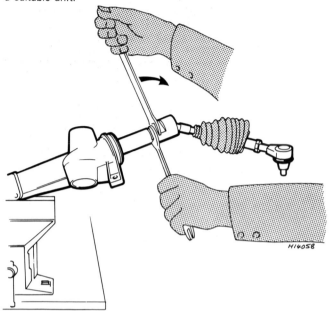

Fig. 8.8 Unscrewing the track rod inner end balljoints (Sec 5)

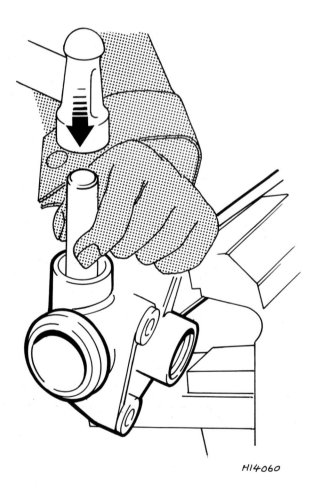

Fig. 8.10 Drifting out the pinion bearing (Sec 5)

13 At the other end of the pinion housing, extract the circlip using a screwdriver and drive out the anti-friction bush, again using a hammer and suitable drift. Hook out the O-ring seal from the pinion housing using a small screwdriver.
14 Finally extract the circlip and washer from the end of the rack housing furthest from the pinion. Withdraw the rubber bush and where fitted prise out the outer track (early models only).
15 Wash all the parts in paraffin and dry with a non-fluffy cloth.
16 Carefully examine the rack and the pinion teeth for chipping, scoring or wear ridges. Also check the rack for straightness by rolling it on a flat surface. Inspect the pinion bearing for slackness, roughness or signs of lack of lubrication, and the rubber gaiters for splits or deterioration. Renew any worn components. It is recommended that the pinion anti-friction bush and the rack housing rubber bush be renewed as a matter of course.
17 Having inspected thoroughly the steering gear components, consider whether it would be more economical to obtain a factory exchange unit rather than recondition the existing steering gear. This decision will depend largely on the cost and availability of the required new parts.
18 Before commencing reassembly measure out 2.75 oz (80 cc) of the recommended lubricant as shown in the Specifications at the

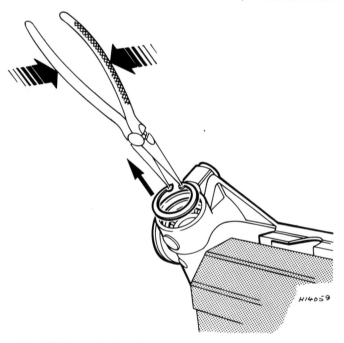

Fig. 8.9 Removing the pinion bearing retaining circlip (Sec 5)

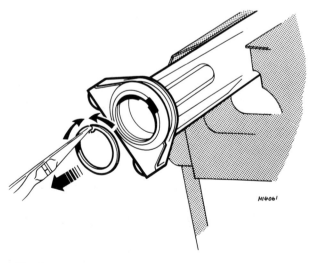

Fig. 8.11 Removing the rubber bush retaining circlip (Sec 5)

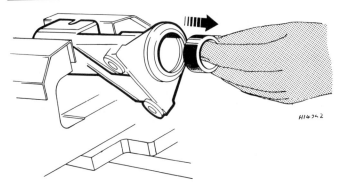

Fig. 8.12 Withdrawing the rubber bush (Sec 5)

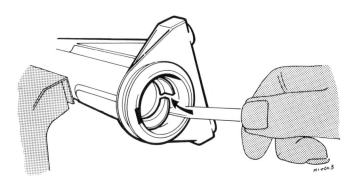

Fig. 8.13 Hooking out the bush outer track (Sec 5)

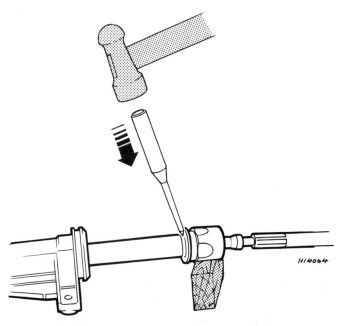

Fig. 8.14 Peening the inner balljoint to the rack (Sec 5)

beginning of this Chapter. During reassembly lubricate all parts from this measured volume and use the remainder to fill the rack on completion.

19 Refit the rack housing rubber bush outer track (where applicable), ensuring that the split of the bush is diametrically opposite the lubrication channel in the end of the housing.

20 Lubricate the rubber bush and insert it in the housing, followed by the washer and circlip.

21 Install the circlip that locates the pinion anti-friction bush into the pinion housing. Drive the anti-friction bush into the housing using a hammer and drift until the outer end of the bush is flush with the edge of the housing.

22 Lubricate a new pinion oil seal and position it over the anti-friction bush.

23 Position the pinion bearing in its recess and drift it fully home.

24 Fit adjustment shims above the pinion bearing until there are sufficient shims to prevent the retaining circlip from entering its groove. Remove shims by increments of 0.002 in (0.05 mm) until the circlip can just be fitted. The final fitted clearance between the circlip and the shims must be less than 0.004 in (0.1 mm).

25 Lubricate the rack and insert it into the housing from the pinion end to avoid the teeth damaging the rubber bush.

26 Position the rubber gaiters over the new track rods and then screw the inner balljoints onto the ends of the rack. Using two spanners as before, securely tighten the balljoints and then peen them onto the flats of the rack using a hammer and punch.

27 Position the rack so that the end nearest the pinion is protruding from the housing by the dimension noted during dismantling (paragraph 4).

28 Lubricate the pinion and with the rack held in the correct position, insert the pinion into the housing so that the scribe marks made previously (paragraph 5) are aligned.

29 Fit the washer followed by the locknut and then tighten the nut to the specified torque wrench setting.

30 Fill the pinion housing with lubricant and then carefully tap the sealing cap into place.

31 Inject the remainder of the lubricant from the measured volume into the damper housing and use the damper plunger to force it into the rack housing. Move the rack from side to side to distribute the lubricant.

32 Refit the damper plunger, spring and screwed plug and then adjust the assembly as described in Section 3.

33 Slide the rubber gaiters over the ends of the rack housing and secure with the spring clips.

34 The steering gear can now be refitted to the car as described in Section 4. Ensure that the steering gear and steering wheel are both set to their straight-ahead position before refitting.

35 If the steering gear has been completely dismantled or if an exchange unit is being fitted the front wheel alignment must be checked and if necessary reset as described in Section 11, after installing the steering gear in the car.

6 Steering wheel – removal and refitting

1 Prise up and remove the steering wheel central motif carefully, using a screwdriver (photo).

2 Using a socket and extension bar, undo and remove the steering wheel retaining nut (photo). Have an assistant hold the wheel as the nut is undone and make sure that the ignition key is in the switch and the steering lock is released. Excessive strain on the steering column lock could cause irreparable damage.

3 Now lift off the steering wheel, tapping it upwards with the palm of your hand if necessary.

4 To refit the wheel, ensure that the roadwheels are in the straight-ahead position and engage the steering wheel with the splines on the shaft. Ensure that the spoke of the wheel is facing downward.

5 Refit the retaining nut and tighten it to the specified torque wrench setting.

6 Refit the centre motif.

7 Steering column – removal and refitting

1 Disconnect the battery earth terminal.

2 If the steering column is to be dismantled after removal, refer to Section 6, and remove the steering wheel. If the column is being removed for access to other components, the steering wheel may be left in position.

3 Undo and remove the three securing screws and lift out the parcel shelf from beneath the steering column.

6.1 Prise up the steering wheel central motif ...

6.2 ... to provide access to the retaining nut

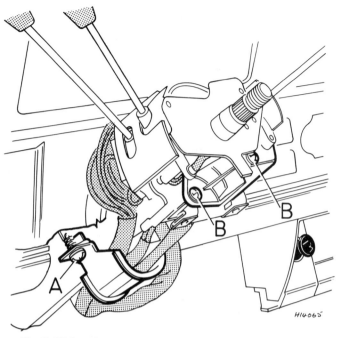

Fig. 8.15 Steering column multi-function switch and harness bracket (Sec 7)

A   Harness bracket retaining screw
B   Switch retaining screws

the cotter pin and tighten the nut to draw out the pin.
15 Release the large rubber grommet from the bulkhead and then withdraw the lower shaft assembly upwards into the car interior.
16 Refitting is the reverse sequence to removal, bearing in mind the following points:

(a) *Set the roadwheels and steering wheel (if in position) to the straight-ahead position before refitting the assembly*
(b) *Engage the steering shafts in their respective couplings, ensuring that the flats on the shafts are aligned with the cotter pin or pinch-bolt holes*
(c) *Refit and tighten the cotter pin or pinch-bolt before fully tightening the steering column mountings*
(d) *Adjust the position of the steering column cowls to avoid fouling the steering wheel*

8   Steering column – dismantling and reassembly

1   The main reason for dismantling the steering column is to renew the top bearing or bottom bush and to do this it is necessary to first remove the steering column assembly from the car as described in Section 7.
2   Mount the column assembly in a vice with protected jaws. Take care not to overtighten the vice.
3   Insert the ignition key into the switch and release the steering column lock. Make sure that the steering shaft is free to turn.
4   Using a hammer and suitable drift, drive out the steering shaft, complete with top bearing, from bottom to top.
5   At the base of the column, straighten the lugs that retain the bottom bush in place. Using a long tube of suitable diameter, drift the bush out of the column.
6   Remove the top bearing from the steering shaft using a universal puller, a press, or by a similar method.
7   With the column assembly dismantled, examine the parts for wear and renew as necessary. Check the straightness of the shaft by rolling it on a flat surface. If distortion is evident the shaft must be renewed.
8   Begin reassembly by positioning the top bearing on the shaft with the raised lip of the bearing towards the bottom. Drive the bearing onto the shaft until the top of the bearing is 3.68 in (93.5 mm) from the top of the shaft (Fig. 8.20).

4   Undo and remove the single screw securing the lower half of the steering column shroud and lift off the shroud.
5   Undo and remove the two securing screws and lift off the column upper shroud.
6   Undo and remove the securing screw and lift off the wiring harness retaining bracket.
7   Disconnect the steering column multi-function switch and ignition switch wires at their respective block connectors under the dash.
8   If the steering column is to be dismantled after removal, undo and remove the securing screws and lift off the multi-function switch. Otherwise leave the switch in position.
9   Undo and remove the locknut and tap out the pinch-bolt securing the upper column shaft to the universal joint.
10 Support the weight of the column and then undo and remove the four bolts securing the column assembly to the mounting bracket beneath the dash.
11 Withdraw the upper shaft from the universal joint by pulling rearwards and then remove the steering column assembly from the car.
12 If it is wished to remove the lower shaft assembly which will be left behind when the column is withdrawn, first jack up the front of the car and support it on stands.
13 From underneath the car undo and remove the locknut on the cotter pin that secures the lower shaft to the steering gear pinion.
14 Screw a suitable nut onto the exposed threads on the other end of

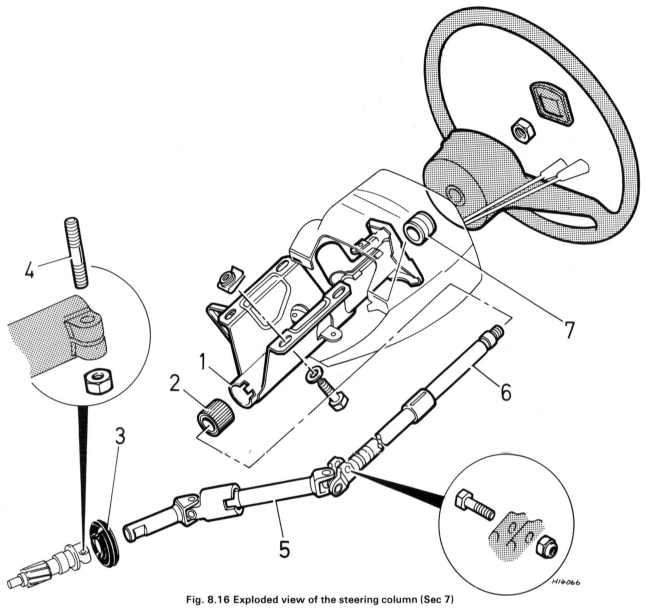

Fig. 8.16 Exploded view of the steering column (Sec 7)

1 Housing
2 Lower bearing
3 Grommet
4 Pinch-bolt

5 Lower shaft assembly
6 Upper shaft assembly
7 Upper bearing

9 Lubricate the bottom bush with molybdenum disulphide grease, insert it in the column and then bend the lugs inward slightly to retain it.
10 Lubricate the shaft and top bearing with molybdenum disulphide grease and insert the shaft into the column. Engage the shaft into the lower bush and the top bearing into the top of the column. Using a suitable tube in contact with the bearing outer track, tap the bearing and shaft into the column until the bearing contacts the ridge pressed in the column circumference.
11 Rotate the shaft to check for free movement and operate the steering lock, checking for positive engagement. If satisfactory refit the column assembly to the car as described in Section 7.

9 Track rod end balljoint – removal and refitting

1 Jack up the front of the car and support it on axle stands. Remove the appropriate front roadwheel.
2 Using a stiff wire brush, thoroughly clean off all dirt and grit from

the track rod end so that the threads are clearly visible.
3 Undo and remove the nut securing the balljoint to the steering arm. Extract the tapered ball-pin shank using a universal separator, or by striking the end of the steering arm with a few sharp hammer blows until the shock frees the taper.
4 Count and record the number of exposed threads between the end of the balljoint and the locknut that secures it to the track rod.
5 Slacken the locknut and then unscrew the balljoint from the track rod. Now remove the locknut.
6 Screw the locknut onto the new balljoint until it is in approximately the same position as it was on the old one.
7 Screw the balljoint onto the track rod until the locknut abuts the end of the rod. Hold the balljoint in the correct position and tighten the locknut.
8 Refit the ball-pin shank into the steering arm and refit the retaining nut, tightened to the specified torque wrench setting.
9 The method described will provide an approximate setting of the original front wheel alignment, but this setting should be accurately checked as described in Section 11, as soon as possible.

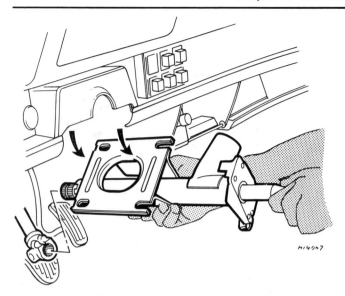

Fig. 8.17 Withdrawing the upper column (Sec 7)

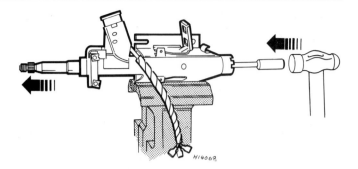

Fig. 8.18 Drifting out the shaft and top bearing (Sec 8)

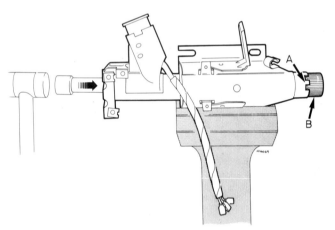

Fig. 8.19 Removing the bottom bush (Sec 8)

A   *Retaining lugs*
B   *Bottom bush*

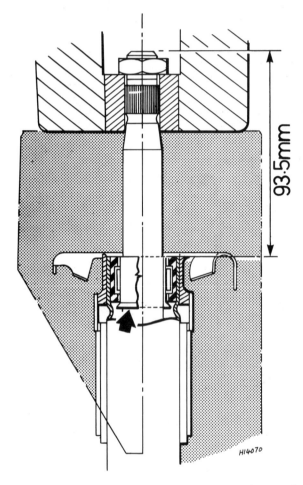

Fig. 8.20 Correct fitted position of the top bearing (arrowed) on the shaft. Dimension in mm (Sec 8)

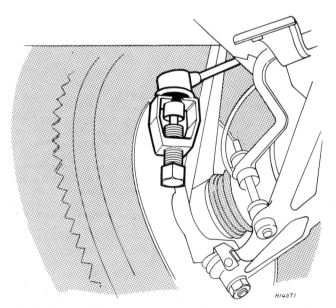

Fig. 8.21 Removing a track rod end balljoint using an extractor (Sec 9)

10 Steering geometry – general

1   Accurate front wheel alignment is essential for good steering and minimum tyre wear.
2   Wheel alignment embraces four factors:
   Camber which is the angle at which the front wheels are set from the vertical, when viewed from the front of the vehicle. Positive camber is the amount (in degrees) that the wheels are inclined outwards from the vertical at their tops.
   Castor is the angle between the steering axis and a vertical line when viewed from each side of the vehicle. Positive castor is when the steering axis is inclined rearwards at the top.
   Steering axis inclination is the angle, when viewed from the front of the vehicle, between the vertical and an imaginary line drawn between the upper and lower hub carrier swivel balljoints.

Toe-in is the amount by which the distance between the front inside edges of the roadwheels (measured at hub height) is less than the diametrically opposite distance measured between the rear inside edges of the roadwheels. A zero setting is specified for Horizon models, with an allowable tolerance, and this means that the wheels are parallel, ie the distance measured between the front inside edges of the roadwheels is the same as the distance measured at the rear inside edges.

3   Checking and adjustment of toe-in (also known as tracking, or front wheel alignment) is described in the next Section.

4   The other steering angles just described are either set during manufacture or in the case of the camber angle, this can be altered by varying the shims described in the preceding Chapter. Any variation of the camber angle should be left to your Talbot dealer who will have the necessary equipment for measuring these critical angles.

5   Two steering angles are shown in diagrammatic form in Fig. 8.22 and reference should be made to the Specifications Section of this Chapter for the precise angles (in degrees).

11 Front wheel alignment – checking and adjusting

1   As stated previously, the front wheel alignment is the difference between measurements taken between the front and rear inside edges of the front road wheels. On Horizon models there is an additional factor to be considered and this is the height and lateral position of the steering gear. If the position of the steering gear is incorrect, the front wheel alignment will alter as the suspension travels up and down, causing insensitive steering and excessive tyre wear.

2   Adjustment of the steering gear position should only be necessary if the unit has been removed from the car or if new or reconditioned steering gear has been fitted.

3   Although it is preferable to leave both these operations to your Talbot dealer, an approximate setting may be made which will be useful after renewal of any of the steering or suspension components and will at lease permit the car to be driven to the dealer's for a more accurate check to be made.

4   Obtain or make an alignment gauge. One may be easily made up from a length of tubing or bar, cranked to clear the engine/transmission unit and with a bolt and locknut at one end to permit adjustment of its overall length.

5   Position the car on level ground with the tyres correctly inflated and preferably with a full fuel tank. Set the front wheels to the straight-ahead position.

6   Drive the car forward so that the wheels make at least one complete revolution before making the following checks. Always drive the car forward when making subsequent checks, never push it backward or make a check immediately after jacking the car up as the wheels and suspension will not be in their correct driving attitude.

7   Using the gauge, measure the distance between the two inner wheel rims (at hub height) at the front of the roadwheels.

8   Now measure the distance between the two inner wheel rims, again at hub height, at the rear of the roadwheels.

9   The second measurement should be the same as the first measurement, ie the wheels are parallel to each other, plus or minus the tolerance given in the Specifications.

10   It is advisable to make three checks, driving the car forward each time, so that the wheels turn by approximately 120° between checks. Then take an average of the three.

11   If the alignment is incorrect, slacken the locknuts that secure both track rod end balljoints to the track rods. Turn both track rods by equal amounts, a fraction of a turn at a time, in the desired direction; clockwise (viewed from the centre of the car) to increase the toe-in, anti-clockwise to increase the toe-out.

12   Recheck the measurements and continue making adjustments as necessary until the alignment is correct. When satisfactory tighten the locknuts and ensure that the rubber gaiters on the end of the steering rack and track rods have not distorted as the track rods have been turned.

12 Wheels and tyres – general

1   The roadwheels fitted to Horizon models are either of pressed steel or alloy construction with four bolt fixing.

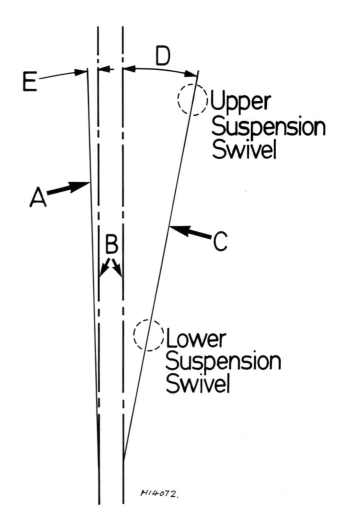

Fig. 8.22 Diagram of steering angles (Sec 10)

A   *Wheel camber*
B   *Vertical lines*
C   *Steering axis inclination*
D   *Angle of inclination*
E   *Positive camber angle*

2   According to model year, wheels having an offset of 1.4 in (36 mm) or 1.7 in (45 mm) may be fitted. It is most important that wheels of the same offset are always fitted to the car. In case of damage to a wheel, ensure that the replacement is of the same type.

3   From time to time check the security of the fixing bolts and check that the bolt head recess in the wheel has not become enlarged or elongated. Where this is the case, the roadwheel must be renewed.

4   To minimise tyre wear and prevent steering wobble and vibration, the tyres should be balanced periodically. Tyre wear can affect balance and the balance of new tyres can also alter after the tyre beds in and settles on the wheel. This usually takes approximately 100 miles.

5   Radial ply tyres should always be fitted, preferably all of the same make. Do not mix different types or makes of tyre on one axle. Also avoid mixing steel-braced and fabric-braced types.

6   It is acceptable to rotate the wheels to obtain maximum life from the tyres, but ensure that this is done front to rear only, never diagonally. This is to ensure that the direction of rotation of the tyres is kept constant.

7   Always keep a close check on tyre wear, noting that any deviation from an even tread wear pattern will indicate the need for rebalancing, or checking and adjusting of the front wheel alignment or steering geometry.

13 Fault diagnosis – steering, wheels and tyres

Before diagnosing faults from the following chart, check that any irregularities are not caused by:

1   *Binding brakes*
2   *Incorrect 'mix' of radial or crossply tyres*
3   *Incorrect tyre pressures*
4   *Misalignment of bodyframe*

Symptom	Reason(s)
Excessive free play at steering wheel	Loose steering shaft cotter pin or pinch-bolt
	Wear in lower steering shaft universal joint
	Incorrect steering rack damper adjustment
	Worn track rod inner or outer end balljoints
	See also Chapter 7
Steering stiff and heavy	Incorrect front tyre pressures
	Lack of steering gear lubricant
	Incorrect rack damper adjustment
	Incorrect front wheel alignment
	Bent or damaged steering rack or steering shaft
Car wanders and is affected by road undulations	Steering gear height or lateral position incorrect
	Wear in steering linkages or suspension components
	Incorrect front wheel alignment
Wheel wobble and vibration	Roadwheels and tyres out of balance
	Damaged or buckled wheel
	Faulty tyre
	Wear in steering linkages
	See also Chapter 7

Chapter 9 Rear suspension and hubs

Contents

Specifications

General
Rear suspension type .... Independent with trailing arms, coil springs, anti-roll bar and telescopic shock absorbers

Coil springs
Free length .... 13.58 in (345 mm)

Hub bearings
Lubricant type .... Multi-purpose medium grease

Torque wrench settings

	lbf ft	Nm
Shock absorber lower mountings	17	22.5
Shock absorber upper mountings	9	12.5
Anti-roll bar mountings	15	20
Suspension arm pivots at crossmember	48	65
Crossmember brackets to body	31	42.5
Roadwheel bolts	46	63
Rear hub nut	See text (Section 2)	

1 General description

The rear suspension on Horizon models is of the independent type utilizing two trailing suspension arms, coil springs and telescopic double-acting shock absorbers. An anti-roll bar is also fitted to minimise body roll when cornering.

The forward ends of each trailing arm pivot on rubber bushes attached to a tubular crossmember. The crossmember is in turn attached to the body underframe through rubber mountings.

The anti-roll bar is attached to a brake pressure reducing valve which alters the braking force available at the rear wheels according to the load being carried in the car.

Each rear suspension arm carries a stub axle which supports the rear hubs through tapered roller bearings.

Caution: *When jacking up the rear of the car, the jack must be positioned beneath the jacking points at the outer ends of the crossmember only. Do not use the crossmember, rear floor or suspension arms as jacking points. Support the raised car on axle stands positioned under the side channel sections and use suitable packing to spread the load.*

2 Rear hubs and bearings – removal, inspection and refitting

1 Jack up the rear of the car and support it on axle stands. Remove the appropriate rear roadwheel.
2 Undo and remove the retaining screws and lift off the brake drum. If difficulty is experienced removing the drum, refer to Chapter 10.
3 By judicious tapping and levering, withdraw the dust cap from the centre of the hub.
4 Raise the peening on the hub retaining nut using a hammer and

small chisel. Undo and remove the nut and thrust washer.
5 Carefully withdraw the hub assembly complete with bearings, ensuring that the inner race of the outer bearing does not drop out onto the floor.
6 To dismantle the hub assembly first lift out the inner race of the outer bearing (if it has not already fallen out).
7 Support the hub in a vice with the inner bearing facing upward.
8 Using a stout screwdriver, prise out the rear oil seal and then lift out the inner bearing inner race.
9 Remove the two outer races from the hub using a hammer and suitably sized pieces of tubing.
10 Thoroughly clean all the parts using petrol or paraffin and then dry with a non-fluffy cloth. Make sure all traces of the old grease are removed, especially from the centre of the hub.
11 Inspect the bearings for the slightest sign of pitting, scoring or wear ridges on the surface of the rollers and the outer races. Renew the bearings as necessary. The oil seal should always be renewed as it was probably damaged during removal.
12 Begin reassembly by removing any burrs from the hub that may have been caused during bearing removal. Use a small file or fine emery cloth for this.
13 Carefully press or drift the outer races into the hub, making sure they are kept absolutely square and level. If they tip slightly they will bind and it is very easy to crack them. If they don't go in squarely, tap them out and start again. The outer races must be installed with their larger diameter facing outward.
14 Spread a liberal amount of the specified grease into the centre of the hub between the bearings.
15 Lubricate the inner race of the inner bearing and position it in the hub.
16 Carefully tap a new oil seal into position with the lip of the seal toward the bearing.

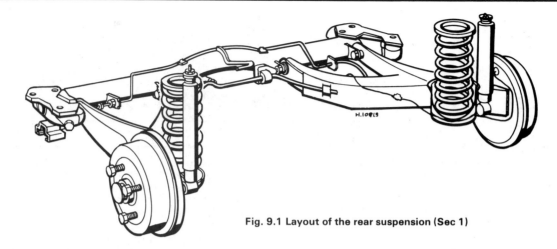

Fig. 9.1 Layout of the rear suspension (Sec 1)

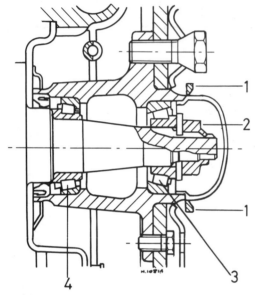

Fig. 9.2 Sectional view of the rear hub and bearings (Sec 2)

1 Dust cap	3 Outer bearing
2 Hub retaining nut	4 Inner bearing

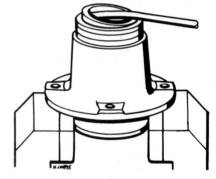

Fig. 9.3 Prising out the rear oil seal (Sec 2)

Fig. 9.4 Withdrawing the inner bearing inner race (Sec 2)

17 Lubricate the inner race of the outer bearing and position it in the hub also.

18 Slide the assembled hub onto the stub axle, followed by the washer and a new retaining nut. Do not tighten the nut at this stage.

19 Refit the brake drum and roadwheel, but with the hub cap of the roadwheel removed.

20 Tighten the hub nut, while rotating the wheel, to a torque wrench setting of 11 lbf ft (15 Nm).

21 Now turn the nut back by half a turn (three flats).

22 Tighten the nut by hand until there is just a trace of endfloat, felt by rocking the wheel.

23 Using a punch, peen the hub nut into the groove on the stub axle.

24 Place a quantity of the recommended lubricant in the hub dust cap and then tap it into place on the hub.

25 Refer to Chapter 10 and readjust the handbrake cable (if it was slackened to remove the drum) or reset the automatic brake adjuster by operating the footbrake.

26 Refit the roadwheel hub cap and lower the car to the ground.

---

3 Rear spring – removal and refitting

1 Jack up the rear of the car and support it on axle stands.

2 Take the weight of the rear suspension arm by placing a suitable jack beneath the spring pan.

3 Undo and remove the bolt securing the lower end of the shock absorber to the suspension arm.

4 Lower the jack slowly and carefully, pull the suspension arm down and then lift out the spring from its seats in the arm and underbody.

5 Refitting the spring is the reverse sequence to removal.

---

4 Rear shock absorbers – removal, testing and refitting

1 From inside the car remove the protective cap and undo the shock absorber upper retaining nut (photo). Retrieve the rubber bushes and spacers noting their sequence of assembly.

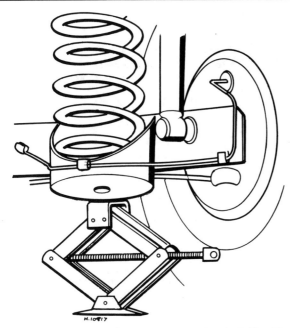

Fig. 9.5 Rear suspension arm supported on jack (Sec 3)

4.1 Rear shock absorber upper ...

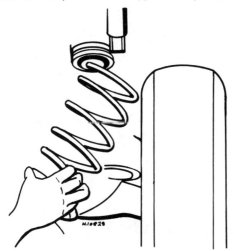

Fig. 9.6 Removing the rear spring (Sec 3)

4.2 ... and lower mountings

2   Undo and remove the lower shock absorber retaining bolt (photo), withdraw the unit from the car and retrieve the rubber bushes and spacers. **Note**: *Only remove the shock absorber mountings with the roadwheels on the ground or if jacked up, with the appropriate suspension arm well supported.* If this precaution is not taken the coil spring will be released, resulting in damage or personal injury.

3   Having removed the shock absorber from the car, the procedure for testing is described fully in Chapter 7 for the front shock absorbers.

4   Refitting is the reverse sequence to removal, ensuring that the rubber bushes and spacers are refitted as noted during removal.

5   Anti-roll bar – removal and refitting

1   Jack up the rear of the car and support it on axle stands.

2   Working underneath the car, secure the operating arm of the brake pressure reducing valve to the valve body using string or wire. This will prevent the rubber boot from being displaced when the operating spring is removed.

3   Disconnect the brake pressure reducing valve operating spring from the lever on the anti-roll bar.

4   Undo and remove the bolts securing the anti-roll bar links to the rear suspension arms (photo).

5   Detach the exhaust tailpipe rear support rubber rings.

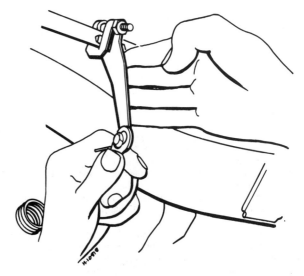

Fig. 9.7 Detaching the brake pressure reducing valve spring
(Sec 5)

5.4 Anti-roll bar-to-rear suspension arm links

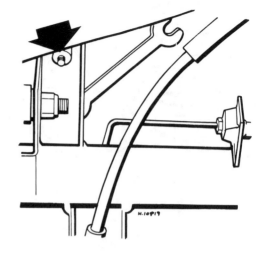

Fig. 9.8 Removing the anti-roll bar-to-crossmember retaining bolts (arrowed) (Sec 5)

6   Undo and remove the bolts securing the anti-roll bar brackets to the crossmember and withdraw the bar from under the car.
7   Refitting the anti-roll bar is the reverse sequence to removal, bearing in mind the following points:

(a)   *Ensure that the rubber boot is correctly positioned over the brake pressure reducing valve body*
(b)   *Check the setting of the valve as described in Chapter 10, after refitting*

6   Rear suspension arm – removal and refitting

1   Jack up the rear of the car and support it on axle stands. Remove the appropriate rear roadwheel.
2   Refer to Section 3, and remove the rear spring.
3   Undo and remove the securing screws and withdraw the rear brake drum. If difficulty is experienced removing the drum refer to Chapter 10.
4   With the brake drum removed, detach the handbrake cable from the operating arm on the rear brake shoe. To do this move the arm toward the hub with a screwdriver and lift the cable up with pliers.
5   Working underneath the car, detach the handbrake cable from the support clip on the underside of the suspension arm (photo). Now pull the cable out of its location in the brake backplate.
6   Using a brake hose clamp or a self-grip wrench with suitably protected jaws, clamp the flexible brake hose at a point midway along its length. This will prevent loss of hydraulic fluid when the hose is disconnected.
7   Undo and remove the metal brake pipe union where it joins the flexible hose on the suspension arm. Withdraw the clip and slide the hose out of the suspension arm bracket. Plug the pipe and hose ends.
8   Undo and remove the nuts from the suspension arm pivot bolts and anti-roll bar link retaining bolt.
9   Support the arm and remove the pivot bolts by tapping them out using a hammer and soft metal drift.
10   Withdraw the suspension arm from under the car.
11   If the rear suspension arm has been removed for the purpose of renewing the mounting bushes only, refer to paragraph 14. If the arm is to be renewed, further dismantling is necessary as follows.
12   Refer to Section 2, and remove the hub assembly.
13   Detach the brake pipe from its support clips on the arm, undo and remove the brake backplate retaining bolts and lift off the backplate complete with brake shoes and brake pipe.
14   The mounting bushes can be removed using a piece of metal tube of suitable length and diameter, a long bolt, nut, and packing washers. This method should prove suitable for drawing out the old bushes and also fitting new ones. However if difficulty is experienced due to corrosion an alternative method may be used for removal.
15   Carefully cut through the inner steel sleeve and rubber bush with

6.5 Rear suspension arm removal

A   *Handbrake cable support clip*
B   *Brake pipe union*
C   *Suspension arm pivot bolt*
D   *Anti-roll bar link mounting bolt*

a hacksaw blade and then collapse the outer sleeve and drive it out using a suitable drift. Take great care not to damage the actual suspension arm assembly.
16   Draw the new bushes into position using the extractor tool made up for removal, or drive them in using a tube and hammer.
17   Refitting the rear suspension arm is the reverse sequence to removal, bearing in mind the following points:

(a)   *Before tightening the suspension arm pivot bolts load the car with heavy friends, or suitable weights in the luggage compartment, until the distance from the rear crossmember bracket reinforcement plate to the ground is 8.1 in (207 mm). Tighten the pivots with the car in this position. If only one arm has been removed, slacken and then retighten the pivots on both arms*
(b)   *Bleed the rear hydraulic system on completion of reassembly as described in Chapter 10*
(c)   *If necessary adjust the handbrake cable as described in Chapter 10. Take up the automatic brake adjusters by operating the footbrake*

7 Rear suspension assembly – removal and refitting

1 Jack up the rear of the car and support it on axle stands.
2 Undo and remove the handbrake cable adjusting nut and lift off the cable and equaliser from the threaded rod.
3 Secure the operating arm of the brake pressure reducing valve to the valve body using string or wire. This will prevent the rubber boot from being displaced when the operating spring is removed.
4 Disconnect the brake pressure reducing valve operating spring from the lever on the anti-roll bar.
5 Undo and remove the bolts securing the anti-roll bar links to the suspension arms.
6 Refer to Section 3, and remove both rear springs.
7 Undo and remove the brake hydraulic fluid supply pipe from the union on the pressure reducing valve. Plug the pipe immediately to prevent loss of fluid and dirt ingress.
8 Disconnect the exhaust system mountings at the rear suspension crossmember, side member and rear body crossmember. Lower the system onto blocks, taking care not to place excessive strain on the flexible front joint.
9 Support the crossmember with a trolley jack at the centre.
10 Undo and remove the three bolts each side securing the crossmember support brackets to the body.
11 Lower the jack and complete rear suspension assembly and roll it out from under the car on its wheels.
12 Refitting the rear suspension assembly is the reverse sequence to removal, bearing in mind the following points:

(a) On completion of the installation, bleed the rear hydraulic system as described in Chapter 10
(b) Check the setting of the brake pressure reducing valve as described in Chapter 10
(c) Make sure that the rubber boot is correctly fitted to the reducing valve body

8 Rear suspension crossmember – removal and refitting

1 Begin by removing the complete rear suspension assembly from the car as described in the previous Section.
2 Undo and remove the metal brake pipes from their unions with the flexible hoses on the crossmember. Withdraw the clips and lift the ends of the hoses from their support brackets. Plug the ends of the pipes and hoses.
3 Release the brake pipes from their clips on the crossmember, undo and remove the securing bolts and lift off the brake pressure reducing valve complete with pipes.
4 Detach the handbrake outer cables from their brackets on the crossmember.
5 Undo and remove the rear suspension arm pivot bolt securing nuts and then tap out the bolts using a hammer and soft metal drift. Withdraw the arms from the crossmember.
6 Undo and remove the two nuts and bolts each side securing the crossmember to the support brackets and lift off the brackets.
7 Renewal of the crossmember bushes follows the same procedure as described in Section 6, for renewal of the suspension arm bushes. Note however that when fitted the bushes must protrude from the front of the boss on the bush housing by 0.60 in (15 mm).
8 Refitting the crossmember is the reverse sequence to removal, bearing in mind the following points:

(a) When refitting the suspension arms initially tighten the mounting pivot bolts finger tight only
(b) Refit the assembled rear suspension to the car as described in Section 7
(c) Adjust the handbrake as described in Chapter 10
(d) Tighten the pivot bolts as described in Section 6, paragraph 17

9 Rear wheel alignment

1 The suspension angles at the rear are all set during manufacture

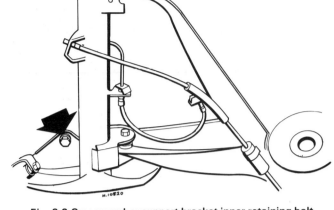

Fig. 9.9 Crossmember support bracket inner retaining bolt (arrowed) (Sec 7)

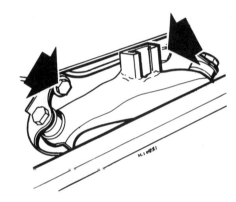

Fig. 9.10 Crossmember support bracket outer retaining bolts (arrowed) (Sec 7)

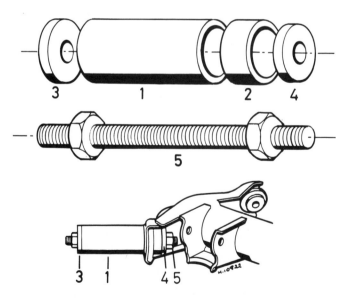

Fig. 9.11 Tool that can be made up for extracting the crossmember or suspension arm bushes (Sec 8)

1 Tube
2 Tube
3 Packing washer
4 Packing washer
5 Threaded rod

and no adjustment is possible.

2 Should the track or other angles be suspect and be reflected in abnormal wear to the rear tyres (and there is no distortion of the suspension components due to collision damage), the hub bearings and the suspension rubber bushes should be checked for wear and renewed if necessary.

10 Fault diagnosis – rear suspension and hubs

Symptom	Reason(s)
Knocking or clunking noises from rear over rough roads	Worn or damaged suspension arm or crossmember bushes Defective shock absorber Broken rear spring Loose or worn anti-roll bar bushes or links
Excessive rear end bouncing, pitching or rolling	Weak or defective shock absorbers Loose or worn anti-roll bar bushes or links Wear in suspension arm bushes
Wheel wobble and vibration	Roadwheels and tyres out of balance Bent or distorted roadwheel Defective tyre Excessively worn hub bearings
Excessive tyre wear	Incorrect tyre pressures Wear in suspension arm bushes Worn hub bearings Roadwheels and tyres out of balance Rear wheel alignment incorrect (accident damage)

Chapter 10 Braking system

For modifications, and information applicable to later models, see Supplement at end of manual

Contents

Specifications

General
System type .... Disc front, drum rear, dual hydraulic circuit, servo-assisted

TWO SIZES. TAKE SAMPLE

Front brakes
Type .... Disc with twin piston caliper *GIRLING* Pads *FERODO*
Manufacture .... Girling, DBA, or Teves *FDB269 ?*
Minimum thickness of brake pad and backing plate .... 0.28 in (7 mm)
Minimum thickness of disc after resurfacing .... 0.35 in (8.9 mm)
Maximum disc run-out .... 0.008 in (0.2 mm)

Rear brakes
Type .... Self-adjusting, single leading and trailing shoe drum
Manufacture .... Girling, DBA, or Teves *GIRLING FERODO FSB 47*
Minimum brake lining thickness .... 0.10 in (2.5 mm)
Nominal drum diameter .... 9 in (228.6 mm)
Maximum oversize after resurfacing .... 0.040 in (1.0 mm)

Master cylinder
Type .... Dual circuit with low fluid level warning actuator
Manufacture .... Automotive products, Teves, or DBA
Master cylinder bore diameter .... 0.81 in (20.6 mm)

Brake servo
Type .... Vacuum, 7 in (178 mm) diameter
Manufacture .... Girling, DBA, or Teves

Torque wrench settings

Front brakes	lbf ft	Nm
Brake disc-to-hub	35	47.5
Caliper mounting bolts	46	62.5
Hose and pipe unions	7	10
Bleed screw	5	6.5

Rear brakes		
Backplate-to-suspension arm	22	30
Wheel cylinder-to-backplate	7	10
Drum-to-hub	11	15
Bleed screw	4	6
Pipe-to-wheel cylinder	7	10

Controls

	lbf ft	Nm
Brake pipe unions at master cylinder and reducing valve	7	10
Reducing valve-to-crossmember	16	22
Servo unit-to-bulkhead	9	12.5
Master cylinder-to-servo unit	7	10
Handbrake lever-to-body	13	17.5
Handbrake adjuster locknut	7	10
Reducing valve adjusting screw locknut	7	10
Reducing valve lever-to-anti-roll bar	16	22

1   General description

The braking system is hydraulically operated with servo-assisted disc brakes on the front wheels and drum brakes on the rear. Both the front and rear brakes are of the self-adjusting type.

A cable-operated handbrake provides an independent mechanical means of rear brake application.

The master cylinder is of the dual circuit tandem type. The primary cylinder supplies the rear brakes and the secondary cylinder supplies the front brakes. Both circuits are independent of each other so that in the event of a hydraulic leak occurring in one circuit, the other circuit will remain fully operative although the brake pedal travel will increase.

A low fluid level indicator consisting of a float and spindle is incorporated in the master cylinder reservoir filler cap. Should the fluid level in the reservoir fall below a predetermined level, the float will close an electrical contact, causing a warning light on the instrument panel to be illuminated.

A brake pressure reducing valve is mounted on the rear suspension crossmember and is actuated by the position of the anti-roll bar under varying loads. The valve automatically varies the braking effort to the rear wheels according to the vehicle load. Adjustment of the valve is critical to ensure that the correct braking forces are applied under all loading and road surface conditions.

2   Disc brake pads – removal, inspection and refitting

1   Either Girling, DBA, or Teves brake calipers may be fitted. All three are identical in operation, but with slight differences in construction. The relevant procedures for removal of the brake pads are therefore described separately.

2   First jack up the front of the car and support it on axle stands. Undo the wheel retaining bolts and lift off the appropriate front roadwheel.

3   Disconnect the brake pad wear warning light wire at the spade connector (photo) and then release the retaining clip or tape.

Girling and DBA calipers

4   Withdraw the two small spring clips from the pad retaining pins, tap the pins out slightly using a thin punch and then remove them completely using a pair of pliers (photos).

5   Lift off the cruciform pad retaining plate and then withdraw the brake pads one at a time from the caliper (photo). If the pads are initially tight, use a screwdriver inserted in the pad retaining pin hole and lever against the edge of the caliper. Once they are free they can be drawn out the rest of the way with pliers.

6   With the pads removed lift out the anti-rattle shims, fitted to Girling calipers, if not already removed with the pads.

Teves calipers

7   Remove the steel deflector plate over the caliper aperture to gain access to the brake pads.

8   Using a thin punch and hammer, drive out the pad retaining pins toward the centre of the car.

9   Lift off the cruciform pad retaining plate and then withdraw the pads using a pair of pliers. If they are initially tight, use a screwdriver inserted in the retaining pin hole on the pad and lever against the edge of the caliper.

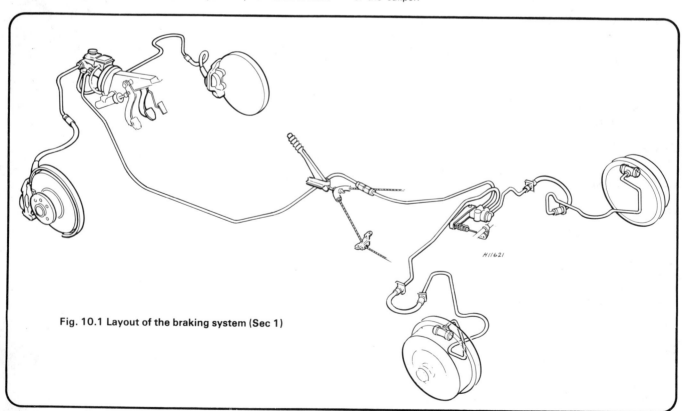

Fig. 10.1 Layout of the braking system (Sec 1)

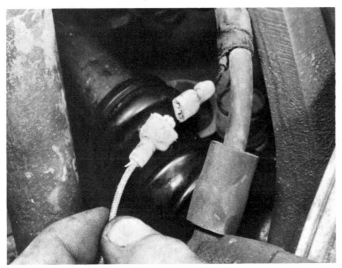
2.3 Disconnect the pad wear warning light lead

2.4a Extract the spring clips from the retaining pins ...

2.4b ... and withdraw the pins

2.5 Removing the brake pads

All calipers
10 With the brake pads removed inspect the thickness of the pad friction material. If it is less than 2 mm (0.07 in) the pads must be renewed. They must also be renewed if there is any sign of oil or hydraulic fluid contamination of the friction material, or if any heavy scoring or cracking is visible on the pad face.
11 When renewing brake pads they should always be renewed as a complete set (4 pads); uneven braking and pulling to one side may otherwise occur.
12 With the pads removed, carefully inspect the surface of the brake disc. Concentric scores up to 0.4 mm (0.015 in) are likely to be apparent and are acceptable. However if deeper scores are found, the brake disc must either be skimmed or preferably renewed.
13 Before refitting the pads, clean away all traces of dust, road grit and corrosion from the area of the caliper in which the pads locate. Carefully inspect the rubber dust seals around the caliper pistons for signs of splits, cracking or deterioration of the rubber. If this is the case it is advisable to renew the dust covers now before any permanent damage to the pistons and seals occurs. If there is evidence of hydraulic fluid leakage from the pistons they must be attended to immediately before refitting the pads. These operations are described in Section 4.
14 To enable the new pads to be fitted, if this is being done, the pistons must be moved back into their cylinders to accommodate the

new, thicker, pads. Using a flat bar as a lever, gently push the pistons into their cylinders as far as they will go. This operation will cause a quantity of hydraulic fluid to be returned to the master cylinder via the hydraulic pipes. Place absorbent rags around the master cylinder to collect any fluid that may overflow and remove the reservoir filler cap. Preferably, drain off a small quantity of fluid from the master cylinder reservoir before retracting the caliper pistons.
15 The pads can now be refitted according to caliper type as follows.

Girling caliper
16 Smear a small amount of the special grease, supplied with the new anti-rattle shims, on both sides of the shims and on the metal backing of the pads. Make sure that none of the grease comes into contact with the pad friction material.
17 Insert the pads followed by the anti-rattle shims. Note that the arrow on each shim must point downward (photo).
18 Line up the retaining pin holes on the pads and shims and insert the upper retaining pin. Place the cruciform spring in position, depress its centre and refit the lower retaining pin (photos).
19 Refit the small spring clips, reconnect the warning light wire and secure with the retaining clip.

Teves calipers
20 Before fitting the pads, check that the relieved portion of each

2.17 Insert the pads and anti-rattle shims with the arrow pointing downward

2.18a Refit the upper retaining pin and cruciform spring ...

2.18b ... followed by the lower pin and warning light lead retaining clip

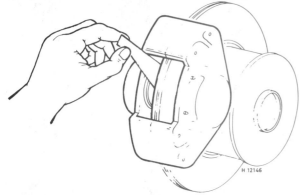

Fig. 10.2 Checking the piston positions on the Teves caliper (Sec 2)

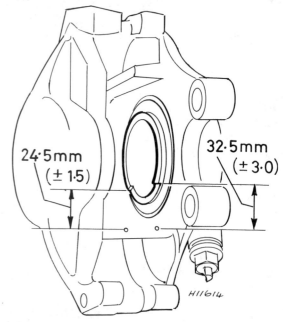

Fig. 10.3 Correct piston positioning on the DBA caliper (Sec 2)

caliper piston adopts an angle of 20° to the horizontal. Fig. 10.2 shows a special tool for checking this angle which can be easily made from a piece of tin or thin metal. If necessary, rotate the piston slightly using a screwdriver.

21 Insert the new pads and refit the upper retaining pin. Place the cruciform spring in position, depress its centre and refit the lower retaining pin.

22 Reconnect and secure the pad wear warning light wire. Refit the steel deflector plate.

DBA caliper

23 Check the position of the caliper pistons against the dimension shown in Fig.10.3, and rotate the pistons slightly if necessary using a screwdriver.

24 Insert the pads and refit the retaining pins and spring clips. Connect and secure the pad wear warning light wires.

All models

25 Depress the brake pedal several times to bring the pads into contact with the disc, refit the roadwheel and lower the car. Check and if necessary top up the fluid in the master cylinder reservoir.

---

3 Front disc brake caliper – removal and refitting

1 Jack up the front of the car and support it on stands. Remove the appropriate front roadwheel.

2 Remove the front brake pads as described in the previous Section and store them in a safe place, face up, to avoid contamination of the friction material.

3 Undo and remove the metal brake pipe at its union with the front flexible hose. To avoid excessive loss of hydraulic fluid as the pipe is undone, either plug its end as soon as it is removed, or preferably fit a dummy master cylinder filler cap, on which the air vent hole has been blocked, in place on the reservoir. This will create an air lock in the system and reduce fluid loss when the pipe is disconnected.

4 Having detached the metal pipe from the hose, plug the end of the

hose to prevent dirt ingress and then withdraw the metal spring clip securing the hose to its mounting bracket.

5 Undo and remove the two bolts securing the caliper to the hub carrier and lift off the caliper, complete with hose.

6 Refitting is the reverse sequence to removal, bearing in mind the following points:

(a) Tighten the caliper retaining bolts to the torque wrench settings shown in the Specifications

(b) When installed, ensure that the brake hose is not twisted or deformed. There is a paint stripe along its length as a guide for checking this

(c) Bleed the front hydraulic circuit after refitting the caliper as described in Section 14

---

4 Front disc brake caliper – dismantling, inspection and re-assembly

1 With the caliper removed from the car as described in the previous Section, begin dismantling by hooking out the piston dust cover retaining rings with a small screwdriver. The rubber dust covers can then be removed.

2 Unscrew the brake hose from the caliper and then using compressed air or the nozzle of a tyre foot pump held firmly against the brake hose union, eject the pistons from the caliper. Once the pistons have been eased part way out they can be removed the rest of the way using the fingers.

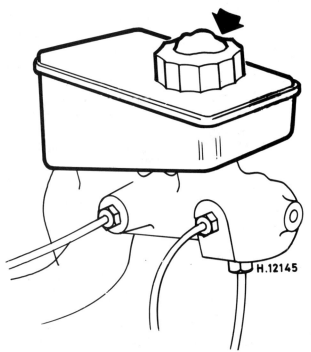

Fig. 10.4 Dummy reservoir filler cap (arrowed) with blocked air vent hole in position (Sec 3)

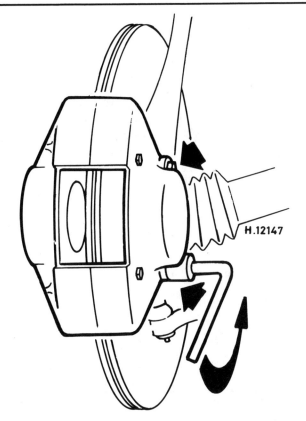

Fig. 10.5 Removing the caliper retaining bolts (Sec 3)

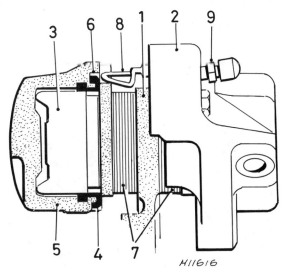

Fig. 10.6 Details of front brake caliper (Sec 4)

1	Disc	6	Dust cover clip
2	Caliper	7	Brake pad
3	Piston	8	Cruciform spring
4	Seal	9	Bleed screw
5	Dust covers		

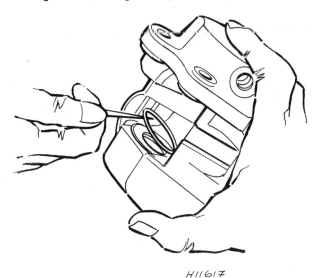

Fig. 10.7 Removing the piston dust cover retaining rings (Sec 4)

3   Release the two piston seals from their grooves in the cylinders using a thin blunt instrument such as a plastic knitting needle.

4   Thoroughly clean the caliper and pistons using clean hydraulic fluid or methylated spirit. Under no circumstances should the two halves of the caliper be separated.

5   Inspect the dismantled components carefully for corrosion, scratches or wear. New seals are available in the form of a repair kit and should be renewed as a matter of course. The pistons are also renewable and should be if they are at all scratched or corroded. If however the cylinders are in any way damaged or if hydraulic fluid has been seen leaking from the joint face between the two caliper halves, a new caliper must be obtained.

6   Begin reassembly by immersing the new piston seals in clean hydraulic fluid, and then carefully fit them to the annular grooves in the cylinders using the fingers only.

7   Liberally coat the pistons with clean hydraulic fluid and then insert each piston by hand squarely into its cylinder bore. Rotate the pistons during insertion to help engagement of the seal. Push the pistons fully down into their cylinders.

8   If working on the Teves brake caliper, finally position the piston so that its relieved edge adopts an angle of 20° to the horizontal. A tool can be made from a piece of tin or thin metal to set the piston edge angle accurately.

9   If working on the DBA caliper, position the piston as shown in Fig. 10.3.

10 With the pistons installed, slide the new dust covers into position

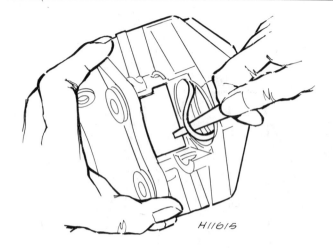

Fig. 10.8 Hooking out the piston seals from the cylinders (Sec 4)

over each piston.
11 Refit the brake hose and then refit the caliper to the car as described in Section 3.

5 Front brake disc – removal and refitting

To enable a front disc to be removed it is first necessary to remove the hub carrier assembly from the car and then remove the hub. As the hub is removed the inner and outer tracks of the double row hub bearing will separate causing damage to the integral oil seal. The bearing cannot then be satisfactorily refitted. Therefore if the disc is to be removed it will be necessary to obtain a new hub bearing before refitting. Full information on the above procedures will be found in Chapter 7, Section 6.

6 Rear brake shoes (Girling) – removal, inspection and refitting

1 Jack up the rear of the car and securely support it on axle stands. Remove the appropriate rear roadwheel.
2 Release the handbrake, undo and remove the securing screws and lift off the brake drum. If the drum is tight, remove the small plastic cover from the rear of the backplate and insert a screwdriver through the aperture. Push outward on the handbrake actuating lever with the screwdriver until a click is heard as the lever stop disengages. With the self-adjusting mechanism now released, the brake shoes will move inwards slightly enabling the drum to be withdrawn.
3 Before dismantling the brake shoes, observe the components in their assembled condition. Make a note of the position of the brake shoe return springs and handbrake linkage, noting also which way round the various parts are fitted. Check for any hydraulic fluid leaks from the wheel cylinder or oil leaks from the hub bearing seals. Have an assistant slowly depress the brake pedal, and observe the action of the wheel cylinder pistons. See that they are both free to operate and that they return under the action of the brake shoe return springs, when the pedal is released. Check also that the self-adjusting mechanism operates when the pedal is depressed. The condition of the brake shoe friction linings and drum can also be inspected at this time. If the friction linings are less than 0.10 in (2.5 mm) thick at their thinnest point, where bonded linings are fitted, or less than 0.06 in (1.5 mm) above the rivet heads, where riveted linings are used, or if there is any sign of oil or grease contamination, they must be renewed. Always renew brake shoes in complete sets (four shoes) even if only one shoe is worn; uneven braking and imbalance may otherwise occur.
4 To remove the brake shoes first disengage and remove the adjuster lever return spring and then slide the adjuster lever off its pivot pin on the leading (front) brake shoe.
5 Rotate the serrated adjuster nut in the appropriate direction to reduce the adjuster pushrod to its minimum length. **Note:** *On the left side of the car the adjuster nut has a left-hand thread and on the right*

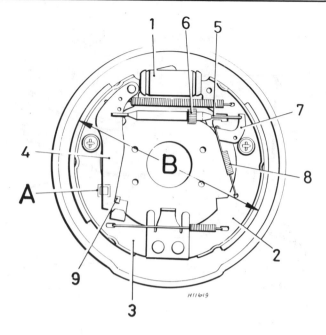

Fig. 10.9 Girling rear brake assembly (Sec 6)

1 Wheel cylinder
2 Leading (primary) shoe
3 Trailing (secondary) shoe
4 Handbrake lever
5 Adjuster pushrod
6 Serrated nut
7 Adjuster lever

8 Spring, adjuster lever
9 Stop, handbrake lever
A Aperture, adjuster release
B Overall diameter of shoes prior to fitting drum – 227 to 227.9 mm $(8\frac{5}{16}$ to $8\frac{31}{32}$ in)

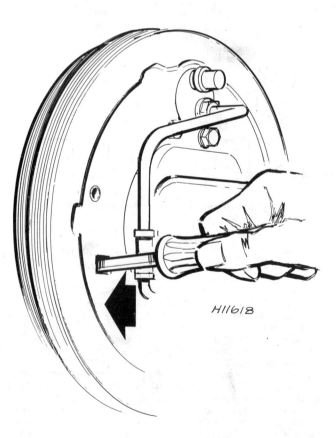

Fig. 10.10 Releasing the automatic brake adjuster (Sec 6)

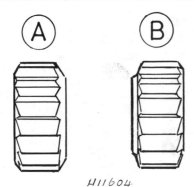

Fig. 10.11 Identification of brake adjuster serrated nuts (Sec 6)

A   Right-hand side
B · Left-hand side

side it has a right-hand thread.

6   Push the handbrake operating lever forward using a screwdriver as a lever and disengage the nipple of the handbrake cable.

7   Using a pair of pliers, depress the cups over the brake shoe steady springs while holding the steady pins from the rear of the backplate with your fingers. Rotate the cups through 90° and lift off. Recover the springs and steady pins.

8   Lift the trailing (rear) shoe off its lower pivot post, move it toward the leading shoe slightly and detach the lower pull-off spring.

9   Lift the leading shoe off its lower pivot post and carefully ease its upper end out of the wheel cylinder, taking care not to damage the rubber boot.

10 Now lift the trailing shoe out of its wheel cylinder location and withdraw both shoes, upper spring and adjuster as a complete assembly from the backplate.

11 Using pliers disengage the upper spring from the leading shoe and separate the two shoes and adjuster.

12 Remove the spring clip from the pivot pin on the trailing shoe and withdraw the handbrake actuating lever.

13 Place a strong rubber band around the wheel cylinder to prevent the pistons being pushed out and subsequent loss of hydraulic fluid. Do not press the brake pedal whilst the shoes are removed.

14 Thoroughly clean all traces of dust from the brake shoes, backplate, and drum, using a cloth and stiff brush. Brake dust is the prime cause of judder and squeal, and therefore it is important to clean away all traces. *Ensure that the working area is well ventilated during this operation as asbestos dust is harmful and should not be inhaled.*

15 Check the operation of the serrated nut on the shoe adjuster mechanism and ensure tht it is free to turn on the full length of thread. Lubricate the mechanism with brake grease.

16 Check the brake backplate and wheel cylinder for security and if necessary tighten the retaining bolts. If any hydraulic fluid or oil leaks are apparent, or if any defects were noticed during initial inspection, they should now be rectified before refitting the brake shoes.

17 To refit the brake shoes first screw the serrated nut of the adjuster mechanism as far as possible onto the threaded rod. Note that the serrated nut fitted to the right-hand side adjuster has a chamfer on its face while the left-hand side serrated nut is identified by a boss on its face.

18 Refit the handbrake actuating lever and pivot pin to the trailing shoe and secure with the spring clip. Engage the forked ends of the adjuster mechanism with the handbrake actuating lever and with the slot on the leading shoe, and then refit the upper brake shoe return spring.

19 Lubricate the tips of the brake shoes and the shoe contact points on the backplate with brake grease, taking care not to allow any grease to come into contact with the friction material.

20 Remove the rubber band from the wheel cylinder and slide the partially assembled brake shoe components into position on the backplate.

21 Place one brake shoe tip on its wheel cylinder piston and then ease the tip of the other shoe into engagement with the remaining piston.

22 Position the lower return spring in its slots in the two brake shoes and then engage the lower tips of the shoes with the lower pivot post.

23 Push the handbrake actuating lever forward and engage the nipple of the handbrake cable. Release the lever and ensure that its stop rests against the edge of the trailing brake shoe. In this position the handbrake cable should be just taut without pulling the lever from its stop. If necessary slacken the cable adjuster.

24 Refit the adjuster lever to its pivot pin, locating it between the brake shoe and the adjuster pushrod. Engage the return spring with the adjuster lever and brake shoe.

25 Refit the steady springs, cups and pins to both brake shoes.

26 Turn the serrated nut on the adjuster mechanism to expand the brake shoes until it is just possible to slide on the brake drum without binding. It may be necessary to move the shoes up or down very slightly to centralise them and enable the drum to be fitted.

27 Having done this, remove the drum again, hold the adjuster lever away from the serrated nut and then rotate the nut inwards two full turns to increase the clearance between the brake drum and shoes.

28 Refit the brake drum and securing screws and then the roadwheel. Start the engine and depress the footbrake hard, thirty times, to operate the automatic adjuster. It should be possible to hear a definite clicking from the brake drum which will indicate that the mechanism is working correctly.

29 Having completed these operations, check and if necessary adjust the handbrake as described in Section 18, and then lower the car to the ground. If new shoes have been fitted, repeat the operations on the opposite rear wheel.

7   Rear brake shoes (DBA) – removal, inspection and refitting

1   Jack up the rear of the car and securely support it on axle stands. Remove the appropriate rear roadwheel.

2   Release the handbrake, undo and remove the securing screws and lift off the brake drum (photos). If the drum is tight, insert a small screwdriver into the hole in the rear of the brake backplate. Press the pawl of the automatic adjuster downward, against spring pressure, to release the adjuster lever. With the mechanism released the brake shoes will move inwards slightly enabling the drum to be withdrawn.

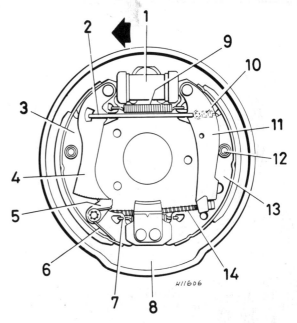

Fig. 10.12 DBA rear brake assembly (Sec 7)

1 Wheel cylinder	9 Upper shoe return spring
2 Link rod	10 Spring link rod and
3 Primary (leading) shoe	handbrake lever
4 Adjuster lever	11 Handbrake lever
5 Adjuster pawl	12 Shoe steady spring
6 Adjuster pawl return spring	13 Secondary (trailing) shoe
7 Lower shoe return spring	14 Handbrake cable
8 Backplate	

7.2a Removing the brake drum securing screw ...

7.2b ... and the drum

7.4 Disconnect the upper return spring (arrowed) from both brake shoes, ...

7.5 ... detach the handbrake cable nipple (arrowed) from the lever, ...

7.6 ... release the lower spring (arrowed) from each shoe ...

7.7 ... and, finally, remove the steady springs and lift off the shoes

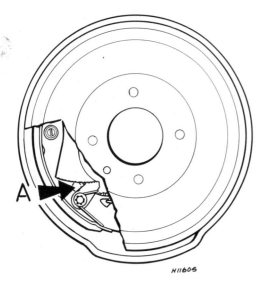

Fig. 10.13 Aperture in backplate (A), for releasing adjusting mechanism (Sec 7)

Fig. 10.14 Removing the retaining clip and adjuster lever (Sec 7)

3   Before removing or dismantling the brake shoe assemblies, refer to paragraph 3 of Section 6.

4   Using a pair of pliers or a screwdriver, disconnect the upper brake shoe return spring from both shoes and lift off the spring (photo).

5   Move the handbrake actuating lever forward and detach the nipple of the handbrake cable (photo).

6   Using a screwdriver, prise the ends of the lower return spring from their locations in the two brake shoes (photo).

7   Depress the centre of the brake shoe steady springs, using a thin screwdriver or similar tool, and then turn the springs to unhook them from the backplate (photo).

8   Move the brake shoe adjusting lever inwards, lift up both shoes

from the bottom and withdraw them, complete with levers and link rod, from the backplate.

9   Place a strong rubber band around the wheel cylinder to prevent the pistons being pushed out and subsequent loss of hydraulic fluid. Do not depress the brake pedal whilst the shoes are removed.

10   To dismantle the brake shoes completely, first extract the retaining clip and washer and then lift off the adjuster lever from the leading shoe. Prise off the adjuster pawl retainer and remove the return spring and pawl.

11   On the trailing shoe, unhook the retaining spring using a screwdriver, and lift away the link rod. Extract the retaining clip and take off the handbrake actuating lever.

12   Thoroughly clean all traces of dust from the brake shoes, backplate, and drum, using a cloth and stiff brush. Brake dust is the prime cause of judder and squeal and therefore it is important to clean away all traces. *Ensure that the working area is well ventilated during*

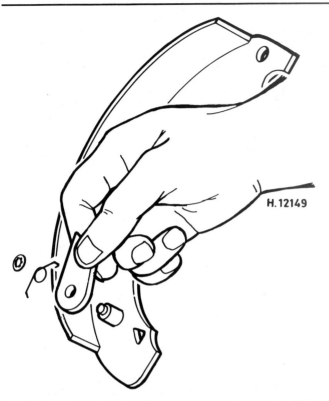

Fig. 10.15 Removing the adjuster pawl and return spring (Sec 7)

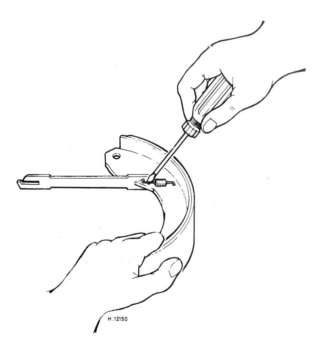

Fig. 10.16 Disengaging the retaining spring from the link rod (Sec 7)

15 Place the pawl and spring in position on the leading (front) shoe and then fit a new retainer to the pivot pin, pushing it on with a piece of tube of suitable diameter.

16 Refit the adjuster lever and pivot pin and secure with the spring clip.

17 Refit the handbrake actuating lever and secure its pivot pin with the spring clip.

18 Hook the link rod retaining spring into the trailing shoe, and then engage the link rod with the other end of the spring. Ease the link rod into its location in the trailing shoe.

19 To refit the brake shoes, first place the trialing shoe complete with handbrake lever and link rod in position on the backplate and retain it by refitting the steady spring. Engage the nipple on the handbrake cable with the actuating lever on the trailing shoe.

20 Position the leading shoe on the backplate, engage the link rod end with the slot in the adjuster lever and then secure the shoe with the steady spring.

21 Remove the rubber band around the wheel cylinder.

22 Engage one end of the lower return spring with its slot in either shoe and then with the aid of a screwdriver, lever the other end into position.

23 Engage the inner hooked end of the upper retaining spring with its slot in either shoe and then using a loop of cord or wire pull the outer hooked end into engagement with the slot in the other shoe.

24 With the brake shoes in position, move the adjuster lever on the leading shoe outward (minimum adjustment position), engage the first few teeth with the pawl and ensure that the pawl return spring is holding the pawl in contact with the lever.

25 Refit the brake drum and roadwheel and depress the brake pedal fully ten times to operate the adjuster.

26 Check and if necessary adjust the handbrake cable as described in Section 18, and then lower the car to the ground.

8 Rear brake shoes (Teves) – removal, inspection and refitting

1 Jack up the rear of the car and securely support it on axle stands. Remove the appropriate rear roadwheel.

2 Release the handbrake, undo and remove the securing screws and lift off the brake drum. If the drum is tight, remove the small plastic cover from the rear of the backplate. Insert a thin screwdriver through one of the wheel bolt holes in the drum and hub, and push the adjuster lever toward the backplate to disengage the adjuster pawl. At the same time insert a second screwdriver through the hole in the backplate and rotate the serrated adjuster nut by pushing downward on the side of the nut nearest the backplate. Rotate the nut until the brake shoes are at their minimum adjustment position and then withdraw the brake drum.

3 With the drum removed, refer to paragraph 3 of Section 6, before

this operation as asbestos dust is harmful and should not be inhaled.
13 Carry out a careful inspection of the dismantled components and renew any that are worn or defective. Check the brake backplate and wheel cylinder for security and if necessary tighten the retaining bolts. Any oil, grease or hydraulic fluid leaks or any other faults noticed during initial inspection must be rectified now before refitting the brake shoes.

14 Lubricate the brake shoe ends, the adjusting mechanism, the lever pivot pins and the contact areas on the brake backplate with brake grease and then reassemble the shoes as follows.

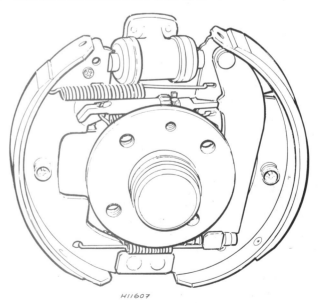

Fig. 10.17 Teves rear brake assembly (Sec 8)

removing or dismantling any of the brake shoe components.

4   To remove the brake shoes first make sure that the adjuster mechanism is in its minimum position. Push the adjuster lever pawl towards the backplate and rotate the serrated nut to reduce the adjuster pushrod to its minimum length. *Note that the adjuster pushrods fitted to the right and left sides of the car have right-hand and left-hand threads, respectively, and are not interchangeable.*

5   To remove the brake shoes, first move the handbrake actuating lever forward and disengage the nipple of the handbrake cable.

6   Using pliers depress and turn through 90° the brake shoe steady spring cup on the leading shoe, while holding the steady pin from behind the backplate. Lift off the cup, spring, and pin, and then repeat this operation on the trailing shoe.

7   Lever the trailing shoe off the lower pivot post and remove the lower brake shoe return spring.

8   Ease the leading shoe off the lower pivot post and lever the top of the shoe out of its location in the wheel cylinder piston. Lift both brake shoes, the adjuster mechanism and upper springs, as a complete assembly, off the backplate.

9   Using pliers, disengage the upper brake shoe return spring and the adjuster pushrod return spring, then lift away the trailing shoe and handbrake actuating lever.

10   Pivot the adjuster mechanism on the leading shoe upwards and disengage the adjuster pushrod.

11   Place a strong rubber band around the wheel cylinder to retain the pistons and prevent loss of hydraulic fluid. Do not press the brake pedal whilst the shoes are removed.

12   Before refitting the brake shoes carry out the inspection and cleaning operations described in Section 6, paragraphs 14 to 16 inclusive.

13   Begin refitting by screwing the serrated nut as far as possible onto the adjuster pushrod and then reassemble the pushrod to the adjuster lever.

14   Engage the trailing shoe with the adjuster pushrod ensuring that the longer fork of the pushrod goes behind the shoe, ie towards the backplate. Move the two shoes together at the bottom and refit the pushrod return spring.

15   Move the two shoes apart at the bottom, against spring tension, and refit the upper brake shoe return spring.

16   Position the brake shoe assembly on the backplate and engage the top of one of the shoes with the wheel cylinder piston. Lever the other shoe outward and engage its top with the other piston.

17   Move the bottom of the two shoes together, refit the lower return spring and then lever the shoes onto the lower pivot post. Remove the rubber band from the wheel cylinder.

18   Refit the two brake shoe steady pins, springs and cups and then reconnect the handbrake cable nipple to the actuating lever. Position the lever so that its stop rests against the edge of the trailing shoe. In this position the cable should be just taut without pulling the lever off its stop. If necessary slacken the handbrake cable adjuster.

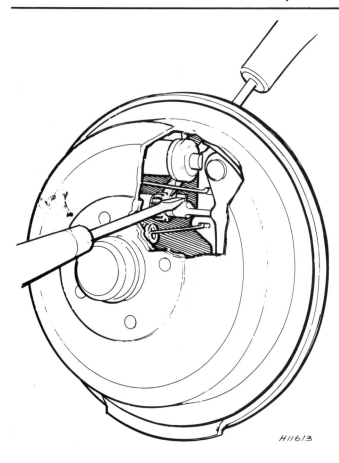

H11613

Fig. 10.18 Releasing the adjuster pawl and rotating the serrated nut (Sec 8)

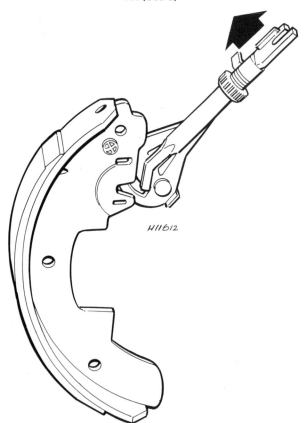

H11612

Fig. 10.19 Disengaging the adjuster pushrod (Sec 8)

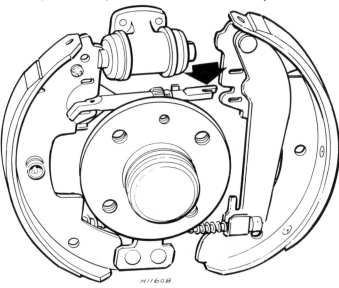

H11608

Fig. 10.20 Positioning longer end of adjuster pushrod (arrowed) behind trailing shoe (Sec 8)

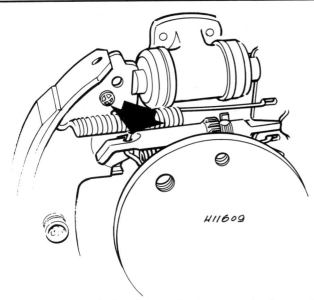

Fig. 10.21 Correct fitting of the pushrod return spring (arrowed) (Sec 8)

19 Refit the brake drum and carry out the initial brake shoe adjustment as described in Section 6, paragraphs 26 to 29 inclusive.

9 Rear brake wheel cylinder – removal, overhaul and refitting

1   Wheel cylinders of either Girling, DBA, or Teves manufacture may be fitted to Horizon models. The cylinders are all similar in design and construction but are not interchangeable. If a wheel cylinder is to be renewed, take the old one along to your Talbot dealer to ensure that the replacement is of the correct type. The removal, overhaul and refitting procedures are virtually identical for all three units and providing reference is made to the appropriate illustration, no difficulties should arise.
2   Begin by jacking up the rear of the car and securely supporting it on axle stands. Remove the appropriate rear roadwheel.
3   Undo and remove the securing screws and withdraw the brake

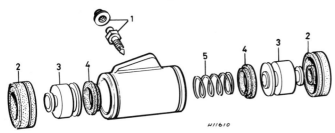

Fig. 10.22 Exploded view of the Girling wheel cylinder (Sec 9)

1 Bleed screw and cap   4 Seals
2 Dust covers   5 Spring
3 Pistons

Fig. 10.23 The DBA wheel cylinder components (Sec 9)

A Support cups under rubber seals

drum. If the drum is tight it will be necessary to release the brake self-adjusting mechanism to remove it, and this information will be found at the beginning of Section 6, 7, or 8, depending on type fitted.
4   Working underneath the car, compress the flexible rear brake hose using a brake hose clamp or a self-grip wrench with its jaws suitably protected. This will prevent loss of hydraulic fluid when the pipe union is undone.
5   At the rear of the wheel cylinder clean away all dirt and road grit from around the pipe connection and then undo and remove the brake pipe. Plug or tape over the pipe and wheel cylinder to prevent dirt ingress.
6   Undo and remove the two bolts securing the wheel cylinder to the backplate. Ease the top of the brake shoes away from the wheel cylinder pistons and withdraw the cylinder from the backplate.
7   With the cylinder removed and laid out on a clean uncluttered working area, proceed by removing the rubber dust covers, pistons, piston seals and spring. On the Girling and Teves cylinders, remove the seals from the pistons.
8   Thoroughly clean all the parts in clean hydraulic fluid or methylated spirit. Carefully examine the pistons and cylinder bore for scuff marks, wear ridges or scoring and if evident, renew the complete wheel cylinder. If the components are in a satisfactory condition, a new set of seals, available in the form of a wheel cylinder repair kit, must be obtained. Never re-use old seals.
9   Begin reassembly by thoroughly lubricating all the parts in clean hydraulic fluid. If working on the Girling or Teves cylinders fit the new seals to the pistons, using the fingers only and ensuring that the larger seal diameter is toward the inner end of the piston. Place the spring in the centre of the cylinder bore and then insert the pistons (one either side), seal end first. Ensure that the lip of the seal does not fold over as it enters the bore. Fit the new dust covers onto the pistons, and over the lip on each end of the cylinder.
10 If working on the DBA cylinder, first fit the new dust covers onto the ends of the pistons using the fingers only. Insert the spring and support cups into the cylinder bore followed by a rubber seal and piston inserted at each end. Make sure that the seals are fitted with their larger diameter toward the centre, and that the dust covers engage the recess in the end of the cylinder.
11 The assembled wheel cylinder may now be refitted to the car using the reverse sequence to removal. If the brake self-adjusting mechanism was disturbed during removal of the brake drum or wheel cylinder, refer to Section 6, 7, or 8, depending on system type, for drum refitting and initial adjustment procedures.
12 On completion of refitting it will be necessary to bleed the rear brakes as described in Section 14.

10 Master cylinder – removal and refitting

1   Master cylinders of either Teves, Automotive Products (Lockheed), or DBA manufacture may be fitted to Horizon models. The removal and refitting procedure for all three is identical as described below.
2   Unscrew the master cylinder reservoir filler cap and fit a dummy cap in which the air vent hole has been blocked. This will prevent loss of fluid when the pipe connections are undone. If a dummy cap is not available, plug the master cylinder unions upon removal of the pipes to keep hydraulic fluid loss to a minimum.
3   Slacken the hose clip and detach the clutch master cylinder supply pipe from the reservoir.
4   Undo and remove the three brake pipe union nuts (photo) and then carefully ease the pipes out of the master cylinder.
5   Undo and remove the two nuts and washers securing the master cylinder to the servo unit and lift off the cylinder. Take care not to spill any hydraulic fluid on the car's paintwork.
6   Refitting is the reverse sequence to removal. On completion it will be necessary to bleed the complete brake hydraulic system as described in Section 14, and also the clutch hydraulic system as described in Chapter 5.

11 Master cylinder – dismantling, inspection and reassembly

1   As stated previously, Horizon models may be fitted with either a Teves, Automotive Products, or DBA master cylinder. The DBA master cylinder is not repairable and if trouble is experienced on this unit it will be necessary to renew the complete master cyliinder assembly. The Teves and Automotive Products master cylinders are similar in

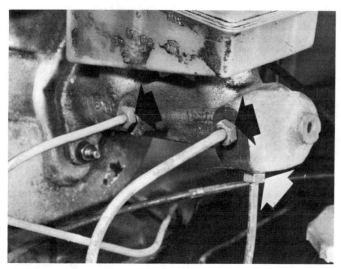

10.4 Master cylinder brake pipe unions (arrowed)

on the retaining circlip. Remove the circlip and stop washer (where fitted) and then withdraw the primary piston and spring.

5   Push the secondary piston down the bore slightly and remove the stop screw and sealing washer (Teves) or the stop pin from the secondary inlet port (Automotive Products).

6   Release the secondary piston and withdraw it from the cylinder bore. If necessary tap the end of the cylinder on a block of wood to dislodge the piston. Recover the piston spring from the cylinder bore.

7   Using the fingers only remove the rubber seals from the pistons, laying them out in the order of removal, and recover the washers and expanders, where fitted.

8   Thoroughly clean all components in methylated spirit or clean hydraulic fluid, and dry with a lint-free cloth.

9   Carefully examine the cylinder bore and pistons for scoring or wear, and all components for damage or distortion. In order that the seals may adequately maintain hydraulic fluid pressure without leakage, the condition of the pistons and cylinder bore must be perfect. If in any doubt whatsoever about the condition of these components, renew the complete master cylinder.

10 If the master cylinder is in a satisfactory condition, a new set of seals *must* be obtained before reassembly. These are available in the form of a repair kit obtainable from your local Talbot dealer.

11 Make sure that all the ports and drillings in the master cylinder are clean and if necessary blow them out using air from a tyre foot pump.

12 Begin reassembly by liberally lubricating the new seals, all the internal components and the cylinder bore with clean hydraulic fluid.

13 Using the fingers only, fit the new washers and expanders (where fitted) and the new rubber seals to the pistons, using the appropriate illustration and the previous removal sequence, as a guide to their correct fitting.

14 Fit the secondary piston spring and secondary piston into the cylinder bore, taking care not to turn back the lips of the seals as they are inserted. On the Teves cylinder, push the secondary piston to the end of its stroke and refit the stop screw with a new seal. With the

construction and the dismantling, inspection and reassembly procedures for both units are described below. Any differences between the two will be indicated where necessary.

2   With the cylinder removed from the car, unscrew the reservoir filler cap and drain the hydraulic fluid into a suitable container.

3   Pull the reservoir off the master cylinder and withdraw the sealing rings from the inlet ports.

4   Push the primary piston down the bore slightly to relieve pressure

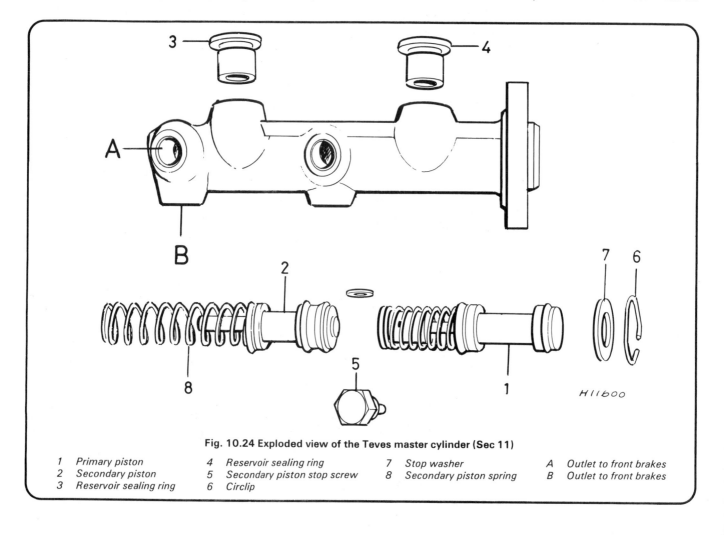

Fig. 10.24 Exploded view of the Teves master cylinder (Sec 11)

1	Primary piston	4	Reservoir sealing ring	7	Stop washer	A	Outlet to front brakes
2	Secondary piston	5	Secondary piston stop screw	8	Secondary piston spring	B	Outlet to front brakes
3	Reservoir sealing ring	6	Circlip				

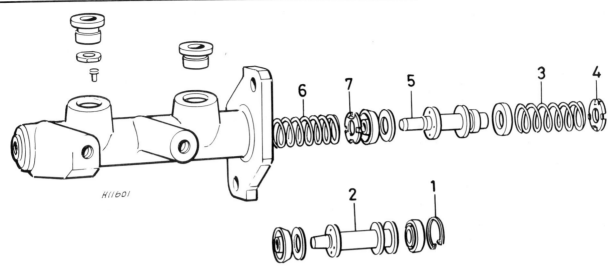

Fig. 10.25 Exploded view of the Automotive Products master cylinder (Sec 11)

1 Circlip	3 Primary piston spring	5 Secondary piston	7 Cup expander
2 Primary piston	4 Cup expander	6 Secondary piston spring	

Automotive Products master cylinder, push the secondary piston down until the first main seal and piston head are seen to pass the secondary supply port, and then insert the stop pin.

15 Insert the primary piston spring and piston assembly into the bore, push it down against spring pressure and refit the stop washer (where applicable) and retaining circlip.

16 Insert two new seals, coated in hydraulic fluid, into the inlet ports and then press the reservoir into position on the master cylinder.

17 The master cylinder can now be refitted to the car as described in Section 10.

12 Brake servo unit – description and maintenance

Description

A vacuum servo unit is fitted into the brake hydraulic circuit in series with the master cylinder, to provide power assistance to the driver when the brake pedal is depressed.

The unit operates by vacuum obtained from the induction manifold and comprises, basically, a booster diaphragm and a non-return valve.

The servo unit and hydraulic master cylinder are connected together so that the servo unit piston rod acts as the master cylinder pushrod. The driver's braking effort is transmitted through another pushrod to the servo unit piston and its built-in control system. The servo unit piston does not fit tightly into the cylinder, but has a strong diaphragm to keep its edges in constant contact with the cylinder wall, so assuring an airtight seal between the two parts. The forward chamber is held under vacuum conditions created in the inlet manifold of the engine and, during periods when the brake pedal is not in use, the controls open a passage to the rear chamber so placing it under vacuum. When the brake pedal is depressed, the vacuum passage to the rear chamber is cut off and the chamber opened to atmospheric pressure. The consequent rush of air pushes the servo piston forward in the vacuum chamber and operates the main pushrod to the master cylinder. The controls are designed so that assistance is given under all conditions and, when the brakes are not required, vacuum in the rear chamber is established when the brake pedal is released. Air from the atmosphere entering the rear chamber is passed through a small air filter.

Two types of servo units are fitted to the Horizon, however the method of operation, removal and servicing procedures are identical.

Maintenance and adjustments

1 The brake servo unit operation can be checked easily without any special tools. Proceed as follows.

2 Stop the engine and clear the servo of any vacuum by depressing the brake pedal several times.

3 Once the servo is cleared, keep the brake pedal depressed and start the engine. If the servo unit is in proper working order, the brake pedal should move further downwards, under even foot pressure, due to the effect of the inlet manifold vacuum of the servo diaphragms.

4 If the brake pedal does not move further downwards the servo system is not operating properly, and the vacuum hoses from the inlet manifold to the servo should be inspected. The vacuum control valve should also be checked. This valve is in the vacuum hose to prevent air flowing into the vacuum side of the servo from the inlet manifold when the engine stops. It is in effect a one-way valve.

5 If the brake servo operates properly in the test, but still gives less effective service on the road, the air filter through which air flows into the servo should be inspected. A dirty filter will limit the formation of a difference in pressure across the servo diaphragm.

6 The servo unit itself cannot be repaired and therefore a complete renewal is necessary if the measures described are not effective.

Air filter renewal

7 Remove the servo unit as described in the following Section.

8 Remove the rubber boot from the pushrod and then ease the filter retainer out of the end of the valve body.

9 Hook out the filter and push in a new one. Refit the retainer and rubber boot.

Non-return valve

10 The non-return valve is fitted on the front face of the servo unit and is connected to the vacuum inlet hose.

11 The valve is not repairable and if suspect should be renewed.

13 Brake servo unit – removal and refitting

1 Unscrew the master cylinder reservoir filler cap and fit a dummy cap in which the air vent hole has been blocked.

2 Slacken the hose clip and detach the clutch hydraulic fluid supply hose from the reservoir. Plug the end of the hose and the reservoir union to prevent dirt ingress.

3 Carefully, using two screwdrivers, prise the non-return valve complete with vacuum hose out of its location on the front face of the servo unit.

4 Undo and remove the two nuts and washer securing the master cylinder to the servo unit. Withdraw the master cylinder off its mounting studs, taking care not to place excessive strain on the brake pipes.

5 From inside the car, remove the trim panel (where fitted) from above the pedal assembly.

6 Extract the retaining spring wire clip and then slide out the clevis pin securing the servo pushrod to the brake pedal.

7 Undo and remove the four securing nuts and washers and then

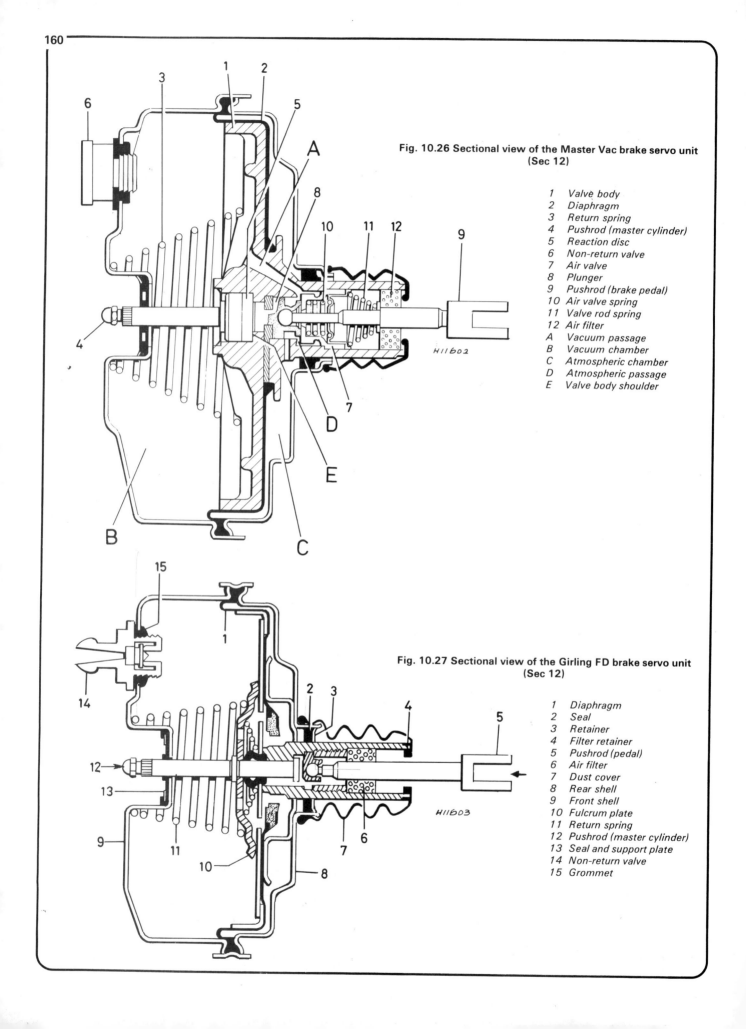

Fig. 10.26 Sectional view of the Master Vac brake servo unit (Sec 12)

1 Valve body
2 Diaphragm
3 Return spring
4 Pushrod (master cylinder)
5 Reaction disc
6 Non-return valve
7 Air valve
8 Plunger
9 Pushrod (brake pedal)
10 Air valve spring
11 Valve rod spring
12 Air filter
A Vacuum passage
B Vacuum chamber
C Atmospheric chamber
D Atmospheric passage
E Valve body shoulder

Fig. 10.27 Sectional view of the Girling FD brake servo unit (Sec 12)

1 Diaphragm
2 Seal
3 Retainer
4 Filter retainer
5 Pushrod (pedal)
6 Air filter
7 Dust cover
8 Rear shell
9 Front shell
10 Fulcrum plate
11 Return spring
12 Pushrod (master cylinder)
13 Seal and support plate
14 Non-return valve
15 Grommet

Fig. 10.28 Brake servo unit attachments (Sec 13)

A   Pushrod clevis pin and retaining clip
B   Servo unit retaining nuts

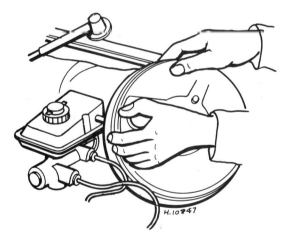

Fig. 10.29 Servo unit removal (Sec 13)

withdraw the servo unit off the bulkhead and into the engine compartment.

8   Refitting the servo unit is the reverse sequence to removal. It will be necessary to bleed the clutch hydraulic system on completion of the installation.

14 Hydraulic system – bleeding

1   If any of the hydraulic components in the braking system have been removed or disconnected, or if the fluid level in the master cylinder reservoir has been allowed to fall appreciably, it is inevitable that air will have been introduced into the system. The removal of all this air is essential if the brakes are to function correctly, and the process of removing it is known as bleeding.

2   As the Horizon utilizes a split braking system with two completely independent hydraulic circuits, it will only be necessary to bleed the complete system if the master cylinder has been disconnected. In all other cases bleeding will only be necessary on the circuit that has been disturbed.

3   There are a number of one-man, do-it-yourself, brake bleeding kits currently available from motor accessory shops. It is recommended that one of these kits should be used wherever possible as they greatly simplify the bleeding operation and also reduce the risk of expelled air and fluid being drawn back into the system.

4   If one of these kits is not available then it will be necessary to gather together a clean jar and a suitable length of clear plastic tubing which is a tight fit over the bleed screw, and also to engage the help of an assistant.

5   Before commencing the bleeding operation, check that all rigid pipes and flexible hoses are in good condition and that all hydraulic unions are tight. Take great care not to allow hydraulic fluid to come into contact with the vehicle paintwork, otherwise the finish will be seriously damaged. Wash off any spilled fluid immediately with cold water.

6   If hydraulic fluid has been lost from the master cylinder, due to a leak in the system, ensure that the cause is traced and rectified before proceeding further or a serious malfunction of the braking system may occur.

7   To bleed the system first remove the master cylinder filler cap and top up the reservoir. Periodically check the fluid level during the bleeding operation and top up as necessary.

8   With the engine stopped, fully depress the brake pedal at least 6 times to completely exhaust the vacuum in the brake servo.

9   Clean the area around the bleed screw at the wheel cylinder or brake caliper to be bled (photo). Always start with the left-hand wheel and finish with the right. If bleeding the complete system it is of no significance whether the front or rear circuit is bled first.

10   If a one-man brake bleeding kit is being used, connect the outlet tube to the bleed screw and then open the screw one full turn (photo). If possible position the unit so that it can be viewed from the car, then depress the brake pedal to the floor and slowly release it. The one-way valve in the kit will prevent expelled air from returning to the system at the end of each stroke. Repeat this operation until clean hydraulic fluid, free from air bubbles, can be seen coming through the tube. Now tighten the bleed screw and remove the outlet tube.

11   If a one-man brake bleeding kit is not available, connect one end of the plastic tubing to the bleed screw and immerse the other end in the jar containing sufficient clean hydraulic fluid to keep the end of the tube submerged. Open the bleed screw one full turn and have your assistant depress the brake pedal to the floor and then slowly release it. Tighten the bleed screw at the end of each downstroke to prevent expelled air and fluid from being drawn back into the system. Repeat this operation until clean hydraulic fluid, free from air bubbles, can be seen coming through the tube. Now tighten the bleed screw and remove the plastic tube.

12   Repeat this procedure for the right-hand wheel and then if bleeding the complete system, carry out the above operations on the other hydraulic circuit. Do not forget to recheck the fluid level in the master cylinder at regular intervals and top up as necessary.

13   When completed, recheck the fluid level in the master cylinder, top up if necessary and refit the cap. Check the 'feel' of the brake pedal which should be firm and free from any 'sponginess' which would indicate air still present in the system.

14   Discard any expelled hydraulic fluid as it is likely to be contaminated with moisture, air and dirt which makes it unsuitable for further use.

15 Hydraulic pipes and hoses – inspection, removal and refitting

Note: All hydraulic pipe and flexible hose connections on the Horizon have a metric thread, M10 x 1 mm pitch, as opposed to the ⅜ in UNF thread used on some other Talbot cars. The metric pipe unions, hoses, etc, are identified by a black or olive paint mark and care must be taken to ensure that new items have the correct fittings.

1   Periodically, and certainly well in advance of the MOT Test, all brake pipes, connections and unions should be completely and carefully examined.

2   Examine first all the unions for signs of leaks (photo). Then look at the flexible hoses for signs of fraying and chafing (as well as for leaks). This is only a preliminary inspection of the flexible hoses, as exterior condition does not necessarily indicate interior condition which will be considered later.

3   The steel pipes must be examined equally carefully. They must be

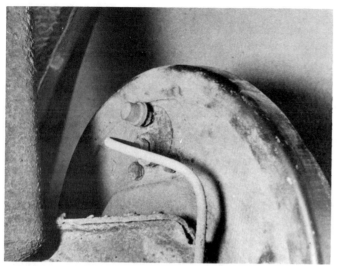

14.9 Protective cap over rear wheel cylinder bleed screw

14.10 One-man bleeding kit connected to front caliper bleed screw

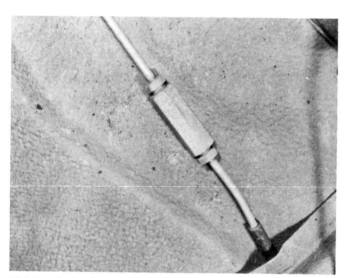

15.2 Rear brake pipe union connector

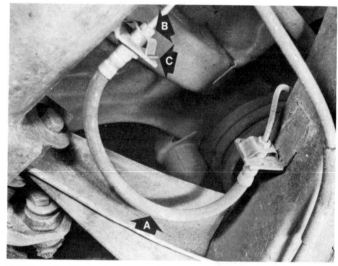

15.6 Rear flexible brake hose and connections

A   Hose   B   Pipe union   C   Spring clips

thoroughly cleaned and examined for signs of dents or other percussive damage, rust and corrosion. Rust and corrosion should be scraped off, and, if the depth of pitting in the pipes is significant, they will require renewal. This is most likely in those areas underneath the chassis and along the rear suspension arms where the pipes are exposed to the full force of road and weather conditions.

4   If any of the hoses or sections of pipe are to be disconnected or removed, first unscrew the master cylinder filler cap and fit a dummy cap in which the vent hole has been blocked. This will create a vacuum in the reservoir and reduce fluid loss when the pipe unions are undone.

5   Rigid pipe removal is usually quite straightforward. The unions at each end are undone and the pipe drawn out of the connection. The clips which may hold it to the car body are bent back and it is then removed. Underneath the car the exposed union can be particularly stubborn, defying the efforts of an open ended spanner. As few people will have the special split ring spanner required, a self-grip wrench is the only answer. If the pipe is being renewed, new unions will be provided. If not, then one will have to put up with the possibility of burring over the flats on the unions and of using a self-grip wrench for refitting.

6   Flexible hoses are always fitted to a rigid support bracket where they join a rigid pipe, the bracket being fixed to the chassis or suspension arms. The rigid pipe union must first be unscrewed from the flexible hose and then the retaining spring clip securing the hose to the bracket is simply withdrawn with a pair of pliers (photo).

7   Once the flexible hose is removed, examine the internal bore. If clear of fluid it should be possible to see through it. Any specks of rubber that come out, or signs of restriction in the bore, mean that the inner lining is breaking up and the hose must be renewed.

8   Rigid pipes which need renewing can usually be purchased at your local garage where they have the pipe, unions and special tools to make them up. All that they need to know is the pipe length required and the type of flare used at the ends of the pipe. These may be different at each end of the same pipe. If possible, it is a good idea to take the old pipe along as a pattern.

9   Refitting of the pipes is a straightforward reversal of the removal procedure. It is best to get all the sets (bends) made prior to fitting. Also, any acute bends should be put in by the garage on a bending machine otherwise there is the possibility of kinking them, and restricting the bore area and thus, fluid flow.

10   With the pipes or hoses refitted, remove the dummy filler cap from the reservoir and bleed the appropriate circuit of the hydraulic system as desribed in Section 14.

---

16 Brake pressure reducing valve – description and adjustment

1   Incorporated in the rear brake hydraulic circuit is a pressure reducing valve that regulates the hydraulic fluid pressure to the rear

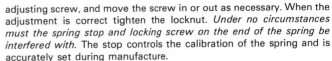

wheel cylinders according to vehicle load.

2   When the car is lightly loaded, hydraulic fluid supplied to the rear wheel cylinders is shut off at a predetermined pressure. This prevents the rear wheels from locking prematurely and reduces the risk of a rear wheel skid.

3   When heavy loads ae being carried, no reduction in pressure takes place and the available braking force at the rear wheels is the same as at the front.

4   The valve is mounted on the rear suspension crossmember and is actuated by the pull of a spring fitted between the valve operating lever and an arm on the rear anti-roll bar.

5   For safe and efficient operation of the rear brakes the pressure reducing valve adjustment must be checked and if necessary reset whenever the valve assembly, rear anti-roll bar, rear crossmember or front torsion bar have been removed, refitted or renewed. It must also be reset if the vehicle ride height has been altered.

6   Checking and adjusting of the valve must take place with the car at kerb weight, with a full fuel tank and with a 176 lb (80 kg) load at the extreme rear of the luggage compartment.

7   Before making any adjustments, ensure that the valve assembly and its associated components are clean and free to operate. It is particularly important to ensure that the operating lever is free to move on its pivot pin. The arm and pin should be periodically lubricated with a few drops of engine oil.

8   To adjust the reducing valve, position the car on level ground and ensure that it is loaded as described previously.

9   Measure the length of the sensing spring as shown in Fig. 10.30. The dimension A should be 6.6 to 6.7 in (167.5 to 170.5 mm). If adjustment is necessary slacken the locknut on the operating arm

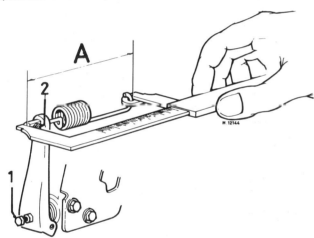

Fig. 10.30 Measuring the length of the brake pressure reducing valve sensing spring (Sec 16)

1   *Adjusting screw*
2   *Spring locking screw must not be altered)*
A   *See text*

adjusting screw, and move the screw in or out as necessary. When the adjustment is correct tighten the locknut. *Under no circumstances must the spring stop and locking screw on the end of the spring be interfered with.* The stop controls the calibration of the spring and is accurately set during manufacture.

10   Having adjusted the valve, a road test should be carried out on a quiet straight stretch of road. Drive the car at approximately 20 to 25 mph and apply the brakes hard. Examine the relative lengths of the front and rear skid marks which should be the same.

11   If the rear brake bias is too great, ie a longer rear skid mark, slacken the locknut and unscrew the adjusting screw by one flat of the hexagon only. Tighten the locknut and repeat the test.

12   If the front/rear brake balance is still biased toward the rear, and after ensuring that each brake is in a satisfactory condition and operating correctly, it is likely that the reducing valve is at fault. It is not possible to repair the reducing valve and if the unit is suspect, it must be renewed.

17 Brake pressure reducing valve – removal and refitting

1   Unscrew the master cylinder reservoir filler cap and fit a dummy cap in which the vent hole has been blocked.

2   Jack up the rear of the car and support it on stands.

3   Secure the operating arm to the valve body with wire or string. This will prevent the rubber boot being dislodged by the arm moving out as the sensing spring is released.

4   Disconnect the sensing spring from the lever on the anti-roll bar (photo).

5   Undo and remove the inlet and outlet hydraulic pipe unions from the valve body (photo). Tape or plug the unions to prevent dirt ingress.

6   Undo and remove the two securing bolts and lift off the reducing valve, operating arm and sensing spring as a complete assembly.

7   Refitting the valve assembly is the reverse sequence to removal. On completion of the installation bleed the rear hydraulic circuit as described in Section 14, and adjust the reducing valve as described in Section 16.

18 Handbrake – adjustment

1   The correct tension in the handbrake cable is automatically maintained by the self-adjusting mechanism of the rear brakes and further adjustment is not usually required. However, after extended service slight stretching of the cable may occur and the following procedure should be carried out. This method should also be used when a new cable or handbrake assembly has been fitted.

2   The normal free travel of the handbrake lever is five to seven notches of the ratchet. If the travel of the lever is greater than this, first make sure that the rear brakes are in satisfactory working order and that the self-adjusting mechanism is operating correctly.

3   Assuming the rear brakes to be in order, jack up the rear of the car and support it on axle stands.

4   Release the handbrake lever and then pull it up five notches.

5   Working under the car, slacken the locknut on the handbrake lever pullrod and screw on the adjusting nut until the cable is just taut (photo).

17.4 Brake pressure reducing valve sensing spring and anti-roll bar connection

17.5 Brake pressure reducing valve pipe unions (A) and retaining bolts (B)

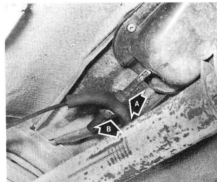

18.5 Handbrake cable locknut (A) and cable adjuster (B)

6   Tighten the locknut, without moving the adjusting nut, and then check that the cable is free to slide in the equaliser.
7   With the cable correctly adjusted the rear wheels should be locked when the handbrake lever is pulled up to the sixth notch.

19 Handbrake assembly – removal and refitting

1   The handbrake assembly comprises three subassemblies, the lever, the operating rod and yoke and the cable.
2   A broken or overstretched cable can only be renewed as a unit as fittings and ends are not detachable.
3   To remove the cable first detach the two ends from the brake shoes as described in Sections 6, 7, or 8, according to brake shoe type.
4   Pull the ends of the cable through the rear brake backplate and remove the two clips securing the cable to the underside of the car.
5   Detach the equalising yoke from the handbrake operating rod, unhook the cable from the front clips and remove it from beneath the car (photo).
6   Refit the new cable using the reverse procedure to that of removal, and adjust it as described in the previous Section.
7   Wear or damage to the rod and yoke can be repaired by renewal

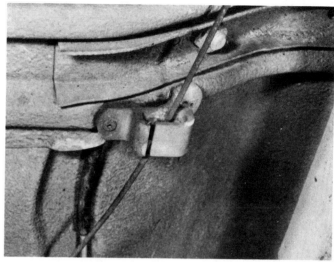

19.5 Handbrake cable front steady clip

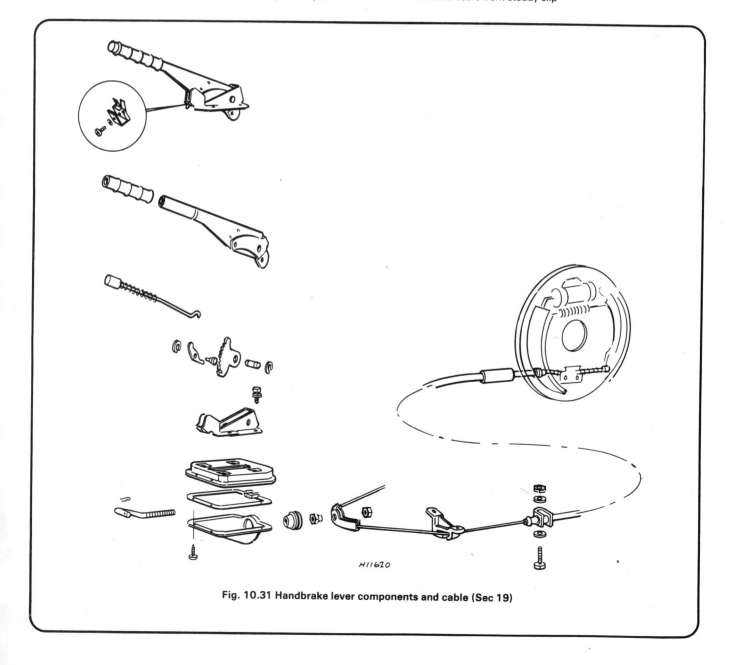

H11620

Fig. 10.31 Handbrake lever components and cable (Sec 19)

of components affected.

8   It is possible to renew the lever ratchet as a separate component after dismantling by removal of the circlips and crosspins. Occasional application of grease to the ratchet and quadrant notches will help to reduce wear. Application of the handbrake with the ratchet button depressed will also increase the life of the lever components.

9   Details of the handbrake assembly are shown in Fig. 10.31.

20 Brake pedal – removal and refitting

1   The brake pedal operates on a common cross-shaft with the clutch.

2   The method of removal and refitting is the same as described for the clutch pedal in Chapter 5.

21 Fault diagnosis – braking system

Symptom	Reason(s)
Brake pedal travels almost to floor before brakes operate	Rear brakes out of adjustment (automatic adjusters inoperative or incorrectly assembled) Failure of front or rear hydraulic circuit Excessive wear in front wheel bearings Excessive front disc run-out Master cylinder faulty
Vehicle pulls to one side under braking	Front disc pads contaminated with grease or hydraulic fluid on one side Disc brake caliper pistons seized or partially seized on one side Excessive wear of pad friction material or brake disc on one side A mixture of brake pad types fitted between sides Rear brake shoes contaminated with grease or hydraulic fluid Rear wheel cylinder seized or partially seized Worn, incorrect or out-of-adjustment steering or suspension components, tyres or tyre pressures
Judder felt through brake pedal and/or steering wheel under braking	Excessive run-out of front discs Front discs worn, scored or grooved Excessively worn front brake pads Front brake caliper mountings loose Rear brake drums worn, scored or out-of-round Rear brake backplate or wheel cylinder insecure Wear in steering and/or suspension linkages
Brake pedal feels 'spongy'	Air in hydraulic system Bulging in brake flexible hose(s) Master cylinder or servo mountings insecure Master cylinder faulty
Excessive effort required to stop car	Servo unit not functioning Failure of front or rear hydraulic circuit One or more wheel cylinders or caliper pistons seized Excessively worn brake pads or linings Brake pads or linings contaminated with grease or hydraulic fluid Faulty brake pressure reducing valve
Loss of hydraulic fluid from reservoir	Leaking rear wheel cylinder(s) Leak from hydraulic pipe, hose or union Faulty master cylinder Leak in clutch hydraulic system
Brakes tend to bind, drag or lock-on	Rear brakes over adjusted Incorrect adjustment of handbrake cable Wheel cylinder or caliper pistons seized Master cylinder faulty Servo unit faulty Brake pressure reducing valve incorrectly adjusted

Chapter 11 Electrical system

For modifications, and information applicable to later models, see Supplement at end of manual

Contents

Specifications

General
System type .... 12 volt, negative earth

Battery
Type .... Lead acid
Capacity .... 40 amp hour

Alternator
Make .... Paris-Rhone, Ducellier or Motorola
Type:
    9 Series models (1978-1979) .... Three phase with separate voltage regulator
    A Series models (1979-1980) .... Three phase with integral voltage regulator
Output .... 50 amps at 15 volts
Field resistance .... 5.5 ohms
Voltage regulator ('9' series models):
    Make .... Paris-Rhone or Ducellier
    Field current .... 1.7 amps
    Regulated voltage .... 13.8 to 14.4 volts

Starter motor
Make .... Paris-Rhone, Ducellier, Bosch or Mitsubishi
Type .... Pre-engaged
Lock torque .... 7 lbf ft (10 Nm)
Maximum power .... 0.8 kW at 8 volts
Light running current .... 50 to 70 amps at 7000 to 10 000 rpm
No of teeth (drive pinion) 9

Windscreen wiper motor

Make	Bosch, Marchal or Siam
Speeds	2

Bulb application

	Wattage
Headlights	40/45 or 50/60 (Halogen)
Sidelamps	4
Front indicators	21
Rear indicators	21
Reverse lamps	21
Rear foglamps	21
Stop/tail lamps	21/5
Rear number plate lamp	5
Interior courtesy lamp	5
Luggage compartment lamp	4
Instrument panel warning lamps	2

Torque wrench settings

	lbf ft	Nm
Starter motor securing bolts	15	21
Alternator-to-mounting bracket	30	41.5
Mounting bracket-to-crankcase	15	21
Adjusting strap-to-alternator	15	21

---

1 General description

The electrical system is of the 12 volt negative earth type and the major components comprise a 12 volt battery of which the negative terminal is earthed, an alternator which is driven from the crankshaft pulley, and a starter motor.

The battery supplies a steady amount of current for the ignition lighting and other electrical circuits and provides a reserve of electricity when the current consumed by the electrical equipment exceeds that being produced by the alternator.

The alternator voltage regulator ensures a high output if the battery is in a low state of charge or the demand from the electrical equipment is high, and a low output if the battery is fully charged and there is little demand for the electrical equipment.

When fitting electrical accessories to cars with a negative earth system it is important, if they contain silicon diodes or transistors, that they are connected correctly, otherwise serious damage may result to the components concerned. Items such as radios, tape players, electronic tachometer, automatic dipping etc, should all be checked for correct polarity.

It is important that the battery is disconnected before removing the alternator output lead as this is live at all times. Also, if body repairs are to be carried out using electric arc welding equipment, the alternator must be disconnected otherwise serious damage can be caused to the more delicate instruments. Whenever the battery has to be disconnected it must always be reconnected with the negative terminal connected last and the cable well earthed. **Do not** disconnect the battery with the engine running. If jumper cables are used to start the car, they *must* be connected correctly – positive to positive and negative to negative.

---

2 Battery – removal and refitting

1 It is advisable to remove the battery once every three months for cleaning and testing. Detach the negative lead and then the positive lead from the battery by compressing the lugs on the clamps with pliers and then lifting the clamps upwards off the terminals (photo).

2 Remove the battery retaining clamp and carefully lift the battery from its tray, holding it upright to ensure that none of the electrolyte is spilled (photo).

3 Refitting is a direct reversal of the removal sequence. Smear the terminals and clamps with petroleum jelly to prevent corrosion. Never use an ordinary grease.

---

3 Battery – maintenance and inspection

1 Check the battery electrolyte level weekly, by lifting off the cover or removing the individual cell plugs. The tops of the plates should be just covered by the electrolyte. If not, add distilled water so that they

2.1 Removing the battery earth terminal

2.2 Battery retaining clamp and bolt

are. *Do not add extra water with the idea of reducing the intervals of topping up.* This will merely dilute the electrolyte and reduce charging and current retention efficiency. On batteries fitted with patent covers, troughs, glass balls and so on, follow the instructions marked on the cover of the battery to ensure correct addition of water.

2 Keep the battery clean and dry all over by wiping it with a dry cloth. A damp top surface could cause tracking between the two terminal posts with consequent draining of power.

3 Every three months, remove the battery and check the support tray clamp and battery terminal connections for signs of corrosion – usually indicated by a whitish green deposit. Wash this off with clean water to which a little ammonia or washing soda has been added. Then treat the terminals with petroleum jelly and the battery mounting with suitable protective paint to prevent the metal being eaten away.

4 If the electrolyte level needs an excessive amount of replenishment but no leaks are apparent, it could be due to over-charging as a result of the battery having been run down and then left to recharge from the vehicle rather than an outside source. If the battery has been heavily discharged for one reason or another, it is best to have it continuously charged at a low amperage for a period of many hours. If it is charged from the car's system under such conditions, the charging will be intermittent and greatly varied in intensity. This does not do the battery any good at all. If the battery needs topping up frequently, even when it is known to be in good condition and not too old, then the voltage regulator should be checked to ensure that the charging output is being correctly controlled. An elderly battery, however, may need topping up more than a new one, because it needs to take in more charging current. Do not worry about this, provided it gives satisfactory service.

5 When checking a battery's condition, a hydrometer should be used. On some batteries, where the terminals of each of the six cells are exposed, a discharge tester can be used to check the condition of any one cell also. On modern batteries, the use of a discharge tester is no longer regarded as useful, as the renewal or repair of cells is not an economic proposition. The tables in the following Section give the hydrometer readings for various states of charge. A further check can be made when the battery is undergoing a charge. If, towards the end of the charge, when the cells are meant to be 'gassing' (bubbling), one cell appears not to be, this indicates the cell or cells in question are probably breaking down and the life of the battery is limited.

4 Battery – charging and electrolyte replenishment

1 It is possible that in winter, when the load on the battery cannot be recuperated during normal driving time, external charging is desirable. This is best done overnight at a 'trickle' rate of 1 to 1.5 amps. Alternatively, a 3 to 4 amp rate can be used over a period of four hours or so. Check the specific gravity in the latter case and stop the charge when the reading is correct. Most modern charging sets reduce the rate automatically when the fully charged state is neared. Rapid boost charges of 30 to 60 amps or more may get you out of trouble or can be used on a battery that has seen better days anyhow. They are not advised for a good battery that may have run flat for some reason.

2 Electrolyte replenishment should not normally be necessary unless an accident or some other cause, such as contamination, arises. If it is necessary then it is best first to discharge the battery completely and then tip out all the remaining liquid from all cells. Then acquire a quantity of mixed electrolyte from a battery shop or garage according to the specifications in the table given next. The quantity required will depend on the type of battery but three or four pints should be more than enough for most. When the electrolyte has been put into the battery, a slow charge – not exceeding one amp – should be given for as long as is necessary to fully charge the battery. This could be up to thirty six hours.

3 Specific gravities for hydrometer readings (check each cell) are as follows:

	Climate below 80°F (26.7°C)	Climate above 80°F (26.7°C)
Fully charged	1.270 to 1.290	1.210 to 1.230
Half-charged	1.190 to 1.210	1.120 to 1.150
Discharged completely	1.110 to 1.130	1.050 to 1.070

Note: *If the electrolyte temperature is significantly different from 60°F (15.6°C), then the specific gravity will be affected. For every 5°F*

(2.8°C) it will increase or decrease inversely with the temperature by 0.020.

When the vehicle is being used in cold climates, it is essential to maintain the battery fully charged because the charge affects the freezing point of the electrolyte. The densities below have been corrected to suit measurement at 80°F (26.7°C):

Specific gravity 1.200 freezes at –35°F
Specific gravity 1.160 freezes at 0°F

5 Alternator – routine maintenance

1 The equipment has been designed for the minimum amount of maintenance in service, the only items subject to wear being the brushes and bearings.

2 Brushes should be examined after about 75 000 miles (120 000 km) and renewed if necessary. The bearings are pre-packed with grease for life and should not require further attention.

3 Check the drivebelt every 3000 miles (5000 km) for correct adjustment, which should be 0.5 in (13 mm) total deflection under firm thumb pressure at the centre of the run between the crankshaft and alternator pulleys.

4 The procedure for adjusting or renewing the alternator drivebelt is given in Chapter 2.

6 Alternator – special precautions

Whenever the electrical system of the car is being attended to, or external means of starting the engine are used, these are certain precautions that must be taken otherwise serious and expensive damage can result.

1 Always make sure that the negative terminal of the battery is earthed. If the terminal connections are accidentally reversed the alternator diodes will be destroyed.

2 Whenever the alternator is to be removed, or when disconnecting the terminals of the alternator circuit, always disconnect the battery earth terminal first.

3 Never disconnect the battery terminals when the engine is running.

4 Should it be necessary to use a booster charger or booster battery to start the engine, always double check that the negative cable is connected to the negative terminal and the positive cable to the positive terminal.

5 Do not attempt to test the alternator output by earthing its terminals, even momentarily.

7 Alternator – removal and refitting

1 Disconnect the leads from the battery terminals.

2 Undo the bolts and remove the alternator guard from under the right-hand wheel arch (photos).

3 Slacken the alternator mounting bolts and adjustment strap bolt (photo).

4 Move the alternator in towards the engine and slip the drivebelt off the crankshaft, water pump and alternator pulleys.

5 Make a note of the position of the electrical connections at the rear of the alternator and disconect them (photo).

6 Remove the adjustment strap bolt and nut, noting that the large washer is positioned against the strap. Now remove the mounting bolt and nut and withdraw the alternator.

7 Refitting is the reverse of the removal procedure. Adjust the tension of the drivebelt so that it is possible to deflect the belt by 0.5 in (13 mm) using finger pressure at a point midway between the crankshaft and alternator pulleys.

8 Alternator – fault finding and repair

Owing to the specialist knowledge and equipment required to test or service an alternator it is recommended that if the performance is suspect, the car be taken to an automobile electrician who will have the facilities for such work. Because of this recommendation, information is limited to the inspection and renewal of the brushes. Should the alternator not charge or the system be suspect, the following

7.2a Remove the retaining bolts ...

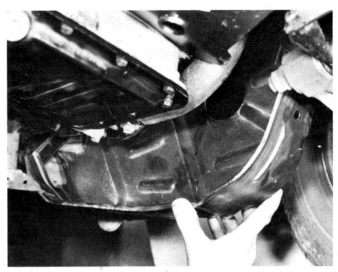
7.2b ... and withdraw the alternator guard

7.3 Alternator adjustment strap bolt

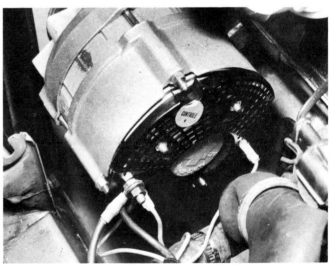
7.5 Electrical connections at the rear of the alternator

points may be checked before seeking further assistance.
1   Check the drivebelt tension, as described in Section 7.
2   Check the battery, as described in Section 3.
3   Check all electrical cable connections for cleanliness and security.

9 Alternator brushes (Paris-Rhone) – removal, inspection and refitting

1   Remove the alternator from the car as described in Section 7.
2   Undo and remove the two screws at the rear of the alternator and lift off the brush holder assembly.
3   Withdraw the brushes from their locations in the holder.
4   Clean the brush holder and brushes with a petrol-soaked rag and check that the brushes slide easily in the holder.
5   Compare the length of the brushes with new ones at the stores of your Talbot dealer and if more than two-thirds worn, renew them.
6   Refitting the brushes and brush holder is the reverse sequence to removal.

10 Alternator brushes (Ducellier) – removal, inspection and refitting

1   Remove the alternator from the car as described in Section 7.

2   Undo and remove the two screws securing the brush holder to the rear of the alternator and withdraw the holder.
3   Lift out the earth brush from the holder, followed by the second brush after removing the securing screw.
4   Refer to paragraphs 4, 5 and 6 of the preceding Section.

11 Alternator brushes (Motorola) – removal, inspection and refitting

1   Remove the alternator from the car as described in Section 7.
2   Undo and remove the two screws securing the cover plate to the rear of the alternator. Lift off the plate, taking care not to strain the connecting wire.
3   Undo and remove the two screws and lift out the brush holder, taking care not to damage the brushes.
4   Refer to paragraphs 4, 5 and 6 cf Section 9.

12 Alternator voltage regulator – description

1   Where an alternator having an external voltage regulator is fitted, the regulator is located in the engine compartment on the left-hand wing valance (photo).
2   The unit comprises a vibrating contact that controls the alternator

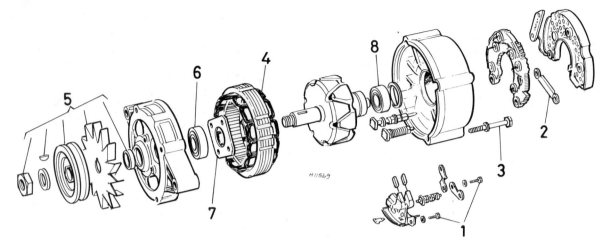

Fig. 11.1 Exploded view of the Paris-Rhone alternator (Sec 9)

1 Brush holder retaining screws	3 Through-bolts	6 Drive end bearing
2 Capacitor	4 Stator	7 Bearing retainer
	5 Fan and pulley assembly	8 Slip ring end bearing

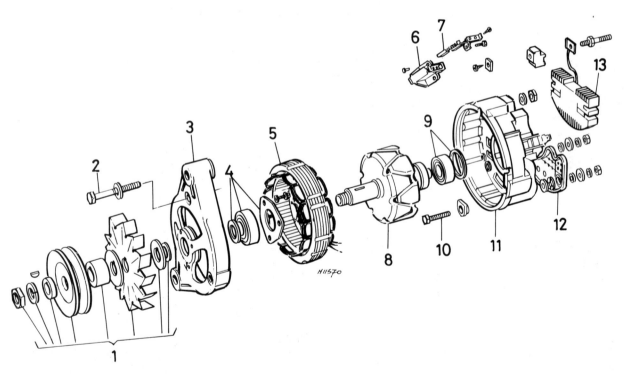

Fig. 11.2 Exploded view of the Ducellier alternator (Sec 10)

1 Fan and pulley assembly	6 Brush holder	10 Terminal bolt
2 Through-bolt	7 Brush assembly	11 Slip ring end bracket
3 Drive end bracket	8 Rotor	12 Cover
4 Drive end bearing assembly	9 Slip ring end bearing assembly	13 Diode assembly
5 Stator		

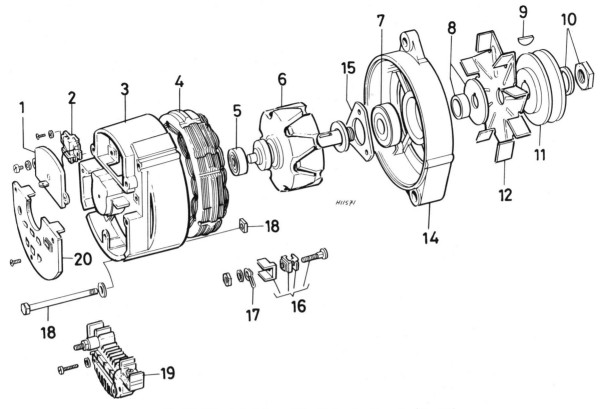

Fig. 11.3 Exploded view of the Motorola alternator (Sec 11)

1	Brush holder plate	5 Slip ring end bearing
2	Brush holder	6 Rotor
3	Slip ring end bracket	7 Drive end bearing
4	Stator	8 Washer and spacer

9	Driving key
10	Pulley nut and washer
11	Pulley
12	Fan

13	Retaining screw
14	Drive end bracket
15	Bearing retainer
16	Terminal screw

17	Warning light terminal
18	Through-bolt and nut
19	Diode assembly
20	Rear cover

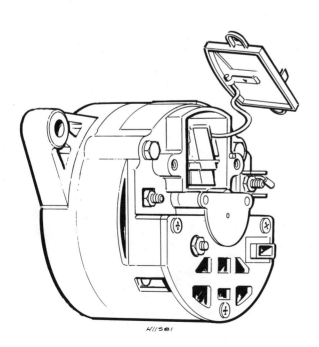

Fig. 11.4 Brush holder cover plate on the Motorola alternator (Sec 11)

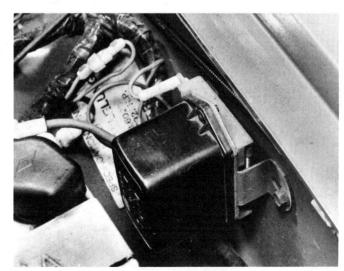

12.1 Alternator external voltage regulator on left-hand wing valance

output by limiting the current in the field windings.

3   The voltage regulator is a sealed unit. If suspect it should be tested by substitution and if faulty, renewed.

13 Starter motor – general description

Horizon models are fitted with pre-engaged starter motors of either Paris-Rhone, Ducellier, Bosch or Mitsubishi manufacture. These motors are all of series wound, four-pole, four-brush design and are fully serviceable.

The operation of the starter motor is as follows. With the ignition switched on, current flows from the solenoid which is mounted on the top of the starter motor body. Contained within the solenoid is a plunger which moves inward so causing a centrally pivoted engagement lever to move in such a manner that the forked end pushes the drive pinion into mesh with the starter ring gear. When the solenoid plunger reaches the end of its travel, it closes an internal contact and full starting current flows to the starter field coils. The armature is then able to rotate the crankshaft so starting the engine.

A one-way clutch is fitted to the starter drive pinion so that when the engine fires and starts to operate on its own, it does not drive the starter motor.

14 Starter motor – testing on engine

1   If the starter motor fails to turn the engine when the switch is operated there are four possible reasons why:

(a)   *The battery is faulty*
(b)   *The electrical connections between the switch, solenoid, battery and starter motor are somewhere failing to pass the necessary current from the battery through the starter to earth*
(c)   *The solenoid switch is faulty*
(d)   *The starter motor is either jammed or electrically defective*

2   To check the battery, switch on the headlights. If they dim after a few seconds, the battery is in a discharged state. If the lights glow brightly, operate the starter switch and see what happens to the lights. If they dim, power is reaching the starter motor but failing to turn it. Therefore check it is not jammed by placing the car in gear (manual transmission only) and rocking it to and fro. Should the motor not be jammed, it will have to be removed for proper inspection. If the starter turns slowly when switched on, proceed to the next check.

3   If, when the starter switch is operated, the lights stay bright, insufficient power is reaching the motor. Remove the battery connections, starter/solenoid power connections and the engine earth strap and thoroughly clean and refit them. Smear petroleum jelly around the battery connections to prevent corrosion. Corroded connections are the most frequent cause of electric system malfunctions.

4   When the above checks and cleaning tasks have been carried out, but without success, you will have possibly heard a clicking noise each time the starter switch is operated. This is the solenoid switch operating, but it does not necessarily follow that the main contacts are closing properly (if no clicking has been heard from the solenoid, it is certainly defective). The solenoid contact can be checked by putting a voltmeter or bulb across the main cable connection of the starter side of the solenoid and earth. When the switch is operated, there should be a reading or lighted bulb. If there is no reading or lighted bulb, the solenoid unit is faulty and should be renewed.

5   Finally, if it is established that the solenoid is not faulty and 12 volts are getting to the starter, then the motor is faulty and should be removed for inspection.

15 Starter motor – removal and refitting

1   Disconnect the battery earth terminal.
2   Make a note of the electrical connections at the starter solenoid and disconnect them (photo).
3   Undo and remove the bolts securing the starter motor to the clutch housing and the additional support bolt securing the motor to the cylinder block (photo). Access to these securing bolts is best gained from under the front of the car.
4   Carefully manipulate the starter motor to clear the alternator, water hoses and engine mounting and withdraw the unit from the engine.
5   Refitting is the reverse sequence to removal. **Note:** *If the motor has been dismantled, or if a new or reconditioned unit is being fitted, check and if necessary adjust the drive pinion travel as described in Section 20, before refitting the starter motor.*

16 Starter solenoid – removal and refitting

1   The procedure for removal of the solenoid is basically the same for all four types of starter motors that may be fitted. In all cases, once the starter motor has been removed from the car the solenoid can be removed without further dismantling of the motor. Consult the relevant illustration for the type of motor you are working on and proceed as follows.
2   First undo the terminal nut and then lift off the wire that connects the solenoid to the motor field coils.
3   Next undo and remove the nuts on the retaining studs, or the screws, that secure the solenoid to the end housing.
4   Now slide the solenoid rearward, taking care not to lose the return spring, shims or washers (where fitted). Note that on the Bosch unit the solenoid armature must be unhooked from the pinion carriage actuating arm as the solenoid is removed.
5   Refitting the solenoid is the reverse sequence to removal. Adjust the drive pinion travel as described in Section 20, before refitting the starter motor to the car.

15.2 Electrical connections at the starter solenoid

15.3 Starter motor lower support bolt

17 Starter motor brushes – inspection and renewal

1   Begin by removing the starter motor from the car and placing it on a clean uncluttered work bench. Have some containers handy to store the small screws, washers and circlips that may otherwise be easily lost.

Paris-Rhone
2   Remove the small cap from the centre of the commutator end cover.
3   Undo and remove the armature end bolt and recover the washer.
4   Undo and remove the two long end cover retaining bolts and carefully withdraw the end cover from the armature and starter motor body. As the end cover is withdrawn, lift up the springs and slide the two field coil brushes out of the end cover.
5   If the brushes are suspect, compare their length against new ones and renew them if worn excessively. To do this, cut off the old brush flexible lead flush with the end of the field coil. Solder the new brush lead onto the severed end of the old one. Take care to localise the heat during the operation and do not damage the insulation of the field coils.

6   Wipe the starter motor armature and commutator clean with a non-fluffy rag, wetted with carbon tetrachloride, or other similar solvent.
7   Refit the brushes into their holders and then reassemble the starter motor using the reverse sequence to removal.

Ducellier
8   Undo and remove the two nuts and lift off the commutator end cover retaining bracket.
9   Undo and remove the armature end bolt and recover the washers.
10 Undo the second pair of retaining nuts and carefully lift off the end cover followed by the brush holders, taking care not to lose the tension springs.
11 The procedure is now the same as for the Paris-Rhone motor described in paragraphs 5 to 7 inclusive.

Bosch
12 Undo and remove the two small screws and lift off the armature end cap.
13 Extract the circlip from the end of the armature and lift off the washers and rubber sealing ring.
14 Undo and remove the two long bolts which hold the motor

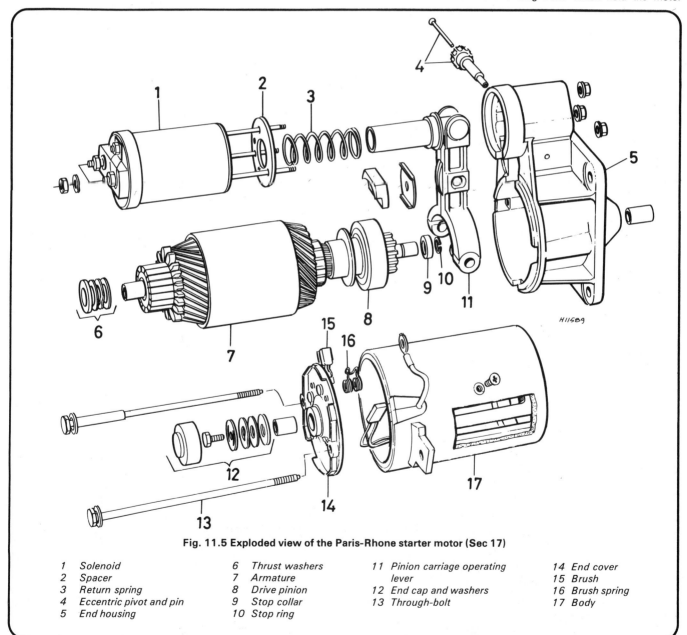

Fig. 11.5 Exploded view of the Paris-Rhone starter motor (Sec 17)

1 Solenoid	6 Thrust washers	11 Pinion carriage operating lever	14 End cover
2 Spacer	7 Armature		15 Brush
3 Return spring	8 Drive pinion	12 End cap and washers	16 Brush spring
4 Eccentric pivot and pin	9 Stop collar	13 Through-bolt	17 Body
5 End housing	10 Stop ring		

assembly together. The commutator end cover can now be withdrawn to reveal the brushes and brush mounting plate.

15 Lift up the springs and slide the field coil brushes out of the mounting plate, then remove the mounting plate from the motor. Retrieve the spacer washers from the end of the armature.

16 The procedure is now the same as for the Paris-Rhone motor described in paragraphs 5 to 7 inclusive.

Mitsubishi

17 Undo and remove the two long bolts which hold the motor assembly together.

18 Lift off the rear support bracket and the commutator end cover.

19 Release the springs on the two field coil brushes and slip these brushes out of their holders. Now lift off the brush holder assembly.

20 The procedure is now the same as for the Paris-Rhone motor described in paragraphs 5 to 7 inclusive.

---

18 Starter motor pinion carriage mechanism – removal and refitting

---

1 With the starter motor removed from the car begin by removing

the solenoid as described in Section 16. Next remove the end cover and brush gear as described in Section 17, according to starter motor type.

2 Having carried out these operations the starter motor body can now be carefully slid rearwards off the armature.

3 The procedure now varies slightly according to motor type as described below.

Paris-Rhone

4 Drive out the expansion pin and then withdraw the pin from the end housing.

5 Slide the armature and pinion carriage operating lever out of the end housing and then lift the lever off the armature.

Ducellier

6 Drive out the pinion carriage operating lever pivot pin from the end housing and then slide the armature and operating lever out of the housing. Lift the lever off the armature.

Bosch

7 Undo and remove the nut from the pinion carriage operating lever pivot bolt. Now withdraw the bolt from the end housing.

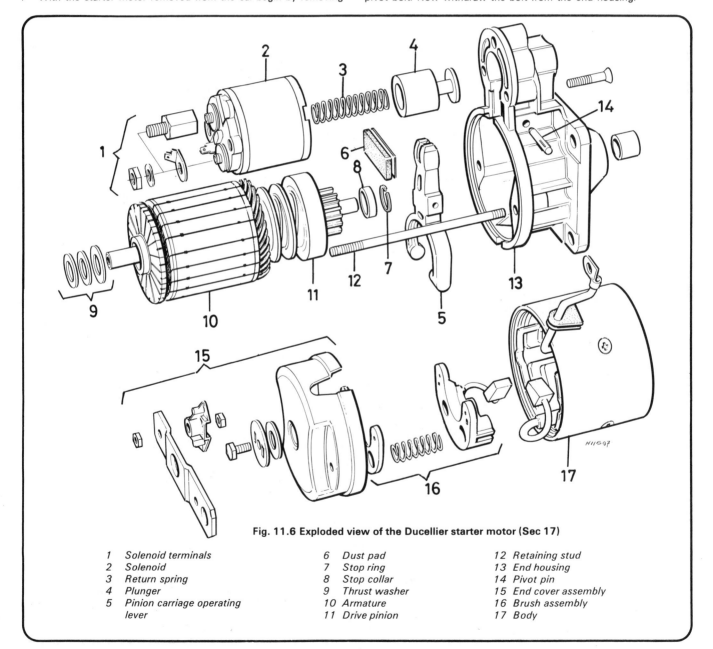

Fig. 11.6 Exploded view of the Ducellier starter motor (Sec 17)

1	Solenoid terminals	6	Dust pad	12	Retaining stud
2	Solenoid	7	Stop ring	13	End housing
3	Return spring	8	Stop collar	14	Pivot pin
4	Plunger	9	Thrust washer	15	End cover assembly
5	Pinion carriage operating	10	Armature	16	Brush assembly
	lever	11	Drive pinion	17	Body

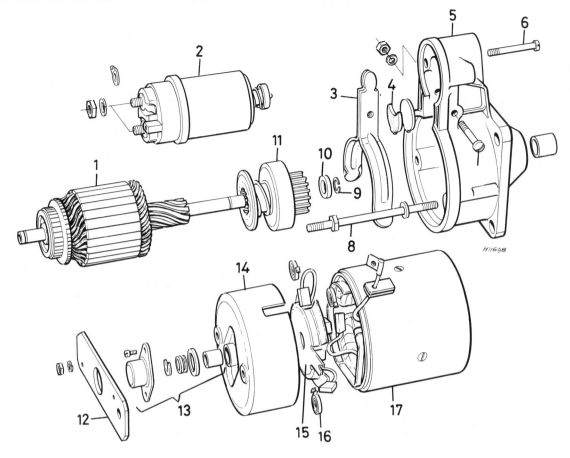

Fig. 11.7 Exploded view of the Bosch starter motor (Sec 17)

1	Armature	5	End housing	10	Stop collar	14	End cover
2	Solenoid	6	Solenoid retaining screw	11	Drive pinion	15	Brush holder
3	Pinion carriage operating lever	7	Pivot pin	12	Bracket	16	Brush spring
4	Dust cover	8	Retaining stud	13	End cap assembly	17	Field coils and body
		9	Stop ring				

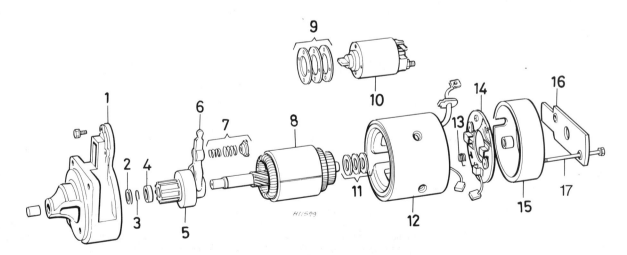

Fig. 11.8 Exploded view of the Mitsubishi starter motor (Sec 17)

1	End housing	5	Drive pinion	8	Armature	12	Body	15	End cover
2	Thrust washer	6	Pinion carriage operating lever	9	Solenoid shims	13	Brush spring	16	End bracket
3	Stop ring	7	Return springs	10	Solenoid	14	Brush and holder	17	Retaining bolt
4	Stop collar			11	Thrust washers				

8   Withdraw the armature and operating lever from the housing and separate the two components.

Mitsubishi

9   On these motors the pinion carriage operating lever is retained by a spring and clip. Extract the clip and spring and then slide the operating lever and armature out of the end housing.

All starter motors

10 Support the armature in a vice, vertically, taking care not to damage the commutator.
11 Using a hammer and tube of suitable diameter, tap the stop collar on the end of the armature shaft down just far enough to reveal the stop ring.
12 Hook out the stop ring, slide off the stop collar and then withdraw the pinion carriage mechanism.
13 The pinion carriage cannot be dismantled and if deemed faulty should be renewed. The armature shaft and spiral spline on which the pinion runs should be thoroughly cleaned and then lubricated with a light grade of engine oil.
14 Reassemble the pinion carriage to the armature shaft, followed by the stop collar. Refit the stop ring, ensuring that it fits tightly in its groove, and then pull the stop collar up over it to lock it in position.
15 The remainder of reassembly is a direct reversal of the dismantling sequence. **Note**: *Before refitting the starter motor to the car, check and if necessary adjust the drive pinion travel as described in Section 20.*

---

19 Starter motor – checking armature and static field windings

1   Follow the instructions given in Section 18 of this Chapter and dismantle the motor to gain access to the armature and the motor casing with the static field windings attached.
2   The armature windings may be checked for a short onto the motor shaft/armature core, and for an open-circuit in the windings.
3   Using a test circuit comprising two probes, a bulb and 12v battery, touch the commutator bars with one probe, whilst holding the other against the armature metal. The test bulb should not light up.
4   To check the armature windings for open circuit, replace the bulb with an ammeter (0 to 10 amp). Touch commutator bars (90° spaced) with the probes and note the ammeter reading. The readings should all be the same; considerable deviation (25%) indicates open-circuits or windings insulation breakdown.
5   The battery and bulb circuit is used to check the static field windings. Touch one probe onto each winding termination and hold the other against the metal of the motor casing. The test bulb must not light up. Remember to touch the positive brushes to check for short-circuits properly.
6   Faulty armatures or field windings should be renewed, though individual new spares may be difficult to obtain, and it will possibly be necessary to purchase an exchange motor unit.

---

20 Starter motor – drive pinion travel adjustment

1   Whenever the starter motor has been dismantled, or if a new or reconditioned unit is being fitted, it is necessary to adjust the drive pinion travel to obtain the correct mesh and clearance between the pinion teeth and the teeth on the flywheel ring gear.
2   With the starter solenoid at rest, the dimension from the end housing flange to the outer edge of the pinion must be 0.55 in (14 mm).
3   With the solenoid energized, the clearance between the end of the pinion and the pinion stop must be 0.019 to 0.059 in (0.5 to 1.5 mm). To energize the solenoid and enable this check to be carried out, connect one lead from a 12 volt battery to the small spade terminal on the solenoid. Using a switch in the circuit, connect the other battery terminal lead to one of the solenoid fixing studs.
4   If the pinion travel is incorrect, the adjustment procedure is as follows.

Paris-Rhone

5   Drive out the steel locking pin and rotate the plastic pivot pin until the 'at rest' dimension is obtained. Check that the clearance with the solenoid energized is satisfactory and then refit the locking pin.

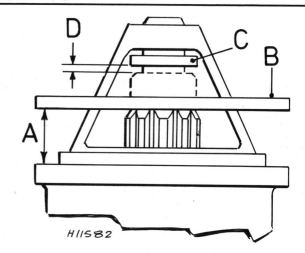

Fig. 11.9 Drive pinion meshing and clearance dimensions (Sec 20)

A   *Dimension with solenoid at rest = 0.55 in (14 mm)*
B   *Straight-edge*
C   *Pinion stop*
D   *Clearance with solenoid energized = 0.019 to 0.059 in (0.5 to 1.5 mm)*

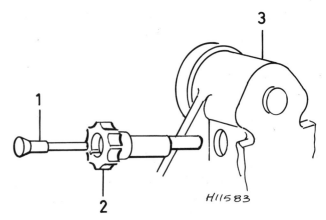

Fig. 11.10 Pinion mesh adjustment – Paris Rhone starter motor (Sec 20)

1   *Expansion pin*
2   *Eccentric pin*
3   *End housing*

Ducellier

6   Remove the plastic dust cover located between the solenoid mounting bolts in the end housing.
7   Using a suitable socket turn the adjusting bolt in the required direction, clockwise to decrease the 'at rest' dimension, anti-clockwise to increase it.
8   Check the clearance with the solenoid energized and if satisfactory refit the dust cover.

Bosch and Mitsubishi

9   If the dimensions are outside the tolerance given, adjustment is by removing the solenoid (see Section 16), and adding or subtracting shims between the solenoid and end housing until the 'at rest' and 'energized' positions of the drive pinion are correct.

---

21 Direction indicator flasher circuit – fault tracing and rectification

1   A flasher unit is located beneath the instrument panel next to the steering column. It plugs into a multi-connector and is retained by a single screw.

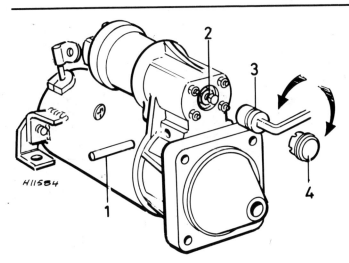

Fig. 11.11 Pinion mesh adjustment – Ducellier starter motor (Sec 20)

1   Pivot pin
2   Adjusting bolt and locknut
3   Socket spanner
4   Dust cap

2   If the flasher unit works twice as fast as usual when indicating either right or left turns, this is an indication that there is a broken filament in the front or rear indicator bulb on the side operating quickly.

3   If the external flashers are working but the internal flasher warning light has ceased to function, check the filament of the warning bulb and renew as necessary.

4   With the aid of the wiring diagram check all the flasher circuit connections if a flasher bulb is sound but does not work.

5   With the ignition switched on check that the current is reaching the flasher unit by connecting a voltmeter between the 'plus' teminal and earth. If it is found that current is reaching the unit, connect the two flasher unit terminals together and operate the direction indicator switch. If one of the flasher warning lights comes on this proves that the flasher unit itself is at fault and must be renewed as it is not possible to dismantle and repair it.

6   Do not overlook the earth connections of the flasher unit and the bulb holders when diagnosing faults.

22 Windscreen wiper mechanism – fault tracing and rectification

1   Should the windscreen wipers fail, or work very slowly, then check the terminals on the motor for loose connections and make sure that insulation of all wiring has not been damaged thus causing a short circuit. If this is in order then check the current the motor is taking by connecting an ammeter in the circuit and turning on the wiper switch. Consumption should be between 2.3 and 3.1 amps.

2   If no current is passing through the motor, check that the switch is operating correctly.

3   If the wiper motor takes a very high current check the wiper blades for freedom of movement. If this is satisfactory check the gearbox cover and gear assembly for damage.

4   If the motor takes a very low current ensure that the battery is fully charged. Check the brush gear and ensure the brushes are bearing on the commutator. If not, check the brushes for freedom of movement and, if necessary, renew the tension springs. If the brushes are very worn they should be replaced with new ones. Check the armature by substitution if this part is suspect.

23 Windscreen wiper components – removal and refitting

Wiper blades

1   To remove the wiper blades lift the arm up off the windscreen, rotate the blade through 90° and ease it off the end of the arm (photo).

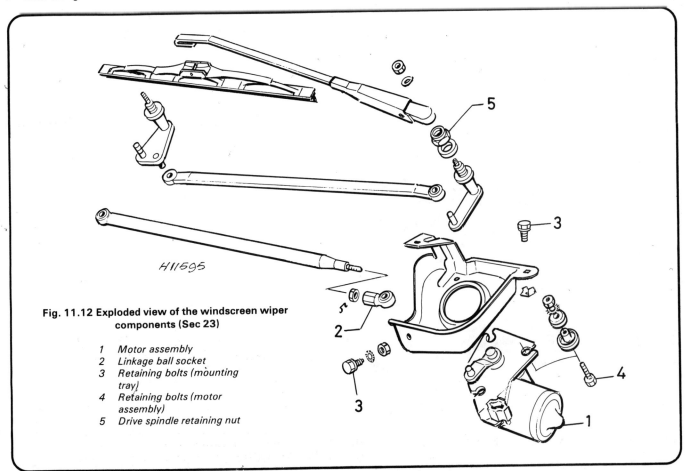

Fig. 11.12 Exploded view of the windscreen wiper components (Sec 23)

1   Motor assembly
2   Linkage ball socket
3   Retaining bolts (mounting tray)
4   Retaining bolts (motor assembly)
5   Drive spindle retaining nut

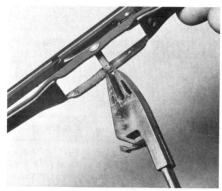

23.1 Removal of a windscreen wiper blade

23.5 Removal of a windscreen wiper arm

23.8 Detach the wiper linkage ballsocket ...

23.9 ... undo and remove the three tray retaining bolts (arrowed) ...

23.10 ... and disconnect the electrical multi-plug

23.11 Undo and remove three nuts and washers (arrowed) to separate motor from tray

2   Refit the blades using the reverse procedure to removal and ensure that the blade is pushed fully home into the slot on the end of the wiper arm.

Wiper arms
3   Before removing a wiper arm, turn the windscreen wiper switch on and off (ignition on) to ensure the arms are in their normal parked position parallel with the bottom of the windscreen.
4   To remove the arm, pivot the cap back to expose the retaining nut.
5   Undo and remove the nut and then withdraw the wiper arm off the splined drive spindle (photo).

24.1 Windscreen washer pump location in engine compartment

6   When refitting an arm, position it so that it is in the correct relative parked position, then press the arm head onto the splined spindle and refit the nut.

Wiper motor
7   Disconnect the battery earth terminal.
8   Disengage the ball connection of the linkage at the motor (photo).
9   Undo and remove the three bolts that secure the wiper motor tray to the bulkhead and valance (photo).
10   Lift out the tray and motor assembly and disconnect the wiring harness plug (photo).
11   Undo and remove the three nuts, washers and bolts, and lift the motor off the mounting tray (photo).
12   Refitting is the reverse sequence to removal.

Wiper linkage
13   Remove both wiper arms from their drive spindles as described previously.
14   Disengage the ball connection of the linkage at the motor.
15   Undo and remove the nut and spacing washer securing each drive spindle to the front scuttle.
16   Lift out the complete linkage assembly from under the scuttle.
17   Refitting the linkage is the reverse sequence to removal.

24 Windscreen washer – description and servicing

1   The washer motor is attached to the right-hand valance inside the engine compartment (photo). It cannot be repaired and if faulty must be renewed.
2   Servicing should be limited to occasionally checking the security of the tubes and connectors and the security of the electrical leads to the switch and pump motor. Keep the washer fluid container topped up.
3   The spray pattern can be adjusted by inserting a pin in the jet orifice and swivelling the jet(s) in the required direction.

25 Rear window wiper mechanism – fault tracing and rectification

The fault diagnosis and rectification for the rear window wiper mechanism is the same as described in Section 22, for the windscreen wiper.

26 Rear window wiper components – removal and refitting

Wiper blade

1　Lift the wiper arm off the window, depress the catch on the side of the wiper arm (where applicable) and slide off the blade.
2　Refitting is the reverse of the removal procedure.

Wiper arm

3　Undo and remove the nut securing the arm to the motor spindle, recover the washer and lift off the arm.
4　Refitting the arm is the reverse of the above.

Wiper motor

5　Disconnect the battery earth terminal.
6　Remove the wiper arm as described in paragraph 3.
7　Undo and remove the motor spindle retaining nut, distance piece and seal.
8　Open the tailgate and lift off the motor housing cover.
9　Disconnect the electrical leads at the connectors and then undo the bolt securing the earth lead to the tailgate interior.
10　Undo and remove the two motor retaining bolts and withdraw the unit (photo).
11　Refitting the wiper motor is the reverse sequence to removal.

27 Rear window washer – description and servicing

1　The rear window washer reservoir, pump and delay switch are contained within the space between the rear inner and outer panel. Access to the components may be gained after removing the left-hand rear light cluster.
2　The servicing requirements are similar to those of the windscreen washer and reference should be made to Section 24.

28 Horn – description, fault tracing and rectification

1　The horn is located in the engine compartment and is bolted to a bracket to the front engine mounting support.
2　If the horn fails to operate, disconnect the horn feed wire and connect a test light between the feed wire and earth.
3　Have an assistant operate the horn switch, with the ignition on, and check that the test light illuminates,
4　If the test lamp lights but the horn (when connected) does not operate, the horn is faulty and as it is a sealed unit must therefore be renewed.

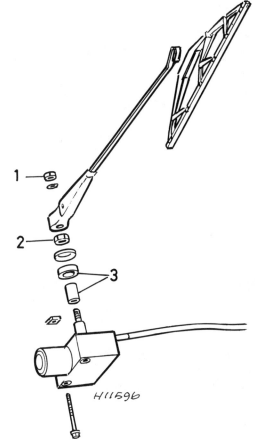

Fig. 11.13 Rear window wiper mountings (Sec 26)

1　Wiper arm retaining nut
2　Motor spindle retaining nut
3　Distance piece and seal

5　If the test lamp fails to light, check the wiring for loose or corroded connections, check for a blown fuse, clean the horn terminals and re-test.

29 Headlights – bulb renewal

1　Open the bonnet and pull the electrical plug off the rear of the headlight bulb (photo).
2　Withdraw the rubber water guard, release the spring clips and lift out the bulb (photos). On some Halogen type bulbs it is necessary to

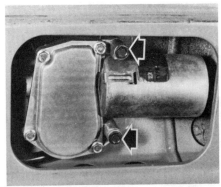

26.10 Rear window wiper motor retaining bolts (arrowed)

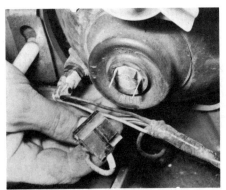

29.1 Detach the electrical plug ...

29.2a ... remove the rubber guard ...

29.2b ... release the spring clip ...

29.2c ... and lift out the headlight bulb

30.3 Withdraw the two retaining clips ...

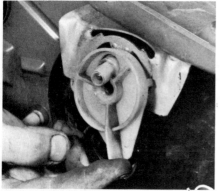

30.4 ... remove the height control wheel from the vertical adjuster ...

30.5 ... and lift out the headlight unit

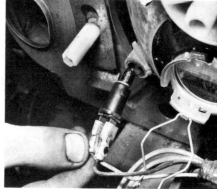

32.1 Sidelight bulb renewal

33.1a Remove the screws and lens ...

33.1b ... to renew the indicator bulb

34.1 Remove the three screws and the lens ...

34.2 ... to gain access to the rear lamp cluster

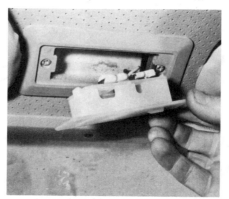

35.1 Ease out the interior lamp lens ...

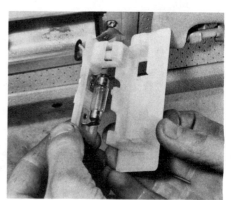

35.2 ... and separate the lens from the bulb holder

turn the bulb outer ring so that the tags are aligned with the notches.
Caution: *With all headlight bulbs, and Halogen types, particularly, avoid touching the glass of the bulb with your fingers as this could cause premature failure of the bulb.* If a bulb is accidentally touched, clean it with methylated spirit.
3   Refit the bulb using the reverse procedure to that of removal.

30 Headlight unit – removal and refitting

1   Remove the front finishing strip from below the front of the headlight unit by unclipping the side fastener and then sliding the strap sideways.
2   Pull the electrical plug off the rear of the headlight bulb and pull the sidelight bulb holder out of its location in the headlight unit.
3   Push the two spring clips upwards to release them from the side adjusting knobs (photo).
4   Press the upper front part of the headlight unit inward and remove the nylon height control wheel from the vertical adjustment knob (photo).
5   Withdraw the headlight unit complete with adjusters from the front of the car (photo).
6   Refit the headlight unit using the reverse of the removal procedure and adjust the headlight alignment as described in the following Section.

31 Headlights – alignment

1   To compensate for the different height of the vehicle when it is either loaded or unloaded, there is a two-position nylon control knob at the rear of the headlight unit. When rotating the control knob, press the headlight lens inwards slightly to relieve the tension of the spring.
2   Completely resetting the headlight alignment is achieved by rotating the three nylon knobs on the rear of the light only.
3   It is always advisable to have the headlamps aligned on proper optical beam setting equipment but if this is not available the following procedures may be used.
4   Position the car on level ground 30 feet (9 metres) in front of a dark wall or board. The wall or board must be at right angles to the centre line of the car.
5   Draw a vertical line on the board in line with the centre line of the car.
6   Bounce the car on its suspension to ensure correct settlement and then measure the height between the ground and the centre of the headlamps.
7   Draw a horizontal line across the board at this measured height. On this horizontal line mark a cross at a point equal to half the distance between the headlamp centres either side of the vertical centre line.
8   Adjust the headlight position by rotating the lower nylon knobs in the required direction for lateral alignment, and the top knob for vertical alignment. The knobs have slotted ends and can be turned using a coin.
9   If a beamsetter is used the top knob must be in the unloaded position prior to adjustment

32 Front sidelamp – bulb renewal

1   Access to the bulb is gained by pulling the bulb holder from the lower rear end of the headlight unit (photo).
2   Renew the bulb with one of the same wattage and push the holder back into place.

33 Front indicator – bulb renewal

1   Access is obtained simply by removing the two lens securing screws (photos).
2   Renew the bulbs with ones of the same type and wattage. Do not overtighten the lens securing screws.

34 Rear lamp cluster – bulb renewal

1   Remove the three retaining screws and withdraw the rear lens (photo).
2   Renew any defective bulbs with ones of the same wattage, do not overtighten the lens retaining screws (photo).
3   The complete bulb holder assembly can be removed if required by pressing down the six retaining clips and withdrawing the unit from the car body aperture.

35 Interior lamps – bulb renewal

1   Carefully lever out the lens using a small screwdriver (photo).
2   Separate the lens from the bulb holder and lift out the bulb (photo).
3   After renewing the bulb ensure that the wire is tucked inside and not trapped before pushing the lens back into place.

36 Push-push switches – removal and refitting

1   To remove a push-push switch illuminating bulb, withdraw the switch button and lift out the bulb (photo).
2   To remove the switch, ease the switch body out of the panel carefully with a small screwdriver or pliers.
3   Disconnect the electrical connections before dismantling the switch.
4   Refitting is the reverse sequence to removal.

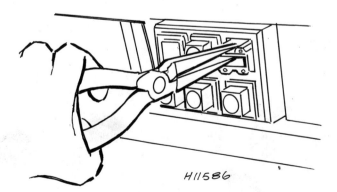

Fig. 11.14 Push-push switch body removal (Sec 36)

36.1 Removing a push-push switch button

37 Steering column multi-function switch – removal and refitting

1   Disconnect the battery earth terminal.
2   Refer to Chapter 8, and remove the steering wheel.
3   Undo and remove the retaining screws and lift off the steering column lower shroud (photo).
4   Undo and remove the two screws securing the upper shroud and remove it from the column (photo).
5   Undo and remove the screw securing the wiring harness support bracket and lift off the bracket.
6   Disconnect the wiring harness multi-plug connectors and line connectors located under the dash.
7   Undo and remove the three screws securing the multi-function switch and lift the switch off the steering column (photo).
8   Refitting the switch is the reverse sequence to removal.

38 Instrument panel warning light bulbs – renewal

1   Disconnect the battery earth terminal.
2   Withdraw the locking pin from each side of the instrument panel window lower edge (photo).
3   Pull the window downward to disengage the two upper retaining clips and lift it off (photo).
4   The warning light bulbs are simply a push fit in their holders (photo).
5   Refit the instrument panel window in the reverse order to removal.

39 Instrument panel – removal and refitting

1   Disconnect the battery earth terminal.
2   Withdraw the locking pin from each side of the instrument panel window lower edge.
3   Pull the window downward to disengage the two upper retaining clips and lift it off.
4   Undo the two screws which secure the lower part, and remove the

two pegs which retain the upper part, of the instrument panel in the binnacle.
5   Tip the instrument panel at the top, away from the windscreen and remove the speedometer cable from the rear of the speedometer by depressing the catch on the side of the cable head connector (photo).
6   Now lift the instrument panel further forward, pull out the wiring harness plug connectors and withdraw the panel from the car.
7   Refitting is the direct reversal of the foregoing procedure.

40 Instrument panel – dismantling and reassembly

1   Having removed the instrument panel from the car, the following components can now be removed.

Instruments
2   Each instrument is retained by two small bolts accessible from the front of the panel. With the bolts removed the instrument is simply lifted out. Refit the instruments in the same manner (Fig. 11.15).

Panel illuminating bulbs
3   From the rear of the panel the bulb holders are removed by turning anti-clockwise and lifting out. The bulbs are a push fit in the holders (photo).
4   Refit the bulb holders by depressing and turning clockwise slightly.

Voltage regulator
5   The voltage regulator is fitted to early Horizon models only (photo). Later versions are fitted with electro-magnetic instruments which are not affected by slight voltage fluctuation.
6   The voltage regulator is retained by a single screw.

Printed circuit
7   Having removed all the instruments, bulb holders and voltage regulator (where fitted), depress the tags and lift the printed circuit off the rear of the panel (photo).
8   Refitting is the reverse sequence to removal.

37.3 Removing the steering column lower shroud retaining screws

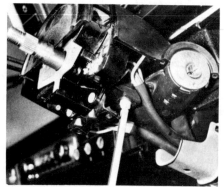

37.4 Removing the steering column upper shroud retaining screws

37.7 The multi-function switch is retained by three screws (arrowed)

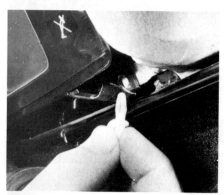

38.2 Withdraw the instrument panel window locking pins ...

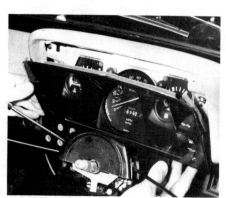

38.3 ... and lift off the window

38.4 The bulbs are a simple push fit in their holders

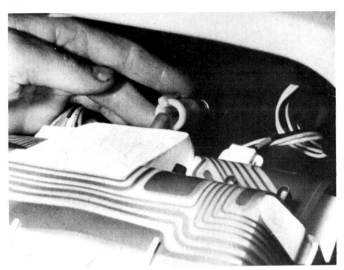

39.5 Disconnecting the speedometer cable from the rear of the instrument panel

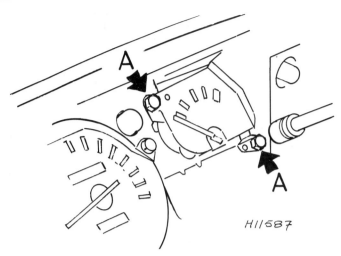

Fig. 11.15 Removal of an instrument (Sec 40)

A   Securing bolts

40.2 The instruments are each secured to the panel with two small bolts (arrowed)

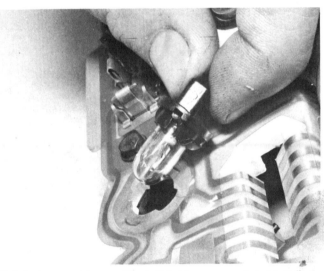

40.3 At the rear of the panel the bulb holders are a push and turn fit

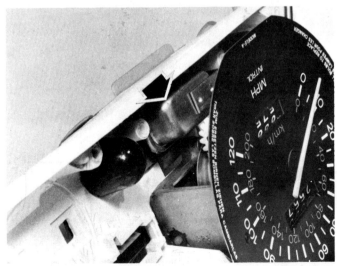

40.5 The instrument voltage regulator (arrowed) is located behind the speedometer

41 Speedometer cable – removal and refitting

1   Disconnect the battery earth terminal.
2   Refer to Section 39, and withdraw the instrument panel sufficiently to enable the speedometer cable to be detached from the rear of the speedometer.
3   Undo and remove the bolt securing the other end of the cable to the adaptor on the differential housing.
4   Lift the cable out of the adaptor (photo) and draw the speedometer end through the bulkhead grommet and into the engine compartment. The complete cable can now be removed from the car.
5   Refitting is the reverse sequence to removal. Take care not to twist or kink the cable when fitting and ensure that the grommet in the bulkhead is properly in position when the cable is installed.

42 Stop-light switch – removal, refitting and adjustment

1   The stop-light switch is a mechanical unit, screwed into a bracket above the brake pedal and activated by brake pedal movement.
2   To remove the switch, first disconnect the electrical connections and then slacken the adjusting locknut. The switch can now be unscrewed from the bracket.

3   Refitting the stop-light switch is the reverse sequence to removal. Once in position it must be adjusted as follows.
4   Depress the brake pedal at least six times (engine stopped) to exhaust the vacuum in the servo unit.
5   Switch on the ignition but do not start the engine.
6   Depress the brake pedal pad slowly by hand. The stop-lights must remain off while the centre of the pedal pad moves approximately $\frac{1}{8}$ in (3 mm) and must illuminate by the time the pedal pad has moved $\frac{5}{8}$ in (15 mm).
7   If necessary, slacken the switch locknut, disconnect the wires and screw the switch in or out of its bracket until the operating distances are correct. Then tighten the locknut, reconnect the wires and recheck.

43 Door pillar switches – removal and refitting

1   Undo and remove the single screw securing the switch to the bodywork and withdraw the switch (photo).
2   Disconnect the electrical lead and lift away the switch.
3   Refitting is the reverse sequence to removal. Spray the switch with a water-repelling electrical lubricant before refitting.

40.7 Printed circuit location at rear of instrument panel

41.4 Removing the speedometer cable from the adaptor on the final drive housing

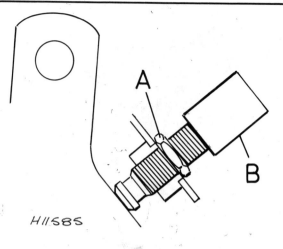

Fig. 11.16 Sectional view of the stop-light switch mounting (Sec 42)

A   Switch locknut
B   Stop-light switch

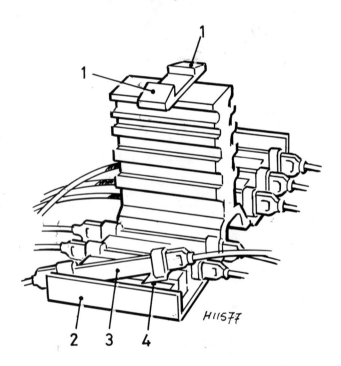

Fig. 11.17 Fuse holder assembly (Sec 44)

1   Retaining clips
2   Fuse holder
3   Fuse
4   Fuse locating claw

44 Fuses – general

1   The fuse block is located in the engine compartment on the right-hand side wing valance.
2   To gain access to the six fuses, unclip the fuse block from its holder and then depress the two projections inwards to open the fuse block. Spread the clips on the fuse holders and lift them out of the block.
3   Fuse failure may be diagnosed by the simultaneous failure of several electrical systems.
4   If a fuse blows, it must be replaced with a fuse of the same rating.

43.1 Door pillar switch removal

If the new fuse blows immediately the particular electrical service is operated, there is a fault in that component or its system and the circuit must be carefully inspected to find the cause of the trouble.

5   The fuses and their respective circuits are shown in the following table. The first colour referred to in the table is the cable colour, the second colour is the colour of the small dot on the cable insulator.

9 Series models (1978–1979)

Colour code		Fuse rating	Circuits protected
Cable in	Cable out		
Red/yellow	White/yellow	16A	Heated rear window
Red/red	White/red	10A	Electric clock Interior lamp and map lamp Luggage compartment lamp Control box, engine oil level warning indicator Direction indicator flasher unit
Grey/Grey	Grey/grey	10A	Windscreen wiper motor and washer pump Reversing lamps Stop-lamps Control box, engine oil level indicator
Purple/purple	Purple/purple	10A*	Tailgate wiper* Digital clock Cigar lighter Heater blower motor
Blue/brown	Blue/brown	10A	Rear foglamps
Green/green	Green/green	10A	Cigar lighter and ashtray illumination Heater controls and switch illumination Instrument and clock illumination Side and rear lamps, number plate illumination

Note: *This fuse may be uprated to 16A where frequent fuse blowing is occurring on this circuit. On later 9 Series models a 5A in-line fuse located adjacent to the cigar lighter behind the facia protects the tailgate wiper motor.*

A separate 1.6A in-line fuse mounted on the heater control panel behind the facia is used to protect the radio/cassette player.

All models 1980 on

Colour code		Fuse rating	Circuits protected
Cable in	Cable out		
Red/yellow	White/yellow	16A	Heated rear window
Red/red	White/red	10A	Electric clock Interior lamp and map lamp Direction indicator flasher unit Luggage compartment lamp control box, engine oil level indicator
Slate/slate	Slate/slate	10A	Windscreen wiper motor and washer pump Headlight wash/wipe and tailgate washer pump Reversing lamps Stop-lamps Control box, engine oil level indicator Speed control Photo-electric cell, fuel meter Automatic transmission selector lever illumination
Purple/purple	Purple/purple	16A	Heater blower motor Cigar lighter Digital clock and trip computer Headlight wash/wipe
Blue/brown	Blue/brown	10A	Rear foglamps
Green/green	Green/green	10A	Side and rear lamps Number plate illumination Instrument and clock illumination Heater control and switch illumination Cigar lighter and ashtray illumination

In-line fuses

The in-line fuses used on A Series models are identical to those listed previously for 9 Series Horizon models.

6   Never be tempted to bypass a persistently blowing fuse with tinfoil or wire, or substitute a fuse of a higher rating (except as mentioned above for 9 Series models). Serious electrical damage, or even fire, may result.

45 Electronic oil level indicator system – general description

The electronic oil level indicator system consists of a sensor in the dipstick, a control unit mounted under the dash, a warning light on the instrument panel and associated wiring. The circuit diagram is included in Fig. 11.32.

The dipstick sensor is a resistor which will be completely or partially immersed in oil depending on the level in the sump. When the engine is started, a small electric current is passed through the resistor, causing its temperature to rise. If the oil level in the sump is correct, the resistor will be completely submerged in oil which will dissipate the heat. The temperature increase will therefore be very small. If the oil level is low, the resistor will not be cooled and a large increase in temperature will occur. This will cause an increase in resistance of the sensor and thus of the voltage at its terminals in the control unit. The voltage increase will trigger an electronic circuit in the control unit, causing the warning light on the instrument panel to flash,

48.3 Cruise control servo unit

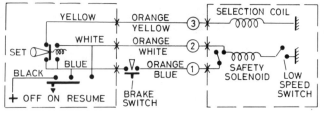

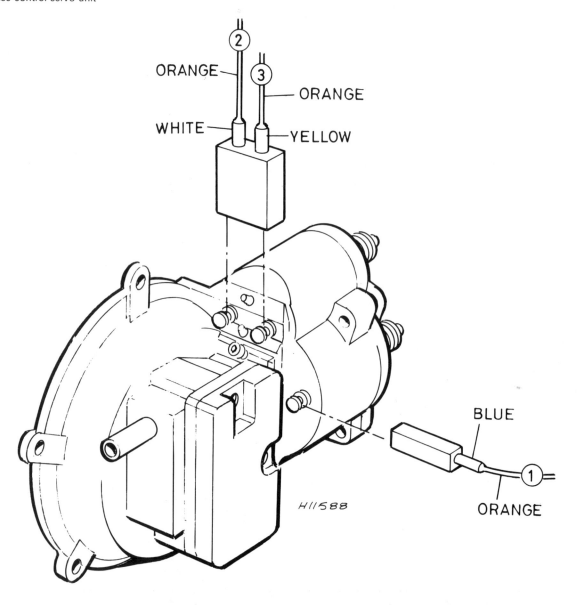

Fig. 11.18 Cruise control servo unit and control unit, showing interconnecting wiring diagram (Sec 48)

thus informing the driver of low oil level in the sump.

46 Electronic oil level indicator system – fault tracing

1   Due to the complex nature of the circuitry, other than checking that all electrical connections are clean and tight, the tracing of faults on this system is considered to be beyond the scope of this manual and should be entrusted to a Talbot dealer.
2   The dipstick may be tested by substitution but it is not recommended that this method be used for the control unit as a fault in the wiring harness may damage the new unit.
3   If, however, the control unit is known to be faulty it may be removed and a new unit fitted as described in the following Section.
4   Do not overlook the fact that the oil level indication will not be correct when the vehicle is parked on a slope.

47 Electronic oil level indicator control unit – removal and refitting

1   Disconnect the battery earth terminal.
2   Undo and remove the three securing screws and one clip and lift off the facia panel surrounding the heater controls.
3   Undo and remove the two securing screws and ease the heater control bracket forward.
4   Release the retaining clip and lift out the trim panel beneath the heater control aperture.
5   Undo and remove the screw securing the right-hand edge of the parcel tray and push the tray down.
6   Make a note of the position of the multi-plug on the oil level indicator control unit and then disconnect the plug.
7   Undo and remove the two control unit securing screws and withdraw the unit from under the dash.
8   Refitting is the reverse sequence to removal.

48 Cruise control (SX models) – description and maintenance

1   The cruise control allows the driver to programme a suitable cruising speed (above 30 mph) into the unit's electronic memory; that speed will then be maintained, regardless of road conditions, until the driver switches the unit off or operates the throttle or brake pedals. The control should only be used under conditions that permit steady speed driving – eg motorway or open road cruising.
2   Operation of the cruise control is as follows. With the vehicle travelling at the desired speed and with the switch in the ON position, the driver presses the SET button to enter the speed into the unit's memory. If the throttle pedal is now released, the set speed will be maintained. Acceleration can take place normally, eg for overtaking, and the set speed will be resumed when the accelerator is released. Operation of the brakes will temporarily disengage the unit until the switch is moved to the RESUME position momentarily. The set speed can be changed by accelerating or braking to the new desired speed and again depressing the SET button. The memory is cleared when the ignition is turned off or when the switch is moved to the OFF position.
3   The components of the cruise control are the switch, the control unit and the servo unit. These last two items have a common mounting. The control unit receives information of vehicle speed and commands from the control switch and the stop-light switch; the servo is vacuum-operated (photo).
4   Maintenance is confined to checking the security and cleanliness of all electrical connections, and verifying the mechanical condition of all other components. Adjustment of the servo cable is described in Chapter 6. Fault diagnosis and rectification should be entrusted to your Talbot dealer, due to the specialised knowledge and test equipment required; repair is by renewal of faulty units.

49 Trip computer – description and maintenance

Fitted to SX models as standard equipment, and to certain other models as an optional extra, the trip computer provides information relating to time, distance and fuel consumption. Apart from the computer itself, the other components of the systems are a fuel flow meter, a speed sensor, and associated wiring.

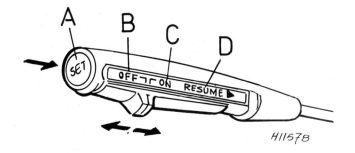

Fig. 11.19 Cruise control operating switch (Sec 48)

A   *SET button*
B   *OFF position*
C   *ON position*
D   *RESUME position*

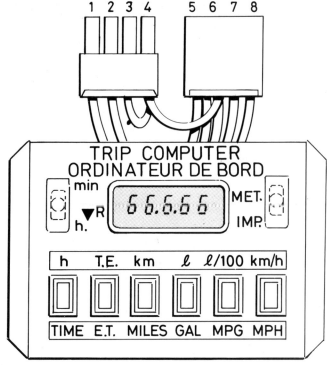

Fig. 11.20 Trip computer and connecting plugs (Sec 49)

1	*(Brown)*	*Fuel flow meter*
2	*(Yellow)*	*Speed sensor*
3	*(Black)*	*Fuel flow meter earth*
4	*(Black)*	*Speed sensor earth*
5	*(Yellow/Orange)*	*Sidelights*
6	*(Black/Black)*	*Earth*
7	*(Blue)*	*Ignition*
8	*(Red)*	*Battery+*

The computer is set up initially by switching on the ignition, pressing the E/T (elapsed time) button and simultaneously pressing the RESET control downwards. Clock time can be set (if necessary) by pressing the TIME button and moving the RESET control upwards to alter minutes, downwards to alter hours. The computer now stores all information fed to it until it is reset (or until the memory is saturated) and at the push of the appropriate button will display elapsed journey time (time with ignition on), total distance, total fuel consumption, average fuel consumption and average speed. The average fuel consumption and speed figures will not be significant on short journeys and should in any case be disregarded for the first couple of minutes of operation.

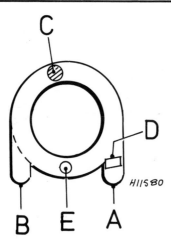

Fig. 11.21 Fuel flow meter – principle of operation. There is a light bulb opposite the photo-electric cell (Sec 49)

A   Fuel inlet
B   Fuel outlet
C   Ball
D   Restrictor
E   Photo-electric cell

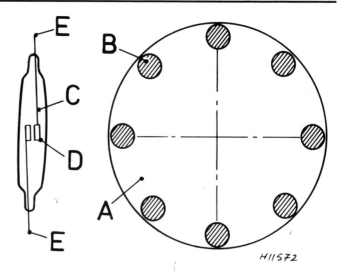

Fig. 11.23 Speed sensor – principle of operation. The magnets close the reed switch contacts as they pass (Sec 49)

A   Internal rotor
B   Magnet
C   Reed switch
D   Contact blade
E   Feed wires

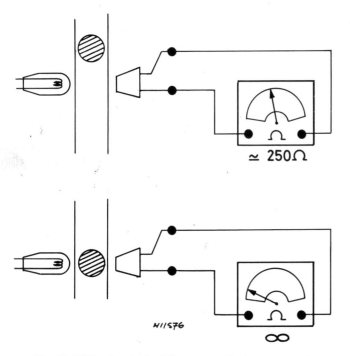

Fig. 11.22 Testing the fuel flow meter. Resistance should fluctuate as shown as ball passes photo-electric cell (Sec 49)

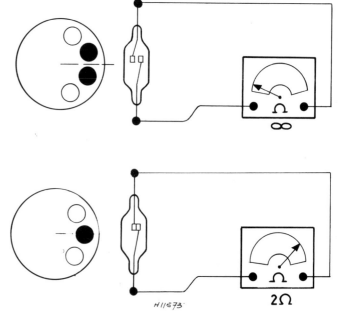

Fig. 11.24 Testing the speed sensor. Resistance should fluctuate as shown as magnets pass reed switch (Sec 49)

As with the cruise control, maintenance is confined to checking the security and cleanliness of electrical connections and the good mechanical condition of other components. The fuel flow meter, mounted on the output side of the fuel pump, can be removed for cleaning if desired. Note that the light bulb in the fuel flow meter must be working in order for the meter to function. The speed sensor unit, mounted between the speedometer cable and the speedometer drive on the transmission, cannot be repaired and if faulty must be renewed. Consult your Talbot dealer before condemning any unit. Replacements are unlikely to be cheap! If an ohmmeter is available, the sender units can be checked with reference to Figs. 11.22 and 11.24.

50 Radios and tape players – fitting (general)

A radio is fitted as standard equipment to all later models. On vehicles not so equipped use the following installation procedure.

A radio or tape player is an expensive item to buy and will only give its best performance if fitted properly. It is useless to expect concert hall performance from a unit that is suspended from the dash panel on string with its speaker resting on the back seat or parcel shelf! If you do not wish to do the fitting yourself there are many in-car entertainment specialists who can do the fitting for you.

Make sure the unit purchased is of the same polarity as the car, and ensure that units with adjustable polarity are correctly set before commencing fitting. All Horizon models (and most modern car radios) are negative earth.

Radios

Most radios are a standardised size of 7 in wide, by 2 in deep – this ensures that they will fit into the radio aperture provided in the Horizon. Some radios will have mounting brackets provided together with instructions: others will need to be fitted using drilled and slotted metal strips, bent to form mounting brackets – these strips are available from most accessory shops. The unit must be properly earthed, by fitting a separate earthing lead between the casing of the radio and the vehicle frame.

Use the radio manufacturer's instructions when wiring the radio into the vehicle's electrical system. If no instructions are available, refer to the relevant wiring diagram to find the location of the radio 'feed' connection in the vehicle's wiring circuit. A 1 to 2 amp 'in-line' fuse must be fitted in the radio's feed wire – a choke may also be necessary (see next Section).

The type of aerial used, and its fitted position is a matter of personal preference. In general the taller the aerial, the better the reception. It is best to fit a fully retractable aerial – expecially if a mechanical car-wash is used or if you live in an area where cars tend to be vandalised. In this respect electric aerials which are raised and lowered automatically when switching the radio on and off are convenient, but are more likely to give trouble than the manual type.

When choosing a site for the aerial the following points should be considered:

(a) *The aerial lead should be as short as possible – this means that the aerial should be mounted at the front of the car*
(b) *The aerial must be mounted as far away from the distributor and HT leads as possible*
(c) *The part of the aerial which protrudes beneath the mounting point must not foul the roadwheels, or anything else*
(d) *If possible the aerial should be positioned so that the coaxial lead does not have to be routed through the engine compartment*
(e) *The plane of the panel on which the aerial is mounted should not be so steeply angled that the aerial cannot be mounted vertically (in relation to the 'end-on' aspect of the car). Most aerials have a small amount of adjustment available.*

Having decided on a mounting position, a relatively large hole will have to be made in the panel. The exact size of the hole will depend upon the specific aerial being fitted, although, generally, the hole required is of 19 mm (0.75 in) diameter. On metal bodied cars, a 'tank-cutter' of the relevant diameter is the best tool to use for making the hole. This tool needs a small diameter pilot hole drilled through the panel, through which the tool clamping bolt is inserted. When the hole has been made the raw edges should be de-burred with a file and then painted, to prevent corrosion.

Fit the aerial according to the manufacturer's instructions. If the aerial is very tall, or if it protrudes beneath the mounting panel for a considerable distance, it is a good idea to fit a stay between the aerial and the vehicle's frame. This stay can be manufactured from the slotted and drilled metal strips previously mentioned. The stay should be securely screwed or bolted in place. For best reception, it is advisable to fit an earth lead between the aerial and the vehicle frame.

It will probably be necessary to drill one or two holes through bodywork panels in order to feed the aerial lead into the interior of the car. Where this is the case, ensure that the holes are fitted with rubber grommets to protect the cable, and to stop possible entry of water.

Positioning and fitting of the speaker depends mainly on its type. The speakers supplied with a factory-installed radio are mounted in the door trim. It is a good idea to fit a 'gasket' between the speaker frame and the mounting panel, in order to prevent vibration – some speakers will already have such a gasket fitted.

When connecting a rear mounted speaker to the radio, the wires should be routed through the vehicle beneath the carpets or floor mats – preferably the middle, or along the side of the floorpan, where they will not be trodden on by passengers. Make the relevant connections as directed by the radio manufacturer.

By now you will have several yards of additional wiring in the car;

use PVC tape to secure this wiring out of harm's way. Do not leave electrical leads dangling. Ensure that all new electrical connections are properly made (wires twisted together will not do) and completely secure.

The radio should now be working, but before you pack away your tools it will be necessary to 'trim' the radio to the aerial. If specific instructions are not provided by the radio manufacturer, proceed as follows. Find a station with a low signal strength on the medium wave band, slowly turn the trim screw of the radio in, or out, until the loudest reception of the selected station is obtained – the set is then trimmed to the aerial.

Tape players

Fitting instructions for both cartridges and cassette stereo type players are the same, and in general the same rules apply as when fitting a radio. Tape players are not usually prone to electrical interference like radios – although it can occur – so positioning is not so critical. If possible, the player should be mounted on an even keel. Also, it must be possible for a driver wearing a seat belt to reach the unit in order to change or turn over tapes.

For the best results from speakers designed to be recessed into a panel, mount them so that the back of the speaker protrudes into an enclosed chamber within the car (eg door interiors or the boot cavity).

To fit recessed type speakers in the front doors, first check that there is sufficient room to mount a speaker in each door without it fouling the latch or window winding mechanism. Hold the speaker against the skin of the door, and draw a line around the periphery of the speaker. With the speaker removed draw a second 'cutting' line, within the first, to allow enough room for the entry of the speaker back, but, at the same time, providing a broad seat for the speaker flange. When you are sure that the 'cutting-line' is correct, drill a series of holes around its periphery. Pass a hacksaw blade through one of the holes and then cut through the metal between the holes until the centre section of the panel falls out.

De-burr the edges of the hole, then paint the raw metal to prevent corrosion. Cut a corresponding hole in the door trim panel – ensuring that it will be completely covered by the speaker grille. Now drill a hole in the door edge and a corresponding hole in the door surround. These holes are to feed the speaker leads through – so fit grommets. Pass the speaker leads through the door trim, door skin and out through the holes in the side of the door and door surround. Refit the door trim panel, then secure the speaker to the door using self-tapping screws. Note that if the speaker is fitted with a shield to prevent water dripping on it, ensure that this shield is at the top.

51 Radios and tape players – suppression of interference (general)

To eliminate buzzes and other unwanted noises costs very little and is not as difficult as sometimes thought. With a modicum of common sense and patience, and following the instructions in the following paragraphs, interferences can be virtually eliminated.

The first cause for concern is the generator. The noise this makes over the radio is like an electric mixer and the noise speeds up when you rev up (if you wish to prove the point, you can remove the drivebelt and try it). The remedy for this is simple; connect a 1.0 μf to 3.0 μf capacitor between earth, probably the bolt that holds down the generator base, and the *large* terminal on the alternator. **This is most important:** *If you connect it to the small terminal, you will probably damage the generator permanently (see Fig. 11.25).*

A second common cause of electrical interference is the ignition system. Here a 1.0 μf capacitor must be connected between earth and the 'SW' or '+' terminal on the coil (see Fig. 11.26). This may stop the 'tick-tick-tick' sound that comes over the speaker. Resistive HT leads are fitted to the Horizon as standard equipment, and provided that no non-standard substitutes have been made, further suppression of the ignition system is neither necessary nor desirable.

At this stage, it is advisable to check that the radio is well earthed, also the aerial, and to see that the aerial plug is pushed well into the set and that the radio is properly trimmed (see preceding Section). In addition, check that the wire which supplies the power to the set is as short as possible and does not wander all over the car.

At this point, the more usual causes of interference have been suppressed. If the problem still exists, a look at the cause of

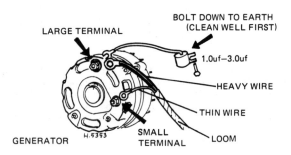

Fig. 11.25 The correct way to connect a capacitor to the alternator (Sec 51)

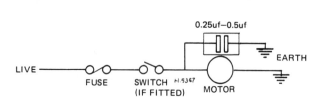

Fig. 11.27 Suppression of electric motors (Sec 51)

Fig. 11.26 Correct connection of a suppressor capacitor to the coil (Sec 51)

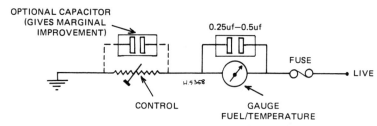

Fig. 11.28 Suppression of fuel or temperature gauge (Sec 51)

Fig. 11.29 Correct fitting of an in-line choke (Sec 51)

interference may help to pinpoint the component generating the stray electrical discharges.

The radio picks up electromagnetic waves in the air; now some are made by radio stations and other broadcasters and some, not wanted, are made by the car. The home made signals are produced by stray electrical discharges floating around the car. Common producers of these signals are electric motors; ie, the windscreen wipers, electric screen washers, electric window winders, heater fan or an electric aerial if fitted. Other sources of interference are flashing turn signals and instruments. The remedy for these cases is shown in Fig. 11.27 for an electric motor whose interference is not too bad and Fig. 11.28 for instrument suppression. Turn signals are not normally suppressed. In recent years, radio manufacturers have included in the line (live) of the radio, in addition to the fuse, an 'in-line' choke. If your installation lacks one of these put one in as shown in Fig. 11.29. All the foregoing components are available from radio shops or accessory shops. For a transistor radio, a 2A choke should be adequate.

If after all this, you are still experiencing radio interference, first assess how bad it is, for the human ear can filter out unobtrusive unwanted noses quite easily. But if you are still adamant about eradicating the noise, then continue.

As a first step, a few 'experts' seem to favour a screen between the radio and the engine. This is OK as far as it goes, literally! – for the whole set is screened and if interference can get past that, then a small piece of aluminium is not going to stop it.

A more sensible way of screening is to discover if interference is coming down the wires. First, take the live lead; interference can get between the set and the choke (hence the reason for keeping the wires short). One remedy here is to screen the wire and this is done by buying screened wire and fitting that. The loudspeaker lead could be screened also to prevent 'pick-up' getting back to the radio – although this is unlikely.

Without doubt, the worst source of radio interference is the ignition HT leads, even if they have been suppressed. The ideal way of suppressing these is to slide screening tubes over the leads themselves. As this is impractical, we can place an aluminium shield over the majority of the lead areas. In a V- or twin-cam engine, this is relatively easy but for a straight engine the results are not particularly good.

Now for the really impossible cases, here are a few tips to try out. Where metal comes into contact with metal, an electrical disturbance is caused which is why good clean connections are essential. To remove interference due to overlapping or butting panels, you must bridge the join with a wide braided earth strap (like that from the frame to the engine/transmission). The most common moving parts that could create noise and should be strapped are, in order of importance:

(a) Silencer-to-frame
(b) Exhaust pipe-to-engine block and frame
(c) Air cleaner-to-frame
(d) Front and rear bumpers-to-frame
(e) Steering column to frame
(f) Bonnet and doors-to-frame

These faults are most pronounced when the engine is either idling or labouring under loads. Although the moving parts are already connected with nuts, bolts, etc, these do tend to rust and corrode, thus creating a high resistance interference source.

If you have a 'ragged' sounding pulse when mobile, this could be wheel or tyre static. This can be cured by buying some anti-static powder and sprinkling it liberally inside the tyres.

If the interference takes the shape of a high pitched screeching noise that changes its note when the car is in motion and only comes now and then, this could be related to the aerial, especially if it is of the telescopic or whip type. This source can be cured quite simply by pushing a small rubber ball on top of the aerial (yes really!) as this breaks the electric field before it can form; but it would be much better to buy yourself a new aerial of a reputable brand. If, on the other hand, you are getting a loud rushing sound every time you brake, then this is brake static. This effect is most prominent on hot dry days and is cured only by fitting a special kit, which is quite expensive.

In conclusion, it is pointed out that it is relatively easy, and therefore cheap, to eliminate 95 per cent of all noises, but to eliminate the final 5 per cent is time and money consuming. It is up to the individual to decide if it is worth it. Please remember also, that you will not get concert hall performance from a cheap radio.

Finally, at the beginning of this Section are mentioned tape players; these are not usually affected by interference but in a very bad case, the best remedies are the first two suggestions plus using a 3 to 5 amp choke in the 'live' line, and in uncured cases screen the live and speaker wires.

52 Fault diagnosis — electrical system

Symptom	Reason(s)
Starter motor fails to turn engine	Battery discharged Battery defective internally Battery terminal clamps loose or corroded Engine earth strap broken or insecure Loose or broken connections in starter motor circuit Starter solenoid faulty Starter pinion jammed in mesh with flywheel ring gear Starter motor brushes worn, sticking or brush wires loose Commutator dirty, worn or burnt Starter motor armature faulty Field coils earthed
Starter motor turns engine very slowly	Battery discharged Engine earth strap broken or insecure Starter motor brushes worn, sticking or brush wires loose Starter motor armature faulty
Starter motor noisy or excessively rough in engagement	Starter motor pinion travel incorrect Starter pinion or flywheel ring gear teeth worn or broken Starter motor retaining bolts loose
Battery will not hold charge	Electrolyte level too low Electrolyte too weak (see Section 4) Battery plate separators ineffective Battery plates severely sulphated
Insufficient current flow to keep battery charged	Alternator drivebelt slipping Alternator not charging properly Alternator regulator faulty Loose, broken, or defective wiring in charging circuit
Alternator not charging	Alternator drivebelt loose, slipping or broken Brushes worn, sticking, broken or dirty Brush springs weak or broken Other internal defect in alternator or regulator (consult an automobile electrician)
Ignition light fails to go out, battery runs flat in a few days	Alternator drivebelt loose, slipping or broken Alternator or regulator faulty
Direction indicator flashers inoperative	Blown fuse Faulty multi-function switch Faulty flasher unit Wiring loose, disconnected or broken Bulb filaments burnt out on both sides of car
Direction indicator flashers work one side only	Bulb filament burnt out Bulb or bulb holder not making good earth connection Wiring loose, disconnected or broken

Symptom	Reason(s)
Fuel gauge gives no reading	Fuel tank empty! Fuel gauge tank unit faulty Wiring fault between tank and gauge Fuel gauge faulty Burnt out track in printed circuit
Fuel gauge registers full all the time	Fuel gauge tank unit faulty Fuel gauge faulty Wiring fault between tank and gauge
Horn emits intermittent or unsatisfactory noise	Cable connection loose Horn retaining bolt loose Horn faulty
Horn fails to operate	Blown fuse Cable connection loose, broken or disconnected Multi-function switch faulty Horn faulty
Horn operates all the time	Horn push in multi-function switch earthed or stuck down
Instrument readings erratic	Instrument voltage regulator faulty
Lights come on but fade out	If engine not running, battery discharged
Lights do not come on	If engine not running, battery discharged Light bulb filament burnt out or bulbs broken Blown fuse Wiring loose, disconnected, or broken Fault in multi-function switch
Lights give very poor ilumination	Lamp glasses dirty Reflector tarnished or dirty Poor electrical or physical earth connection Incorrect wattage bulb fitted Existing bulb discoloured
Temperature gauge gives no reading	Wiring disconnected or broken Temperature gauge transmitter faulty Temperature gauge faulty Burnt out track in printed circuit
Temperature gauge registers maximum all the time	Temperature gauge transmitter faulty Wiring fault between transmitter and gauge Temperature gauge faulty
Wiper motor fails to work	Blown fuse Wiring loose, disconnected or broken Brushes badly worn Motor faulty
Wiper motor works but blades remain static	Linkage disconnected Wiper arms slipping on drive spindle Worn gears in wiper gearbox
Wiper motor works slowly and takes little current	Brushes badly worn Commutator dirty, worn or burnt Armature faulty
Wiper motor works very slowly and takes excessive current	Wiper linkage binding or damaged Drive spindle binding or partially seized Armature faulty

Key to wiring diagrams. Not all items are fitted to all models

1 Battery
2 Starter motor
3 Alternator
4 Voltage regulator
5 Control unit, electronic ignition
6 Ignition coil
7 Distributor
8 Ignition switch
9 Diagnostic socket
10 Fuse unit
11 Headlamp main beam
12 Headlamp dip beam
13 Sidelamps
14 Tail lamps and number plate lamp
15 Column switch
16 Stop-lamp switch
17 Stop-lamps
18 Direction indicator unit
19 Hazard warning switch
20 Front RH direction indicator
21 Front LH direction indicator
22 Rear RH direction indicator
23 Rear LH direction indicator
24 Rear foglamp switch
25 Rear foglamps
26 Reverse lamp switch
27 Reverse lamps
28 Horns
29 Boot lamp switch
30 Boot lamp
31 Illumination, instrument panel
32 Illumination, facia switches
33 Illumination, heater controls
34 Illumination, ashtray/cigar lighter
35 Courtesy lamp switches
36 Front interior/map reading lamp
37 Warning lamp, side and tail lamps
38 Warning lamp, headlamp main beam
39 Warning lamp, direction indicator
40 Warning lamp, choke control
41 Warning lamp, low oil pressure and low oil level
42 Warning lamp, low fuel
43 Warning lamp, handbrake and low fluid level
44 Switch, rear window heater element
45 Relay, rear window heater element
46 Rear window heater element
47 Windscreen wiper motor
48 Windscreen washer pump

49 Tailgate wiper switch
50 Tailgate wiper motor
51 Tailgate washer pump
52 Fuel gauge
53 Fuel gauge sender unit
54 Switch on choke control
55 Heater blower motor switch
56 Heater blower motor
57 Resistor block, heater blower motor
58 Test switch, brake pad wear indicator
59 Brake pad wear indicators
60 Brake fluid level indicator
61 Switch, handbrake warning lamp
62 Control box, engine oil level indicator
63 Sender unit, oil warning lamp
64 Sender unit, oil pressure gauge
65 Engine oil level indicator, dipstick
66 Oil pressure gauge
67 Switch, electric fan
68 Electric fan, engine cooling
69 Water temperature gauge
70 Sender unit, water temperature gauge
71 Voltage stabiliser (instruments)
72 Voltmeter (battery condition indicator)
73 Cigar lighter
74 Clock, analogue
75 Clock, digital
76 Connector, grey, instrument panel
77 Connector, green, instrument panel
78 Connector, green, column switch
79 Connector, yellow instrument panel
80 Connector, white instrument panel
81 Connector, instrument panel printed circuit
82 Connection to radio
83 Connections to inhibitor switch, automatic transmission
84 Warning lamp, no charge

Colour Code

BK	Black
BL	Blue
BR	Brown
GR	Green
GY	Grey
R	Red
Y	Yellow
P	Purple
W	White
O	Orange

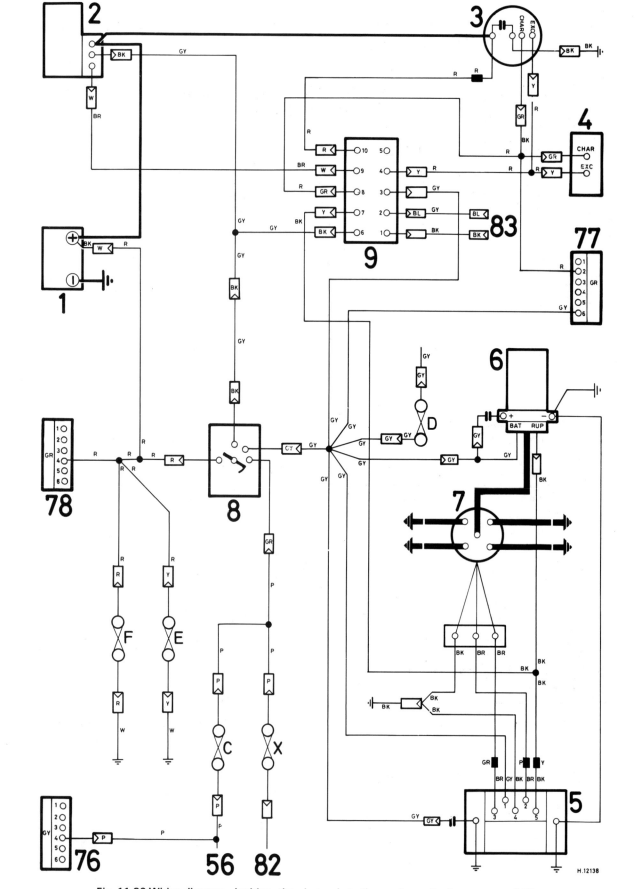

Fig. 11.30 Wiring diagram – ignition, charging and starting systems. For key see page 193

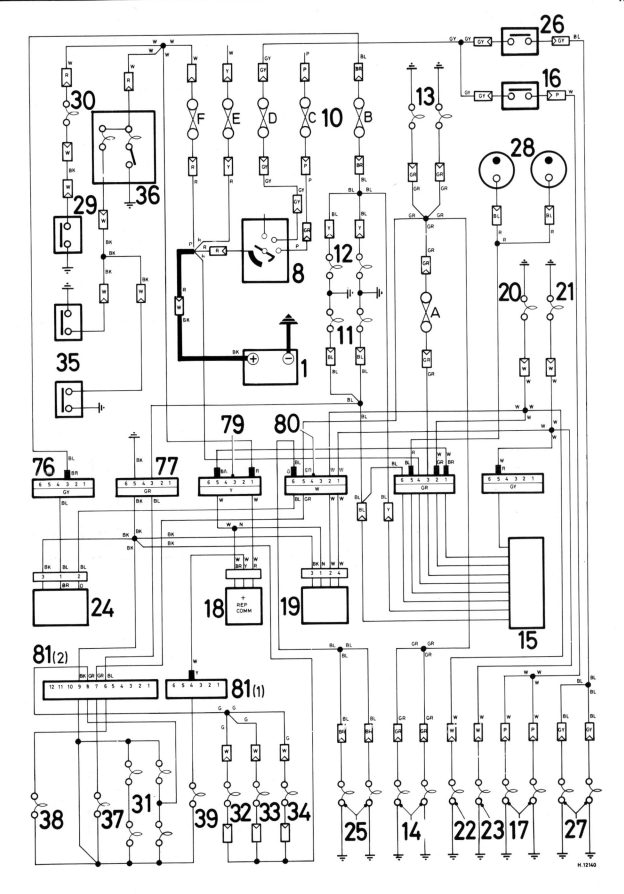

Fig. 11.31 Wiring diagram – lighting and signalling systems. For key see page 193

H.12140

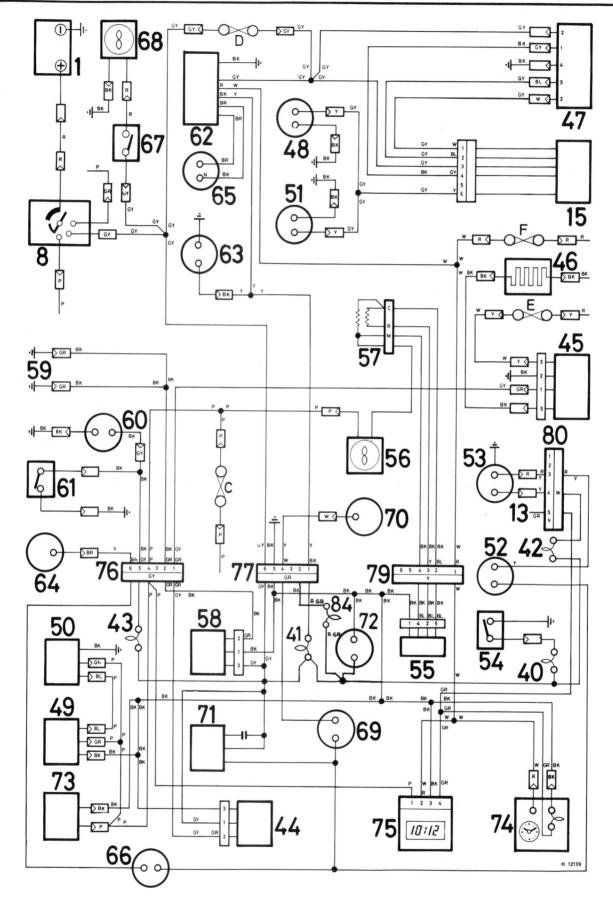

Fig. 11.32 Wiring diagram – instrumentation, warning lamps and accessories. For key see page 193

H. 12139

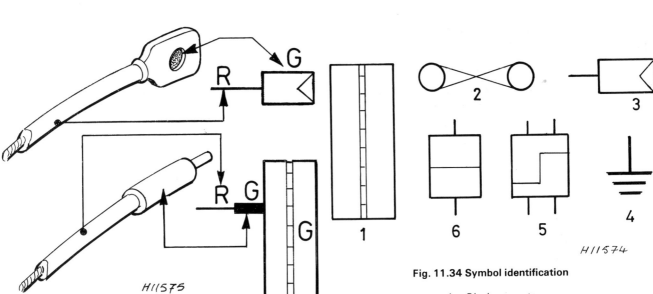

H11575

Fig. 11.33 Colour identification of connector block, terminals and cables

H11574

Fig. 11.34 Symbol identification

1   Block connector
2   Fuse
3   Connector
4   Earth
5   Two-pin connector
6   Single pin connector

Chapter 12 Bodywork and fittings

Contents

1 General description

The vehicle body structure is a welded fabrication of many individual shaped panels to form a 'monocoque' bodyshell. Certain areas are strengthened locally to provide for suspension system, steering system, engine support anchorages and transmission. The resultant structure is very strong and rigid.

It is as well to remember that monocoque structures have no load paths and all metal is stressed to an extent. It is essential therefore to maintain the whole bodyshell top and underside, inside and outside, clean and corrosion free. Every effort shoiuld be made to keep the

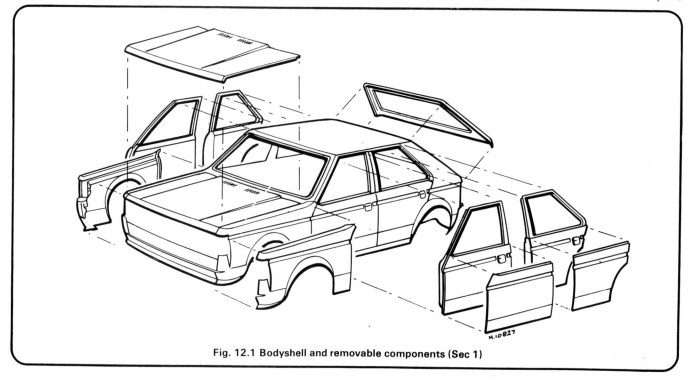

Fig. 12.1 Bodyshell and removable components (Sec 1)

underside of the car as clear of mud and dirt accumulations as possible. If you are fortunate enough to acquire a new car then it is advisable to have it rustproofed and undersealed at one of the specialist workshops who guarantee their work.

2 Maintenance – bodywork and underframe

1   The general condition of a car's bodywork is the thing that significantly affects its value. Maintenance is easy but needs to be regular. Neglect, particularly after minor damage, can lead quickly to further deterioration and costly repair bills. It is important also to keep watch on those parts of the car not immediately visible, for instance the underside, inside all the wheel arches and the lower part of the engine compartment.

2   The basic maintenance routine for the bodywork is washing – preferably with a lot of water, from a hose. This will remove all the loose solids which may have stuck to the car. It is important to flush these off in such a way as to prevent grit from scratching the finish. The wheel arches and underframe need washing in the same way to remove any accumulated mud which will retain moisture and tend to encourage rust. Paradoxically enough, the best time to clean the underframe and wheel arches is in wet weather when the mud is thoroughly wet and soft. In very wet weather the underframe is usually cleaned of large accumulations automatically and this is a good time for inspection.

3   Periodically, it is a good idea to have the whole of the underframe of the car steam cleaned, engine compartment included, so that a thorough inspection can be carried out to see what minor repairs and renovations are necessary. Steam cleaning is available at many garages and is necessary for removal of the accumulation of oily grime which sometimes is allowed to become thick in certain areas. If steam cleaning facilities are not available, there are one or two excellent grease solvents available which can be brush applied. The dirt can then be simply hosed off.

4   After washing paintwork, wipe off with a chamois leather to give an unspotted clear finish. A coat of clear protective wax polish will give added protection against chemical pollutants in the air. If the paintwork sheen has dulled or oxidised, use a cleaner/polisher combination to restore the brilliance of the shine. This requires a little effort, but such dulling is usually caused because regular washing has been neglected. Always check that the door and ventilator opening drain holes and pipes are completely clear so that water can be drained out. Bright work should be treated in the same way as paintwork. Windscreens and windows can be kept clear of the smeary film which often appears, by adding a little ammonia to the water. If they are scratched, a good rub with a proprietary metal polish will often clear them. Never use any form of wax or other body or chromium polish on glass.

3 Maintenance – upholstery and carpets

1   Mats and carpets should be brushed or vacuum cleaned regularly to keep them free of grit. If they are badly stained remove them from the car for scrubbing or sponging and make quite sure they are dry before refitting. Seats and interior trim panels can be kept clean by a wipe over with a damp cloth. If they do become stained (which can be more apparent on light coloured upholstery) use a little liquid detergent and a soft nail brush to scour the grime out of the grain of the material. Do not forget to keep the head lining clean in the same way as the upholstery. When using liquid cleaners inside the car do not over-wet the surfaces being cleaned. Excessive damp could get into the seams and padded interior causing stains, offensive odours or even rot. If the inside of the car gets wet accidentally it is worthwhile taking some trouble to dry it out properly, particularly where carpets are involved. *Do not leave oil or electric heaters inside the car for this purpose.*

4 Minor body damage – repair

    The photographic sequences on pages 206 and 207 illustrate the operations detailed in the following sub-sections.

Repair of minor scratches in the car's bodywork

    If the scratch is very superficial, and does not penetrate to the metal of the bodywork, repair is very simple. Lightly rub the area of the scratch with a paintwork renovator, or a very fine cutting paste, to remove loose paint from the scratch and to clear the surrounding bodywork of wax polish. Rinse the area with clean water.

    Apply touch-up paint to the scratch using a thin paint brush; continue to apply thin layers of paint until the surface of the paint in the scratch is level with the surrounding paintwork. Allow the new paint at least two weeks to harden: then blend it into the surrounding paintwork by rubbing the paintwork, in the scratch area, with a paintwork renovator or a very fine cutting paste. Finally, apply wax polish.

    Where the scratch has penetrated right through to the metal of the bodywork, causing the metal to rust, a different repair technique is required. Remove any loose rust from the bottom of the scratch with a penknife, then apply rust inhibiting paint to prevent the formation of rust in the future. Using a rubber or nylon applicator fill the scratch with bodystopper paste. If required, this paste can be mixed with cellulose thinners to provide a very thin paste which is ideal for filling narrow scratches. Before the stopper-paste in the scratch hardens, wrap a piece of smooth cotton rag around the top of a finger. Dip the finger in cellulose thinners and then quickly sweep it across the surface of the stopper-paste in the scratch; this will ensure that the surface of the stopper-paste is slightly hollowed. The scratch can now be painted over as described earlier in this Section.

Repair of dents in the car's bodywork

    When deep denting of the car's bodywork has taken place, the first task is to pull the dent out, until the affected bodywork almost attains its original shape. There is little point in trying to restore the original shape completely, as the metal in the damaged area will have stretched on impact and cannot be reshaped fully to its original contour. It is better to bring the level of the dent up to a point which is about $\frac{1}{8}$ in (3 mm) below the level of the surrounding bodywork. In cases where the dent is very shallow anyway, it is not worth trying to pull it out at all. If the underside of the dent is accessible, it can be hammered out gently from behind, using a mallet with a wooden or plastic head. Whilst doing this, hold a suitable block of wood firmly against the outside of the panel to absorb the impact from the hammer blows and thus prevent a large area of the bodywork from being 'belled-out'.

    Should the dent be in a section of the bodywork which has double skin or some other factor making it inaccessible from behind, a different technique is called for. Drill several small holes through the metal inside the area – particularly in the deeper section. Then screw long self-tapping screws into the holes just sufficiently for them to gain a good purchase in the metal. Now the dent can be pulled out by pulling on the protruding heads of the screws with a pair of pliers.

    The next stage of the repair is the removal of the paint from the damaged area, and from an inch or so of the surrounding 'sound' bodywork. This is accomplished most easily by using a wire brush or abrasive pad on a power drill, although it can be done just as effectively by hand using sheets of abrasive paper. To complete the preparation for filling, score the surface of the bare metal with a screwdriver or the tang of a file, or alternatively, drill small holes in the affected area. This will provide a really good 'key' for the filler paste.

    To complete the repair see the Section on filling and re-spraying.

Repair of rust holes or gashes in the car's bodywork

    Remove all paint from the affected area and from an inch or so of the surrounding 'sound' bodywork, using an abrasive pad or a wire brush on a power drill. If these are not available a few sheets of abrasive paper will do the job just as effectively. With the paint removed you will be able to gauge the severity of the corrosion and therefore decide whether to renew the whole panel (if this is possible) or to repair the affected area. New body panels are not as expensive as most people think and it is often quicker and more satisfactory to fit a new panel than to attempt to repair large areas of corrosion.

    Remove all fittings from the affected area except those which will act as a guide to the original shape of the damaged bodywork (eg headlamp shells etc). Then, using tin snips or a hacksaw blade, remove all loose metal and any other metal badly affected by corrosion. Hammer the edges of the hole inwards in order to create a slight depression for the filler paste.

    Wire brush the affected area to remove the powdery rust from the surface of the remaining metal. Paint the affected area with rust inhibiting paint; if the back of the rusted area is accessible treat this also.

Before filling can take place it will be necessary to block the hole in some way. This can be achieved by the use of zinc gauze or aluminium tape.

Zinc gauze is probably the best material to use for a large hole. Cut a piece to the approximate size and shape of the hole to be filled, then position it in the hole so that its edges are below the level of the surrounding bodywork. It can be retained in position by several blobs of filler paste around its periphery.

Aluminium tape should be used for small or very narrow holes. Pull a piece off the roll and trim it to the approximate size and shape required, then pull off the backing paper (if used) and stick the tape over the hole; it can be overlapped if the thickness of one piece is insufficient. Burnish down the edges of the tape with the handle of a screwdriver or similar, to ensure that the tape is securely attached to the metal underneath.

Bodywork repairs – filling and re-spraying

Before using this Section, see the Sections on dent, deep scratch, rust holes and gash repairs.

Many types of bodyfiller are available, but generally speaking those proprietary kits which contain a tin of filler paste and a tube of resin hardener are best for this type of repair. A wide, flexible plastic or nylon applicator will be found invaluable for imparting a smooth and well contoured finish to the surface of the filler.

Mix up a little filler on a clean piece of card or board – measure the hardener carefully (follow the maker's instructions on the pack) otherwise the filler will set too rapidly or too slowly.

Using the applicator apply the filler paste to the prepared area; draw the applicator across the surface of the filler to achieve the correct contour and to level the filler surface. As soon as a contour that approximates the correct one is achieved, stop working the paste – if you carry on too long the paste will become sticky and begin to 'pick up' on the applicator. Continue to add thin layers of filler paste at twenty-minute intervals until the level of the filler is just proud of the surrounding bodywork.

Once the filler has hardened, excess can be removed using a metal plane or file. From then on, progressively finer grades of sandpaper should be used, starting with a 40 grade production paper and finishing with 400 grade wet-and-dry paper. Always wrap the abrasive paper around a flat rubber, cork, or wooden block – otherwise the surface of the filler will not be completely flat. During the smoothing of the filler surface the wet-and-dry paper should be periodically rinsed in water. This will ensure that a very smooth finish is imparted to the filler at the final stage.

At this stage the dent should be surrounded by a ring of bare metal, which in turn should be encircled by the finely 'feathered' edge of the good paintwork. Rinse the repair area with clean water, until all of the dust produced by the rubbing-down operation has gone.

Spray the whole repair area with a light coat of primer – this will show up any imperfections in the surface of the filler. Repair these imperfections with fresh filler paste or bodystopper, and once more smooth the surface with abrasive paper. If bodystopper is used, it can be mixed with cellulose thinners to form a really thin paste which is ideal for filling small holes. Repeat this spray and repair procedure until you are satisfied that the surface of the filler, and the feathered edge of the paintwork are perfect. Clean the repair area with clean water and allow to dry fully.

The repair area is now ready for final spraying. Paint spraying must be carried out in warm, dry, windless and dust free atmosphere. This condition can be created artificially if you have access to a large indoor working area, but if you are forced to work in the open, you will have to pick your day very carefully. If you are working indoors, dousing the floor in the work area with water will help to settle the dust which would otherwise be in the atmosphere. If the repair area is confined to one body panel, mask off the surrounding panels; this will help to minimise the effects of a slight mis-match in paint colours. Bodywork fittings (eg chrome strips, door handles etc) will also need to be masked off. Use genuine masking tape and several thicknesses of newspaper for the masking operations.

Before commencing to spray, agitate the aerosol can thoroughly, then spray a test area (an old tin, or similar) until the technique is mastered. Cover the repair area with a thick coat of primer; the thickness should be built up using several thin layers of paint rather

than one thick one. Using 400 grade wet-and-dry paper, rub down the surface of the primer until it is really smooth. While doing this, the work area should be thoroughly doused with water, and the wet-and-dry paper periodically rinsed in water. Allow to dry before spraying on more paint.

Spray on the top coat, again building up the thickness by using several thin layers of paint. Start spraying in the centre of the repair area and then, using a circular motion, work outwards until the whole repair area and about 2 inches of the surrounding original paintwork is covered. Remove all masking material 10 to 15 minutes after spraying on the final coat of paint.

Allow the new paint at least two weeks to harden, then, using a paintwork renovator or a very fine cutting paste, blend the edges of the paint into the existing paintwork. Finally, apply wax polish.

5   Major body repairs

Where serious damage has occurred or large areas need renewal due to neglect, it means certainly that completely new sections or panels will need welding in and this is best left to professionals. If the damage is due to impact it will also be necessary to completely check the alignment of the body shell structure. Due to the principle of construction the strength and shape of the whole can be affected by damage to a part. In such instances the services of a Talbot agent with specialist checking jigs are essential. If a body is left misaligned it is first of all dangerous as the car will not handle properly and secondly uneven stresses will be imposed on the steering, engine and transmission, causing abnormal wear or complete failure. Tyre wear may also be excessive.

6   Maintenance – hinges and locks

1   Oil the hinges of the bonnet, tailgate and doors with a drop or two of light oil periodically. A good time is after the car has been washed.
2   Oil the bonnet release catch pivot pin and the safety catch pivot pin periodically.
3   Do not overlubricate door latches and strikers. Normally a little oil on the rotary cam spindle alone is sufficient.

7   Doors – tracing rattles and their rectification

1   Check first that the door is not loose at the hinges and that the latch is holding the door firmly in position. Check also that the door lines up with the aperture in the body.
2   If the hinges are loose or the door is out of alignment it will be necessary to reset the hinge positions.
3   If the latch is holding the door properly it should hold the door tightly when fully latched and the door should line up with the body. If it is out of alignment it needs adjustment. If loose, some part of the lock mechanism must be worn out and requiring renewal.
4   Other rattles from the door would be caused by wear or looseness in the window winder, the glass channels and sill strips or the door buttons and interior latch release mechanism.

8   Front wings – removal and refitting

1   The front wings are bolted in position and are fairly easy to remove and refit.
2   First disconnect the battery earth terminal.
3   Remove the bonnet as described in Section 26.
4   Remove the headlight unit and direction indicator assembly (see Chapter 11).
5   Remove the front bumper as described in Section 30.
6   Jack up the front of the car and support it on axle stands. Remove the appropriate front roadwheel.
7   Undo and remove the bolts securing the front wing to the front panel, inner wing and front pillar. Withdraw the wing from the car, cutting through the wing-to-body sealing mastic if necessary.
8   Clean all traces of sealing mastic from the body mating flanges.
9   Place a bead of sealing compound on the whole length of the body-to-wing mating flange and then locate the front wing in position.

Screw in the securing bolts, with their threads well greased, finger tight.

10 Move the wing slightly as required to obtain an exact and flush fit with adjacent body panels and then tighten the securing bolts.

11 As new wings are supplied in primer, the external surface will now have to be sprayed in cellulose to match the body. If the vehicle is reasonably new this can be carried out using home spraying equipment but if the body paint is badly faded it is advisable to leave the refinishing to a professional bodyshop.

12 Once the wing is sprayed and the finishing complete, the previously removed components may be refitted using the reverse sequence to removal.

9 Front door inner trim panel – removal and refitting

1 Pull the interior door latch open and remove the screw securing it to the handle (photo).

2 Press the window winder handle escutcheon plate inwards and remove the spring clip which retains the handle to the winder mechanism shaft, using a hooked piece of wire.

3 Undo and remove the armrest securing screws and lift off the armrest (photo).

4 If a radio speaker is fitted to the trim panel, disconnect the battery earth terminal first. Insert a screwdriver between the trim panel and the door and lever the panel clips from their locations. Once the first securing clip has been displaced, use the fingers instead of the screwdriver and by giving the panel a sharp jerk, the remaining clips can be removed in succession (photo).

5 When all the retaining clips are free, carefully lift off the panel. If a radio speaker is fitted, disconnect the leads at the cable connectors.

6 Refitting the trim panel is the reverse sequence to removal. When refitting the window winder handle, position the spring clip into its location in the handle and simply push the handle into place on the window winder mechanism (photos).

10 Front door exterior handle – removal and refitting

1 Remove the front door inner trim panel as described in Section 9, and then carefully lift up the plastic sheet water barrier and paper sheets (photo).

2 Working through the aperture on the door, undo and remove the exterior handle retaining nuts and then disengage the handle from its operating rod. The handle can now be removed.

3 Refitting the handle is the reverse sequence to removal.

11 Front door interior handle remote control assembly – removal and refitting

1 Remove the front door inner trim panel as described in Section 9, and then carefully lift up the plastic sheet water barrier and paper sheets.

2 Unhook the return spring from the lever on the remote control assembly.

3 Undo and remove the two securing bolts and withdraw the remote control assembly. Disengage the operating rod from its retaining clips on the door inner skin and also the end of the rod from the remote control assembly. The assembly can now be removed from the door.

4 Refitting is the reverse sequence to removal.

12 Front door private lock and barrel – removal and refitting

1 Remove the front door inner trim panel as described in Section 9, and then carefully lift up the plastic sheet water barrier and paper sheets.

2 Disconnect the private lock catch link from its nylon keeper on the door lock (photo).

3 Extract the lock retaining spring clip and withdraw the lock and barrel from the door.

4 Refitting is the reverse sequence to removal.

9.1 Interior door latch retaining screw

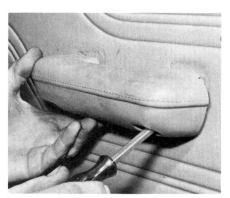
9.3 Removing the armrest securing screws

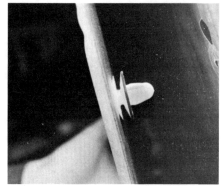
9.4 Interior trim panel retaining clip

9.6a Refit the window winder handle retaining clip ...

9.6b ... and then push the handle into position

10.1 Front door with trim panel and plastic sheet water barrier removed

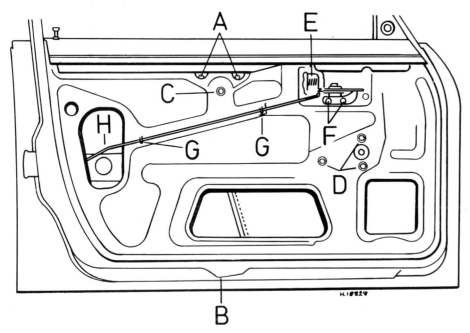

Fig. 12.2 Front door internal
components (Sec 11)

A   Access hole – cam plate-to-
     channel retaining bolts
B   Door glass guide lower retaining
     bolt
C   Door glass guide upper retaining
     bolt
D   Window winder mechanism
     retaining bolts
E   Remote control assembly return
     spring
F   Remote control assembly retaining
     bolts
G   Operating rod retaining clips
H   Operating rod

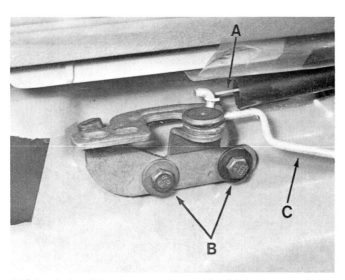

11.2 Interior handle remote control assembly, showing return spring
(A), retaining bolts (B) and operating rod (C)

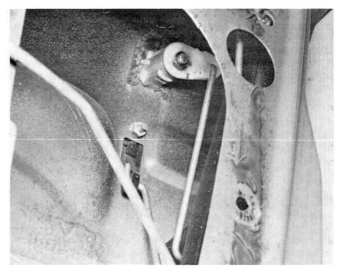

12.2 Front door private lock, operating rod and retaining clip

13 Front door lock – removal and refitting

1   Remove the interior trim panel as description in Section 9, and the
exterior door handle as described in Section 10.
2   Disengage the private lock button operating rod, the private lock
catch link and the interior door handle operating rod from their nylon
keepers on the lock mechanism.
3   Undo and remove the three latch securing screws (photo), lift off
the latch and then withdraw the door lock (photo).
4   Refitting the door lock is the reverse sequence to removal. Apply
medium grease to the lock mechanism before fitting and make sure
that the interior and exterior handles and private lock all operate the
door lock before refitting the trim panel. Adjust the closure position of
the door by repositioning the latch before finally tightening the
retaining screws.

14 Front door window winder mechanism – removal and refitting

1   Ensure that the window glass is in the fully raised position and

then remove the inner trim panel as described in Section 9.
2   Unscrew the private lock pushbutton, undo and remove the four
securing screws and lift the trim capping off the top edge of the door.
3   Using two wooden wedges inserted between the window glass
and the top edge of the door panel, wedge the window glass so that
it does not drop when the winder mechanism is disconnected.
4   Carefully lift back the plastic sheet water barrier and paper sheets
from the inner door panel.
5   Undo and remove the upper and lower retaining bolts securing the
door glass vertical guide to the centre of the door panel.
6   Undo and remove the three bolts securing the mounting plate of
the winder mechanism to the door panel (photo).
7   Using a socket inserted through the access holes near the top of
the door panel, undo and remove the two bolts securing the door glass
lower channel to the winder mechanism cam plate.
8   The window winder mechanism can now be withdrawn through
the large aperture in the door panel.
9   Refitting the winder mechanism is the reverse sequence to
removal. Adjust the position of the door glass guide as necessary to
provide smooth up-and-down travel of the glass after the winder
mechanism is fully installed.

13.3a Front door latch securing screws

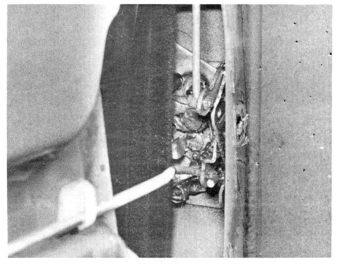

13.3b Internal view of the door lock showing location of operating rods

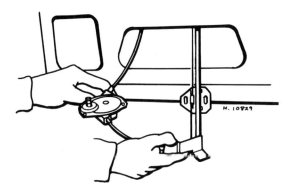

Fig. 12.3 Removing the front door window winder mechanism (Sec 14)

15 Front door window glass – removal and refitting

1   Ensure that the window glass is in the fully open position and then remove the inner trim panel as described in Section 9.
2   Unscrew the private lock pushbutton, undo and remove the four securing screws and lift the trim capping off the top edge of the door.
3   Carefully lift back the plastic sheet water barrier and paper sheets from the inner door panel.
4   Undo and remove the two bolts securing the lower glass channel to the window winder mechanism cam plate (photo). Rotate the glass through 90°, rear end upward, and withdraw it upward and toward the outside of the door.
5   Refitting the glass is the reverse sequence to removal. Adjust the door glass guide as necessary to provide smooth up-and-down movement of the glass.

16 Adjustable rear view mirror – removal and refitting

1   To remove the mirror glass only, ease back the black rubber surround from around the mirror and then undo the screw securing the glass and metal backing to the frame (photo).
2   To remove the complete mirror assembly, first undo and remove the spindle retaining screw followed by the adjustment knob insert and spring (photo).
3   Lift off the small adjustment knob, the snap-ring and then the large adjustment knob (photos).
4   Using a punch and hammer very carefully tap undone the cylindrical inner retaining nut, engaging the punch with one of the four depressions on the nut (photo).

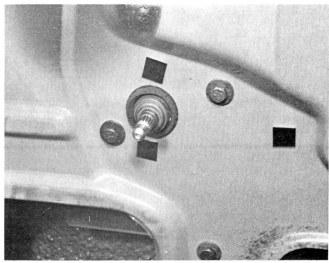

14.6 Window winder mechanism mounting plate retaining bolts

15.4 Window winder mechanism cam plate-to-channel retaining bolts

16.1 Removing the external mirror retaining screw

16.2 Unscrew and remove the spindle retaining screw, insert and spring ...

16.3a ... lift off the small knob ...

16.3b ... and the large adjustment knob ...

16.4 ... then undo the retaining nut to remove the assembly

5   Now lift off the mirror assembly from the outside of the door corner panel.
6   Refitting is the reverse sequence to removal.

17 Front door – removal and refitting

1   Undo and remove the retaining bolt and lift off the rubber door check strap and grommet from the door.
2   If a radio speaker is fitted to the door inner trim panel it will be necessary to remove the panel, as described in Section 9, to enable the speaker wiring to be disconnected.
3   Have an assistant support the weight of the door, and then drive out the upper hinge pin using a hammer and suitable drift.
4   Unless a cranked drift is available the lower pin may prove slightly more difficult. A useful method of removal is to use a length of old accelerator cable or similar having a soldered nipple on one end. Thread the free end of the cable through the hinge until the nipple is in contact with the bottom of the hinge pin. If necessary use a small washer to prevent it pulling through. Now tie, or secure by use of cable clamps, the free end of the cable to a stout bar and lever the hinge pin out of the hinge.
5   With the hinges removed, carefully lift off the door.
6   Refitting is the reverse sequence to removal.

18 Rear door inner trim panel – removal and refitting

The removal and refitting procedure is the same as described in Section 9, for the front door.

19 Rear door exterior handle – removal and refitting

The removal and refitting procedure is the same as described in Section 10, for the front door.

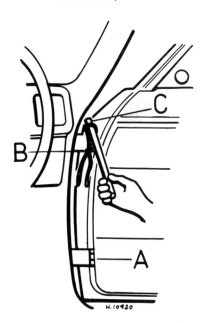

H.10420

Fig. 12.4 Removal of door hinge pin (Sec 17)

A Hinge pin
B Cable
C Lever

20 Rear door interior handle remote control assembly – removal and refitting

The removal and refitting procedure is the same as described in Section 11, for the front door.

21 Rear door lock – removal and refitting

1   Ensure that the door window glass is in the fully raised position and then remove the inner trim panel as described in Section 18.
2   Carefully peel back the plastic sheet water barrier from the inner door panel.
3   Unscrew the private lock button from the operating rod.
4   Remove the door exterior handle as described in Section 19.
5   Disengage the interior handle remote control assembly operating rod from its steady clips along the inner panel and from the interior handle.
6   Using a screwdriver or similar tool with the last inch (25.4 mm) of its blade bent through approximately 90°, push the exterior handle linkage pivot clip lock peg out of its clip and remove it. Access to the peg is gained by inserting the tool through the rear uppermost hole in the inner door panel.
7   Disengage the exterior handle linkage pivot clip from its bracket and the private lock link rod from its steady clips.
8   Undo and remove the screws securing the latch to the door and lock and lift off the latch.
9   Push the lock up into the top rear corner of the door with the private lock operating rod up as far as possible. Now disconnect the private lock linkage pivot from the door.
10   Remove the private lock vertical link and pivot assembly from the horizontal link and then withdraw the links.
11   The lock and linkage assembly can now be removed through the aperture in the inner door panel.
12   Refitting is the reverse sequence to removal. Lubricate the lock with medium grease prior to fitting.

22 Rear door window winder mechanism – removal and refitting

The removal and refitting procedure is the same as described in Section 14, for the front door.

23 Rear door window glass – removal and refitting

1   Open the window and using a block of wood and a mallet, carefully tap the inside of the finisher strips around the upper edges of the window frame until they can be removed. The order of removal is rear, top and the front finisher.
2   Refer to Section 18, and remove the inner trim panel.
3   Starting at the lower rear cover, ease out the window channelling using a screwdriver.
4   Disengage the lock water shield retaining lugs and remove the water shield.
5   Undo and remove the two bolts securing the lower window glass channel and seal to the window winder cam plate. Now carefully withdraw the window glass from the door.
6   Refitting the window glass is the reverse sequence to removal.

24 Rear door fixed quarterlight glass – removal and refitting

1   Begin by removing the door window glass as described in the previous Section.
2   Undo and remove the quarterlight post retaining screw from the top of the window frame.
3   Undo and remove the quarterlight post lower retaining bolts from the inner door panel.
4   Free the quarterlight post from the quarterlight glass and move the post forward until it is clear of the glass.
5   Now ease the quarterlight glass out of the frame and withdraw it from the door.
6   Refitting is the reverse sequence to removal.

25 Rear door – removal and refitting

The procedure for removal and refitting of the rear door is the same as described in Section 17, for the front door. There is however one additional point worth noting. When extracting the lower hinge pin, on some models the pin will foul a ribbed pressing in the door skin

Fig. 12.5 Removing the rear lock pivot clip locking peg (Sec 21)

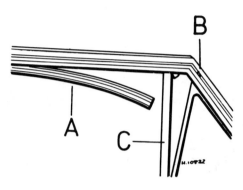

Fig. 12.6 Removing the rear door fixed quarterlight glass (Sec 24)

A   *Window seal*
B   *Quarterlight post*
C   *Upper retaining screw*

immediately above the hinge. Should this occur, extract the pin partially and cut off the top half using a hacksaw. Then remove the remaining portion. A new pin will be required when refitting.

26 Bonnet – removal and refitting

1   Open the bonnet and place pieces of cloth below each rear corner of the bonnet to protect the paintwork.
2   Disconnect the windscreen washer hose from the outlet on the washer pump and detach the hose from the clip on the right-hand bonnet hinge.
3   Lightly pencil a line around each hinge to ensure that the bonnet is refitted in the same position.
4   With the help of an assistant, support the weight of the bonnet, undo and remove the two bolts securing each hinge to the bonnet (photo) and carefully lift the bonnet off the car.
5   Refit the bonnet using the reverse procedure to that of removal. If necessary adjust its position at the hinges to ensure a flush fitting with the front wings and scuttle upper surface.

27 Bonnet lock and cable – removal and refitting

Note: *If the bonnet release cable has broken the bonnet can be opened by inserting a long screwdriver through the radiator grille and operating the release catch.*
1   Remove the radiator grille as described in Section 32.
2   Disconnect the release cable from the lock.
3   Remove the screw securing the interior bonnet release handle to the bracket and withdraw the handle complete with cable.
4   The lock assembly can be removed by unscrewing the four retaining bolts and lifting out the lock asssembly and stiffener plates.
5   Refit the cable and lock assembly using the reverse procedure to that of removal.

This sequence of photographs deals with the repair of the dent and paintwork damage shown in this photo. The procedure will be similar for the repair of a hole. It should be noted that the procedures given here are simplified — more explicit instructions will be found in the text

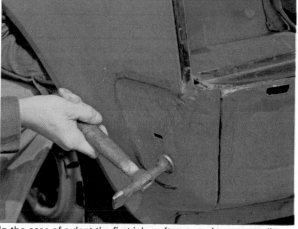

In the case of a dent the first job — after removing surrounding trim — is to hammer out the dent where access is possible. This will minimise filling. Here, the large dent having been hammered out, the damaged area is being made slightly concave

Now all paint must be removed from the damaged area, by rubbing with coarse abrasive paper. Alternatively, a wire brush or abrasive pad can be used in a power drill. Where the repair area meets good paintwork, the edge of the paintwork should be 'feathered', using a finer grade of abrasive paper

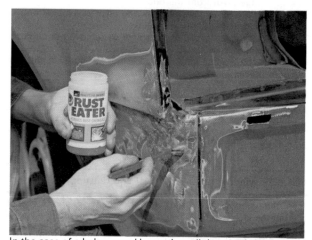

In the case of a hole caused by rusting, all damaged sheet-metal should be cut away before proceeding to this stage. Here, the damaged area is being treated with rust remover and inhibitor before being filled

Mix the body filler according to its manufacturer's instructions. In the case of corrosion damage, it will be necessary to block off any large holes before filling — this can be done with aluminium or plastic mesh, or aluminium tape. Make sure the area is absolutely clean before ...

... applying the filler. Filler should be applied with a flexible applicator, as shown, for best results; the wooden spatula being used for confined areas. Apply thin layers of filler at 20-minute intervals, until the surface of the filler is slightly proud of the surrounding bodywork

Initial shaping can be done with a Surform plane or Dreadnought file. Then, using progressively finer grades of wet-and-dry paper, wrapped around a sanding block, and copious amounts of clean water, rub down the filler until really smooth and flat. Again, feather the edges of adjoining paintwork

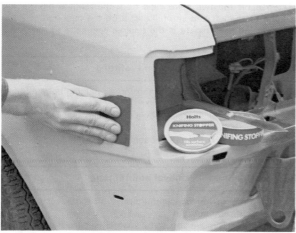

Again, using plenty of water, rub down the primer with a fine grade wet-and-dry paper (400 grade is probably best) until it is really smooth and well blended into the surrounding paintwork. Any remaining imperfections can now be filled by carefully applied knifing stopper paste

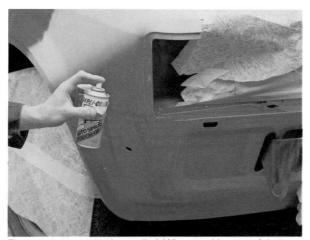

The top coat can now be applied. When working out of doors, pick a dry, warm and wind-free day. Ensure surrounding areas are protected from over-spray. Agitate the aerosol thoroughly, then spray the centre of the repair area, working outwards with a circular motion. Apply the paint as several thin coats

The whole repair area can now be sprayed or brush-painted with primer. If spraying, ensure adjoining areas are protected from over-spray. Note that at least one inch of the surrounding sound paintwork should be coated with primer. Primer has a 'thick' consistency, so will find small imperfections

When the stopper has hardened, rub down the repair area again before applying the final coat of primer. Before rubbing down this last coat of primer, ensure the repair area is blemish-free — use more stopper if necessary. To ensure that the surface of the primer is really smooth use some finishing compound

After a period of about two weeks, which the paint needs to harden fully, the surface of the repaired area can be 'cut' with a mild cutting compound prior to wax polishing. When carrying out bodywork repairs, remember that the quality of the finished job is proportional to the time and effort expended

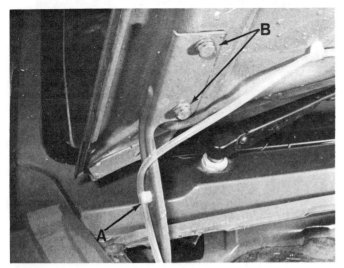

26.4 Windscreen washer hose clip (A) and bonnet hinge retaining bolts (B)

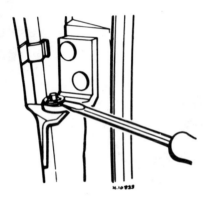

Fig. 12.7 Removing the tailgate hinge retaining clips (Sec 28)

28 Tailgate – removal and refitting

1   Disconnect the battery earth terminal.
2   Open the tailgate and disconnect the parcel shelf strings.
3   Lift off the left-hand side access cover on the tailgate inner panel.
4   Remove the wiper motor wires from their clips and disconnect the wires from the wiper motor (if applicable).
5   Disconnect the wire to the heated rear window from the wiring harness.
6   Undo and remove the nut and lift off the earth wires from the earthing terminal.
7   Attach a long length of string or wire to the disconnected end of the wiring harness. Release the grommet from the top edge of the tailgate and release the wiring harness from the clip on the left-hand side. Carefully pull the harness out of the tailgate until the string or wire appears. Disconnect the harness from the string, leaving the string in position. This will enable the harness to be drawn back through when the tailgate is refitted.
8   Disengage the nylon pipe of the tailgate washer from the washer jet (if applicable).
9   Have an assistant take the weight of the tailgate. Loosen the lock peg of the gas strut at the swivel joint on the tailgate and disconnect the strut.
10   Prise off the two spire clips from the tailgate hinges, move the tailgate to the left and carefully lift it off the car.
11   Refitting the tailgate is the reverse sequence to removal.

29 Tailgate lock – removal and refitting

1   Open the tailgate, remove the three retaining bolts and lift off the lock.
2   The lock barrel is retained by a spring clip accessible after removal of the lock.
3   Refitting is the reverse sequence to removal.

30 Front bumper – removal and refitting

1   Using a screwdriver, carefully prise off the cover plates from the bumper side sections.
2   Undo and remove the screws which secure the side sections to the front wings.
3   Remove the plastic rivets which secure the side sections to the bumper centre section. To do this, push the pin right through the

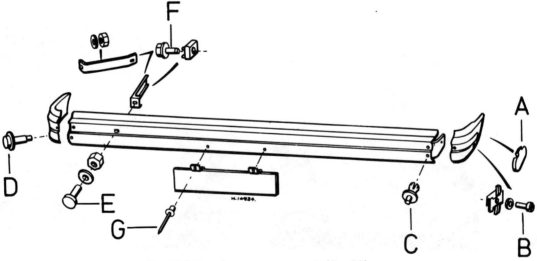

Fig. 12.8 Front bumper components (Sec 30)

A Cover plate
B Screw
C Plastic rivet
D Retaining bolt – side
    sections

E Retaining bolt – support
    brackets
F Retaining bolt – front
    sections
G Rivet

centre of the rivet and lift the rivet off.

4   Undo and remove the four bolts securing the bumper centre section to the mounting brackets and withdraw the bumper from the car.

5   Refitting is the reverse sequence to removal.

31 Rear bumper – removal and refitting

Removal and refitting of the rear bumper follows the same procedure as described in the previous Section, for the front bumper.

32 Radiator grille – removal and refitting

1   Remove the right-hand and left-hand finishing strips below the headlights by easing out the side retaining clip and sliding the strip sideways (photo).

2   Undo and remove the single retaining screw at the centre top of the grille panel (photo).

3   Disengage the upper clips at each side of the grille, move the grille forward to release the lower locating peg and lift off the grille (photo).

4   Refitting is the reverse sequence to removal.

33 Centre console – removal and refitting

1   Unscrew the gear lever knob from the end of the gear lever.

2   Carefully prise up the four retaining clips and lift out the front console base (photo).

3   Undo and remove the two screws at the front of the console, disengage the mounting lug at the rear and then lift the console up over the gear lever to withdraw it.

4   Refitting is the reverse sequence to removal.

34 Facia panel

1   Open the bonnet and disconnect the battery earth terminal.

2   Remove the instrument panel as described in Chapter 11.

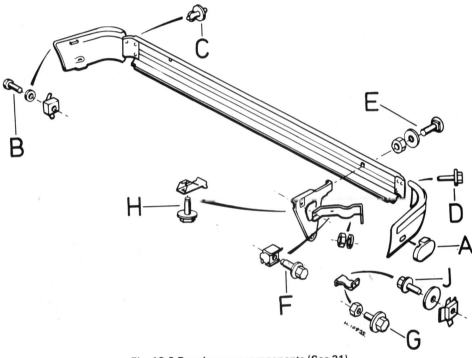

Fig. 12.9 Rear bumper components (Sec 31)

A Cover plate
B Retaining bolt – side section
C Plastic rivet
D Retaining bolt – front section
E Retaining bolt – front section
F Retaining bolt – side support
G Retaining bolt – side support
H Retaining bolt – rear bracket
J Retaining bolt – side section

32.1 Slide out the front finishing strips ...

32.2 ... unscrew the upper retaining screw ...

32.3 ... disengage the locating pegs and lift off the grille

33.2 Lift up the console base to access the front centre console retaining screws

Fig. 12.10 Removing the facia capping securing screws (Sec 34)

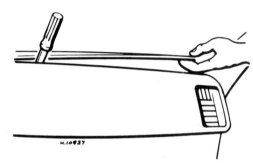

Fig. 12.11 Easing off the facia capping (Sec 34)

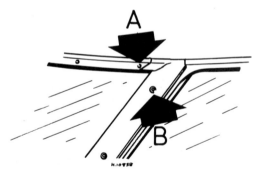

Fig. 12.12 Location of upper (A) and side (B) trim securing screws (Sec 34)

3   Undo and remove the two screws, one in each demister vent, which secure the facia capping. Insert a spatula or screwdriver and carefully lever the capping up to disengage the four retaining clips, then withdraw the capping.
4   Undo and remove the screw at each end of the trim strip over the top of the windscreen. Now undo and remove the two screws securing the windscreen side trims to each pillar. Lift up the upper trim carefully and disengage both side trims.
5   Slide out the ashtray and then undo and remove the three screws and one clip that secure the driver's parcel tray in position. Take out the tray.
6   Undo and remove the two screws and lift off the steering column lower shroud.
7   Undo and remove the bolt securing the column cable guard, lift off the guard and then disconnect the steering column switch multi-plug connectors.
8   Undo and remove the four bolts securing the steering column mounting bracket to the pedal bracket and lower the column. Release any cable clips as necessary to avoid straining the wiring harness. **Note**: *The ignition switch should be in the 'accessories' position to allow free movement of the column and bracket as it is lowered.*
9   Unclip and lift out the radio blanking panel, or if a radio is fitted, remove the radio escutcheon plate.
10 Withdraw the clock and after making a note of their positions, disconnect the wires at the rear.
11 Prise off the fresh air vent control knob, release the retaining lugs on the vent control and press it clear of the facia finisher panel.
12 Withdraw the facia finisher panel after undoing the seven screws and removing one clip. The screws are situated as follows: at the far left of the finisher panel; at the middle of the glovebox hinge; right-hand side bottom corner of the glovebox; top and bottom of the auxiliary switch panel; top left of clock aperture; adjacent to glovebox striker. The clip is located at the far left upper rear of the panel.
13 Undo and remove the screws securing the radio mounting tray and supporting strut, then remove the tray. Disconnect the aerial, speakers, and electrical supply plugs from the radio (if fitted).
14 Undo and remove the three screws, one in the carpet tread plate and two in the kick pad panel, that secure the kick pads on each side of the footwells.
15 Undo and remove the three screws and one clip securing the heater control access panel. The screws are located as follows: one in the left-hand side top corner and two in the bottom. The clip is positioned in the right-hand side top corner. Lift away the panel and then detach the two clips and remove the finisher panel from beneath the heater controls.
16 Undo and remove the two screws, one each side, securing the heater control panel.
17 Make a note of their positions and then disconnect the two vacuum pipes from the temperature control.
18 Disconnect the wires to the heater control illumination bulb, move

the control panel forward slightly and then disconnect the blower motor multi-pin plug.
19 Release the radio in-line fuse holder from its clip on the heater control plate.
20 Detach the heater control cables from their retaining clips and then disconnect them from their respective levers.
21 Disconnect the five or six multi-plugs, according to model, from behind the heater control panel.
22 Disconnect the choke cable from the carburettor and detach it from the clip on the wing valance. Pull the cable free from the brake fluid reservoir.
23 Undo and remove the screw fitted vertically above the heater vent outlet at the rear of the ashtray.
24 Undo and remove the three screws and one clip and withdraw the passenger parcel tray. The screws are positioned as follows: one at the top left-hand corner and two by the heater vent control. The clip is situated at the rear centre of the tray.
25 Undo and remove the two screws securing the stiffener plate located to the left of the clutch pedal pivot shaft. Lift off the plate rearwards.
26 Slacken but do not remove the two screws, one each side,

securing the facia lower brackets to the body pillars.
27 Undo and remove the four bolts securing the forward top edge of the facia to the bulkhead. Ease the bellows off the heater duct and pull the choke cable through the pedal bracket. Carefully lift off the facia panel, tilting it rearwards away from the windscreen, and withdraw it from the car.
28 Refitting the facia panel is a direct reversal of the foregoing procedure.

35 Air Diffuser – removal and refitting

1 The air diffusers, situated on the left and right-hand sides of the facia, are each held in place by a simple retaining clip positioned mid-way up the side of the diffuser nearest the car centre.
2 To remove a diffuser, depress the retaining clip and slide the diffuser out of its location in the facia.
3 To refit the diffuser, position the retaining clip on the diffuser body (if it became detached during removal) and press the diffuser into place.

36 Heating and ventilation – general description

The heater unit is mounted below the facia and is supplied with fresh air via the intake grille panels on the bonnet. The air passes through the heater matrix and then depending on the position of the heater distribution control, is directed to the car interior or windscreen and side window demister outlets.
The temperature of the air entering the car is controlled by the heater temperature control lever. When the lever is set to the cold position, a valve in the heater return hose closes and water is prevented from circulating within the heater matrix. When the control is moved to any other position the valve opens and engine cooling water is allowed to circulate. A flap valve within the heater blends cool air with the warm air from the matrix to produce the desired temperature.
A four speed blower motor provides a boosted air flow if required.
Fresh air can also be admitted to the car, independently of the heater unit, via air diffusers at each end of the facia and by a vent below it. Airflow from these outlets is only available when the car is moving.

37 Heater unit vacuum control system – description and testing

1 The flow of engine coolant through the heater matrix is controlled by three valves, all of which are actuated by engine manifold vacuum according to the position of the heater unit temperature control.
2 The system operates as follows. With the temperature control lever in the cold position, manifold vacuum is applied to the on/off valve behind the heater control panel, via a plastic tube. From here vacuum is passed by another tube to the coolant control valve on the front suspension crossmember (photo). The vacuum acts on the valve, preventing coolant circulation through the heater matrix.
3 When the temperature control lever is moved to any other position, the manifold vacuum is isolated, allowing the coolant control valve to open. Circulation of coolant now takes place through the heater matrix. Intermediate temperatures are catered for by blending warm and cool air within the heater unit.
4 An additional one-way valve, also located at the rear of the heater control panel, maintains manifold vacuum at the coolant control valve (assuming the temperature control to be set to the cold position) when the engine is stopped for short periods.
5 Should a leak develop in the system it will be difficult to obtain a flow of cold air from the heater as the coolant control valve will remain open. It may also be noticed that engine idling becomes erratic and servo assistance to the brake pedal may be reduced.
6 Should the one-way valve fail, warm air will be emitted from the heater, irrespective of control position, whenever the engine is started after a short stoppage.
7 It is advisable periodically to check the condition of the vacuum tubes and their connections, making sure that the tubes are well supported and not subject to chafing.
8 The valves themselves can be removed from their locations and tested by sucking the outlet connections. If resistance to suction is not

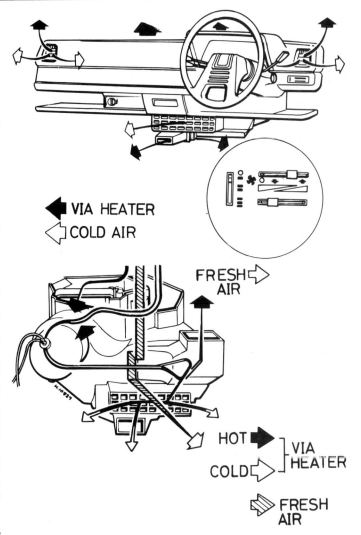

Fig. 12.13 Air circulation through the heating and ventilation system (Sec 36)

37.2 Vacuum-operated coolant control valve on the front suspension crossmember

felt, or in the case of the coolant control valve, if movement of the valve is not observed, the valves are faulty and must be renewed. Repair of the valves is not possible as they are sealed units.

38 Heater blower motor – removal and refitting

1   The heater blower motor can be removed with the heater still in position in the car as follows.
2   Open the bonnet and disconnect the battery earth terminal.
3   Slide the ashtray out of its housing, undo and remove the three screws and one retaining clip and withdraw the driver's parcel tray from under the facia.
4   Now undo and remove the three screws and one retaining clip securing the passenger's parcel tray in position and lift out the tray.
5   Remove the radio blanking plate, or if a radio is fitted, pull off the control knobs and lift off the escutcheon plate.
6   Withdraw the clock (if fitted) and after making a note of their positions, disconnect the wires at the rear.
7   Prise off the fresh air vent control knob, release the retaining lugs on the vent control and push it clear of the facia finisher panel.
8   Withdraw the facia finisher panel after undoing the seven screws and removing one clip. The screws are situated as follows: far left of the finisher panel; middle of the glovebox hinge; right-hand side bottom corner of the glovebox striker. The clip is located at the far left upper rear of the panel.
9   Undo and remove the screws securing the radio mounting tray and supporting strut and then remove the tray. If a radio is fitted disconnect the aerial, speaker and electrical supply plugs from the unit.
10 Working through the radio aperture, disconnect the heater motor earth lead connector and then the motor electrical supply feed from the resistor panel.
11 Undo and remove the four screws securing the heater motor in the heater unit and withdraw the motor from under the facia. **Note:** *It may be necessary to gently prise the motor out of the heater unit if a sealer has been used on manufacture.*
12 After removing the motor assembly from the heater unit, remove the fan, lift up the retaining clips and slide the motor out of its mounting.
13 Refitting the heater motor is the reverse sequence to removal.

39 Heater unit – removal and refitting

1   Open the bonnet and disconnect the battery earth terminal.
2   Drain the cooling system as described in Chapter 2.
3   Remove the centre console as described in Section 33.
4   Refer to Section 38, and carry out the operations described in paragraphs 3 to 9 inclusive.
5   Undo and remove the vertically positioned screw located behind the ashtray housing.
6   Undo and remove the nut, located behind the master cylinder pushrod pivot of the clutch pedal, that secures the heater to the bulkhead bracket.
7   Disconnect the heater motor earth lead connector and then the motor electrical supply feed from the resistor panel. Access is via the radio aperture in the facia.
8   Disconnect the wiring harness multi-plug from the resistor panel.
9   Spread the clip, located to the right of the heater motor resistor panel, and ease out the air distribution control outer cable. Now disconnect the inner cable thimble and release the cable from the flap actuating lever.
10 Next spread the other clip, located on the rear face of the heater to the left of the steering column universal joint, and ease out the temperature control outer cable. Disconnect the inner cable thimble and release the cable from the control lever.
11 Working in the engine compartment, release the heater supply and return hose clips at their outlet connections just in front of the bulkhead.
12 Detach the upper hose from its outlet connection and then using a suitable length of plastic tubing or old hose, pushed on to the upper outlet, blow through the hose once or twice. This will force the remaining water in the heater matrix back into the engine cooling system and reduce spillage in the car interior as the heater unit is removed.
13 Now remove the hose and also the lower heater supply hose.
14 Place suitable covers or a plastic sheet over the carpets inside the car.
15 Undo and remove the two nuts from the studs protruding into the engine compartment, which secure the heater unit to the bulkhead.

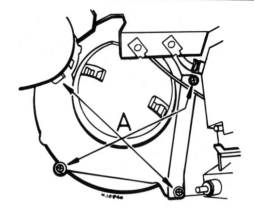

Fig. 12.14 Heater blower motor retaining screws (A) (Sec 38)

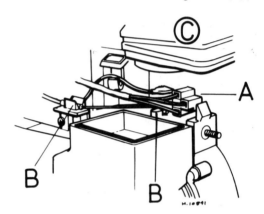

Fig. 12.15 Heater components beneath facia panel (Sec 39)

A Motor electrical plug
B Control cable fixings
C Bellows

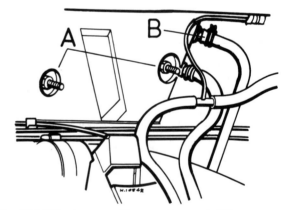

Fig. 12.16 Heater assembly mounting studs (A) and hose connections (B) in engine compartment (Sec 39)

16 Carefully detach the bellows that connects the heater outlet to the windscreen demister duct.
17 Tilt the heater downwards slightly to release the air intake duct from the bulkhead aperture and then ease the unit away from the bulkhead until the mounting studs are clear of their holes in the bulkhead. Be prepared for some spillage of coolant.
18 The heater unit is removed via the left-hand footwell and in order to do this it is necessary to prise the left-hand mounting bracket (from where the nut was removed in paragraph 6) away from the heater. This will release a moulded lug on the heater case from the bracket, enabling the unit to be lowered and withdrawn from the footwell.
19 Refitting the heater unit is the reverse sequence to removal, bearing in mind the following points:

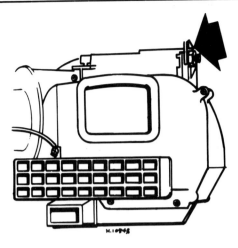

Fig. 12.17 Location of left-hand mounting bracket moulded lug (arrowed) which must be released prior to heater removal (Sec 39)

(a) If any of the control cable clips have become detached, they should be placed in position before refitting the heater
(b) Keep all wiring and loose fittings clear when refitting the heater to avoid trapping them during installation
(c) On completion refill the cooling system as described in Chapter 2

40 Heater matrix – removal and refitting

1 With the heater unit removed from the car as described in the previous Section, the case can be opened and the matrix removed as follows.
2 First lift off the two sponge gaskets from the matrix outlets.
3 Release the seven retaining lugs on the heater unit top cover, lift off the cover and carefully slide the matrix out of its grooves in the

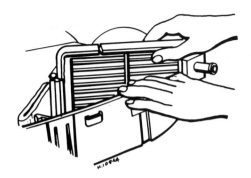

Fig. 12.18 Removing the heater matrix (Sec 40)

heater unit body.
4 Carefully inspect the matrix for signs of water leakage; if evident, the best policy is renewal. Attempts at soldering are seldom satisfactory. If the matrix is blocked it may be possible to clear the blockage by reverse flushing but the use of descaling or cleansing compounds is not recommended as the water tubes are so narrow that any sediment resulting from such treatment will probably only clog the matrix in another position. Again the best course of action is a new matrix.
5 Refitting the heater matrix is the reverse sequence to removal.

41 Windscreen glass – removal and refitting

1 Removal and refitting of the windscreen is considered to be beyond the scope of the average owner. Special tools are required to install the windscreen, as well as a special sealing compound, and if this work is not carried out professionally leaks or possibly even damage to the glass may occur.
2 If you are unfortunate enough to have a windscreen crack or shatter it is recommended that you entrust this job to a Talbot dealer or windscreen replacement specialist.

Chapter 13 Supplement:
Revisions and information on later models

Contents

1 Introduction

Since its introduction in 1978 the Talbot Horizon has had a number of modifications and improvements made in order to keep pace with current technical and servicing innovations.

Those modifications made since the original publication of this manual which affect servicing and/or repairs are included in this supplementary Chapter.

In order to use the supplement to the best advantage it is suggested that it is referred to before the main Chapters of the manual: this will ensure that any relevant information can be collected and incorporated within the procedures given in Chapters 1 to 12. Time and cost will therefore be saved and the particular job will be completed correctly.

2 Specifications

The Specifications listed below are revised or supplementary to the main Specifications listed at the beginning of each Chapter.

Engine
Identification

Engine code	Capacity	Compression ratio	Commencing engine number
2E1 (low comp.)	1118 cc	8.8:1	86800021
2E1A	1118 cc	9.6:1	86600021
2G1	1294 cc	9.5:1	87240021
2Y1 and 2Y2	1442 cc	9.5:1	98400001
2Y1B (economy)	1442 cc	9.5:1	8300021

Performance
Maximum power (DIN):
1118 cc (l.c)	54 bhp (40.5 kW) at 5600 rev/min
1118 cc (h.c)	58 bhp (42.2 kW) at 5600 rev/min
1294 cc	67 bhp (50.1 kW) at 5600 rev/min
1442 cc (economy)	64 bhp (46.4 kW) at 5200 rev/min
1442 cc (single choke carb)	68 bhp (49.3 kW) at 5200 rev/min
1442 cc (dual choke carb)	82 bhp (59.3 kW) at 5600 rev/min

Maximum torque (DIN):
1118 cc (l.c)	67 lbf ft (88 Nm) at 3000 rev/min
1118 cc (h.c)	67 lbf ft (88 Nm) at 3000 rev/min
1294 cc	80 lbf ft (105 Nm) at 2800 rev/min
1442 cc (economy)	85 lbf ft (117 Nm) at 2400 rev/min
1442 cc (single choke carb.)	82 lbf ft (114 Nm) at 3000 rev/min
1442 cc (dual choke carb.)	86 lbf ft (119 Nm) at 3000 rev/min

Piston rings
End gap (compression)	0.25 to 0.45 mm (0.010 to 0.018 in)
End gap (oil control)	0.20 to 0.40 mm (0.008 to 0.016 in)
Ring to groove clearance:	
Top compression	0.25 to 0.45 mm (0.010 to 0.018 in)
Second compression	0.25 to 0.45 mm (0.010 to 0.018 in)
Oil control	0.20 to 0.40 mm (0.008 to 0.016 in)

Fuel system
With the exception of the Solex 32 BISA 8 carburettor, all data for later models is as given in Chapter 3

Solex 32 BISA 8 (single choke)
1442 cc code 2Y1B economy (B, C and D Series)
Engine type	26
Choke tube	2
Secondary venturi	130 ± 5
Main jet	180 ± 10
Air correction jet	EC
Emulsion tube	45 ± 10
Econostat fuel jet	60 ± 10
Econostat air jet	300
Idling fuel jet	46 ± 3
Idling air jet	0.6 x 4.5
Progression slot	40
Pump injector	3 mm
Pump stroke	1.5 mm
Float needle	5.7g
Float weight	

Solex 32 BISA 8 (143)
1294 cc code 2G1E (C and D Series)
Engine type	26
Choke tube	2
Secondary venturi	130 ± 5
Main jet	185 ± 5
Air correction jet	EC
Emulsion tube	60 ± 10
Fuel enricher	50 ± 10
Econostat fuel jet	300
Econostat air jet	45 ± 10
Idling fuel jet	–
Idling air jet	4.5 x 0.6
Progression slot	40 ± 5
Pump injector	3 mm/0.6 ± 0.15 cc
Pump stroke/capacity	1.5
Float needle	5.7g
Float weight	

Ignition system
Ignition timing (dynamic) – vacuum pipe disconnected
C Series 1981 to 82:
    1294 cc engine .... 2° BTDC
    1442 cc engine .... 4° BTDC
D Series, 1982 on:
    1294 cc engine .... 2° BTDC
    1442 cc engine (single choke carb.) .... 4° BTDC
    1442 cc engine (dual choke carb.) .... 12° BTDC

Spark plugs
1983 to 84 .... Champion N10Y
1984 on:
    Champion N281YC
    Bosch W7DC
    PRO (Peugeot) .... CP 10

Transmission
Application (Series 2, 1984 on)
LE .... BE 1/4 (four speed)
LS .... BE 1/5 (five speed)
LS Auto .... A3 (three-speed automatic)
GL, LX, GLX .... BE 1/5 (five-speed)

Ratios (five-speed)
1st 3.308:1
2nd 1.882:1
3rd 1.280:1
4th 0.969:1
5th 0.757:1
Reverse 3.333:1
Final drive 3.812:1

Torque wrench settings

	lbf ft	Nm
Rear cover bolts (use thread locking compound)	9	12
Input and output shaft nuts	40	54
Rear bearing retainer bolts	11	15
Selector rod backplate bolt	11	15
End casing to main casing bolts	9	12
Reverse idler spindle bolt	15	20
Selector shaft spring bracket	11	15
Reverse selector spindle nut	15	20
Breather	11	15
Reversing lamp switch	18	25
Drain plug (gearbox)	7	9
Drain plug (final drive)	22	30
Speedometer pinion adaptor	9	12
Final drive extension housing bolts	11	15
Crownwheel securing bolts	48	65
Final drive half housing bolts, 10 mm	30	41
Final drive half housing bolts, 7 mm	9	12
Clutch release bearing guide tube bolts	9	12
Mounting stud nut	25	34

Suspension
Tyres
Pullman version .... 175 x 70*
Pressures (normal load):
    Front .... 26 lbf/in²
    Rear .... 26 lbf/in²
Pressures (fully loaded with luggage or for sustained high speed
driving):
    Front .... 29 lbf/in²
    Rear .... 29 lbf/in²
* Snow chains cannot be used with this size of tyre, also the spare wheel supplied with vehicles equipped with these tyres is of emergency type for limited road use only.

Torque wrench setting

	lbf ft	Nm
Roadwheels (steel or alloy)	48	65

Dimensions and weights
Dimensions (Series 2)
Front track .... 56.03 in (1422 mm)
Rear track .... 54.18 in (1375 mm)

Kerb weight
Models with manual transmission .... 2084 to 2183 lb (945 to 990 kg)
Models with automatic transmission .... 2194 to 2260 lb (995 to 1025 kg)

3 Vehicle identification

1978 to 79 ....   9 Series
1979 to 80 ....   A Series
1980 to 83 ....   B Series
October 1983 on ....   Series 2 (D Series)

Version

Model	Engine code	Engine capacity
21A041	E1	1118 cc
21A102	G1E	1294 cc
21A106	G1E	1294 cc
21A243	Y2	1442 cc
21A232	Y1	1442 cc

LE ....
LS (manual) ....
EX ....
LS (auto) ....
GL Super EX ....

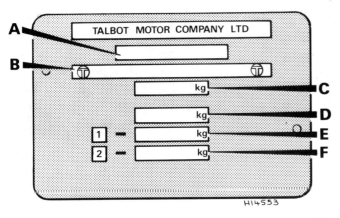

Fig. 13.1 Typical 9 series vehicle identification plate (Sec 3)

A   Type approval
B   VIN
C   Max. gross vehicle weight
D   Max. gross vehicle weight plus trailer weight
E   Front (maximum load on axle)
F   Rear (maximum load on axle)

4 Routine maintenace

1985 model cars have a revised maintenance schedule.

Engine oil change periods extended to every 6000 miles (10 000 km)
Engine oil filter to be renewed every 12 000 miles (20 000 km)
The 10 000 mile (16 000 km) service intervals to be extended to 12 000 miles (20 000 km)

First service (1000 to 1500 miles – 1500 to 2500 km) – new vehicles
Checking the cylinder head bolt torque is no longer necessary (see Section 5, Engine in this Supplement). However, the valve clearances should still be checked and adjusted at this service interval. The extended service interval may be applied to earlier models but excluding the following operation

Disc pad and shoe lining wear check
On pre-1985 models, it is important to check the engine oil level regularly. The fitting of specified copper electrode spark plugs is also recommended.

12 000 miles (20 000 km) service of every twelve months
Check fluid level in power-assisted steering fluid reservoir.

5 Engine

Engine mountings – modifications
1   The right-hand rear engine mounting support securing bolt is 16 to 20 mm longer on later models and therefore if it is found necessary to renew this bolt, be sure to fit one of the correct length.
2   From Series 9 engines on, the engine front support was moved to the right and the attachment brackets changed accordingly. The engine support boss on the crankcase was relocated and is closer to the fuel pump flange.

Crankcase, oil seal housing – modifications
3   The crankshaft oil seal housing location bolt holes for the Number 1 main bearing were changed from 7 mm to 6 mm in diameter. The housing retaining bolts are also shorter being 18 mm long (instead of 20 mm on previous engines).

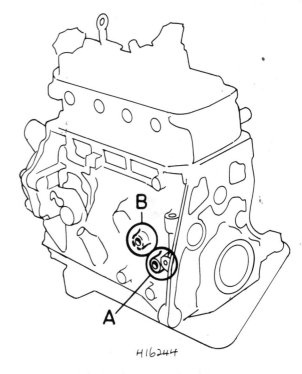

Fig. 13.2 Engine mounting locations (Sec 5)

A   Early models   B   Later models

Crankshaft and flywheel – modifications

4   Previously fitted with a spigot bearing, from Series 9 on the crankshaft is fitted with a spigot bush. The fitting diameter for the bush in the crankshaft is 16 mm instead of 32 mm for the bearing used previously.

5   From Series 9 on, the flywheel circumference has two grooves machined in it to indicate the timing signal to the TDC sensor unit. The groove positions are additional to the TDC dimple.

Oil pump – modification

6   From Series 9 models on, the oil pump unit is fitted with a larger oil pressure relief valve spring and ball and therefore their aperture in the pump body is larger. Whilst early and late type pumps are directly interchangeable as complete units, the individual components of each are not interchangeable.

Timing gears – modifications

7   Later models produced from 1981 onwards have modified timing gears fitted in which the teeth profiles are different from those of earlier models. In addition a flexible rubber ring is fitted to the groove in the camshaft gear to reduce the timing gear noise level. It should be noted however that some later type crankshaft and camshaft gears have been fitted without the rubber ring. In such instances it is recommended that the flexible ring is obtained and fitted during reassembly.

8   The later type timing gears can be fitted during reassembly to earlier engines together with the flexible rubber ring, *but only as a complete set.* The timing procedure is the same for both early and late types during reassembly.

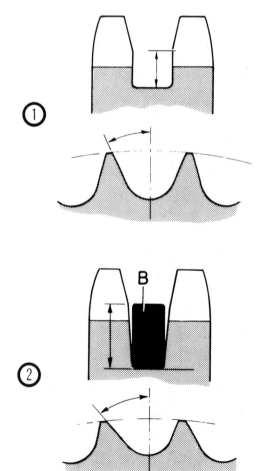

Fig. 13.3 Timing gear profiles (Sec 5)

1   Early models   B   Flexible damper ring
2   Later models

Oil pump – removal and refitting (engine in car)

9   Raise and support the car at the front end. Position a jack under the right-hand side of the sump and raise the jack to support the engine on that side. Locate a suitable flat piece of wood between the jack and the sump to avoid damage to the sump.

10   Unscrew and remove the nut and two bolts which secure the rear engine mounting to engine support bracket and crossmember on the right-hand side.

11   Unscrew the two nuts which hold the driveshaft gaiter heat shield to the exhaust downpipe flange and remove the shield (photo).

12   Unscrew the four right-hand support bracket to engine bolts and remove the bracket and mounting (photo).

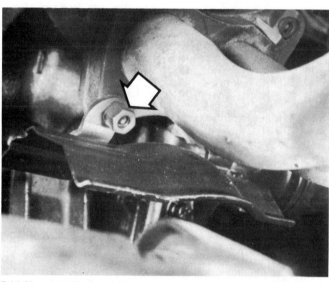

5.11 Heatshield/exhaust flange nut

5.12 Engine rear mounting

13   Unscrew and remove the oil filter cartridge, using a strap wrench if necessary. Allow for a certain amount of oil spillage when released and remove the filter spigot tube.

14   Remove the right-hand driveshaft as described in Chapter 7.

15   Unscrew and remove the bolts securing the oil pump then withdraw the pump cover and body. As the bolts pass through the cover and body they can be removed separately or together as a unit.

16   Carefully scrape old gaskets and any jointing compound from the

mating surfaces. For oil pump examination and renovation refer to Section 32 in Chapter 1.

17 Refitting is a reversal of the removal procedure. Lubricate the pump drivegear and shaft before assembling to the body. Lightly smear the joint surfaces with grease and assemble the gasket to the crankcase side of the pump, locate the spigot of the body into the crankcase and hand fit a location bolt to position the pump.

18 Assemble the drivegear and dog into the pump body and rotate to engage with the drive dog. Smear the gasket surfaces with grease and locate it onto the cover face. Unscrew and remove the temporary location bolt and then fit the driven gear and cover, tightening the retaining bolts to the specified torque setting.

19 With the pump in position, the right-hand rear engine support can now be refitted and the jack removed.

20 Refit the right-hand driveshaft as described in Chapter 7.

21 Fit the oil filter spigot tube and cartridge.

22 On completion run the engine and check for any signs of leaks from around the pump body or filter element joints.

Cylinder head bolt tightening

23 On 1985 models built from August 1984, the cylinder head bolts do not need to have their torque checked at the first service interval (new vehicles).

24 The cylinder head bolt thread length on these engines has been lengthened to 1.97 in (50.0 mm). Note the new position for the cylinder head earth lead (photo).

5.24 Cylinder head earth strap

25 When the cylinder head is being refitted after engine overhaul, carry out the following procedure.

26 Oil the threads and underside of the cylinder head bolts.

27 Tighten the bolts in three stages.

Stage 1	*37 lbf ft*	*50 Nm*
Stage 2	*52 lbf ft*	*71 Nm*

Stage 3 Run until engine fan cuts in, switch off and allow to cool (minimum six hours). Unscrew first bolt in tightening sequence and then retighten to 52 lbf ft (71 Nm). Repeat on the remaining bolts, see Fig. 1.25, Page 47.

28 Adjust the valve clearances.

29 Check the torque of the cylinder head bolts (engine cold) after the first 800 to 1200 miles (1280 to 1930 km).

Piston rings

30 The oil control ring on later model pistons is of two rail and expander type.

Cylinder head

31 A distorted cylinder head may be surface-ground to restore its flatness provided its overall thickness is not reduced by more than 0.6 mm (0.024 in) on 1294 cc and 1442 cc engines or 1.0 mm (0.039 in) on 1118 cc engines.

Diagnostic plug and ignition timing marks

32 An alternative location for the diagnostic plug which is positioned on the front face of the crankcase is on the left side of the engine compartment towards the rear (photo).

33 Ignition timing index (Peugeot BE type transmission) (photo).

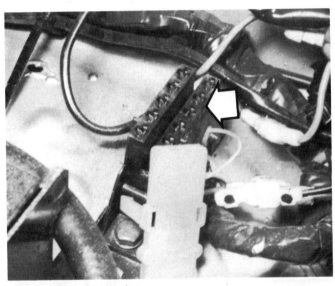

5.32 Diagnostic plug socket

5.33 Ignition timing marks (BE type transmission)

6 Fuel system

Solex 32 BISA 8 carburettor

1 This carburettor is virtually identical to the 32 BISA 6A and 32 BISA 7 types described in Chapter 3. However, the method of adjustment of the idling speed on certain versions of the 32 BISA 8 differs as follows.

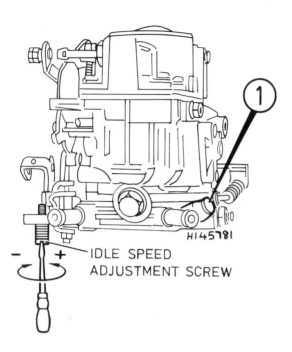

Fig. 13.4 Adjustment screws on Solex 32 BISA 8 carburettor
(Sec 6)

1   Mixture screw

6.2 Throttle cable and bracket on some later models

2   A volume control screw may not be incorporated, in which case the idling speed is adjusted using the screw shown in Fig. 13.4. Otherwise the tuning and adjustment procedure remains as detailed in Chapter 3, Section 14 (photo).

Carburettor adjustment

3   Before making any adjustments to the carburettor it is most important to first ensure that the following associated engine and ancillary items are in good order and where applicable adjusted properly:

   (a) Air cleaner filter element – must be clean and in good condition.
   (b) Crankcase ventilation system – the valve must be cleaned or renewed.

   (c) Check security of carburettor and manifold fastenings.
   (d) The engine must be known to be in good condition and the valves adjusted correctly.
   (e) The spark plugs must be in good condition and correctly adjusted.
   (f) The ignition timing must be correct and the system associated components in good condition.
   (g) The fuel pump and fuel lines must be in good order (photo).

4   Unless the above mentioned items are known to be in good condition then any adjustments made to the carburettor whether for servicing or to correct a malfunction may lead to further problems.

6.3 Fuel line filter

Fuel tank gauge transmitter unit

5   The fuel gauge transmitter unit fitted to later models is manufactured in plastic and has a brass tag connector to earth the unit to the tank.
6   When fitting this type of transmitter unit to the tank, first locate the rubber seal so that its lug is positioned in line with the brass connector. This is necessary to prevent the seal from being wedged between the connector and the tank during fitting, which would in turn prevent the earth circuit from being made.

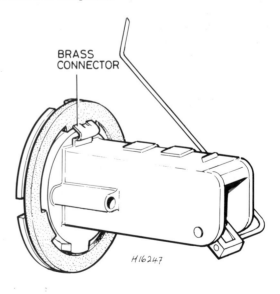

Fig. 13.5 Later type fuel tank transmitter (Sec 6)

Exhaust system – vibration

7 If the special balljoints in the front downpipe of the exhaust system seize a certain amount of vibration may be transmitted at engine speeds of 2000 to 3000 rpm when in gear.

8 To eradicate this, disconnect the exhaust downpipe from the manifold and pull the pipe flange downwards off the mounting studs.

9 Disconnect the balljoint springs using a pair of grips with suitably wide jaws to compress the spring whilst pushing on the inner end of the clips (towards each other) so that one clip may be unhooked from the pipe.

10 Move the downpipes to deflect the balljoints through maximum deflection. While this is being done, apply some anti-seize fluid to the balljoint rubbing surfaces. It should be noted that the balljoint sections cannot be separated from each other and no attempt should be made to prise them apart.

11 Reassembly is a reversal of dismantling, but use a new exhaust flange gasket.

Weber 36 DCA carburettor

12 With this type of carburettor which is fitted to automatic transmission models, the following adjustment may be required if there is a persistent tendency for the engine to stall when driving away immediately after a cold start.

13 Run the engine until it reaches normal operating temperature.

14 Set the idle speed (speed selector in N or P) to 1000 rev/min and the mixture screws to give a smooth idle with specified CO level (refer to Chapter 3).

15 Reset the fast idle cam and choke valve plate gaps to 9.0 mm instead of the 6.0 to 7.0 mm specified in Chapter 3, Section 13, paragraph 18. Carry out the adjustment by bending the lug (2) Fig. 13.6 of the fork lever (1).

16 Make sure that the cam is clear of the fast idle screw when the choke valve plates are fully open (engine at normal operating temperature).

17 Release the three fixing screws which secure the automatic choke housing cover and turn the cover in a clockwise direction until the alignment marks on the cover are 5.0 mm apart.

18 Having left the car overnight, start the engine cold and check the fast idle speed with the selector in N or P. The speed should be between 1700 and 1800 rev/min. If necessary, turn the screw (4) to achieve this.

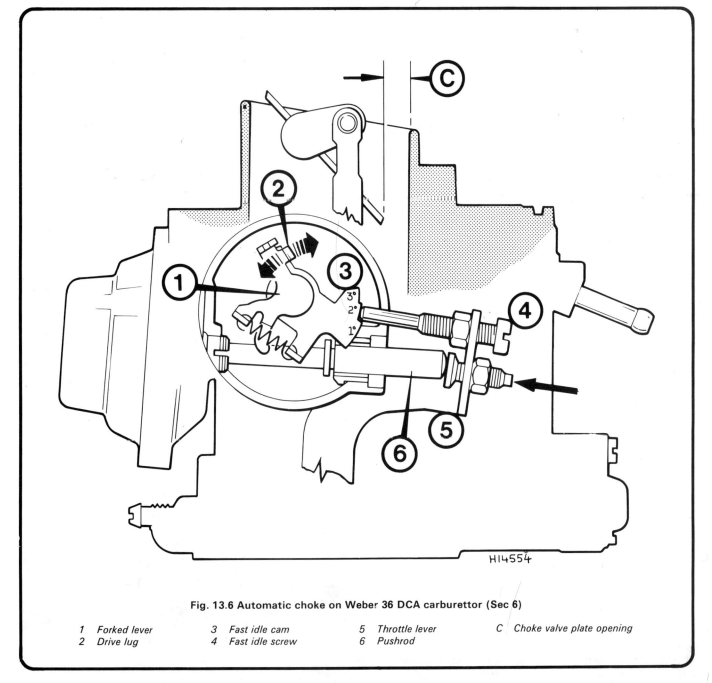

H14554

Fig. 13.6 Automatic choke on Weber 36 DCA carburettor (Sec 6)

1 Forked lever	3 Fast idle cam	5 Throttle lever	C Choke valve plate opening
2 Drive lug	4 Fast idle screw	6 Pushrod	

7 Manual transmission

Internal modifications

1 From September 1979 the dog teeth length of the 4th speed output shaft gear was increased to give a deeper mesh with the sliding gear of the synchromesh. To allow for this the output shaft driven gear teeth length was shortened and the 4th speed gear on the input shaft had its chamfer increased to prevent an interference condition.

2 Whilst the input shaft cluster is interchangeable between the gearboxes built before and after this date, the late type 4th speed driven gear must only be used with the late type input shaft.

3 Another modification made at this time was the introduction of a machined rebate on the 3rd/4th gear synchro sliding sleeve (C). This rebate is to prevent the possibility of the 3rd speed gear fouling with the 3rd speed input shaft gear when 3rd speed is engaged. During reassembly ensure that the rebate on the sliding sleeve faces 3rd gear as shown. A brief mention of this is made in paragraph 8, Section 7, Chapter 6.

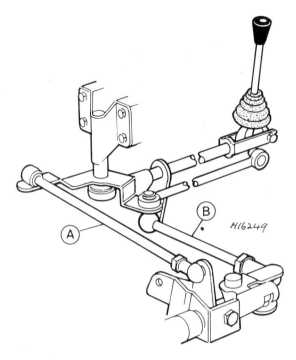

Fig. 13.8 Two rod gearchange linkage on later type M4T Simca type transmission (Sec 7)

A   256 to 266 mm (between balljoint centres)
B   157 to 167 mm (between balljoint centres)

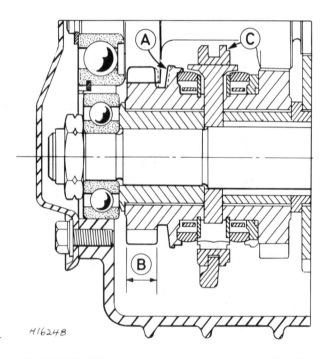

Fig. 13.7 Modified manual gearbox components (Sec 7)

A   *Early and later type dog and driven gear tooth profiles*
B   *Driven gear tooth length*
    Early 13.45 mm
    Late 12.45 mm
C   *Rebate on 3rd/4th gear sliding sleeve*

Peugeot type transmission (BE 1/4 and BE 1/5) – description

9 During 1984, the Peugeot type transmission was introduced on all models in place of the Simca type unit previously fitted (photo).

10 On LE (1118 cc) models the new transmission is of four-speed type BE 1/4 while on the 1294 cc and 1442 cc units, a five-speed unit, the BE 1/5 is used.

11 All forward speed gears are of synchromesh type. The four-speed unit is very similar to the five-speed version except that of course it does not have the 5th gear components which are located on the side of the intermediate plate remote from the main geartrains.

Two-rod gearchange linkage (Simca transmission)

4 Commencing with Series 2 models (October 1983) a two-rod gearchange linkage was fitted in conjunction with the four-speed (M4T) Simca type transmission.

5 Adjustment of this new linkage is carried out in the following way.

6 The length of rod A affects the side movement of the gear lever. This should be adjusted in the manner described in Chapter 6 so that the effective length (ie, between balljoint centres) is between 256 and 266 mm.

7 The length of rod B affects the movement of the gear lever in the fore-and-aft plane. This should be adjusted so that its effective length is between 157 and 167 mm.

8 Note that no adjustment is possible at the base of the gear lever.

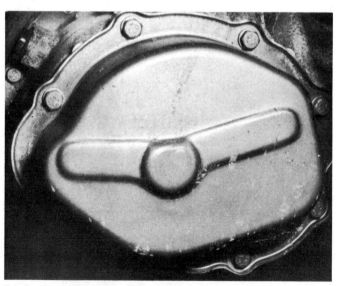

7.9 Gearbox end cover to identify BE type transmission

223

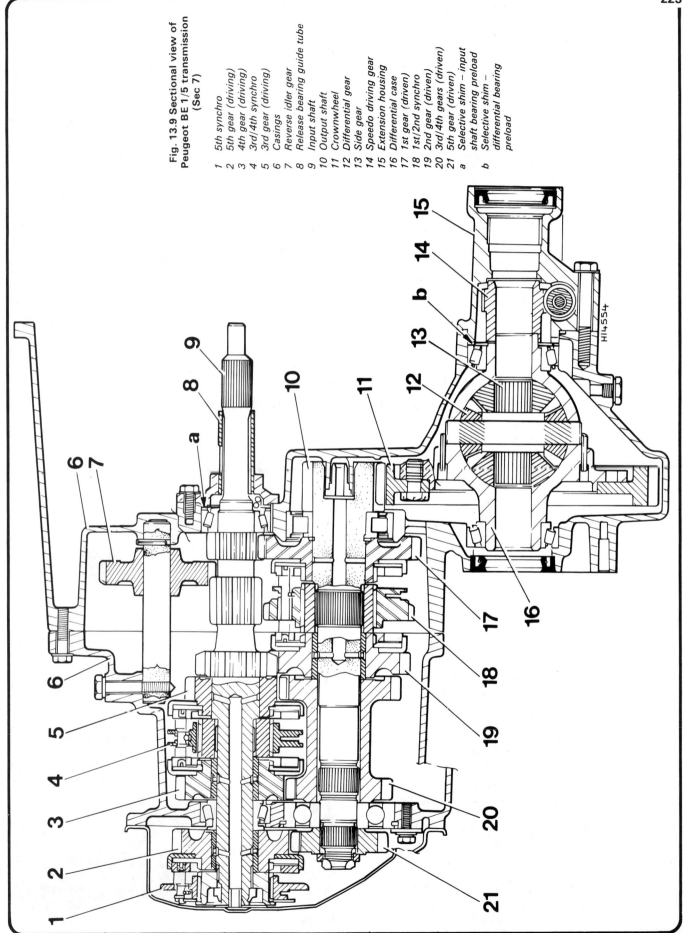

Fig. 13.9 Sectional view of Peugeot BE 1/5 transmission (Sec 7)

1 5th synchro
2 5th gear (driving)
3 4th gear (driving)
4 3rd/4th synchro
5 3rd gear (driving)
6 Casings
7 Reverse idler gear
8 Release bearing guide tube
9 Input shaft
10 Output shaft
11 Crownwheel
12 Differential gear
13 Side gear
14 Speedo driving gear
15 Extension housing
16 Differential case
17 1st gear (driven)
18 1st/2nd synchro
19 2nd gear (driven)
20 3rd/4th gears (driven)
21 5th gear (driven)
a Selective shim – input shaft bearing preload
b Selective shim – differential bearing preload

12 The differential (final drive) unit is contained in its own housing which is bolted to the gearbox casing. The gearbox and differential share the same lubricant.

Routine maintenance

13 The only regular maintenance required is to change the lubricant. *There is no provision for checking the oil level in the gearbox or in the final drive unit.* The oil must therefore be drained completely and the transmission be refilled with a known quantity of oil.

14 Apart from the regular oil change at the specified intervals the oil should be changed in a new or reconditioned unit after the first 1000 to 1500 miles, and in any unit after detection and rectification of an oil leak.

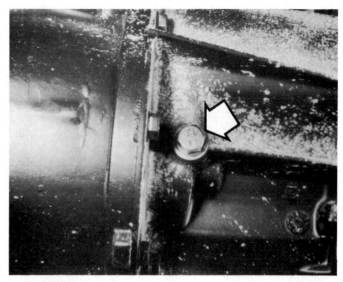

7.15A Gearbox drain plug

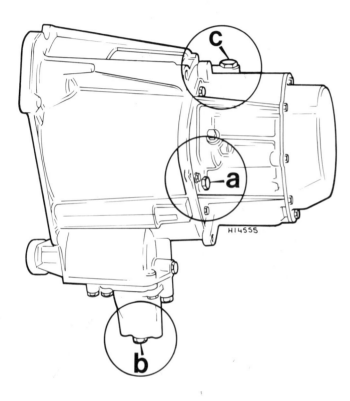

Fig. 13.10 Drain and filler plug locations on Type BE1 transmission (Sec 7)

a   *Gearbox drain plug*   c   *Filler plug*
b   *Final drive drain plug*

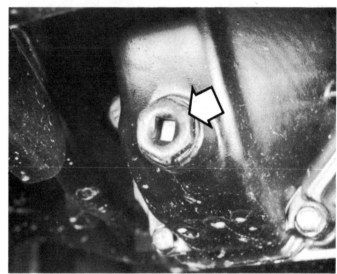

7.15B Final drive drain plug

15 When draining the transmission oil, note that there are two drain plugs, one for the gearbox and one for the final drive. Both plugs must be removed (photos).

16 When refilling the transmission with oil, do so through the filler plug orifice (photo). Remember to measure out the quantity of oil required beforehand.

Gearchange linkage – adjustment

17 With the gearbox in neutral, note that the gearchange levers on the gearbox are in the correct position (Fig. 13.11). There are no master splines so it is easy to put the levers in the wrong position after dismantling.

18 Measure the lengths of the engagement rod and the selection rod and compare them with the values given in Fig. 13.12. Adjust if necessary by slackening the locknut and screwing the rod in or out of the threaded portion of the end fitting. (The balljoints must be disconnected to do this).

19 Inside the car, release the gear lever gaiter and slide it up the gear lever. Engage 2nd gear and let go of the lever.

20 Measure the gap between the plastic cam and the stop in the gear

7.16 Filling BE type transmission

lever housing. If the gap is not as given in Fig. 13.13 remove the spring clip and lift the cam off its splines. Reposition the cam to obtain the correct clearance and secure with the spring clip. Apply a smear of grease to the side of the cam where it rubs against the stop (photo).

21 If after this adjustment it is still difficult to engage 1st and 2nd gears, measure the travel of the gear lever towards the 1st/2nd plane in the following way.

22 Place the gear lever in neutral, then move it gently to the left until the commencement of resistance is felt.

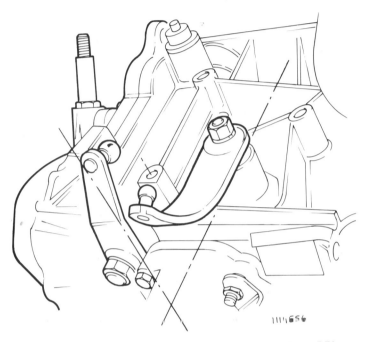

Fig. 13.11 Gearchange levers in neutral position on Type BE1 transmission (Sec 7)

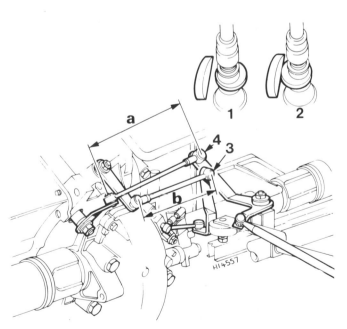

Fig. 13.12 Gearchange linkage adjustment Type BE1 transmission (Sec 7)

1	Eccentric cam in minimum position	3	Selection rod
2	Eccentric cam in maximum position	4	Engagement rod
		a	239 mm
		b	165 mm

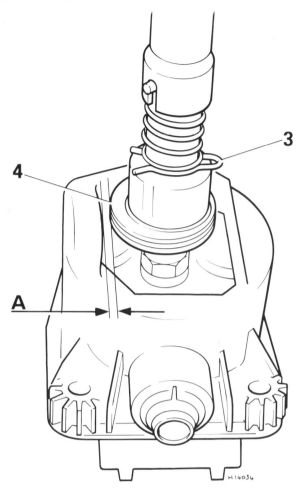

Fig. 13.13 Gearchange lever and housing on Type BE1 transmission (Sec 7)

A	4.5 mm	3	Spring clip
		4	Eccentric cam

7.20 Gearlever stop and cam

23 Position a ruler against the gear knob with the zero marking aligned with the 1/2 mark on the knob.

24 Push the gear lever as far as possible to the left without moving the ruler and note the distance travelled by the knob. Repeat the operation two or three times. The desired travel is 38 ± 2 mm.

25 If necessary, reposition the plastic cam as previously described to achieve the desired travel.

26 If the cam is positioned to give maximum lever travel, but the specified value has not been reached, lengthen the selection rod by 6 mm, then repeat the adjustment.

27 If the cam is positioned to give minimum lever travel, but the specified value is exceeded, shorten the selection rod by 6 mm, then repeat the adjustment.

28 Whatever adjustments have been carried out, check the engagement of all gears. Make sure that reverse gear cannot be engaged without lifting the collar on the gear lever.

29 Refit and secure the gear lever gaiter when adjustment is complete.

Transmission – removal and refitting

30 The transmission can be removed independently or together with the engine as described in Chapter 1.

31 To remove the transmission on its own, first disconnect the battery.

32 Disconnect the leads from the reversing lamp switch (photo).

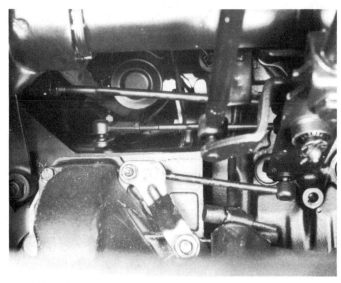
7.34A Gearchange linkage

7.32 Reverse lamp switch

7.34B Gearchange rods

33 Drain the oil from the gearbox and final drive casings.

34 Disconnect the gearchange linkage from the gearbox (photos).

35 Unbolt the clutch cylinder from the bellhousing and tie it to one side.

36 Refer to Chapter 7 and remove both driveshafts.

37 Retain the differential side gears in position by fitting Peugeot/Talbot tools 8.0317M and 8.0317N. *If this is not done, the side gears may fall into the differential housing.* In the absence of the special tools, it is possible to improvise using a length of wooden dowel, 1 inch diameter, ground down slightly at one end to enter the splines in the side gear.

38 Disconnect the speedometer drive cable from the transmission. Also disconnect the earth strap (photo).

39 Unbolt the starter motor and support it away from the engine.

40 Working at the base of the bellhousing, unbolt and remove the cover plate (photo).

41 Support the weight of the engine either on a hoist or by placing a jack and a block of wood as an insulator under the sump pan.

42 Unscrew and remove the bellhousing to engine connecting bolts.

43 Disconnect the transmission mounting from the body member (photo).

7.38 Earth strap on BE type transmission

7.40 Removing flywheel housing plate (spanner arrowed)

7.43 Transmission flexible mounting

44 Pull the gearbox away from the engine until the input shaft is clear of the clutch, then lower the gearbox through the engine compartment and withdraw it from below.

45 Refit in the reverse order to removal, noting the following points:

(a) Apply a smear of molybdenum grease to the gearbox input shaft

(b) Make sure that the gearchange levers are in the neutral position (Fig. 13.11)

(c) If the clutch has been dismantled, make sure that it is centralised as described in Chapter 5 before attempting to connect the transmission to the engine

(d) Tighten all nuts and bolts to the specified torque and use new nuts on the driveshafts, staking them into position. Tighten the drain plugs

(e) Refill the transmission with the specified grade and quantity of oil

(f) Check the operation of the gearchange linkage and adjust it if necessary

Transmission overhaul – general

46 Although the transmission system employed is relatively simple, nevertheless a few words of warning must be stressed, before any inexperienced dismantlers start work, to make sure that they know what they are letting themselves in for.

47 First of all decide whether the fault you wish to repair is worth the time and effort involved. Secondly bear in mind that, if the transmission is well worn, then the cost of the necessary component parts could well exceed the cost of an exchange factory unit and, furthermore, you would get a guaranteed job without the bother of having to do it yourself. Thirdly, if you are intent on doing it yourself, make sure that you understand how the transmission works.

48 Special care must be taken during all dismantling and assembly operations to ensure that the housing is not overstressed or distorted in any way. When dismantled, check the cost and availability of the parts to be renewed and compare this against the cost of a replacement unit, which may not be much more expensive and therefore would be a better proposition.

49 On reassembly, take careful note of the tightening procedures and torque wrench settings of the relevant nuts and bolts. This is most important to prevent overtightening, distortion and oil leakage and also to ensure smooth, trouble-free running of the unit.

50 With the transmission removed from the car, clean away external dirt using paraffin and a stiff brush or a water-soluble solvent.

51 Where possible, avoid dismantling on the floor, but preferably use the bench or a table top as a work surface.

52 Obtain an overhaul repair kit which will contain the necessary oil seals, gaskets, roll pins and other renewable items.

53 Start work with clean tools, clean hands and a plentiful supply of clean rag. To simplify reassembly a methodical work routine is essential. Put parts in small containers, lay the parts out in order of assembly as they are removed, mark individual items, or make sketches as you proceed. In practice most people use a combination of these procedures.

Dismantling into major assemblies

54 Remove the eight bolts and washers which secure the end cover. Remove the cover (photo)

Four-speed transmission

55 On four-speed units, release the nuts on the input and output shafts. In order to prevent the shafts from rotating, engage a gear by moving a selector fork and then hold the input shaft using a tool made up from an old clutch driven plate to which a lever has been welded (Fig. 13.14). Do not grip the shaft splines with a tool.

Five-speed transmission

56 On five-speed units, use a dab of quick drying paint to mark the alignment of the 5th speed gear synchro hub and its sleeve (photos).

57 Engage 5th speed gear by moving the selector fork.

7.54 Removing gearbox end cover

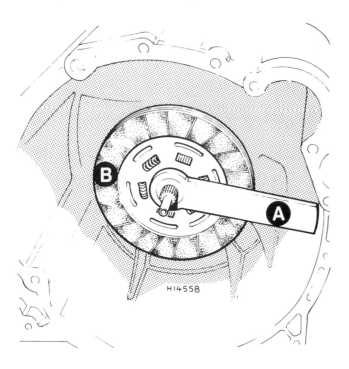

Fig. 13.14 Typical tool for locking input shaft (Sec 7)

A Lever   *B Old clutch driven plate*

58 Drive out the roll pin which secures 5th speed gear fork to its selector rod (photo).

59 Hold 5th gear selector fork in the engaged position and return the gear selector to neutral so that the selector passes through the fork.

60 Engage any other gear to lock up the shafts, then unscrew and remove the 28 mm nut from the end of the input shaft. If the nut is staked in position it may be necessary to relieve the staking (photo).

61 Remove 5th gear synchro hub, sliding sleeve and selector fork from the input shaft. Be prepared for the ejection of the detent ball from the selector fork.

62 Refit the 5th gear sliding sleeve and hub and engage 5th gear again. Relieve the staking from the output shaft nut and remove the nut. Remove the sliding sleeve and hub again (photo).

63 Remove from the input shaft the 5th gear, its bush and the spacer.

Four- and five-speed transmissions

64 Remove the two bolts and washers which secure the output shaft rear bearing.

65 Remove the circlip from the output shaft rear bearing by prising up its ends. The circlip should be renewed anyway, so do not be afraid of breaking it. Raise the output shaft if the circlip is jammed in its groove.

66 Extract its securing bolt and remove the selector rod lockplate (photo).

67 Remove the bolt which retains the reverse idler gear spindle.

68 Remove the thirteen bolts and washers which secure the end casing to the main casing. Withdraw the end casing: it is located by dowels, and may need striking with a wooden or plastic mallet to free it. Do not use a metal hammer, nor lever in between the joint faces.

69 Remove the selector arm and spring from the gear selector shaft. Remove the circlip and washer, push the shaft in and recover the O-ring (photo).

70 Drive out the roll pins which secure the selector finger and the interlock bracket to the selector shaft.

71 Use pliers or a self-gripping wrench to remove the cover from the end of the selector shaft (photo).

72 Press the selector shaft from the casing so that the circlip and washer can be extracted from the end of the shaft (photo).

73 Screw the reverse idler spindle retaining bolt back into the spindle and use it as a lever to extract the spindle. Remove the reverse idler gear itself (photo).

7.56A Unscrewing input shaft nut

7.56B Unscrewing output shaft nut

7.58 5th speed gear selector fork and roll pin (arrowed)

7.66 Selector rod lockplate bolt

7.73 Removing reverse idle spindle

7.71 Selector shaft cover and reverse lamp switch

74 Remove the swarf-collecting magnet from the casing (photo).
75 Carefully lift out the two geartrains with their shafts, the selector forks and the selector rods (photos).
76 Remove the spring support bracket from inside the main casing.
77 If not already removed, drive out the selector shaft end cover, using a drift of diameter no greater than 14 mm.
78 Extract the lubrication jet, using a wire hook.
79 Unscrew and remove the reversing lamp switch.
80 Remove the nut and washer which secure the reverse selector fork spindle. Remove the spindle and selector fork. Recover the detent plunger and spring.
81 Unscrew and remove the breather from the main casing (photo).
82 Turning to the clutch housing, remove the clutch release bearing (if not already done). Pull off the release fork.
83 Unbolt and remove the release bearing guide tube.
84 From behind the tube remove the preload shim and the outer track of the input shaft front bearing.
85 To remove the final drive unit, first unbolt and remove the speedometer pinion and its adaptor (photo).
86 Unbolt and remove the extension housing. Recover the speedometer driving gear and the bearing preload shim (photos).

7.72 Selector shaft projecting for access to circlip and washer

7.74 Casing magnet

7.75A Reverse selector fork

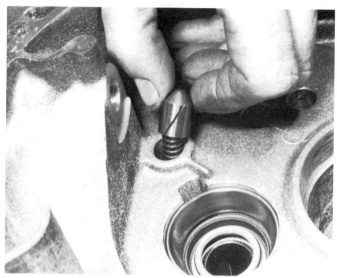

7.75B Reverse detent plunger and spring

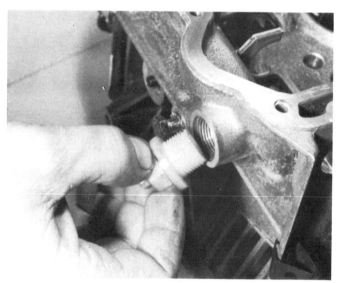

7.81 Removing the breather

7.85 Removing the speedometer drive pinion

7.86A Removing the final drive extension housing

7.86B Removing the speedometer drivegear

87 Unbolt the final drive half housing. Remove the half housing and final drive unit. Note the location of the gearchange pivot bracket.

88 Identify the final drive bearing outer tracks; if they are to be reused they must be refitted on the same sides.

89 Remove the selector lever from the main casing. It is retained by a circlip and a washer.

90 If it is wished to remove the clutch release lever balljoint, do so with a slide hammer having a suitable claw. (A new gearbox will not necessarily be fitted with a balljoint).

91 The gearbox is now dismantled into its major assemblies.

Input shaft – dismantling

92 Remove the 3rd and 4th gear components from the input shaft by supporting the assembly under the 3rd gear and pressing or driving the shaft through. Protect the end of the shaft. Once the rear bearing is free, the other components can be removed from the shaft in order: 4th gear and its bush, 3rd/4th synchro sleeve and hub and 3rd gear (photos).

93 Mark the synchro sleeve and hub relative to each other and to show which side faces 4th gear.

94 Remove the front bearing from the shaft, preferably with a press or a bearing puller. As a last resort it may be possible to support the bearing and drive the shaft through; be sure to protect the end of the shaft if this is done.

7.92C 4th speed gear bush

7.92D 3rd/4th synchro sleeve on input shaft

7.92A Input shaft bearing

7.92B 4th speed gear on input shaft

7.92E 3rd/4th synchro hub on input shaft

7.92F 3rd speed gear on input shaft

7.96 Output shaft rear bearing

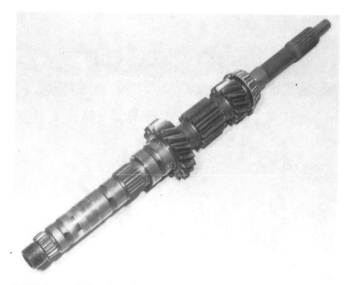

7.92G Input shaft stripped except for front bearing

7.97A 3rd/4th speed gear assembly on output shaft

95 Once the input shaft bearings have been removed, they must be renewed. Press the rear bearing outer track from the end casing and press in the new track, making sure it enters squarely.

Output shaft – dismantling

96 Remove 5th gear (when applicable) and the rear bearing from the output shaft. Use a puller or bearing extractor if they are a tight fit on the shaft (photo).
97 Remove 3rd/4th gear assembly, 2nd gear and its bush (photos).
98 Make alignment marks between the 1st/2nd synchro hub and sleeve, then remove them from the shaft (photos).
99 Remove 1st gear and the thrust bearing. Remove the bearing circlip (photos).
100 Press or drive the shaft out of the pinion end bearing, protecting the end of the shaft.

Differential – dismantling

101 Unbolt the crownwheel from the differential housing.
102 Remove the side gears by pushing them round inside the housing until they can be removed (photo).

7.97B 2nd speed gear on output shaft

7.97C 2nd speed gear bush

7.98 1st/2nd synchro sleeve on output shaft

7.99A 1st speed gear on output shaft

7.99B Needle thrust bearing

7.99C Output shaft bearing circlip

7.102 Removing a differential side gear

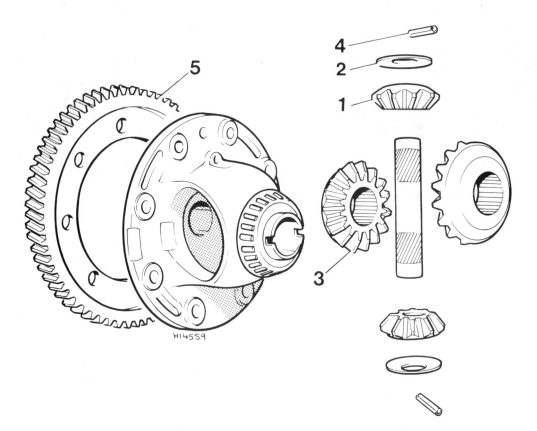

Fig. 13.15 Differential components (Sec 7)

1   Differential gear
2   Thrust washer
3   Side gear
4   Roll pin
5   Crownwheel

H14559

7.104 Differential spindle, gears and thrust washer

103 Drive out the roll pins which secure the differential gear spindle.
104 Remove the spindle, the differential gears and their washers (photo).
105 Use a press or bearing extractor to remove the bearings.

Selector mechanism – dismantling

106 One of the unusual features of this gearbox is that the detent springs and balls are located in the forks (photo). If a spring is weak, the whole fork must be renewed. (This does not apply to 5th gear fork).

107 Rotate the 1st/2nd and 3rd/4th selector rod to disengage the detent slots from the balls, then remove the rod from the forks.
108 Where applicable, remove 5th gear selector rod from the 1st/2nd fork.

Examination and renovation

109 Having removed and dismantled the transmission unit, the various components should be thoroughly washed with a suitable solvent or with petrol and paraffin, and then wiped dry. Take care not to mix components or to lose identification of where they fit and which way round they should be fitted. Don't use hard scrapers or emery cloth to clean the housing mating faces as the surface must be kept perfectly flat and undamaged.
110 Inspect the transmission housing and the differential unit housing for cracks or damage, particularly near bearings or bushes. The transmission housing, differential housing and the mainshaft centre bearing cap are all machined after assembly and none of these parts must be renewed separately.
111 Components requiring special attention will have been noted as a result of the performance of the transmission when installed in the car or will have been noted during dismantling.
112 Examine the teeth of all gears for signs of uneven or excessive wear or chipping. If you find a gear in a bad state have a close look at the gear it engages with – this may have to be renewed as well. All gears should run smoothly on their bushes or in their bearings with no sign of rocking or sloppiness.
113 A not so obvious cause of noise and trouble is bearing wear. Wash and dry the bearings thoroughly and examine them closely for signs of scoring, pitted tracks or blueing. Rotate the races and feel for smooth movement with no grittiness or abnormal noise. A new ball bearing will show no perceptible axial movement between the inner and outer races. As the bearing wears some play will be evident but if this is excessive the bearing must be renewed. After examining bearings they should be lubricated with engine oil to prevent corrosion, and wrapped to avoid contamination with dust and dirt.
114 Carefully inspect the synchromesh units for excessive wear or damage. If weak or ineffective synchromesh action has been experienced, renew the units as complete assemblies.

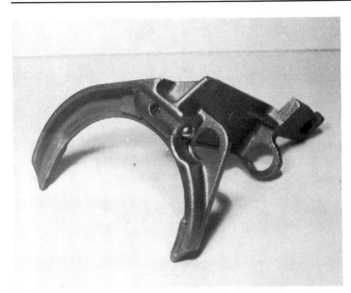

7.106 Gear selector fork with captive detent ball and spring

121 Fit a new front bearing to the shaft, using a suitable tube to press or drive it home.
122 Fit 3rd gear, 3rd/4th synchro hub and sleeve, 4th gear and its bush. Take care not to get 3rd and 4th gears mixed up, they are similar in appearance. (4th gear has more teeth). If the original synchro components are being refitted, observe the mating marks made during dismantling.
123 Fit a new rear bearing to the shaft, again using a piece of tubing.
124 The input shaft is now reassembled.

Output shaft – reassembly

125 Before commencing reassembly, make sure that the shaft is free from burrs or wear marks. Lubricate all parts as they are fitted.
126 Fit the pinion end bearing to the shaft, using a piece of tubing to drive or press it home. Fit a new circlip.
127 Fit the thrust bearing and 1st speed gear.
128 Refit the 1st/2nd synchro unit, observing the mating marks made when dismantling. The chamfer on the external teeth must face towards 1st gear.
129 Fit 2nd gear and its bush.
130 Fit the 3rd/4th gear assembly, making sure it is the right way round.
131 Fit the rear bearing, with the circlip groove nearest the tail of the shaft.
132 On five-speed units, fit the 5th speed gear so that the boss on the gear is towards the shaft bearing.
133 On four-speed units, fit the shaft spacer (Fig. 13.17).
134 Screw on a new nut, but do not tighten at this stage.

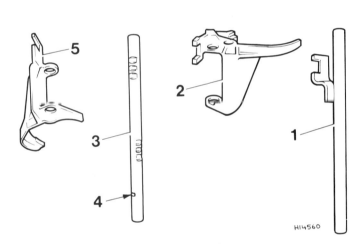

Fig. 13.16 Selector forks and rods (Sec 7)

1	5th rod	4	Rod locking slot
2	1st/2nd fork	5	3rd/4th fork
3	1st/2nd and 3rd/4th rod		

115 Check the selector forks for wear in the areas which contact the synchromesh units. Any wear evident should be minimal; if in doubt renew the forks.
116 Inspect the selector shafts and detents for wear which can cause imprecise gear changing, and renew where necessary.
117 All remaining components such as the speedometer gears, locking plungers, springs, balls, and so on, should be inspected for signs of wear or damage and, where necessary, renewed.
118 It is now worth reviewing the total requirements needed to restore the transmission unit to full serviceability, not forgetting the new lockwashers, circlips, roll pins, seals and gaskets. Compare the cost with that of an overhauled or good condition secondhand unit as it may be more economical to go for one of these alternatives.
119 If new input shaft or differential bearings are to be fitted, a selection of preload shims will be required. Read through the relevant procedures before starting work.

Input shaft – reassembly

120 Before commencing reassembly, make sure that the input shaft is free from burrs and wear marks. Lubricate all parts as they are fitted.

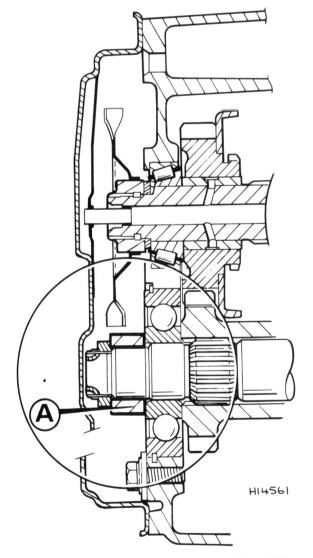

Fig. 13.17 Shaft spacer (A) on four-speed Type BE1 transmission (Sec 7)

Differential – reassembly

135 Fit the bearings, using a piece of tube to press or drive them home.
136 Fit the spindle with the differential gears and washers. Secure the spindle with new roll pins, which should be driven in until they are centrally located in their holes (photo).
137 Fit the side gears, one at a time, and work them into their proper positions. Retain them in this position using tool 8.0317 M or a wooden dowel which is inserted from the crownwheel side (photo).
138 Fit the crownwheel with its chamfer towards the differential housing. Secure with the bolts, tightening them in diagonal sequence to the specified torque.

7.136 Differential spindle roll pin

7.137 Side gear retaining tool

Selector mechanism – reassembly

139 Commence reassembly by inserting 5th gear selector rod into the 1st/2nd fork.
140 Offer the 3rd/4th fork to the 1st/2nd fork so that their holes and selector fingers align.
141 Insert the 1st/2nd and 3rd/4th selector rod, positioning the locking slot as shown. Bring all the selector finger slots into line to position the selectors in neutral (photo).

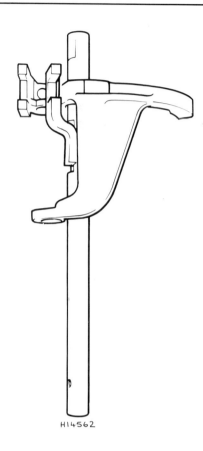

Fig. 13.18 5th selector rod through 1st/2nd fork (Sec 7)

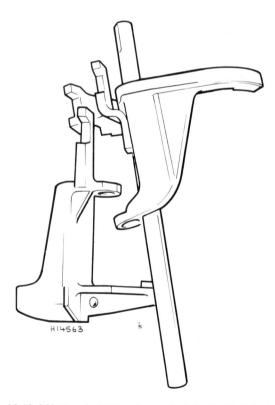

Fig. 13.19 Offering 3rd/4th selector fork to 1st/2nd fork on 5th selector rod (Sec 7)

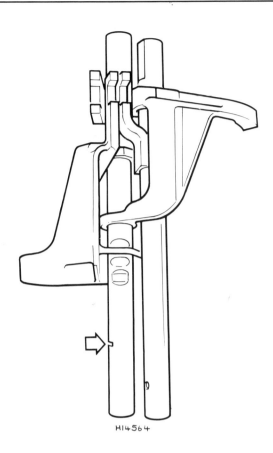

Fig. 13.20 Selector rod/fork assembly. Rod locking slot arrowed (Sec 7)

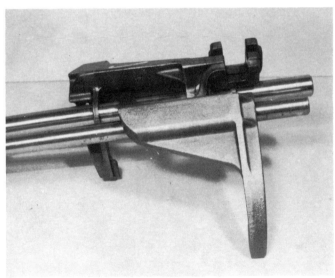

7.141 Selector forks and rods in neutral

Transmission – reassembly

142 The only difference in reassembling the four-speed transmission apart from the obvious absence of 5th gear components, lies in the method of locking the geartrains when tightening the input and output shaft nuts.

143 Refer to paragraph 55 and use the method described there. Remember to stake the nuts after tightening.

144 Commence reassembly by fitting the selector lever into the main

casing. Make sure that the locating dowel is in position in the final drive housing mating face.

145 Apply jointing compound to the mating face, then fit the differential assembly with its bearing tracks (photo).

146 Fit the final drive half housing and the extension housing, but only tighten their securing bolts finger tight at this stage.

147 Fit a new oil seal, lips well greased, to the other side of the final drive housing from the extension.

148 Remove the extension housing, fit a preload shim 2.2 mm thick to the bearing outer track and refit the extension housing (without its O-ring). Rotate the crownwheel while tightening the extension housing bolts until the crownwheel *just* starts to drag. This operation seats the bearings.

149 Remove the extension housing and the preload shim. With an accurate depth gauge, measure the distance from the final drive housing joint face to the bearing outer track. Call this dimension A. Similarly measure the protrusion of the spigot on the extension housing above the joint face. Call this dimension B (photos).

150 The thickness S of preload shim required is determined by the formula:

$$S = (A - B) + 0.10 \text{ mm}$$

The extra 0.10 mm is the preload factor for the bearings. Shims are available in thicknesses of 1.1 to 2.2 mm in steps of 0.1 mm.

7.145 Differential/final drive. Locating dowel arrowed

7.149A Measuring bearing outer track recess

7.149B Measuring extension housing spigot projection

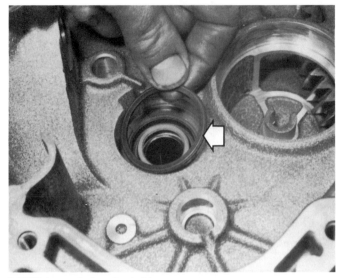

7.156A Input shaft preload shim

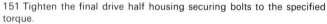

151 Tighten the final drive half housing securing bolts to the specified torque.

152 Fit the preload shim just determined, the speedometer driving gear and the extension housing with a new O-ring. Tighten the securing bolts to the specified torque. Make sure that the crownwheel is still free to rotate (photo).

153 Fit and secure the speedometer pinion and its adaptor.

154 Fit a new oil seal, lips well greased, into the extension housing.

155 Fit a new gear selector shaft oil seal in the main casing.

156 From the clutch housing side, fit the clutch release bearing guide tube. Do not use a gasket under the guide tube flange, and only tighten the bolts finger tight. Invert the casing and fit a preload spacer (any size) and the input shaft bearing outer track (photos).

157 Fit the gear selector shaft spring bracket and tighten its securing bolts to the specified torque.

158 If removed, fit the two locating dowels in the main casing mating face.

159 Fit and tighten the breather.

160 Refit the lubrication jet (photo).

7.156B Input shaft front bearing outer track

7.152 Fitting preload shim

7.160 Fitting the lubrication jet

161 Fit the reverse detent spring and plunger. Depress the plunger and fit the reverse selector fork and its spindle. Tighten the spindle securing nut to the specified torque.

162 Fit the reversing lamp switch using a new copper washer. Tighten it to the specified torque (photo).

163 Assemble the geartrains and the selector forks and rods. Offer the whole assembly to the gearcase (photo).

164 Fit the reverse idler spindle and gear, with the chamfer towards the rear of the gearbox. Make sure the pin in the shaft is correctly located.

165 Refit the swarf-collecting magnet.

166 Insert the spring and washers into the bracket (photo).

167 Enter the selector shaft into the casing, passing it through the compressed spring and washers inside the casing. Also engage the shaft with the selector finger and the interlock bracket. It may be helpful to keep the finger and the bracket together with a short length of rod (maximum diameter 14 mm) which can be withdrawn as the selector shaft enters (photo).

168 Make sure that the flat on the shaft and the roll pin hole are correctly orientated (Fig. 13.21). Secure the selector finger and the interlock bracket with two new roll pins. The slots in the roll pins should be 180° away from each other and in line with the longitudinal axis of the shaft (photo).

7.166 Selector shaft spring, washers and bracket

7.162 Reversing lamp switch

7.167 Fitting the selector shaft

7.163 Fitting the geartrains and selector mechanism

7.168 Selector finger/interlock bracket roll pins

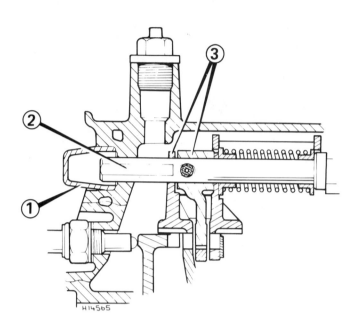

Fig. 13.21 Selector shaft fitting details (Sec 7)
1 Cover
2 Flat on shaft
3 Selector finger and
   interlock bracket

169 Fit the washer and a new circlip to the cover end of the shaft.
170 Refit the selector shaft cover if it was removed.
171 To the lever end of the selector shaft fit a new O-ring, a washer and a new circlip.
172 Apply jointing compound to the main casing/end casing mating face. Fit the end casing, making sure that the input and output shafts and the selector rod pass through their respective holes. Fit the thirteen securing bolts and tighten them progressively to the specified torque.
173 Fit the reverse idler spindle bolt, using a new washer. Tighten the bolt to the specified torque.
174 Fit the drain plugs, using new washers, and tighten them to the specified torque.
175 Fit the selector rod lockplate. Secure it with its bolt and washer, tightening the bolt to the specified torque.
176 Fit the output shaft bearing circlip, making sure it is properly located in the groove.
177 Fit the output shaft rear bearing retaining washers and bolts. Tighten the bolts to the specified torque.
178 On four-speed units, lock up the gearshafts as described in paragraph 55, tighten the shaft nuts to the specified torque and stake the nuts into the shaft grooves.
179 On five-speed units, fit the spacer (shoulder to bearing) then 5th gear bush and 5th speed gear to the input shaft followed by the sliding sleeve and hub, but not the selector fork.
180 Lock up the geartrains by engaging 5th gear with the sliding sleeve and any other gear with the selector shaft. Fit the output shaft nut and tighten it to the specified torque, then lock it by staking its skirt into the groove.
181 Remove the 5th gear sliding sleeve and hub, then refit them with the selector fork. If the original components are being refitted, observe the mating marks made when dismantling. As the fork is being lowered into position, insert the detent ball into its hole. Alternatively extract the roll pin and insert the detent ball and spring from the other end (photos).
182 Engage two gears again, then fit the input shaft nut and tighten it to the specified torque. Lock the nut by staking.
183 Secure 5th gear selector fork to its rod with a new roll pin.
184 Coat the mating faces with jointing compound, then refit the rear cover. Use thread locking compound on the securing bolts and tighten them to the specified torque.
185 Turn to the clutch housing and remove the release bearing guide

7.179A 5th speed gear spacer on input shaft

7.179B 5th speed gear bush on input shaft

7.179C Input shaft 5th speed gear

7.181A 5th speed selector fork detent ball and spring

7.187A Measuring input shaft front bearing outer track recess

7.181B 5th speed selector fork roll pin

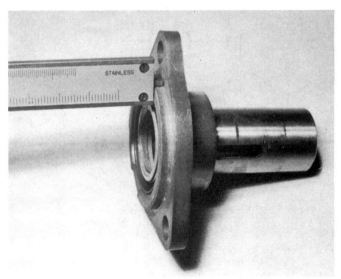

7.187B Measuring guide tube spigot projection

tube. If a new release lever balljoint is to be fitted, do so now; put thread locking compound on its splines and drive it in.

186 Refit the clutch release bearing guide tube with a preload spacer 2.4 mm thick and without a gasket. Insert the retaining bolts and tighten them progressively, at the same time rotating the input shaft. Stop tightening when the shaft *just* starts to drag: the bearings are then correctly seated.

187 Remove the guide tube and the shim. Using a depth gauge, accurately measure the distance from the bearing outer track to the joint face on the casing. Call this dimension C. Similarly measure the protrusion of the spigot on the guide tube flange above the joint face. Call this dimension D (photos).

188 The thickness T of preload shim required is given by the formula:

$$T = (C - D) + 0.15 \text{ mm}$$

The extra 0.15 mm is to provide bearing preload, and allows for the thickness of the gasket which will be fitted. Shims are available in thicknesses from 0.7 to 2.4 mm in steps of 0.1 mm.

189 Fit a new oil seal, lips well greased, to the guide tube.

190 Fit the preload shim (of calculated thickness), a new gasket and the guide tube. Secure with the bolts and tighten them to the specified torque (photo).

7.190 Input shaft front bearing preload shim

191 Refit the clutch release fork and release bearing.
192 If not already done, refit the gearchange levers, making sure that they are in the correct neutral position. Also refit the clutch bellcrank (if removed) and the gearchange pivot bracket.
193 Reassembly of the transmission is now complete. Do not refill it with oil until the driveshafts have been engaged.

8   Automatic transmission

Fluid level 1982 to 1984
1   The dipstick level markings are as shown in Fig. 13.22.
2   The fluid level checking procedure is otherwise the same as that given in Section 15 of Chapter 6.
3   It should be noted that the final drive (differential) unit on automatic transmission models is housed integrally with the transmission, but in a separate compartment which contains its own lubricant.
4   Whilst the transmission unit fluid level is checked with the dipstick, the final drive oil level is checked by unscrewing and removing its filler/level plug (the upper plug when the housing has two fitted). The oil level is correct when it is level with the bottom of the filler/level plug hole.

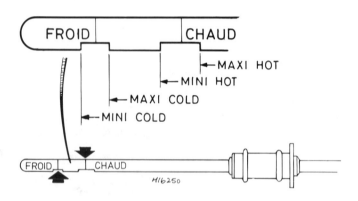

Fig. 13.22 Later type dipstick markings on automatic transmission (Sec 8)

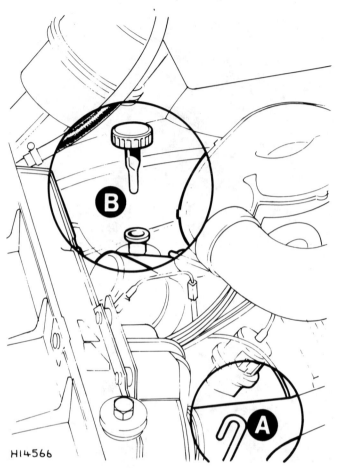

Fig. 13.23 Dipstick locations (Sec 8)

A   Automatic transmission   B   Power steering

Fluid level 1984 and later
5   On these models, the separate final drive filler/level plug is deleted. Check the automatic transmission fluid level using the dipstick. This is all that is needed for checking the gearbox and final drive common fluid supply.

Front brake band – adjustment
6   It is recommended that the front brake band is adjusted at the same time as the transmission fluid is changed.
7   Release the locknut from the adjuster screw which is located adjacent to the fluid dipstick hole.
8   Retighten the adjuster screw to 72 lbf in (8 Nm) and then unscrew it through exactly two and half complete turns.
9   Without moving the position of the adjuster screw, tighten the locknut to 37 lbf ft (47 Nm).

9   Steering, wheels and tyres

Alloy roadwheels
1   Where alloy roadwheels are fitted, their securing bolts should be checked for security after a distance of 100 miles (160 km) has been covered from when the wheel(s) were fitted. This applies whether one or more roadwheels has been removed for any reason at any time. Refer to Chapter 8 for the correct wheel nut torque setting.

Wheels and tyres – care and maintenance
2   Wheels and tyres should give no real problems in use provided that a close eye is kept on them with regard to excessive wear or damage. To this end, the following points should be noted.

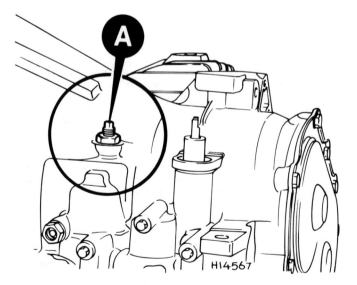

Fig. 13.24 Location of automatic transmission front band adjuster (A) (Sec 8)

3 Ensure that tyre pressures are checked regularly and maintained correctly. Checking should be carried out with the tyres cold and not immediately after the vehicle has been in use. If the pressures are checked with the tyres hot, an apparently high reading will be obtained owing to heat expansion. Under no circumstances should an attempt be made to reduce the pressures to the quoted cold reading in this instance, or effective underinflation will result.
4 Underinflation will cause overheating of the tyre owing to excessive flexing of the casing, and the tread will not sit correctly on the road surface. This will cause a consequent loss of adhesion and excessive wear, not to mention the danger of sudden tyre failure due to heat build-up.
5 Overinflation will cause rapid wear of the centre part of the tyre tread coupled with reduced adhesion, harsher ride, and the danger of shock damage occurring in the tyre casing.
6 Regularly check the tyres for damage in the form of cuts or bulges, especially in the sidewalls. Remove any nails or stones embedded in the tread before they penetrate the tyre to cause deflation. If removal of a nail *does* reveal that the tyre has been punctured, refit the nail so that its point of penetration is marked. Then immediately change the wheel and have the tyre repaired by a tyre dealer. Do *not* drive on a tyre in such a condition. In many cases a puncture can be simply repaired by the use of an inner tube of the correct size and type. If in any doubt as to the possible consequences of any damage found, consult your local tyre dealer for advice.
7 Periodically remove the wheels and clean any dirt or mud from the inside and outside surfaces. Examine the wheel rims for signs of rusting, corrosion or other damage. Light alloy wheels are easily damaged by 'kerbing' whilst parking, and similarly steel wheels may become dented or buckled. Renewal of the wheel is very often the only course of remedial action possible (photo).

9.7 Wheel trim on GLX models

8 The balance of each wheel and tyre assembly should be maintained to avoid excessive wear, not only to the tyres but also to the steering and suspension components. Wheel imbalance is normally signified by vibration through the vehicle's bodyshell, although in many cases it is particularly noticeable through the steering wheel. Conversely, it should be noted that wear or damage in suspension or steering components may cause excessive tyre wear. Out-of-round or out-of-true tyres, damaged wheels and wheel bearing wear/maladjustment also fall into this category. Balancing will not usually cure vibration caused by such wear.
9 Wheel balancing may be carried out with the wheel either on or off the vehicle. If balanced on the vehicle, ensure that the wheel-to-hub relationship is marked in some way prior to subsequent wheel removal so that it may be refitted in its original position.

10 General tyre wear is influenced to a large degree by driving style – harsh braking and acceleration or fast cornering will all produce more rapid tyre wear. Interchanging of tyres may result in more even wear, but this should only be carried out where there is no mix of tyre types on the vehicle. However, it is worth bearing in mind that if this is completely effective, the added expense of replacing a complete set of tyres simultaneously is incurred, which may prove financially restrictive for many owners.
11 Front tyres may wear unevenly as a result of wheel misalignment. The front wheels should always be correctly aligned according to the settings specified by the vehicle manufacturer.
12 Legal restrictions apply to the mixing of the tyre types on a vehicle. Basically this means that a vehicle must not have tyres of differing construction on the same axle. Although it is not recommended to mix tyre types between front axle and rear axle, the only legally permissible combination is crossply at the front and radial at the rear. When mixing radial ply tyres, textile braced radials must always go on the front axle, with steel braced radials at the rear. An obvious disadvantage of such mixing is the necessity to carry two spare tyres to avoid contravening the law in the event of a puncture.
13 In the UK, the Motor Vehicles Construction and Use Regulations apply to many aspects of tyre fitting and usage. It is suggested that a copy of these regulations is obtained from your local police if in doubt as to the current legal requirements with regard to tyre condition, minimum tread depth, etc.

Power-assisted steering – description and maintenance
14 Power-assisted steering is fitted as standard to Pullman and GLX models (photo).
15 At the specified intervals, after coming in off the road with the fluid hot, withdraw the reservoir dipstick, wipe it clean, re-insert it and withdraw it for the second time. If the fluid is not up to the high mark, top it up with Dexron II type automatic transmission fluid (photo).

Power-assisted steering pump drivebelt – tensioning
16 With the pump carrier mounting bolts loose, check that the drivebelt is fully engaged with the pump and crankshaft pulleys (photo).
17 Insert a lever through the pulley guard, and raise the pump until there is 0.5 in (13 mm) of movement halfway along the run of the belt.
18 Tighten the bolts and recheck the tension.
19 Run the engine for two or three minutes, then switch off and recheck the tension.
20 Never pull on the reservoir to adjust the position of the pump. A new drivebelt should be retensioned after 600 miles (1000 km).

Steering pump – removal and refitting
21 Disconnect the battery negative terminal.
22 Loosen the mounting bolts, lower the pump, and remove the drivebelt.

9.14 Power-assisted steering pump and hoses

9.15 Power-assisted steering fluid dipstick

23 Cover the distributor, alternator, and the alternator drivebelt with polythene sheeting.
24 Loosen the feed pipe union.
25 Remove the nuts securing the pump to the carrier.
26 Loosen the hose clip at the base of the reservoir.
27 Remove the pump from the carrier, noting the location of any spacers. Remove the filler cap and empty the fluid into a suitable receptacle.
28 Disconnect the feed and return pipes and withdraw the pump. Drain any remaining fluid and plug all pipes and apertures.
29 Unbolt the belt guard from the pump.
30 Refitting is a reversal of removal, but tension the drivebelt as previously described and then refill the reservoir with specified fluid. Bleed the system in the following way.
31 Refit the reservoir cap and then turn the steering wheel from lock to lock several times. Top up the reservoir until it is half full, then start the engine and again turn the steering wheel from lock to lock several times. When all the air has been purged from the circuit, run the car until the fluid is hot, and top up the level to the FULL mark on the dipstick.

Power-assisted steering gear – removal and refitting
32 The operations are very similar to those described for the manual steering in Chapter 8, Section 4, except that the fluid supply and return

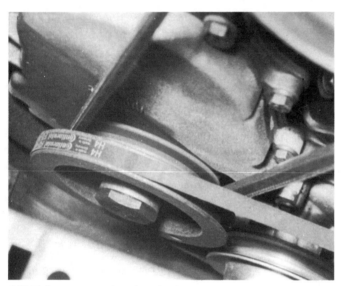

9.16 Twin groove crankshaft pulley for power steering pump drivebelt

9.24 Pipe connection on rear face of power steering pump

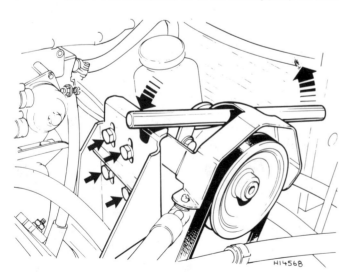

Fig. 13.25 Tensioning power steering pump drivebelt. Pump mounting bolts (arrowed) (Sec 9)

9.32 Pipe connections on steering rack housing

hoses must be disconnected from the steering gear and the fluid drained into a container. Plug the open ends of the hoses.

33 After refitting, fill and bleed the system as described in paragraph 31 of this Section.

10 Braking system

Girling disc brakes

1 Later model Girling calipers have a single piece pad pin retaining clip fitted instead of the two R-clips and a pin used on earlier types. When servicing the earlier brake type, the new clip type should replace the pin and R-clips previously fitted.

2 To prevent brake squeal from the front disc brake units on the Girling type caliper they are modified and have a cutaway section on the leading edge of the pistons. Set at an angle of 20°, this is similar to the Teves/DBA caliper types.

3 On earlier models anti-squeal shims are available for fitting between the piston and pads. Ensure that they are fitted with the arrow marking pointing in the direction of disc rotation.

4 A further modification on later models is in the supply of disc pads with latex-coated backs in order to further reduce brake squeal.

Bendix disc brakes

5 C-Series models fitted with Bendix type front disc brakes incorporate an anti-squeal shim. When refitting this shim during brake pad renewal or a brake unit service operation ensure that the shim is fitted so that the direction of the arrow points in the direction of disc forwards rotation.

6 Girling type shims may be adapted to fit Bendix brakes by cutting them in accordance with the diagram (Fig. 13.27).

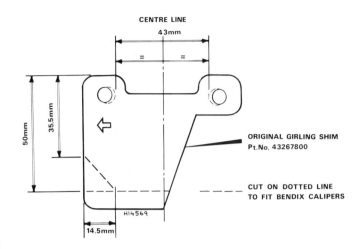

Fig. 13.27 Disc pad anti-squeal shim modification diagram (Sec 10)

Disc brakes – idenfication

7 The three front disc brake unit types used are shown in the accompanying illustrations to assist in identification of the particular type fitted. Identification is important to ensure that the correct replacement parts are obtained since the corresponding parts of each type are not directly interchangeable.

8 Wear sensors are fitted to all later disc pads.

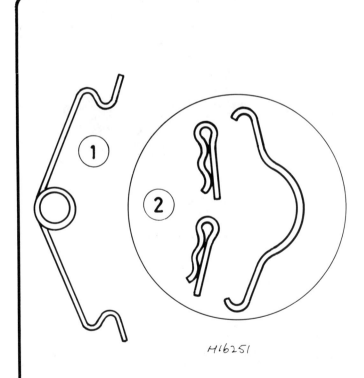

Fig. 13.26 Disc pad retaining clips (Sec 10)

1   Later type   2   Earlier type

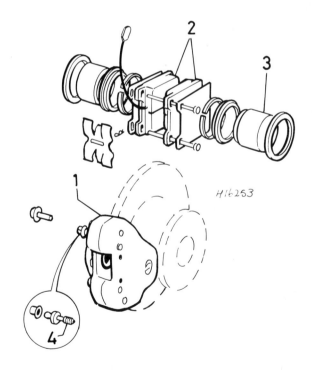

Fig. 13.28 Caliper components (Girling) (Sec 10)

1   Caliper   3   Piston
2   Disc pads   4   Bleed screw

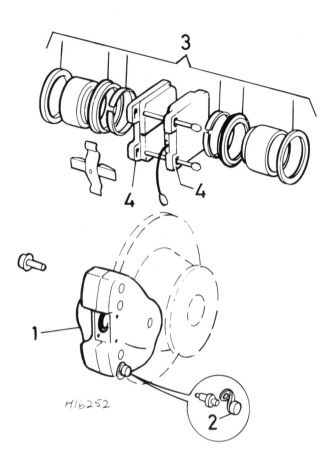

Fig. 13.29 Caliper components (Teves) (Sec 10)

1 Caliper   3 Pistons and seals
2 Bleed screw   4 Pads

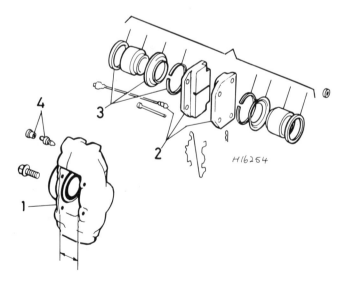

Fig. 13.30 Caliper components (Bendix) (Sec 10)

1 Caliper   3 Piston and seals
2 Pads and wear warning   4 Bleed screw
   lead

11 Electrical system

Alternator (Series 2 cars)

1 To improve the performance of the alternator the drive pulley was reduced in diameter from 70 to 60.5 mm (2.75 to 2.38 in) and this in turn necessitated a shorter drivebelt being fitted, 760 mm (29.9 in) long instead of 775 mm (30.5 in) previously.

2 Whenever the drivebelt is to be renewed check that you have been supplied with a replacement of the correct length.

3 On cars built up to the commencement of D-Series two terminals were fitted to the rear cover of the alternator – (A) 4.8 mm diagnostic and (L) 6.35 mm warning lamp.

4 On D-Series cars, the (A) terminal is no longer fitted and the (L) terminal is moved to a different location on the cover.

5 When replacing an alternator on a D-Series car, if the new unit has two terminals, connect the black/green wire to terminal (L) and ignore the terminal (A).

6 When replacing an alternator on a pre D-Series car with an alternator which has only the (L) terminal, cut off the two pin locking type wiring plug from the diagnostic and warning lamp harness.

7 Tape back the diagnostic plug wire and insulate its cut end. Now change the terminal on the warning lamp wire to a 6.35 female spade terminal and connect to the male terminal on the new alternator.

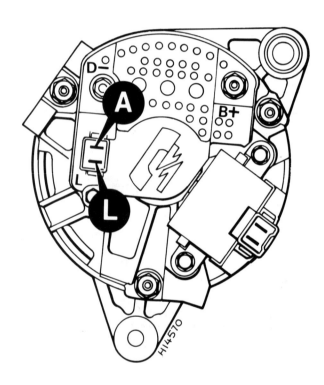

Fig. 13.31 Alternator terminals (Sec 11)

A (Diagnostic) 4.8 mm terminal   L (Warning lamp) 6.35 mm
                                           terminal

Instruments

8 Additional items to the instrumentation on some later models include an Econometer (Econoscope), a Linear Tachometer and a Mk II Trip Computer.

Econometer

9 The Econometer, as its name implies, is an economy aid device which indicates to the driver the most efficient throttle setting in accordance with operating conditions. The system operates by means of a potentiometer pick-up unit located within the engine compartment, which is vacuum controlled from the inlet manifold according to the carburettor throttle opening position. The potentiometer pick-up unit actuates light emitting diodes on the speedometer unit according to output voltage and vacuum variation.

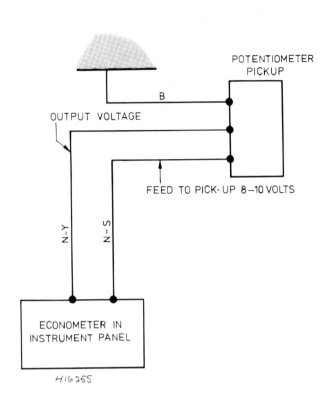

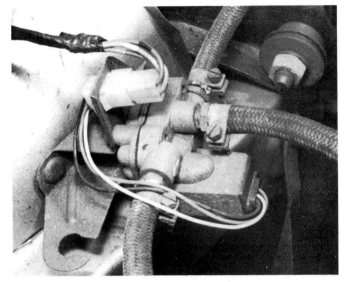

11.11 Fuel sensor

Fig. 13.32 Econometer wiring diagram (Sec 11)

Linear tachometer
10 This indicates engine speed (rpm) and when fitted is located in the upper steering column cowl. The wiring diagram for this instrument is shown in Fig. 13.33.

Mk II Trip computer
11 Similar in operation to that fitted to earlier models, this later type unit displays the average fuel consumption for about 5 seconds after depressing the button. Included in the Mk II unit is a turbo type fuel sensor which incorporates a fuel return system, the sensor being operated by a 5 volt electrical feed from the display unit. The Mk I and Mk II Trip computer types are not interchangeable (photo).
12 The distance sensor is located in the end of the speedometer drive or in series with the drive cable. It provides the computer with the actual distance travelled by the car.

Trip computer – fault diagnosis

Function	Symptom	Reason(s)
Clock	Not operating	No current
	Unintentional return to zero	Time base not operating Intermittent current interruption
	Inaccurate	Defective time base
Elapsed time	Not operating	Time base not operating Defective sensors
	Inaccurate	Defective flow sensor
Distance travelled	Not operating or inaccurate	Defective distance sensor Defective computer
Fuel consumption	Not operating or inaccurate	Defective flow sensor, or computer

Additionally, check that all electrical connections are secure, that the flow sensor is connected the correct way round and that the fuel filter is clean.

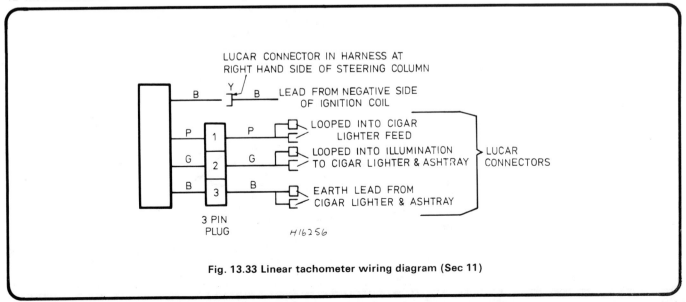

Fig. 13.33 Linear tachometer wiring diagram (Sec 11)

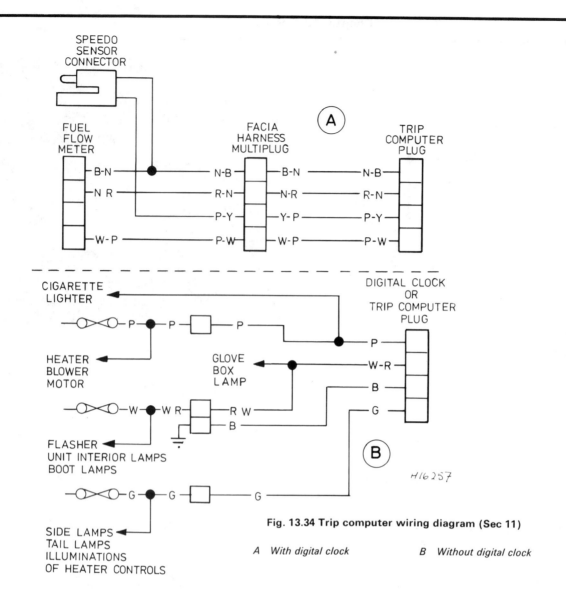

Fig. 13.34 Trip computer wiring diagram (Sec 11)

A   With digital clock   B   Without digital clock

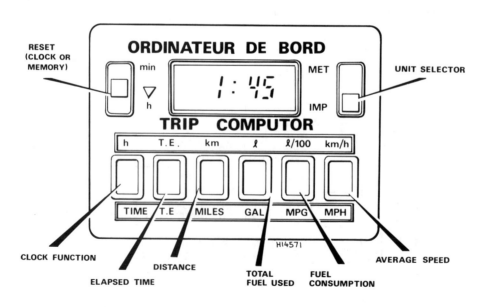

Fig. 13.35 Trip computer (Sec 11)

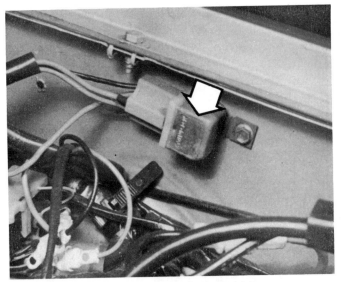

11.20A Tailgate heated window relay (early models)

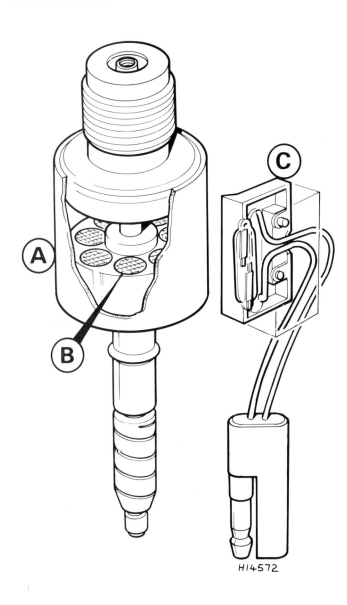

H14572

Fig. 13.36 Trip computer distance sensor (Sec 11)

A *Housing*   C *Microswitch*
B *Permanent magnets*

11.20B Tailgate heated window relay (later models)

Heated tailgate window
13 In order to prevent damage to the heater elements on the inside of the tailgate window, observe the following precautions.
14 Clean the glass with water only to which a little detergent has been added.
15 Wipe the glass in the direction in which the elements run and avoid scratching them with rings on the fingers.
16 Do not stick labels over the heater elements. Prevent articles on the rear parcels shelf from rubbing on the glass.
17 The heated tailgate glass is controlled by an illuminated push-button switch.
18 Renewal of the bulb can be carried out as described in Chapter 11.
19 Only keep the heated tailgate glass switched until the glass is clear, otherwise the battery may become discharged.
20 A relay is incorporated in the electrical circuit and located on the left-hand wing valance (early models) or under the instrument panel (later models) (photos).
21 Repair of a broken element can be carried out using one of the new silver conductive paints available for the purpose. Follow the manufacturer's instructions carefully.

Electrically-operated windows
22 This is a factory-fitted option on certain models. The system is energised when the ignition is on and the door-mounted switches on the driver's side control both front windows.
23 Access to the operating motor is obtained after removal of the door trim panel as described in Chapter 12, Section 9 (photos).
24 The motor is not repairable and if a fault develops, renew it complete.
25 A thermal overload cutout is fitted to the electric motors. The wiring harness is protected by a flexible rubber sheath at the point where it is routed into the door casings.
26 When a window reaches either extremity of travel, the rocker switch must be released. Failure to do this will cause the lift motor overload cutout to operate, putting the system temporarily out of action.

Central door locking system
27 All door locks in this system are controlled from the lock plunger on the driver's door by turning the lock key.
28 Independent override control is provided by the other door lock plungers.

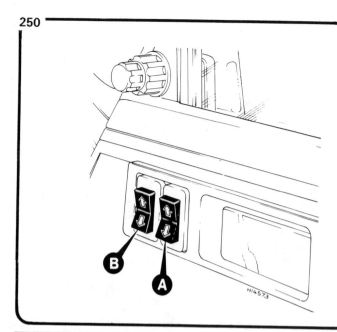

Fig. 13.37 Electric window control switches (Sec 11)

   A   *Driver's window*
   B   *Passenger's window*

11.23A Door arm rest fixing screw

11.23B Speaker mounted on door trim panel

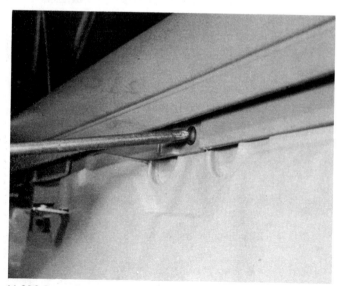

11.23C Door trim capping screw

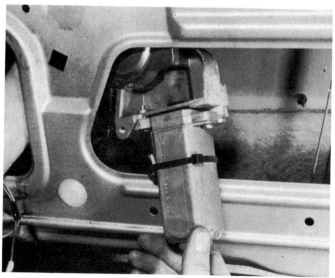

11.23D Removing window winder motor

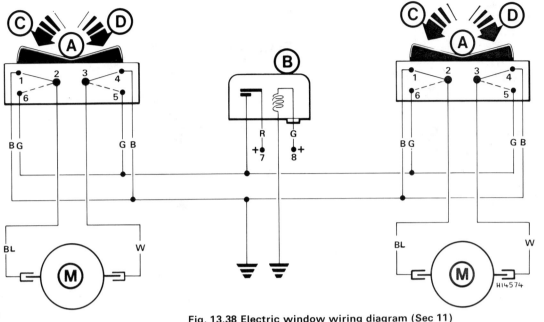

Fig. 13.38 Electric window wiring diagram (Sec 11)

Colour code
BL Blue
W White
G Grey
B Black
R Red

A   Rocker switch
B   Relay

C   Window 'up'
D   Window 'down'

M   Motor
1 to 6 Switch contacts

7   Power supply to motors
8   To ignition switch

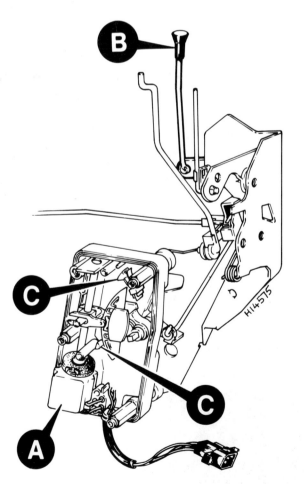

Fig. 13.39 Electric door locking mechanism (Sec 11)

A   Solenoid
B   Control knob

C   Microswitches

Central door lock control box/solenoid – removal and refitting
29 Disconnect the battery negative lead.
30 Remove the door trim panel (Chapter 12).
31 Extract the lock solenoid screws (photo).
32 Unclip the solenoid wiring harness.
33 Disconnect the multi-plug wiring harness, swivel the solenoid to disconnect the hooked link rod and withdraw the solenoid from the door cavity (photos).
34 Refitting is a reversal of removal.

Headlamp wash/wipe system
35 The system is fitted to certain models only.
36 For access to the motor and to remove the wiper arm, first detach the radiator grille (photos).
37 The washer pump is located beside the headlamp reflector within the engine compartment (photo).

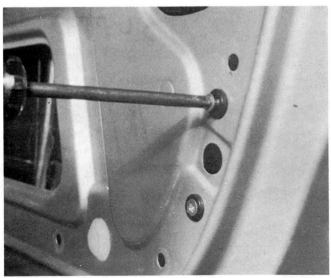

11.31 Door lock solenoid screws

11.33A Door lock solenoid and link rod

11.33B Removing door lock solenoid

11.36A Radiator grille top fixing screw

11.36B Headlamp wiper arm nut

11.37 Headlamp washer pump

Key to typical wiring diagram for Talbot Horizon range

Note: Some items in the diagram may differ within the range

C4	Earth	H40	Illumination, pushbutton switches	M6	Thermostatic switch	M53	Capacitor
C8	Heated rear window			M7	Horn, LH	M54	Motor, windscreen wiper

C4 Earth
C8 Heated rear window
C9 Earth on body
C10 Earth
C14 Illumination, luggage compartment
C16 Rear lamp cluster, LH
C20 Earth on body
C22 Switch, luggage compartment lamp
C24 Fuel tank transmitted unit
C26 Rear lamp cluster, RH
CC2 Connector
CC6 Connector
CR Capacitor
EC Instrument illumination panel lamp
H6 Heater blower motor
H8 Resistor, heater motor
H10 Switch, stop lamps
H12 Relay, heated rear window
H14 Ignition/starter switch
H16 Combination switch
H31 Flasher unit, direction indicators
H32 Illumination, heater controls
H34 Switch, heater blower motor
H36 Switch, choke control
H38 Instrument panel

H40 Illumination, pushbutton switches
H46 Switch, heated rear window
H48 Brake test switch
H50 Switch, hazard warning
H52 Switch, rear fog lamps
H54 Cigar lighter
H56 Illumination, ashtray
H58 Clock
H62 Courtesy switch, LH
H64 Interior lamp
H65 Oil level indicator control unit
H66 Courtesy switch, RH
H67 Earth on body
H70 Switch, handbrake
HC21 Connector
HC24 Multi-pin connector
HC26 Multi-pin connector
HC28 Multi-pin connector
HC30 Multi-pin connector
HC68 Connector
JE Fuel gauge
L1 Rear fog lamp
L3 Reversing lamp
L4 Stop/tail lamp
L5 Direction indicator lamp
L6 Number plate illumination lamp
M3 Horn, RH

M6 Thermostatic switch
M7 Horn, LH
M8 Cooling fan motor
M10 Earth on body
M14 Headlamp, LH
M16 Direction indicator, LH
M19 Indicator repeater, LH
M20 Battery
M22 Voltage regulator
M23 Earth
M26 Switch, reversing lamps
M28 Sender unit, temperature gauge
M30 Ignition coil
M31 Solenoid, idle jet
M32 Sender unit, oil pressure
M34 Sender unit, engine oil level (alternative)
M37 Sender unit, engine oil level
M38 Distributor
M40 Starter motor
M44 Alternator
M45 Diagnostic socket
M47 Wear indicator, LH brake pad
M48 Fuse box
M49 Relay, cooling fan
M50 Control unit, ignition
M50 Indicator repeater, LH

M53 Capacitor
M54 Motor, windscreen wiper
M56 Indicator, brake fluid level
M57 Wear indicator, RH brake pad
M58 Pump, windscreen washer
M59 Indicator repeater, RH
M60 Direction indicator, RH
M62 Headlamp RH
M64 Earth
MC45 Connector
MC46 Connector
MC52 Connector
PH Oil pressure gauge
RV Instrument voltage stabilizer
T1 Warning light, side/tail lamps
T2 Warning light, main beam
T3 Warning light, choke
T4 Warning light, no charge
T5 Warning light, direction indicators
T6 Warning light, low fuel
T7 Warning light, engine oil pressure/level
T8 Warning light, brake pad wear/handbrake
TE Water temperature gauge
VT Voltmeter

Wiring colour code

R	–	Red	S	–	Slate	G	–	Green
N	–	Brown	W	–	White	Y	–	Yellow
B	–	Black	U	–	Blue	P	–	Purple
						O	–	Orange

Use of wiring diagram

At each end of the wire is the symbol of the component or connector to which the wire is attached

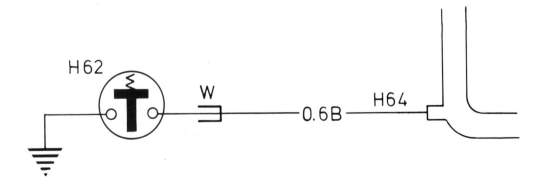

The 0.6 mm² black wire having a white connector sleeve, supplies the door courtesy switch (H62).
Its other end is connected to the interior lamp (H64)

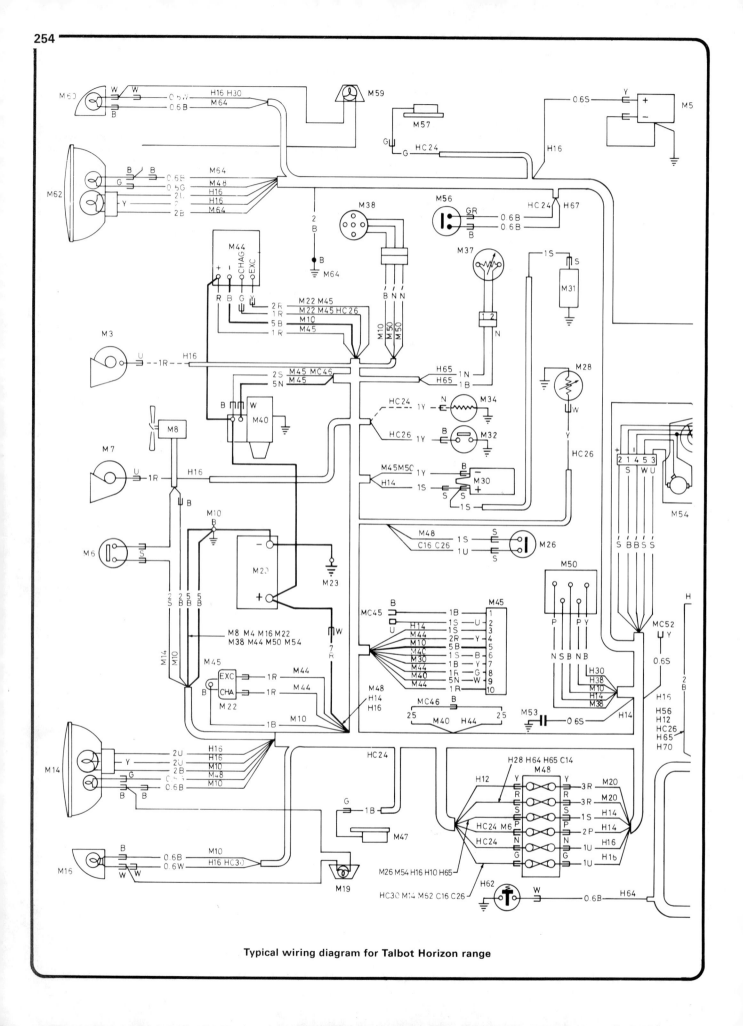

Typical wiring diagram for Talbot Horizon range

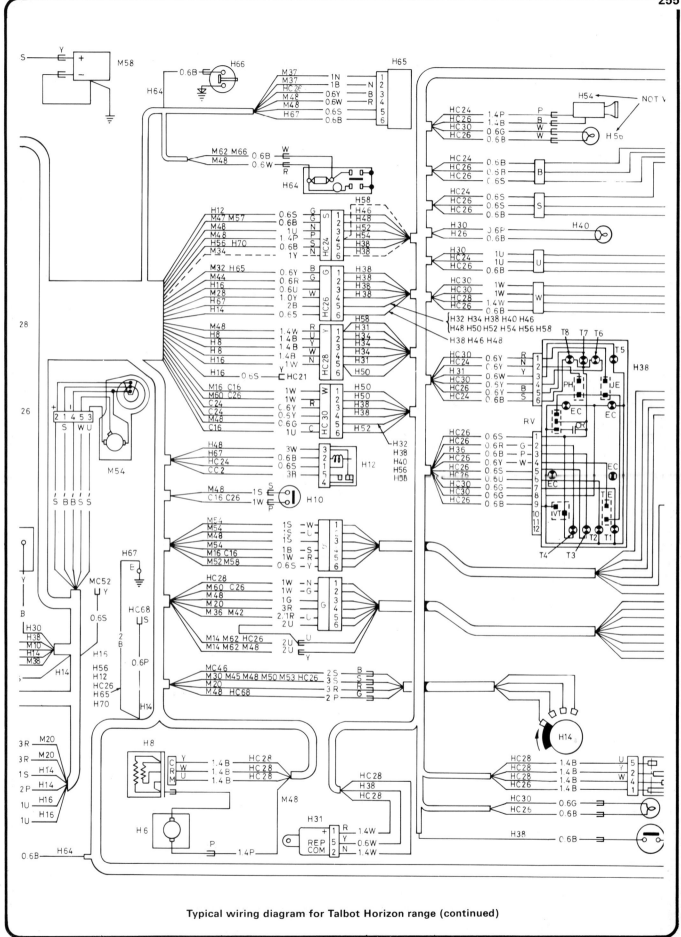

Typical wiring diagram for Talbot Horizon range (continued)

HC30 — 0.6B — B
HC26 — 0.6G — G
HC28 — 0.6W — R
HC24 — U
H58 — NOT VALID FOR LOW MODEL

H54 — NOT VALID FOR LOW-MODEL
H56

0.6G — 4
0.6B — 3
0.6W — R — 2
C.6P — 1
BE:LI
H60

G — S
0.6U 0.6W 0.6B 0.6G
S — S
6 3 1 2 4 5
L4
L5
L3
L6
C 26

G
G
H46 3 2
H48 3 2
N
3 1 2 4
H50
N O
H52
H40

C 24
Y
R

0.6Y — HC30
0.6Y — HC30

T8 T7 T6
T5
H38
PH
IJE
EC
EC
CR
EC
C
T E
VT
T2 T1
T3

A O PV GV
H16
LC OCR

H70
0.6B 0.6B
HC24 H67

B — 3B — B
C 9

C 8

0.5B — C16 / C26
C14 — 0.6B

B
C 20

W
C22
C16

L6
L1
L3
L5 L4
6 3 1 2 4 5
S P C
0.6U 5W 0.6W 5G 1U

3B
13

C10
CC6
CC2 — C4 — 3B — B
3B
B

3B
B
C4 — CC2
3B
B
C10

H14
U — 1.4B — 5
Y — 1.4B — 2
W — 1.4B — 4
1.4B — 1
H34
0.6G — H32
0.6B
0.6B — H36

C14
R — W
0.6 0.6
W B

H12

M26 H56 HC30
20
H10
M48 HC30
G

Typical wiring diagram for Talbot Horizon range (continued)

12.5A Electrically-operated sunroof switch

12.5B Electrically-operated sunroof motor

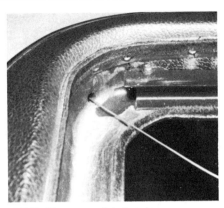
12.7 Probing sunroof drain tube

12 Bodywork

Sunroof (manually-operated)
1   This can be fitted as a factory option.
2   To open, pull the handle A downwards and then forwards and upwards towards the glass until the handle clicks into place.
3   To remove the sunroof panel, pull the handle down to release tension and then extract the pivot pin (C). Using both hands, push the glass panel upwards until it is located vertically over the hinges. Remove the panel upwards.
4   Closure and refitting of the sunroof panel are reversals of opening and removal.

Sunroof (electrically-operated)
5   The switch for this accessory is located on the front face of the centre console and the operating motor is mounted in the rear corner of the luggage area (photos).
6   The sunroof panel is moved by cable drive.
7   Periodically probe the drain holes with a length of wire (photo).
8   Access to the cable can be obtained after removal of the rear quarter interior trim panels.
9   Extract the screws from the front edge of the sliding panel and peel away the lining for access to the operating gear and slides.

Front spoiler
10 On later models, this is of plastic construction and is secured at the edge of the front wheel arches by screws and rivets (photo).

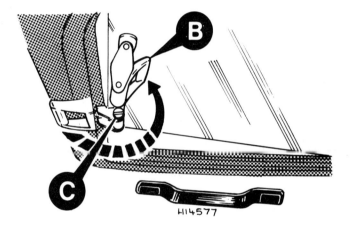
Fig. 13.41 Sunroof handle (B) in open position and pivot pin (C) (Sec 12)

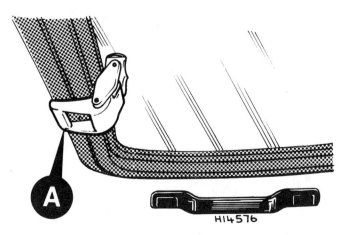
Fig. 13.40 Sunroof operating handle (A) (Sec 12)

12.10 Front spoiler fixings

Conversion factors

Length (distance)

Inches (in)	X	25.4	= Millimetres (mm)	X 0.0394	= Inches (in)
Feet (ft)	X	0.305	= Metres (m)	X 3.281	= Feet (ft)
Miles	X	1.609	= Kilometres (km)	X 0.621	= Miles

Volume (capacity)

Cubic inches (cu in; in³)	X	16.387	= Cubic centimetres (cc; cm³)	X 0.061	= Cubic inches (cu in; in³)
Imperial pints (Imp pt)	X	0.568	= Litres (l)	X 1.76	= Imperial pints (Imp pt)
Imperial quarts (Imp qt)	X	1.137	= Litres (l)	X 0.88	= Imperial quarts (Imp qt)
Imperial quarts (Imp qt)	X	1.201	= US quarts (US qt)	X 0.833	= Imperial quarts (Imp qt)
US quarts (US qt)	X	0.946	= Litres (l)	X 1.057	= US quarts (US qt)
Imperial gallons (Imp gal)	X	4.546	= Litres (l)	X 0.22	= Imperial gallons (Imp gal)
Imperial gallons (Imp gal)	X	1.201	= US gallons (US gal)	X 0.833	= Imperial gallons (Imp gal)
US gallons (US gal)	X	3.785	= Litres (l)	X 0.264	= US gallons (US gal)

Mass (weight)

Ounces (oz)	X	28.35	= Grams (g)	X 0.035	= Ounces (oz)
Pounds (lb)	X	0.454	= Kilograms (kg)	X 2.205	= Pounds (lb)

Force

Ounces-force (ozf; oz)	X	0.278	= Newtons (N)	X 3.6	= Ounces-force (ozf; oz)
Pounds-force (lbf; lb)	X	4.448	= Newtons (N)	X 0.225	= Pounds-force (lbf; lb)
Newtons (N)	X	0.1	= Kilograms-force (kgf; kg)	X 9.81	= Newtons (N)

Pressure

Pounds-force per square inch (psi; lbf/in²; lb/in²)	X	0.070	= Kilograms-force per square centimetre (kgf/cm²; kg/cm²)	X 14.223	= Pounds-force per square inch (psi; lbf/in²; lb/in²)
Pounds-force per square inch (psi; lbf/in²; lb/in²)	X	0.068	= Atmospheres (atm)	X 14.696	= Pounds-force per square inch (psi; lbf/in²; lb/in²)
Pounds-force per square inch (psi; lbf/in²; lb/in²)	X	0.069	= Bars	X 14.5	= Pounds-force per square inch (psi; lbf/in²; lb/in²)
Pounds-force per square inch (psi; lbf/in²; lb/in²)	X	6.895	= Kilopascals (kPa)	X 0.145	= Pounds-force per square inch (psi; lbf/in²; lb/in²)
Kilopascals (kPa)	X	0.01	= Kilograms-force per square centimetre (kgf/cm²; kg/cm²)	X 98.1	= Kilopascals (kPa)

Torque (moment of force)

Pounds-force inches (lbf in; lb in)	X	1.152	= Kilograms-force centimetre (kgf cm; kg cm)	X 0.868	= Pounds-force inches (lbf in; lb in)
Pounds-force inches (lbf in; lb in)	X	0.113	= Newton metres (Nm)	X 8.85	= Pounds-force inches (lbf in; lb in)
Pounds-force inches (lbf in; lb in)	X	0.083	= Pounds-force feet (lbf ft; lb ft)	X 12	= Pounds-force inches (lbf in; lb in)
Pounds-force feet (lbf ft; lb ft)	X	0.138	= Kilograms-force metres (kgf m; kg m)	X 7.233	= Pounds-force feet (lbf ft; lb ft)
Pounds-force feet (lbf ft; lb ft)	X	1.356	= Newton metres (Nm)	X 0.738	= Pounds-force feet (lbf ft; lb ft)
Newton metres (Nm)	X	0.102	= Kilograms-force metres (kgf m; kg m)	X 9.804	= Newton metres (Nm)

Power

Horsepower (hp)	X	745.7	= Watts (W)	X 0.0013	= Horsepower (hp)

Velocity (speed)

Miles per hour (miles/hr; mph)	X	1.609	= Kilometres per hour (km/hr; kph)	X 0.621	= Miles per hour (miles/hr; mph)

Fuel consumption*

Miles per gallon, Imperial (mpg)	X	0.354	= Kilometres per litre (km/l)	X 2.825	= Miles per gallon, Imperial (mpg)
Miles per gallon, US (mpg)	X	0.425	= Kilometres per litre (km/l)	X 2.352	= Miles per gallon, US (mpg)

Temperature

Degrees Fahrenheit = (°C x 1.8) + 32   Degrees Celsius (Degrees Centigrade; °C) = (°F - 32) x 0.56

*It is common practice to convert from miles per gallon (mpg) to litres/100 kilometres (l/100km), where mpg (Imperial) x l/100 km = 282 and mpg (US) x l/100 km = 235

Index

Printed by
J H Haynes & Co Ltd
Sparkford Nr Yeovil
Somerset BA22 7JJ England